FIRST BOOK

B.L. ULLMAN
CHARLES HENDERSON, JR.
NORMAN E. HENRY

SEVENTH EDITION

GLENCOE
McGraw-Hill

New York, New York   Columbus, Ohio   Mission Hills, California   Peoria, Illinois

FIRST BOOK

LATIN

FOR AMERICANS

ABOUT THE AUTHORS:

B.L. Ullman enjoyed a distinguished career of teaching and scholarship at the Universities of Pittsburgh, Iowa, Chicago, and North Carolina. An authority on all aspects of the Roman world, ancient, medieval, and Renaissance, he was also a pioneer in modern methods of teaching elementary Latin.

Charles Henderson, Jr. collaborated with Professor Ullman in the previous revisions of this book. He has taught at New York University, the University of North Carolina, and at Smith College.

Norman E. Henry, collaborator with Professor Ullman in earlier editions of the *Latin for Americans* series, taught for many years at the Peabody High School, Pittsburgh, and contributed material that had been tested in high-school classrooms.

Front cover: The Stabian Baths, Pompeii. This is one of the first baths uncovered after excavations began in the late eighteenth century. The entire grounds encompass 33 acres. The Hot Room (caldārium) contained a basin of cool water for bathers to use if they wished.

Title page: The Appian Way was known as the "Regina Viarum" (Queen of Roads). It was the triumphal road of the victorious Roman armies and an important artery for trade. It extended some 540 miles from Rome to southern Italy. The paving was made of slabs of basalt.

A revision of *Latin for Americans, First Book,* by B.L. Ullman, Charles Henderson, Jr. (1962, 1968, and 1981 editions), and Norman E. Henry, Copyright ©1941, 1950, 1956, 1959, 1962, 1968, and 1981 by Macmillan Publishing Co., Inc.

Send all inquiries to:
GLENCOE/McGraw-Hill
15319 Chatsworth Street
P. O. Box 9609
Mission Hills, CA 91346-9609

ISBN 0-02-646000-9
6 7 8 9   95

CONTENTS

UNIT III–LATIN AND THE ROMANS

UNIT IV–ROMAN LIFE

UNIT V–FAMOUS STORIES

UNIT VII–GAMES AND GODS

UNIT VIII–TRAVEL AND ADVENTURE

UNIT IX–MYTH AND HISTORY

ix

UNIT XII–GREEK MYTHS AND ROMAN HISTORY

UNIT XIII–MEN WHO MADE ROME GREAT

INTRODUCTION

This seventh edition of *Latin for Americans, First Book* reaffirms the time-tested principles upon which Professor B. L. Ullman originally based his highly successful series. From the very start the student is presented with what should be his ultimate goal: reading connected Latin passages with comprehension of the Latin as Latin.

The reading lessons, derived wherever possible from classical literature, provide a solid cultural basis for the student, and afford him or her many comparisons between ancient and modern life. They furnish reading in keeping with the concerns of present-day students and at the same time attempt to develop a sense of our debt to the past. The pupil is repeatedly encouraged to use his or her imagination and common sense in rendering the Latin into good idiomatic English, and to avoid slavish adherence to the literal meaning and word order of the Latin.

In this edition, the reading passages in various lessons have either been replaced or re-written to provide more motivating content and more effective treatment of grammar and vocabulary. New, appealing color photos replace those in earlier editions and serve to further reinforce the unit themes.

Vocabulary is methodically chosen for the frequency of its occurrence in Latin literature and in English derivatives. The simple and informal presentation of the grammar is based on a similarly practical standard of usage. The similarities and differences between English and Latin are regularly stressed, and the reading selections and drill exercises constantly reinforce the mastery of the grammar and vocabulary.

With this revision, teachers will welcome the addition of workbooks as a new ancillary component. The workbooks, authored by Donald Peet and Marcia Stille, offer a rich and varied source of supplemental practice for the grammar, vocabulary and syntax within each lesson. The Teacher's Manual, Teacher's Key, and Teacher's Key to the Progress Tests have been combined into one ancillary component, the *Teacher's Resource Guide*. The *Progress Tests* can be employed profitably for testing on reading, vocabulary, grammar, English derivatives, and civilization. A set of thirteen tapes, with accompanying tape script, is also available from the publisher.

The Arch of Septimius Severus in the Roman Forum was erected in 203 A.D. in honor of the emperor whose name it bears. The arch is seventy-five feet high and eighty-two feet wide with an internal staircase. The monument was constructed to celebrate the military victories of Septimius Severus and his sons in Mesopotamia and Assyria. The Arch of Titus can be seen in the distance. Can you name a more recent arch in the city of Paris erected in honor of the French Emperor Napoleon?

Facing page: The "Arch of Drusus," probably built in the reign of Septimius Severus. It may have been part of an aqueduct. This engraving is the work of the famous eighteenth-century artist G.B. Piranesi.

1. OUR ROMAN HERITAGE

The Romans used great arches as monuments to celebrate military victories or famous heroes. All over the world other peoples have built triumphal arches in imitation of this Roman custom.

Arches are also gateways, and the Latin language is the arch through which countless generations of Western men have been able to enter into their past and discover the ideas and traditions that have shaped their lives. All over the world, for centuries, men have studied Latin because of their curiosity about the ancient world. Now you too stand before that arch. Step right ahead! Just through that arch is the rich inheritance the Romans have left you. It is yours—and all men's—to share.

The first thing you will notice as you begin the study of Latin is the close resemblance between many Latin and English words, for the English language owes a great debt of vocabulary to Latin. But the Roman heritage is not just one of vocabulary; more important are the ways in which the ancient Romans have influenced our forms of government, our social institutions, our habits of thinking, and have provided inspiration to statesmen, writers, artists, architects, engineers, and, in short, to almost all educated men.

But your own greatest reward beyond the arch will be the broadened vision you will find in yourself. Some things in the ancient world will be strikingly familiar to you, others totally new; some things will seem primitive, others remarkably modern. How did an ancient Roman live? What was life like in his family? What were his ideas about government and religion? How could he believe in both freedom and

1

The Emperor Justinian (sixth century) was responsible for the Justinian Code, a collection of Roman laws, edicts, and decisions of the preceding 1000 years. It is still the basic law of many nations. In this mosaic, we see the Emperor Justinian with his court.

slavery? What were the moral qualities and the skills that made him, once a simple farmer, into the master of the world? To all these questions he will give you the answers, in his own language; and the comparisons between his experience and yours will tend to make another person of you. As so many others have learned before you, you too will see that "to learn another language is to gain another soul."

But why study Latin and Rome rather than a modern language and a modern city? Because no other language and no other city have had so much influence—and for so long a time—upon our own culture. More than twenty-seven hundred years ago Rome was an insignificant settlement on the Tiber River in a central district of Italy called Latium (pronounced *Lay´shum*). From small beginnings, the military, political, and cultural power of Rome spread, first throughout Latium, then through Italy and over the Mediterranean. By the second century after the birth of Christ, the Romans dominated almost the entire civilized world; Rome itself was at the same time **urbs et orbis**—*city and world*.

The Romans' language, Latin (which gets its name from Latium), came to be used everywhere, largely displacing the languages of the conquered peoples. (Only Greek, a language much older than Latin, successfully resisted the invasion, mainly because it was the vehicle of a great literature and culture that the Romans admired and imitated. Just as we today study Latin, so did the Romans then study Greek, and for similar reasons.)

From the map on pages 92–93 you can see the stages of growth of the Roman Empire, and from it you can see why the languages of Spain, Portugal, France, Italy, and Romania are called *Romance* languages: they are the living descendants of the Latin spoken by the

Romans who conquered and colonized these lands. And although English is basically a Germanic language, Latin has influenced it so much through the centuries that it would be almost fair to call it a Romance language, too. More than sixty per cent of our English vocabulary has been derived or taken intact from Latin.

Thus the Latin language and the ideas it conveys have actually survived the Roman Empire itself. As the centuries passed, and as the empire was gradually transformed into the beginnings of modern Europe, Latin continued to be the international language of all educated men and women, living a sort of parallel existence with the different national languages that were growing up from and alongside it. When the Middle Ages ended, interest in the classical Latin of Cicero, Caesar, and Virgil gained great impetus from the discovery of more and more works of the ancient authors that had lain entombed in dusty and neglected manuscripts in the monasteries and libraries of Europe. This rebirth of interest in the *ancient* world was one of the major causes for the amazing period of transition to the *modern* world that we call the Renaissance. From their deeper knowledge of the past, the men of the Renaissance found a new confidence in themselves and new horizons to explore. Since the discovery and colonization of the New World were the work of Europeans who were the heirs of the Roman tradition, Latin was transplanted by them to the Western Hemisphere. Even today the people of Mexico, Central America, and South America are called Latins, and the region they live in Latin America.

Our own country was settled under the same influences. The Revolutionary War was led and the Constitution drafted by men who cherished the classical ideals of liberty and the dignity of the individual. The two names by which we refer to our country, America and the United States, are both derived from Latin. Our motto *e pluribus unum* is Latin. In one sense, there could have been no Declaration of Independence without Latin, and its first sentence would have looked like this: "We hold these truths to be self-_____, that all men are _____ _____, that they are _____ by their _____ with _____ _____ rights; that among these are life, _____, and the _____ of happiness." The Romans not only gave us the omitted words, but the ideas themselves, which they in turn had inherited from the Greeks. Hardly one page of this book does not show you some specific example of the way in which classical literature, mythology, art, history, or social custom is still part of our lives in the twentieth century.

To be sure, Latin itself is seldom written or spoken today, outside of ecclesiastical circles. But its immense influence upon English and other languages makes its study a very practical one. Most of the "difficult" words in English come from Latin (or Greek)—in a short time you will see how even an elementary knowledge of Latin makes easy the meaning and spelling of such words as *impecunious, equanimity, collaborate, obdurate,* and many others. Latin abbreviations, words, mottoes, and phrases in common English use will no longer be a mystery. Latin will help to build the technical vocabulary you will need if you are to become a doctor, lawyer, teacher, or scientist— someday it may be you who uses Latin to coin a new word like *astronaut* or *urbiculture!* Practice in translating Latin will give polish and precision to your English style, and will help to do away with the narrow prejudice that our way of saying something is always the easiest or best.

Nevertheless, the best reason for passing through the arch is that you will enter a new and different world that will tell you much about your own, and will thus help to educate you, for understanding what you owe to the past is a major part of being "educated." As the famous Roman orator Cicero said, "Not to know what happened before you were born is to be forever a child."

2. Discussion Questions

1. How many events of Roman history can you list?
2. Which famous Romans can you name?
3. What Roman gods can you recall?
4. What do you know about the city of Rome as it is today?
5. Make a list of the Latin words, phrases, legal terms, scientific terms, mottoes, proverbs, and abbreviations you already know.

3. The Alphabet

Without writing, the continuity of civilization would be impossible. Man can pass on his hard-won experience and his ideas by word of mouth, but only to a few people, in a limited area, and only for a brief time. And what is only heard can easily be misunderstood. But whatever is written down can be read by people far and wide, can be preserved for long periods of time, and can, if it is proved wrong, be changed with later experience. Since writing gives permanence and wide distribution to knowledge and ideas, it is a more effective way to move men's minds than such violent means as war, slavery, and torture. This is what we mean when we say that the pen is mightier than the sword.

There are many forms of writing, some better than others. The earliest, used as long ago as the cave-dwellers, was *pictographic,* in which the stories were told by means of pictures. The ancient Egyp-

A wax-covered tablet, called an abcedarium, from Etruria, in Italy, over 2500 years old. The ABC's were scratched on the wooden rim as a model to imitate, and run from right to left, as in the earlier Semitic alphabets.

tians and Chinese, and even the modern American Indian, have used pictographic writing. But although the pictures are often quite beautiful, they are difficult to draw, they leave a lot out of the story, and, as they become more numerous and complicated, they are too much for any one man to remember. *Ideographic* writing is similar to pictographic: the pictures have gradually been standardized into simpler characters which convey an idea. But they too are often difficult for the untrained reader to understand: for example, a foreign visitor driving along a highway might think that the signpost $+$ stood for a gravestone instead of a crossroad (and in his case indeed it might!). In *logographic* writing the characters are associated with the sounds of the words of which they were originally pictures: if a wavy line represents the "sea" and the figure of a small boy represents a "son," then

$\sim\!\sim$ 尺 becomes "season." When, in this way, a limited number

of characters become firmly fixed as the standard signs for the sounds of the syllables of a language, *syllabic* writing is the result. Many ancient peoples used syllabic writing, often together with the other types; this is the form the Japanese use today.

But the simplest and clearest system of writing is the *alphabetic,* which developed from the syllabic, and in which there is a single character for almost every vowel or consonant sound. This system helps people to "hear" more easily the sounds they see, and thus simplifies learning to read and write. Furthermore, in the alphabetic system the sounds of one language can be represented fairly exactly in the writing of another language, and this makes learning the new language that much simpler. But not even the alphabetic system is perfect; in English we still have difficulty learning to spell because custom often requires

5

TERENTIAE
FLAVOLAE
V V
MAXIMAE
CN STATILIVS
MENANDER
FICTOR
V V
CN STATILI
CERDONIS
FICTORIS
V V
ALVMNVS

us to use a different set of characters for the same sound: compare *debt* and *let*, or *there* and *their*.

Nevertheless, the Roman alphabet which we use and share with so many other countries is the best yet invented, and is one of the Romans' greatest contributions to our culture. Its history is an excellent example of the way in which valuable inventions are passed from one civilization to another. Sometime before 1500 B.C. the Semites, a people of western Asia, developed a syllabic script from Egyptian pictographic characters, and gave these characters names from their own language. The first letter was *aleph* ("ox," because the character looked like the head of an ox, although upside-down); the second was *beth* ("house"), and so forth. The Phoenicians, a sea-faring Semitic people related to the Jews and Arabs, passed this set of characters to the Greeks, who adapted it to their own language, and made the signs for the vowels (*a, e, i, o, u*) separate and distinct (the Semitic alphabet had not done this). *Aleph* became *alpha*, and *beth* became *beta*, and thus the alphabet was born, because *alpha* and *beta* no longer had anything to do with "ox" and "house," but were simply signs for the sounds *A* and *B*. From the Greeks the alphabet was passed to the Etruscans, northern neighbors of the Romans in Italy. When the Romans in turn borrowed it from the Etruscans, they made some changes in the values and forms of the letters, and passed it on to the modern world, where it is used almost universally today. All of Europe, except Greece and Russia

6

Greek inscription spelling Caesar's name *Kaisar*, which shows that C was pronounced *K* in Latin, and *ai* like English *i*. In Latin letters, the inscription reads "o demos sebaston kaisara," "The people (honor) Augustus Caesar."

(which uses a modified Greek alphabet), writes in Latin letters. In the latter half of the twentieth century, almost as a symbol of its emergence into the modern world, Turkey abandoned the Arabic alphabet (a descendant of the ancient Semitic one) in favor of the simpler Latin one. In Japan today, particularly in the business community, "our" Roman alphabet is gaining rapid acceptance. This is, in fact, a trend throughout Asia.

Roman A B C D E F G H I K L M N O P Q R S T V X Y Z

English A B C D E F G H I J K L M N O P Q R S T U V W X Y Z

You can see that the alphabet has changed but little since Roman days. The Romans used *i* for both *i* and *j*. Three centuries ago it became the custom in English to use a long form of *i* for *j*, and thus our *j* was formed. Similarly, the Romans used only one character for *u* and *v*, but we have introduced the useful distinction between them, even in Latin, and in this book *u* is printed for the vowel, *v* for the consonant. The original identity of the two is shown by another modern letter, *w*, which is a double *u* in name and a double *v* in form. (The letters *j* and *w* are not found in Latin words in this book.)

The Romans made no distinction between capitals and small letters. Our small letters gradually developed out of capitals in late antiquity.

4. Pronunciation

The pronunciation of Latin has naturally changed in the course of centuries. During the Middle Ages it was variously pronounced in different countries in accordance with the rules for pronouncing the everyday languages of those countries, and this practice has continued in some places even to the present time. A century ago scholars discovered in various ways how Latin was pronounced in the days of Caesar and Cicero. This "new" ancient pronunciation first came into general use in the United States. It is now fairly general everywhere except in Italy, including Vatican City, where the Pope lives and from which the Roman Catholic Church is administered. According to the ancient pronunciation, Cicero pronounced his name *Ki'kero,* and so you are taught in this book—but once it was pronounced *Si'sero* in England and the United States, *See'sero* in France, *Tsi'tsero* in Germany and Austria, *Chee'chero* in Italy, *Thi'thero* in Spain. But we know that *Kikero* is most nearly correct because, for example, Greek writers spell his name Κικερων (*Kikeron*), and the *k* sound in Greek cannot be confused with the *s* sound, for which there is an entirely different letter. Caesar pronounced his own name *Kysar.* We used to pronounce it in Latin as in English (*Seezer*), and each of the other languages had its own way of saying the word.

The system of pronunciation that you are taught in this book is thus both ancient, "modern," and standard. Pronouncing Latin is not difficult: the rules are few and simple, and, unlike English, each consonant (except *b*) has only one sound, and each vowel at most only two sounds. The rules are given in sections **511–518,** but they are not enough. The best way to get started is by imitating your teacher carefully and by listening to Latin tapes. Pay particular attention to the length (*quantity*) and sound (*quality*) of the vowels, and to the position of the stress (*'*). You will see that Latin is a sonorous and almost musical language.

5. Pronunciation Exercises

1. Each of the first five columns drills a different vowel, either long or short; the sixth column is devoted to the different diphthongs.

   Pronounce:

ā	ē	quī	nōn	ius	aes
Mārs	mē	hīc	prō	cūr	quae
pār	pēs	vīs	mōns	lūx	Aet'nae
ab	ex	in	nox	nunc	aut
iam	sed	quid	post	cum	cau'sa
dat	per	fit	mors	dux	clau'sae
nār'rat	cer'tē	di'gitī	cō'gor	iūs'tus	poe'nae
ma'lā	lē'ge	mī'litis	ro'gō	cur'rū	moe'nia

2. Read the verse. Can you tell from the rhythm and arrangement of words what it is?

   > Mi'cā, mi'cā, par'va stēl'la!
   > Mī'ror quae'nam sīs, tam bel'la,
   > Splen'dēns ē'minus in il'lō,
   > Al'ba ve'lut gem'ma, cae'lō.

3. This is a translation by George D. Kellogg of the first two stanzas of "America":

Tē ca′nō, Pa′tria,	Tē ca′nō, Pa′tria,
Can′dida, lī′bera;	Sem′per et ā′tria
Tē re′feret	Inge′nuum;
Por′tus et ex′ulum	Lau′dō viren′tia
Et tu′mulus se′num;	Cul′mina, flū′mina;
Lī′bera mon′tium	Sen′tiō gau′dia
Vōx re′sonet.	Caeli′colum.

4. Here is part of a translation of Lincoln's Gettysburg Address made by Msgr. Edwin Ryan for the Vatican Library:

Octōgin′tā et sep′tem ab′hinc iam an′nōs rem pū′blicam no′vam, lībertā′te incep′tam at′que homi′nibus nātū′rā pa′ribus dēdicā′tam, maiō′rēs hīs in regiō′nibus ēdidē′runt. . . . Sēn′sū ta′men altiō′re hanc ter′ram dēdicā′re, cōnsecrā′re, sānctificā′re, nō′bīs nōn com′petit. . . . Quō fī′et ut cī′vitās haec De′ō adiuvan′te lībertā′tī renāscē′tur; et di′ciō in po′pulō fundā′ta, ā po′pulō ges′ta, ad po′pulī salū′tem dīrēc′ta, nēquā′quam dē mun′dō tābēs′cēns interī′bit.

5. These are ancient Latin quotations, some of which you probably have seen:

a) **Vē′nī vī′dī, vī′cī,** *I came, I saw, I conquered* (Caesar's famous dispatch to the senate after a victory).

b) **In hōc sig′nō vin′cēs,** *In this sign* (the cross) *you will conquer* (motto of Constantine, the first Christian emperor).

c) **Pos′sunt qui′a pos′se viden′tur,** *They can because they think they can.*

d) **Aman′tium ī′rae amō′ris integrā′tiō est,** *The quarrels of lovers are the renewal of love* (Terence; quoted by Winston Churchill in a message to Franklin D. Roosevelt).

6. The two verses that follow were used by Roman children in some of their games:

a) **Ha′beat sca′biem quis′quis ad mē vē′nerit novis′simus,** *May he have the itch who comes to me last.*

b) **Rēx e′rit quī rēc′tē fa′ciet; quī nōn fa′ciet nōn e′rit,** *He will be king who does right; he who does not will not be king.*

7. Here is the most famous sentence of President John F. Kennedy's Inaugural Address, as it has been translated into Latin by Mrs. Jo Ann Stachniw and the Rev. R. V. Schoder, S.J.:

I′taque concī′vēs me′ī Americā′nī, nē rogē′tis quid pa′tria ves′tra prō vō′bis fa′cere pos′sit, im′mo quid vōs prō pa′triā fa′cere possī′tis, id rogā′te.

9

UNIT I

THE ROMANS' WORLD

Modern Rome goes on among the monuments of its past. Here in the center of the city, we see the Forum of Trajan. When it was completed in 113 A.D., it was richly decorated with marble and sculptures. The two rows of columns form the border of the rectangular forum. Trajan's Forum contained a giant basilica, or public hall, Greek and Latin libraries, and the Emperor's famous Column which we see here covered in scaffolding as it undergoes repair. The Column was dedicated to the Emperor Trajan in honor of his military victories. (See p. 199.) On the right, the semi-circular building is the Market of Trajan.

Lesson I

6. RŌMA ET ITALIA

Rōma est in Italiā. Italia est in Eurōpā. Britannia est in Eurōpā. Britannia est īnsula. Italia nōn est īnsula. Italia paene [1] est īnsula. Italia paenīnsula [2] est. Sicilia et Sardinia sunt īnsulae. Īnsulae in aquā sunt. Austrālia īnsula est, sed Asia nōn est īnsula.

5   Sunt viae et silvae in paenīnsulā Italiā. Viae et silvae et paenīnsulae in Eurōpā sunt. Italia et Graecia et Hispānia paenīnsulae sunt. Rōma nōn in Graeciā sed in Italiā est. Est Graecia in Eurōpā?

Est aqua in Antarcticā, sed nōn sunt silvae in Antarcticā. Silvae in Āfricā sunt. Est America īnsula?

QUESTIONS

1. Can you use other islands, countries, states, and cities whose names end in *–a,* e.g., Bermuda, India, Virginia, Philadelphia, to make up additional Latin sentences?
2. Why do the continents have Latin names?
3. Which of the words above seem totally unrelated to English? *paene sed*

7. Understanding Latin

Here is the easiest method to get the sense and make a good translation of a Latin sentence:

1. Read through the complete sentence aloud in Latin, trying to grasp the meaning of each word as you come to it. At the same time, try to get the general idea of the whole sentence as you go along.

2. Be careful with your pronunciation (remembering that there are no silent syllables) and pay particular attention to the endings of the words. Make your ears help your eyes, and vice versa.

3. Often the meaning of the sentence will become clear from a single reading aloud. But if a word stumps you, try to find a clue to its meaning from some English word which has been formed from the Latin one, as *insular* from **īnsula.** Use the vocabulary only as a last resort.

4. Since Latin has no words for *a, an,* and *the,* you must supply them with the nouns that need them. **Est** means not only *is,* but also *he, she,* or *it is,* and even *there is.* Experience and common sense will tell you which to use.

5. Be patient with the Latin word order, and avoid wild jumping back and forth. English is much more strict about making the sense

---

[1] *almost.*   [2] What do we call an "almost-island" in English?

'depend upon the word order. Compare *Dog bites man* with *Man bites dog*. Latin's flexible word order is made possible by the fact that it changes the *endings* of words to show the relationship between them. A change of ending changes the meaning of word; for example, **insula** is singular, *an island,* but **insulae** is plural, *islands.*

This principle of the change of word endings (called *inflection*) is the most important thing for the beginner to master. Unfamiliar vocabulary can often be worked out (or, as a last resort, looked up) and the now strange word order will soon seem natural; but there is no short cut to learning the various endings, which are the signposts of the sentence.

6. When you have read the whole sentence through and understand it, convert it into the English that is natural to you. Try to be as exact as possible, but do not stick blindly to the English meanings given in the vocabulary. Use synonyms (words of like meaning) whenever they make better sense.

7. Keep in mind that your goal is to understand Latin as Latin, the way the Romans did. Eventually Latin **Britannia insula est** and English *Britain is an island* will have exactly the same meaning to you, without the need for translation.

8. Sentences

The word *sentence* comes from the Latin word **sententia,** which means "thought." In both Latin and English, sentences are words grouped together to express thoughts.

Every sentence has two parts: the *subject,* about which something is said, and the *predicate,* which says something about the subject.

1. *Italy* (subject) *is a peninsula* (predicate), **Italia paeninsula est.**
2. *The girls* (subject) *carry water* (predicate), **Puellae aquam portant.**

9. Nouns

1. *Nouns* are used to name persons, places, or things.
2. A noun is *singular* in *number* when it names one person, place, or thing. It is *plural* in number when it names more than one. Compare **insula,** *island,* in the singular, with **insulae,** *islands,* in the plural. In Latin, as in English, the endings of nouns are changed to show differences in number.

3. The *case* of a noun is determined by its use in a sentence. In Latin, the case of the subject is the *nominative* case. Soon you will learn the *accusative* case, the case of the direct object (which we sometimes call the objective case in English). Remember that in Latin it is a change in the ending of a noun which indicates any

Time

This looks like a painting, but actually it is a mosaic—a decoration made of small pieces of colored glass or stone. This detail of a magnificent floor, found recently in a Roman villa of about 400 A.D. in central Sicily, shows a big game hunt in Africa. Africa came under Roman rule in the second century B.C.

change of case and of number, and these changes tell you what that word means in that particular sentence.

4. A *declension* is a group of nouns which have the same general pattern of case endings. Nouns of the *first declension* end in –a in the nominative singular.

10. Predicate Nominative

After a linking verb (*is, are, seem,* etc.) a noun used in the predicate is in the nominative case. This is called the *predicate nominative.* A linking verb is really nothing more than an equals sign (=).

$$A \quad = \quad B \qquad A \quad = \quad B$$
Britannia est īnsula, *Britain is an island.*

11. Endings

The case endings for the nominative, singular and plural, of nouns of the *first declension* are:

	SINGULAR	PLURAL
	–a	–ae
as in the Latin word	vi a	vi ae

12. English Word Studies

Many Latin words have simply been taken over into English unchanged, but often with a change of meaning. For example, the Latin first-declension noun *larva*, which meant "ghost," now is used to name the just-hatched egg of many insects because, in a pale and formless way, the *larva* "masks" the form of the future insect. The *larva* then grows into a *pupa*, which is the Latin word for "doll," which looks somewhat like a small version of the adult form. The plural of both these words in English is the same as in Latin: *larvae, pupae*.

Other words of this sort are *alumna, antenna, penna, minutiae* (singular rare). But others have adopted the English plural in *–s*: *area, arena, camera, formula, scintilla*.

Since all these words are now "English" words, when the *–ae* ending is used for the plural it is pronounced like the *–e* in *me*. In an English dictionary, look up the present and the former meanings of each of the italicized words above.

13. Vocabulary

a'qua, *water*	(aqueous, aqueduct)
est, *is*	
et, *and*	
īn'sula, *island*	(insulate, isolate)
nōn, *not*	(nonsense)
sed, *but*	
sil'va, *forest, woods*	(Pennsylvania)
sunt, *are*	
vi'a, *road, way, street*	(viaduct)

NOTE. The words in parentheses are English derivatives of the Latin words. Be sure that you understand these derivatives and can use them in English sentences. Write the Latin words of each lesson vocabulary in a notebook together with additional derivatives. Your teacher will give you directions about the notebook.

Isolation = insulation.

Lesson II

14. SICILIA

Sicilia est īnsula magna in Eurōpā. Magna est fāma Siciliae,[1] sed
fortūna Siciliae [1] nōn bona est. In Siciliā vīta est dūra.[2] Terra et aqua
sunt bonae, sed familiae sunt magnae. Magnae silvae in Siciliā nōn
sunt. Viae nōn bonae sed parvae sunt. Vīta est dūra in Siciliā, et
5 fortūna nōn bona est.

In Siciliā sunt parvae puellae. Parvae puellae pūpās [3] amant. Magnae
puellae aquam portant. Familiae puellās amant. Familiae Siciliam et
Siciliae [1] fāmam amant, sed fortūnam dūram nōn amant.

QUESTIONS

1. Why is life hard in Sicily?
2. What is wrong with Sicilian roads?
3. Can you guess why so many Americans are of Sicilian descent?

15. Adjectives

An *adjective* is a word used to describe a noun or to limit its meaning. We say that an adjective *modifies* its noun. Pick out the adjectives
in the second paragraph of page 1.

In English, an adjective is not changed to show number and case.
For example, we say *good dog* and *good dogs,* but not *goods dogs.*
This and *that,* however, change in the plural to *these* and *those.*

In Latin an adjective changes its ending to match both the number
and the case of the noun it modifies.

1. **magna silva,** *a large forest.*
2. **magnae silvae,** *large forests.*
3. **aquam bonam,** *good water.*

An adjective may be used directly with a noun, as in the examples
above, or in the predicate, as follows:

1. **Magna familia est bona,** *A large family is good.*
2. **Magnae silvae sunt bonae,** *Large forests are good.*

[1] *of Sicily.*   [2] *hard.*   [3] *dolls.*

16. Accusative Case: Direct Object

The *direct object* is the word which is directly acted upon by the verb. It is put in the *accusative* case. In English we call this case the objective case.

In Latin, and sometimes in English, the accusative singular ends in *–m,* the plural usually in *–s:*

	SINGULAR	PLURAL
	–am	–ās
as in:	vi**am**	vi**ās**
Compare English:	hi**m**	road**s**

1. **Puellae silvam amant,** *The girls like the forest.*
2. **Familiae viās bonās amant,** *The families like good roads.*
3. (a) *I saw him.* (b) *He saw me.*

Caution. Do not confuse direct object and predicate nominative **(10). Est** and **sunt** are forms of the linking verb *be.* Any noun they link to the subject must be in the same case as the subject.

Scholars have spent lifetimes studying the ruins, or remains, of ancient buildings such as this one. This is a Sicilian temple where Juno, queen of the gods, was worshiped. (See also pp. 18–19.) Compared with many other ruins, this temple is in a good state of preservation.

James Sawders

Seven hundred years before the birth of Christ, Greek civilization flourished in Sicily, an island southwest of Italy. The Romans, who gained control of Sicily, imitated the beautiful temples the Greeks had built, such as the one shown on the facing page. These ruins are in the Sicilian town of Segesta.

Below: Public baths were popular throughout the Roman world. There were warm and hot rooms (heated by hot air ducts), massage rooms, open areas for exercise, lecture halls, and public libraries.

Erich Lessing/PhotoEdit

17. Word Order

1. In English the adjective almost always precedes the noun it modifies; only rarely do we use such expressions as *lady fair, Captains Courageous.*

In Latin the adjective generally precedes in sentences in which it is more important or emphatic than the noun.

2. The greatest difference between English and Latin is this: in English, word order shows the connection between words and therefore determines the meaning; in Latin, the connection and meaning are shown by the endings. It does not make much difference whether you say **Anna occīdit** (*killed*) **Clāram** or **Clāram occīdit Anna,** but it makes a great deal of difference whether you say *Anna killed Clara* or *Clara killed Anna.*

3. The verb usually stands last in the sentence.

18. Exercises

A. Read in Latin and get the meaning; then translate.

1. Via est bona.
2. Silva est parva.
3. Īnsula est magna.
4. Familiae sunt magnae.
5. Fāmam et vītam amant.
6. Familiae īnsulam amant.
7. Puellae Siciliam amant.
8. Parvae puellae sunt bonae.
9. Puellae aquam bonam portant.
10. Crēta et Sicilia sunt magnae īnsulae.

19

B. Copy these sentences and add the correct endings.

1. Vi___ sunt bon___.
2. Īnsula est magn___.
3. Puell___ est parv___.
4. Puell___ sunt parv___.
5. Terr___ nōn bon___ est.
6. Puellae aqu___ portant.

7. Via et silva sunt magn___.
8. Familiae vīt___ bon___ amant.
9. Familiae fortūn___ bon___ amant.

C. For the English words supply Latin words with the correct endings.

1. Puellae (*the land*) amant.
2. Familiae (*water*) portant.
3. Puellae (*the good roads*) amant.
4. (*Large*) familiae (*small lands*) nōn amant.

19. Vocabulary

a′mant, (*they*) *love, like*	(amatory)
bo′na, *good*	(bonus, bonbon)
fā′ma, *report, fame*	(famous, defamation)
fami′lia, *family*	(familiar)
fortū′na, *fortune, luck*	(fortunate, misfortune)
mag′na, *large, great*	(magnitude, magnify)
par′va, *small*	
por′tant, (*they*) *carry*	(portable, porter)
puel′la, *girl*	
ter′ra, *earth, land*	(terrain, Mediterranean)
vī′ta, *life*	(vital)

20. Roman Numerals in English

Roman numerals are often used in English, as in dates, etc. (see the lesson headings of this book): I = 1; V = 5; X = 10; L = 50; C = 100; D = 500; M = 1000. The other numerals are formed: (*a*) by *adding* to a numeral one or more numerals of equal or smaller value after it: II = 2; VII = 7; CCLVIII = 258; (*b*) by *subtracting* from a numeral by placing a smaller numeral before it: IV = 4; IX = 9; XCV = 95. A smaller numeral placed between two larger numerals subtracts from the following numeral: CCCXLV = 345.

Ball III, strike II.

Lesson III

21. ANNA ET RĀNA

Agricolae in[1] Sardiniā labōrant. Feminae[2] etiam[3] labōrant. Sardinia īnsula magna est et terra ibi[4] dūra est. Agricolae terram exarant et irrigant[5]. Puellae parvae agricolās spectant et temptant[6] adiuvāre.[7] Puella nōmine[8] Anna magnam urnam[9] portat.

FĒMINA NŌMINE CLAUDIA: Quid[10] portās, Anna?   5
ANNA: Urnam portō, Claudia.
         (Fēminae et agricolae rīsitant.[11])
FĒMINA NŌMINE SOPHIA: Quid in urnā est, Anna?
ANNA: Aquam in urnā portō.
AGRICOLA NŌMINE SYLVESTER: Mactē![12] Aquam bonam amāmus.   10
In terrā dūrā labōrāmus.
       (Agricolae et fēminae aquam spectant. Iterum[13] rīsitant.)
AGRICOLA NŌMINE LABŌRIŌ: Quid in aquā est, puella?
ANNA: Rāna[14] parva in aquā est.
CLAUDIA: Rānās amās, Anna?   15
ANNA: Sīc![15] Rānās amō. In silvā multa aqua est. In aquā multae rānae sunt. Rānās amātis?
SOPHIA: Minimē![16]
      (Rāna subsultat[17] et Sophia exclāmat.[18] Sylvester rīsitat.)
LABŌRIŌ: Rānās in silvā amāmus, Anna, sed nōn in urnā.   20
       (Anna etiam rīsitat. Urnam novam parat.)

QUESTIONS

1. Why is work difficult for the farmers and their wives?
2. What is wrong with the water in Anna's jar?
3. Why does Sophia shout?

[1] *on*	[2] *women; wives*	[3] *also*	[4] *there*	[5] *plow and irrigate*
[6] *try*	[7] *to help*	[8] *by the name of*	[9] *water jar*	
[10] *what*	[11] *laugh*	[12] *Well done!*	[13] *again*	[14] *frog*	[15] *Yes*
[16] *No*	[17] *jumps up*	[18] *shouts*		

22. Verbs

1. Verbs tell what a subject is or does. The verb is either the whole predicate or part of it.

Puella parva *est*, The girl *is* small.   **Puellae** *labōrant*, The girls *work*.

2. Verbs also indicate the time, or *tense* (from Latin **tempus,** *time*), of an action, i.e., whether the action is past, present, or future. In English the verb is usually changed to show the tense:

> *I see—I saw; I hear—I heard;* but sometimes, *I put—I put.*

Latin verbs regularly change.

3. *a.* Verbs have three *persons,* in both the singular and the plural. English indicates the persons by the use of *personal pronouns:*

	SINGULAR	PLURAL
1st (the person speaking)	*I*	*we*
2nd (the person spoken to)	*you*	*you*
3rd (the person or thing spoken about)	*he, she, it*	*they*

    b. Latin, however, usually omits personal pronouns, and uses *personal endings* to show the person and number of the subject These, in a sense, are the equivalent of personal pronouns. The most common personal endings are:

	SINGULAR	PLURAL
1st person	$-\bar{o}$ (or $-$ m) $= I$	$-$ mus $=$ *we*
2nd person	$-$ s $=$ *you*	$-$ tis $=$ *you*
3rd person	$-$ t $=$ *he, she, it*	$-$ nt $=$ *they*

These endings must become as familiar to you as the personal pronouns in English.

    c. Sometimes English too changes the verb to show differences of person: (*I*) *have,* (*he*) *has,* or of number: (*I*) *am,* (*we*) *are.*

23. Infinitive

In English, the infinitive is the verb form that is introduced by *to: to go, to be, to prepare.* It does not show person or number.

In Latin, there is no separate word corresponding to the English *to.* The present infinitive of all regular Latin verbs ends in **–re:**

parāre $=$ *to get*   **amāre** $=$ *to love*   **portāre** $=$ *to carry*

The House of Representatives in Washington contains marble plaques of men who made important contributions to American law. Among the Romans are (*left*) Papinian (third century A.D.) and the Emperor Justinian (see p. 2).

24. Present Stem

Drop the infinitive ending **–re** and you have the *present stem:*

parā– (from **parā–re**)   **amā–** (from **amā–re**)   **portā–** (from **portā–re**)

25. First Conjugation Present Tense

The hundreds of verbs in Latin are divided, according to the present stem, into four classes called *conjugations.* Verbs with a present stem ending in **–ā** belong to the *first* conjugation.

The present tense of a first-conjugation verb like **portō** (stem **portā–**) is *conjugated* by adding the personal endings to the present stem·

SINGULAR	PLURAL
por′tō, *I carry, am carrying, do carry*	portā′mus, *we carry, are carrying, do carry*
por′tās, *you carry, are carrying, do carry*	portā′tis, *you carry, are carrying, do carry*
por′tat, *he, she, it carries, is carrying, does carry*	por′tant, *they carry, are carrying, do carry*

Excavations of Pompeii, a town near Naples that was buried by a volcano in 79 A.D., tell us much about Roman life. Town water systems were common, but usually the water had to be carried home from public fountains. This is a reconstruction, a modern picture based upon the actual ancient ruins.

1. *Observe* the three ways to translate each Latin verb form—*common, progressive,* and *emphatic.* Unlike English, Latin does not use *do* and *am* as auxiliary verbs. For example, English says *Do you carry? Are you carrying?* Latin says simply **Portās?**

Thus Latin does not have progressive and emphatic verb forms corresponding to English. Do not say **Est portat** for *He is carrying.* **Portat** is quite enough.

2. Remember that when a noun is used as the subject, the personal pronoun should not be expressed. **Puella portat,** *The girl carries,* not *The girl she carries.*

3. Two singular subjects connected by **et** require a plural verb, just as in English when *and* joins two singular subjects.

4. Note that all vowels are shortened before **–nt** and final **–m** and **–t**. In the first person singular, the stem vowel **–ā–** disappears entirely before the personal ending **–ō.**

26. Exercises

A. Read in Latin and get the meaning; then translate.

1. Amō; parās; spectat.
2. Spectās; parō; amat.
3. Portāmus; amātis; parant.
4. Portant; amāmus; parātis.
5. Portat; parat; est; sunt.
6. Puella terram spectat.
7. Multam aquam portant.
8. Puella bona viam dūram spectat.
9. Puellae et agricolae aquam parant.
10. Agricola et puella silvam spectant.

B. For the English words supply Latin words with the correct endings.

1. Puella (*is preparing*).
2. Agricolae (*carry*) aquam.
3. Multās īnsulās (*I look at*).
4. (*You (sing.) like*) parvam puellam.
5. Terram bonam (*we like*).
6. Parat (*to carry*) aquam.
7. (*Are they watching*) agricolam?
8. (*We do love*) puellās; bonae (*they are*).

C. Copy these sentences and add the correct endings.

1. Portā___ (*we*); para___ (*they*); amā___ (*you, plur.*).
2. Vi___ nov___ sunt bon___.
3. Puellae silv___ (*forests*) amant.
4. Agricol___ aquam bonam spectant.
5. Long___ īnsul___ agricolae amant.

This is a reconstruction of a wall painting from Pompeii that creates the effect of a garden. Many Roman houses had pictures painted on the walls. Wallpaper was unknown.

27. Vocabulary

agri′cola, *farmer* (agriculture)

a′mō, amā′re, [amā′vī, amā′tus],[6] *love, like* (amiable, Amy)

dū′ra, *hard* (durable, endure)

labō′rō, labōrā′re, [labōrā′vī, labōrā′tus], *work* (labor)

lon′ga, *long* (longitude, elongated)

mul′ta, *much;* plur., *many* (multitude, multiply)

no′va, *new, strange* (novel, novelty)

pa′rō, parā′re, [parā′vī, parā′tus], *get, get ready, prepare* (preparation)

por′tō, portā′re, [portā′vī, portā′tus], *carry* (import)

spec′tō, spectā′re, [spectā′vī, spectā′tus], *look at, watch* (inspect)

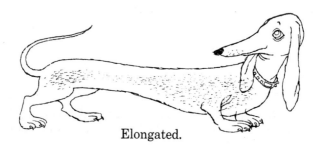

Elongated.

28. English Word Studies

1. An *amiable* person is basically "lovable." What then is a *portable* TV? A *respectable* job? Why do we use *insulation?* What does a *porter* do? An *elaborate* carving is one that required a lot of *work.* An *amateur* pursues his interests for the *love* of it.

2. As we have already seen, many scientific terms in English are *loan words* borrowed straight from the Latin first declension. Here are a few more: *amoeba, amoebae* (or *amoebas*); *nebula, nebulae* (or *nebulas*); *nova, novae* (or *novas*); *scapula, scapulae* (or *scapulas*); *vertebra, vertebrae* (or *vertebras*). Look up the meanings of these words. Remember to pronounce *–ae* as English *–e,* and the rest of the letters as they are pronounced in other English words.

---

[6] The first person singular of the verb is given first, then the present infinitive. The two forms in brackets complete the *principal parts* of the verb. You will not need them for a while, but their regularity and rhythm make them easy to learn now.

Remains of the Milliarium Aureum, the Golden Milestone. The Emperor Augustus erected the column in the Forum to signify the beginning of all the roads of the Empire. Milestones were a common sight on the roads themselves.

Anthony Paccione

Lesson IV

29. VIAE

Multae viae in Italiā erant et sunt. Multae viae Rōmānae erant bonae. Via Appia in Italiā erat et est. Ōlim [1] Via Appia erat via Rōmāna. Nōn nova est sed fāma eius [2] est magna, quod longa et bona via est. Multae viae Americānae ōlim erant malae, sed nunc bonae sunt. In Italiā et in Americā bonās viās laudāmus. Viās malās nōn 5 amāmus. Viās dūrās amātis?

Multī carrī et equī erant in viīs [3] Rōmānīs. Agricolae in Viā Appiā erant. Servī magnī et parvī in viīs erant. Ubi nunc equī sunt? Ubi carrī sunt? Nunc servī nōn sunt.

Agricola carrum bonum parat. Agricola carrum laudat, quod novus 10 et magnus est. Puellae carrōs nōn amant, quod dūrī sunt. Puellae equōs amant, quod bonī sunt. Agricola equōs amat, quod in terrā labōrant. Servum malum nōn laudat, quod nōn labōrat.

QUESTIONS

1. Why is the Appian Way famous?
2. What two great cities did the Appian Way connect? (see map, pp. 92–93).

30. Second Declension Nouns

Nouns of the second declension have these endings:

	SINGULAR	PLURAL
Nominative (subject)	–us	–ī
as in	serv**us**, *slave*	serv**ī**, *slaves*
Accusative (direct object)	–um	–ōs
as in	serv**um**	serv**ōs**

[1] *once.*   [2] *of it = its.*   [3] *on the roads.*

The Appian Way, begun in 312 B.C., was the most important of the ancient Roman roads. It connected Rome with southern Italy. Parts of the Appian Way are lined with tombs of prominent Romans.

Albert Moldvay

31. Gender

In English, and sometimes in Latin, *gender* is a distinction in the form of words corresponding to a distinction of sex. It is shown by change of word (*father,* **pater;** *mother,* **māter**), by change of endings (*master,* **dominus;** *mistress,* **domina**), or by use of a prefix (*he-goat, she-goat*). *Father, master, he-goat* are *masculine* words; *mother, mistress, she-goat* are *feminine* words.

In English, nouns that are the names of sexless things are *neuter*.

In Latin, however, many nouns that would be considered neuter in English are masculine or feminine: **via** (f.), *way;* **carrus** (m.), *cart*. In these cases, the gender is indicated not by the meaning of the word but by its ending. But in other Latin nouns, the sex of the object named determines its gender, as in English.

Nouns of the *first declension* are feminine (except a few that name males); those of the *second declension* ending in **–us** are masculine; the nominative plural ends in **–ī; equus,** *horse;* **equī,** *horses*.

Adjectives have forms to match the gender of the nouns to which they belong: **parva puella, parvus equus, servī bonī.** They therefore *agree* with their nouns in number, case, and gender. We say they *modify* the nouns.

32. Practice

1. Give the nominative plural of **īnsula, equus, fortūna, carrus.**
2. Give the accusative plural of **aqua, servus, fāma, carrus, via.**
3. Give the Latin for *you* (sing.) *get, they are carrying, we do praise, she is working.*

28

33. Exercises

A.
1. Viae sunt malae.
2. Servus erat parvus.
3. Servus nōn est malus.
4. Magnī equī sunt et bonī.
5. Carrī magnī sunt sed equī sunt parvī.
6. Servī aquam laudant.
7. Servus malus in terrā labōrat.
8. Agricola magnōs carrōs spectat.
9. Ubi servī multōs carrōs parant?
10. Puella et agricola longam vītam laudant.

B.
1. (*Wagons*) nunc nōn sunt.
2. Nunc fortūna (*bad*) est.
3. (*The farmer*) equōs bonōs parat.
4. Agricolae (*the good slaves*) laudant.
5. Ubi est (*the large island*)?
6. Amāmus (*the girl*) quod bona est.
7. Aquam (*the large slaves*) portant.
8. (*Large wagons*) agricolae spectant.

C.
1. Bon— est equus.
2. Carrī long— sunt.
3. Serv— aqu— portant.
4. Ubi sunt vi— long—?
5. Puella est parv— et bon—.
6. Puellae īnsulam ama—.
7. Serv— agricola specta—.
8. Servus equum mal— nōn ama—.
9. In īnsulā terr— dūr— erat.
10. Bon— serv— puellam bon— laudat.

34. Vocabulary

car′rus, m.,[4] *cart, wagon*   (car, carriage)
e′quus, m., *horse*   (equine, equestrian)
e′rat, *he, she, it was;* **e′rant,** *they were*
lau′dō, laudā′re, [laudā′vī, laudā′tus], *praise*   (laudatory)
ma′lus, ma′la, *bad* [5]   (malice, malign)
nunc, adverb,[6] *now*
quod, conjunction,[6] *because*
ser′vus, m., *slave*   (servile, servitude)
u′bi, adverb,[6] *where*

---

[4] In the vocabularies the letters *m., f.,* or *n.* will tell you whether the noun is masculine, feminine, or neuter in Latin.
[5] The masculine and feminine nominative singular of adjectives will be given from now on.
[6] For definitions of adverb and conjunction see **526, 528.**

Associated Press

Above: Roman road discovered during the building of a modern highway to Rome's new airport at Fiumicino, near Ostia. **Right:** The ancient Via Tusculana, at modern Frascati, southeast of Rome.

35. English Word Studies

1. It does not take a *genius* to see that a *bonus* is something "good." *Genius* ("inborn talent") and *bonus* are just two of many *loan words* the Latin second declension has given to English in their original form. Here are others. (When the plural ends in the original *–i*, pronounce it like the *–i* in *ripe*.)

> *alumnus, alumni*;
> *bacillus, bacilli*;
> *circus, circuses*;
> *focus, focuses* (or *foci*);
> *stimulus, stimuli* (or *stimuluses*)

Look up the meanings and the plurals of: *campus, fungus, gladiolus, humus, locus, quietus*.

2. Here are the names of some American cities and towns with Latin names that show the influence of Rome on the building of this country: *Alma, Americus, Augusta, Aurora, Cincinnati, Columbia, Columbus, Concordia, Paramus, Pomona, Urbana, Utica*. There are many more; for example, at least ten towns, from Maine to California, are called *Aetna* (or *Etna*, the English spelling). Perhaps your hometown has a classical name.

Glimpses of Roman Life

36. ROMAN ROADS AND TRAVEL

Perhaps nothing better demonstrates the industry, thoroughness, and engineering skill of the Romans than the system of roads with which they linked their empire. Built like walls as much as three feet deep into the ground, and running in straight lines across all but the most difficult terrain, many of these roads are still in use today, an example to the modern world. For they are more than monuments to Roman skills, they are testimony to the practical vision of a people who quickly saw that their military conquests would be made permanent, and commerce and colonization flourish, only with extensive and efficient means of communication. So they built nearly 50,000 miles of hard-surface highways—enough to circle the globe twice—radiating out from Rome through Italy and beyond. For a faster means of travel the world had to wait until the eighteenth century, when the invention of the steam engine made possible railroads and steamships.

The construction of our railroads is an earlier and perhaps better parallel to the Romans' efforts than our system of superhighways, for petroleum and the automobile have come late in history, and until very recently our own highways have been built in a most haphazard manner. Even as the twenty-first century approaches, America's system of interstate highways is still being completed.

The queen of Roman highways (**rēgīna viārum,** as the Roman poet Statius said) was the Appian Way, built in 312 B.C., just after the Romans had subdued Latium. Like most Roman roads, it took its name from its builder, the magistrate Appius Claudius. (For convenience we number our highways, but we also often give them names as memorials to prominent citizens.) The **Via Appia** stretched about 130 miles from Rome to Capua, the most important city in southern Italy. Later it was extended more than 200 miles across Italy to Brundisium, the seaport gateway to Greece and the Orient. Much of it is still in use.

It is not difficult to imagine the bustle and confusion of these great arteries of commerce, crowded with all sorts of travelers and vehicles. Horses, mules, carriages or omnibuses, and litters were used by those who did not wish to journey on foot. All along the roads there were milestones to indicate distances (see p. 27). There were benches and fountains where the weary might refresh themselves, and watering troughs for the animals. Still, travel was slow and difficult (the word *travel* basically means "torture"; compare the related word *travail*). Fifty to sixty miles a day was a fast rate for people in a great hurry.

Half that speed was a fair average. Compare this with the speeds of jet planes and space capsules.

But if the roads were good, the hotel accommodations were poor. Those who could afford it shunned the cramped, dirty, and uncomfortable inns, and stayed overnight at country villas belonging to themselves or their friends (a wealthy Roman might have half a dozen or more villas scattered throughout Italy).

Travel by water was avoided if possible, but there were fortunes to be made in overseas trade, and merchants swallowed their fear and took their cargoes to sea in small vessels propelled by sails and oars. Sailing was always dangerous, so the ships skirted the coast as much as possible, and almost never put to sea during the winter months.

All these roads, by land or sea, led back to Rome as well. Along them came not just men and goods, but ideas too: Greek art and literature, Eastern religions, eventually Christianity itself.

DISCUSSION QUESTIONS

1. The Romans were great road builders—why?
2. What effect has rapid transportation had on the development of the United States, Canada, and modern western Europe?
3. For centuries, man could travel no faster than the horse he rode. What discoveries have enabled him to move faster?

A modern thoroughfare in Rome. On the left are the ruins of the Temple of Venus and Rome, with some of the columns at one side.

Servizio Editorio Fotografico/Art Resource

UNIT I REVIEW

37. VOCABULARY

The English meanings of these Latin words will be found with corresponding numbers on the following page. Study both pages and drill yourself on the words. You will find it helpful to ask someone to test you by reading the words in the Latin list. As each word is read, give the English meaning.

NOUNS

1. **agricola**	5. **fāma**	9. **puella**	13. **via**
2. **aqua**	6. **familia**	10. **servus**	14. **vīta**
3. **carrus**	7. **fortūna**	11. **silva**	
4. **equus**	8. **īnsula**	12. **terra**	

ADJECTIVES

15. **bonus**	17. **longus**	19. **malus**	21. **novus**
16. **dūrus**	18. **magnus**	20. **multus**	22. **parvus**

VERBS

23. **amō**	25. **est, sunt**	27. **laudō**	29. **portō**
24. **erat, erant**	26. **labōrō**	28. **parō**	30. **spectō**

ADVERBS

31. **nōn**	32. **nunc**	33. **ubi**

CONJUNCTIONS

34. **et**	35. **quod**	36. **sed**

38. GRAMMAR SUMMARIES

A. Nouns

In Latin	*In English*
1. Show person and number by their endings.	1. Show person and number in only a few endings.
2. Usually omit pronoun subjects.	2. Regularly use pronoun subjects.

B. Adjectives

In Latin	In English
1. Change form to agree with the noun they modify in number, gender, and case.	1. Do not change form to agree with the noun they modify.
2. Generally follow the noun.	2. Regularly precede the noun.

C. Verbs

In Latin	In English
1. Endings to show person and number.	1. Few endings to show person and number.
2. Pronoun subjects usually omitted.	2. Pronoun subjects regularly used.

39. VOCABULARY (English Meanings)

NOUNS

1. *farmer*	5. *report*	9. *girl*	13. *road, way*
2. *water*	6. *family*	10. *slave*	14. *life*
3. *cart, wagon*	7. *fortune*	11. *forest*	
4. *horse*	8. *island*	12. *land, earth*	

ADJECTIVES

15. *good*	17. *long*	19. *bad*	21. *new*
16. *hard*	18. *large*	20. *much*	22. *little*

VERBS

23. *love, like*	25. *is, are*	27. *praise*	29. *carry*
24. *was, were*	26. *work*	28. *get, prepare*	30. *look at*

ADVERBS

31. *not*	32. *now*	33. *where*

CONJUNCTIONS

34. *and*	35. *because*	36. *but*

40. ENDINGS AND STEMS

1. What are the endings of the nominative case, singular and plural, in the first declension? In the second declension?

2. What are the endings of the accusative case, singular and plural, in the first declension? In the second declension?
3. How do you find the present stem of a Latin verb? With what letter does the stem of a first-conjugation verb end? What are the six personal endings?

41. UNIT PRACTICE

A. In each of the sentences below, identify the subject, the verb, and the object (when there is one). Translate each sentence.

1. Equus est parvus.
2. Longam viam nunc parātis.
3. Parvī carrī equōs nōn portant.
4. Agricola fortūnam bonam laudat.
5. Servus et puella multam aquam portant.
6. Anna puellās spectat.
7. In Siciliā viae sunt parvae.
8. Virginia et Anna equōs amant.
9. Silvae erant magnae et longae.
10. In silvā aquam bonam parātis?

B. Give the Latin for the words in italic type:

1. Anna loved *horses.*
2. It was *a long road.*
3. My sons are *small.*
4. Anna is *a good girl.*
5. I saw *large wagons.*
6. These horses are *small.*
7. He owned *a small island.*
8. We must have *good water.*

C. In what number and case are each of the following: **fortūna, īnsulam, equī, servōs, via?** Give the correct form of **magnus** with each of the above words.

D. 1. Give the present tense of **amō** and translate each form in three ways.
2. Translate: **sunt, parant, laudāmus, est, portātis.**

42. ENGLISH WORD STUDIES

1. What is a *loan word?* How should *–ae* be pronuonced in the English word *fibulae?* How should *–i* be pronounced in English *fungi?*

2. Judging from the meaning of their Latin roots, what do you think the following italicized words mean?

a *laudable* success; *conservation* of energy; to live in *amity;* a *multitude* of errors; *aquatic* sports.

UNIT II

ROME AND AMERICA

The square building known as the Senate House, or *Curia* in the Roman Forum, is where the Roman lawmakers assembled. This building was the scene of all the major decisions which made Rome a great power. Modern public buildings often recall ideas that were important in ancient Rome. The classical design of the Capitol Building (insert) in Washington, D.C., suggests the dignity of government and the majesty of the law.

Scala/Art Resource

Washington, D.C. Tourism Office

Roma regina terrarum. A modern museum outside Rome contains this small-scale model of the ancient city. The round building in the background is the famous amphitheater (round theater) called the Colosseum. Dedicated in 80 A.D., the Colosseum was the scene of fights between gladiators, exhibits of wild animals, and mock sea battles.

Museo della Civiltà Romana

Lesson V

43. RŌMA

Rōma prīmō[1] parva erat et Rōmānī[2] nōn multī erant. Propter Septimontium,[3] urbs[4] nōn plāna erat, sed fōrma Rōmae quadrāta[5] erat. Posteā[6] urbs magna et clāra erat; regīna terrārum erat. Fortūna Rōmae et Rōmānōrum bona erat.

5   Viae Romanae multae et longae erant. Regīna viārum erat Via Appia. Olim[7] erat magnus numerus carrōrum et equōrum in Viā Appiā. Nunc in viīs[8] Italiae nōn multī carrī et equī sunt. Olim multī servī erant in viīs Rōmānīs, sed nōn iam.[9]

    Quod aqua bona erat magna cura Rōmānōrum, erant multae et longae
10 aquaeductiōnēs[10] in Latiō antīquō.[11] Etiam[12] nunc copia aquae clārae est cūra multōrum Italiānōrum et multōrum Americānōrum.

    Fāma Rōmae magna est. Fāma Americae etiam magna est. Rōmam et Americam laudāmus, quod clārae sunt et erant. Rōma regīna terrārum erat. Est America nunc regīna terrārum? Tōtus orbis terrārum[13] est cūra
15 Americae.

    Multī Americānī Rōmam laudant; ruīnās antīquās Rōmae spectant et laudant. Fōrmam Rōmae antīquae et novae spectant. Pictūrās ruīnārum Rōmānārum amātis?

QUESTIONS

1. What was Rome's original size and shape?
2. What did Rome's water supply have to do with its growth?
3. What attraction does Rome have for tourists?

[1] *at first*   [2] *Romans*   [3] *on account of its seven hills*   [4] *city*   [5] *square*
[6] *afterwards*   [7] *once*   [8] *on the roads*   [9] *not now = no longer*
[10] *aqueducts*   [11] *ancient Latium*   [12] *even, also*   [13] *the whole world*

44. Genitive Case

In English, the objective case with *of* shows various relations between nouns, including possession; there is also a possessive case:

SINGULAR	PLURAL
1. *the father of the boy*	*the father of the boys*
2. *the boy's father*	*the boys' father*

In Latin, these various relations are shown by the *genitive* case. Its endings in the first and second declensions are:

	SINGULAR		PLURAL	
Declension:	FIRST	SECOND	FIRST	SECOND
	–ae	–ī	–ārum	–ōrum
as in:	viae	servī	viārum	servōrum

1. **equus agricolae,** *the horse of the farmer, the farmer's horse.*
2. **cōpia cibī,** *a supply of food.*

Translation Hint. In English, when the subject follows the verb, the sentence (unless it is a question) begins with *there*. In Latin, no such word is used (see section **7**):

Sunt multae viae, *There are many roads.*

Practice

Give the Latin nominative, genitive, and accusative, singular and plural, of *water, supply, wagon, land, number.*

45. Exercises

A. 1. Equōs amāmus.
2. Cōpia est aquae bonae.
3. Fōrma terrae plāna nōn est.
4. Cūrae puellārum parvae sunt.
5. Numerus servōrum magnus erat.
6. Silvās clārās īnsulae magnae spectātis.

B. 1. Cōpiam (*of good water*) portāmus.
2. Terram novam (*we are looking at*).
3. (*There is not*) rēgīna Americae.
4. Parvus est numerus (*of the girls*).
5. Cibus (*of the slaves*) parvus erat.

C. 1. Ann___ (*Anna's*) cūrae erant mult___.
2. Numerus equ___ (*of the horses*) erat magn___.
3. Cōpiam cib___ bon___ para___ (*they are preparing*).
4. Agricol___ (*the farmers'*) cōpiam cibī equus portat.
5. Fāma īnsul___ parv___ (*of the small islands*) magna erat.

46. Vocabulary

ci′bus, ci′bī, m., *food*	
clā′rus, clā′ra, *clear, famous*	(clarify)
cō′pia, cō′piae, f., *supply, abundance*	(copious)
cū′ra, cū′rae, f., *care, concern*	(curator, curious)
fōr′ma, fōr′mae, f., *shape*	(formal, reformatory)
nu′merus, nu′merī, m., *number*	(numerical, enumerate)
plā′nus, plā′na, *level*	(plain, aquaplane)
rēgī′na, rēgī′nae, f., *queen*	

Important! Beginning with this vocabulary you are given the four things which you must memorize about each noun in the lesson vocabularies:

1. the nominative singular
2. the genitive singular
3. the gender
4. the basic meaning(s)

These four things, and your knowledge of the standard endings of the declension to which a noun belongs, give you control over that noun.

47. Latin Phrases and Abbreviations in English

i.e. (id est), *that is.*
cf. (confer), *compare.*
Fortuna caeca est, *Fortune is blind.*
etc. (et cetera), *and the rest, and so forth.*
Magna Charta, *the Great Paper,* the document, signed in 1215, that is one of the cornerstones of English civil liberties.

A detail of Magna Charta. Which of these Latin words are familiar to you?

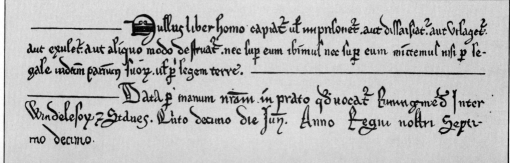

Commisariat General Tourism (Nimes)

Rome's empire outside Italy was divided into provinces (see map, pages 92–93). All of Gaul (ancient France) was finally made a Roman province by Julius Caesar in the first century B.C. This Roman amphitheater at Nîmes, France, is sometimes used for bullfights, not unlike the shows held there in ancient times.

Lesson VI

48. EURŌPA

Ad Eurōpam nāvigābō; tōta [1] familia nāvigābit. Nautae nāvem [2] novam parābunt. Magnam pecūniam ad Eurōpam portābimus. Cibum nōn parābimus, quod in nāvī [3] magna cōpia cibī bonī est. Pecūnia cibum parābit.

Magnās undās spectābimus; sed aquam plānam, nōn magnās undās, 5 amāmus. Ad īnsulam clāram Britanniam nāvigābimus. In Britanniā familia domum [4] rēgīnae spectābit. Ruīnās Rōmānās in Britanniā spectābō. Tum ad Galliam tōta [1] familia nāvigābit. In Galliā rēgīna nōn est, sed familia multās pictūrās spectābit. Ruīnās Rōmānās in Galliā spectābō. 10

[1] whole.　　　[2] Accusative singular: ship.　　　[3] on the ship.
[4] house. What would be a better translation here?

41

Tum ad Germāniam et ad Austriam ībimus.[5] Familia pictūrās et statuās in Germāniā et in Austriā spectābit, sed ego [6] ruīnās Rōmānās spectābō. Tum ad Italiam ībimus.[5] In Italiā tōta [1] familia ruīnās Rōmānās spectābit.

15 Rēgīnās et pictūrās et statuās et terrās novās spectābō, sed ruīnās Rōmānās amō et amābō.

QUESTIONS

1. Who is going to Europe?
2. Where can one find Roman ruins in Europe?
3. What does the speaker in this story especially like?

49. Future Tense

The *future* tense refers to something that *will* happen at some *future* time.

In Latin, the future of the first conjugation is formed by adding the tense sign **–bi–** (corresponding to *shall* and *will* in English) to the present stem and then attaching the same personal endings as in the present:

SINGULAR	PLURAL
portā**bō**, *I shall carry*	portā**bimus**, *we shall carry*
portā**bis**, *you will carry*	portā**bitis**, *you will carry*
portā**bit**, *he, she, it will carry*	portā**bunt**, *they will carry*

Observe that the future sign **–bi–** loses **i** before **–ō** in the first person singular and changes to **–bu–** before **–nt** in the third person plural.

Practice

1. Give the future indicative of **labōrō** and **nāvigō**, and translate.
2. Tell the form of **labōrātis, portābit, nāvigāmus, parant, spectābitis.**

[5] *we shall go.*   [6] *I.*

Pecunia. A hoard of Roman coins found recently in a jar. Ancient coins reveal many items of political interest, since they commonly portray famous men and events and were often used for purposes of propaganda. Do we put our own coins to a similar use?

Museo Civico, Padua

50. Exercises

A. 1. Ad silvam cibum portābunt.
2. Nunc carrum rēgīnae laudāmus.
3. Ad terram novam nāvigābimus.
4. Magnae undae ad īnsulam sunt.
5. Ubi magnam cōpiam cibī parābis?
6. Nautae ad īnsulam plānam nāvigābunt.
7. Anna ad familiam cōpiam aquae portābit.
8. Ubi undae erant, fōrma terrae plāna est.

B. 1. Ad terrās novās (*we shall sail*).
2. Multōs carrōs (*he will prepare*).
3. Undās magnās (*they will look at*).
4. Ad familiam nautae pecūniam (*I shall carry*).
5. Numerus undārum magnus (*was*).

C. 1. Est cōpia cib__ bon__.
2. Ubi sunt silv__ īnsul__ (*of the island*)?
3. Cōpiam pecūni__ parā__ (*we shall get*).
4. Familia naut__ (*sailor's*) ad īnsul__ nāvigā__ (*will sail*).
5. Terr__ plān__ agricolae amā__ (*will like*).

51. Vocabulary

ad, preposition [7] with acc., *to, toward* (with verbs of "coming" and "going"); *near* (with verbs of rest)
nau′ta, nau′tae, m., *sailor* (nautical)
nā′vigō, nāvigā′re, [nāvigā′vī, nāvigā′tus], *sail* (navigation)
pecū′nia, pecū′niae, f., *sum of money, money* (pecuniary)
tum, adverb, *then*
un′da, un′dae, f., *wave* (undulate, inundate)

52. English Word Studies

From what Latin word does *impecunious* come? What does this sentence mean? The town was *inundated* by the river, and the river itself was not *navigable*.

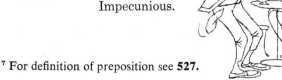

Impecunious.

43

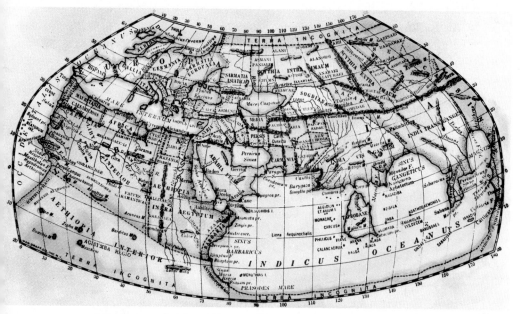

Columbus probably used this kind of map, based on a fifteenth-century Latin translation of the geography of the ancient Greek Ptolemy. Note the prominence of India, which Columbus thought he had reached; hence he called the American natives Indians.

Lesson VII

53. COLUMBUS

Columbus ad Hispāniam nāvigat. Isabellae, rēgīnae Hispāniae, nūntiat: "Terra nōn plāna est; id [1] probābō et terrās novās mōnstrābō. Ad Indiam nāvigābō: viam novam mōnstrābō." Sed Isabella pecūniam nōn dōnat. Tum amīcus Columbī litterās ad Isabellam portat, et 5 Isabella Columbō pecūniam mandat. Columbus grātus amīcō fortūnam bonam nūntiat.

Annō Dominī [2] MCCCCXCII Columbus nāvigat, sed via longa est et cūrae multae sunt. Vīta nautārum dūra est. Magnus numerus nautārum malōrum Columbum accūsat: [3] "Īnsānus est! Ubinam 10 gentium sumus? [4] Terra plāna est. Indiam numquam [5] spectābimus."

[1] *it.*   [2] *in the year of our Lord.* What abbreviation is used in English?
[3] *criticize.*   [4] *where in the world are we;* literally, *where of nations.*
[5] *never.*

44

Columbus nautīs malīs nūntiat: "Ad terrās novās nāvigābimus. Vōbīs [6] praedam magnam dōnābō."

Sed subitō [7] nauta terram grātam Columbō mōnstrat. Columbus cūram nāvis [8] nautīs mandat et terram novam spectat. Īnsula parva est, sed grāta nautīs, quod terra firma est. Tum Columbus litterās ad 15 Isabellam portat et Isabellae praedam dōnat. Nautīs praedam dōnat?

QUESTIONS

1. What caused the queen to grant Columbus' request?
2. What caused the sailors to mutiny?
3. Find in an encyclopedia where Columbus got the idea that the earth was round.

54. Dative Case: Indirect Object

The direct object takes the force of the verb directly, *He tells a story*. Verbs that mean give, show, tell, etc., often carry this direct action over *to* (or *for*) another noun, which is the *indirect object* and is in the *dative* case, *He tells the girl a story*.

In Latin, the endings of the dative in the first and second declensions are:

	SINGULAR		PLURAL	
Declension:	FIRST	SECOND	FIRST	SECOND
	–ae	–ō	–īs	–īs
as in:	viae	servō	viīs	servīs

Nautae pecūniam dōnō, *I give money to the sailor,* or *I give the sailor money.*

Observe the following points:

1. The direct object (**pecūniam,** *money*) is in the accusative; an indirect object (**nautae,** *sailor*) to show the receiver may be used.

2. In Latin the indirect object is expressed by the dative, but in English it may be expressed either by the dative, as in the second translation, or by the objective case with *to* (or *for*).

3. In English there is no separate form for the dative.

4. In English, and often in Latin, the dative is placed before the accusative.

5. In Latin the genitive and dative singular of the first declension have the same ending. In both declensions the dative plural has the same ending.

[6] *to you.*   [7] *suddenly.*   [8] *of the ship.*

Caution. After verbs of motion like "come" and "go, *to* is expressed in Latin by a preposition (**ad** with the acc.):

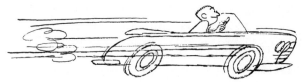

1. He went *to the city* as fast as he could (accusative with **ad**).

UBI IGNIS EST?

2. He told his story *to the officer* and showed *him* his driver's license (datives of indirect object).

55. Practice

A. Give the Latin nominative, genitive, dative, and accusative, singular and plural, of *shape, money, horse, care, number.*

B. Tell the case to be used in Latin in translating the words in italics:
1. Forgive *us* our debts.
2. I showed *Anna* the book.
3. I told my *friend* the whole story.
4. We carried our bags to the *station.*
5. He presented his library to the *city.*
6. He told *me* how to go to the *wharf.*
7. They moved to *California.*
8. Do it for *me.*
9. Show *him* to *me.*

56. Exercises

A.
1. Familiae pecūniam dōnābit.
2. Puellae litterās mandāmus.
3. Servō praedam nōn mōnstrābimus.
4. Amīcīs bonīs litterās mandābis.
5. Anna Clārae magnam pecūniam dōnābit.
6. Carrī ad silvam parvam aquam clāram portant.
7. Columbō magnam pecūniam Isabella rēgīna mandat.
8. Annae viās silvae mōnstrābō.

B.
1. (*To many lands*) nāvigābimus.
2. (*To the sailor*) litterās mandābō.
3. (*To the sailors*) viam mōnstrant.
4. (*To Anna*) fortūnam bonam nūntiābit.
5. (*To many families*) pecūniam dōnat.

Above: The *Santa Maria,* largest of Columbus' three ships.
Right: Model of a Roman freighter, based on mosaics from Ostia, the seaport of Rome.

C. 1. Naut___ (*sing.*) litterās mandābō.
2. Naut___ (*plur.*) pecūniam dōnābimus.
3. Nautae _____ (*to the islands*) nāvigābunt.
4. _____ (*to Clara*) cibum dōna___ (*she gives*).
5. _____ (*to Anna*) litterās portā___ (*she will carry*).

57. Vocabulary

amī′cus, amī′cī, m., *friend*   [amo] [9]
dō′nō, dōnā′re, [dōnā′vī, dōnā′tus], *give, present*   (donation)
grā′tus, grā′ta, *pleasing, grateful*   (gratitude, gratify)
lit′tera, lit′terae, f., *letter* (of the alphabet); plur.,
    a letter (epistle), *letters* (if modified by an adjective
    such as **multae**)   (literary) [10]
man′dō, mandā′re, [mandā′vī, mandā′tus], *entrust*   (mandate)
mōns′trō, mōnstrā′re, [mōnstrā′vī, mōnstrā′tus], *point out,*
    show   (demonstration)
nūn′tiō, nūntiā′re, [nūntiā′vī, nūntiā′tus], *report, announce*
                                              (pronunciation)
prae′da, prae′dae, f., *loot*   (predatory)
pro′bō, probā′re, [probā′vī, probā′tus], *test, prove, approve*
                                              (probation)

---

[9] When a new word in the vocabulary is related to a word previously studied, the latter instead of an English derivative is given in brackets.

[10] Except for *letter,* all the English derivatives have one *t,* based on an older spelling **lītera.**

58. English Word Studies

Try to see the relation between the meaning of the English derivative and the Latin word from which it comes, and then use the derivative in a sentence:

1. A "literary" man is a man of *letters;* a "literal" translation is one that is almost *letter for letter.*

2. A "mandate" is something *entrusted* to a person or a group, as the government of a weak nation.

3. A "novelty" is something *new.*

4. A person who is on "probation" is being *tested.*

In the same way explain a *familiar* friend, an *undulating* river, an *amicable* attitude, an interested *spectator.*

Hadrian's Villa. The Emperor Hadrian (117–138 A.D.) built a splendid summer palace, really a small town, about 18 miles from Rome, near the town of Tivoli. In it he imitated some of the fine buildings he had seen in Athens, Egypt, and elsewhere.

Susan McCartney/Photo Researchers, Inc.

Lesson VIII

59. GALLIA

Rōmānī Galliam occupant et magnam praedam parant. Gallī [1] fortūnās et familiās silvīs mandant. Rōmānī magnās poenās Gallīs parant. Poenae dūrae sunt. Tum memoria iniūriārum prōvinciam Galliam ad pugnam incitat. Gallī Rōmānīs nūntiant: "Terram nostram [2] pugnīs occupātis. Praedam magnam ad Italiam 5 multīs carrīs portātis. Poenae nostrae [2] dūrae sunt. Sed pugnābimus et victōriīs nostrīs [2] vītam [3] et pecūniam nostram servābimus. Iniūriīs et poenīs nōs [4] ad pugnam incitātis. Pugnāre parāmus. Victōriās grātās familiīs nostrīs nūntiābimus, sed vōs [5] victōriās grātās Rōmae nōn nūntiābitis." 10

Gallī diū et fortiter [6] pugnant, sed multae et clārae sunt victōriae Rōmānōrum. Pugnīs Gallī vītam et terram nōn servant.

Ubi est prōvincia Gallia? Gallōs accūsātis quod pugnāvērunt? [7] Animum [8] Gallōrum nōn laudātis? Pugnās Gallōrum memoriae mandābitis? 15

QUESTIONS

1. What did the Gauls do with their families?
2. What did the Romans do to Gaul?
3. Why is France today called a Latin country?

60. Ablative Case

In English, the object of any preposition is in the objective (accusative) case.

In Latin, the object of some prepositions is in the accusative case; of others, in a case called the *ablative,* which has these endings:

Declension:	SINGULAR		PLURAL	
	FIRST	SECOND	FIRST	SECOND
	−ā	−ō	−īs	−īs
as in:	viā	servō	viīs	servīs

---

[1] *the Gauls,* i.e., the people of Gaul (**Gallia**).
[2] *our.*
[3] In English we use the plural.
[4] *us.*
[5] *you.*
[6] *long and bravely.*
[7] *they fought.*
[8] *courage.*

The famous church of the Madeleine in Paris is built like a Roman temple, with highly ornate (Corinthian) columns, a Latin inscription, and sculpture in the triangular space known as the pediment.

61. Ablative of Means

Many ideas expressed in English by a noun preceded by a preposition are expressed in Latin by a noun in the ablative case without a preposition, as the following common type:

Litterīs victōriam nūntiant, *They report the victory by* (*means of*) *a letter,* or *with a letter.*

Observe that **litterīs** (abl.) shows *by what means* they report, and that no preposition is used.

Practice

1. Translate and tell the case and number of **memoriam, amīcōrum, iniūriā, fōrmae, numerō, poenīs.** Notice that some of these may require more than one answer.

2. Translate and tell the person, number, and tense of **occupābis, pugnātis, incitāmus, servāmus, mōnstrābō, dōnat.**

62. Exercises

A. 1. Pugnīs īnsulam occupātis.
2. Cibō multās familiās servābitis.
3. Victōriīs vītam et prōvinciam servant.
4. Memoriā iniūriae nautās incitās.
5. Aquā vītam equōrum servābimus.
6. Puella memoriae litterās mandābit.
7. Litterīs magnam victōriam rēgīnae nūntiābit.

B. 1. (*With money*) nautās incitāmus.
2. (*To friends*) victōriam nūntiābō.
3. (*With care*) vītam amīcī servābō.
4. (*By the victory*) prōvinciam servābimus.
5. Memoria iniūriārum et poenārum nautās (*arouses*).

C. 1. Pecūni___ nautās incitā___ (*I shall urge on*).
2. Serv___ (*of the slaves*) poenam nōn probāmus.
3. Aqu___ (*with water*) silvam serva___ (*they save*).
4. Victōri___ (*by victory*) prōvinciam servā___ (*they will save*).
5. Amīc___ (*to friends*) pecūniam dōnā___ (*I shall give*).

63. Vocabulary

in'citō, incitā're, [incitā'vī, incitā'tus], *urge on, arouse*
(incitement)
iniū'ria, iniū'riae, f., *wrong, injustice* (injurious)
memo'ria, memo'riae, f., *memory* (memorable, memorial)
oc'cupō, occupā're, [occupā'vī, occupā'tus], *seize* (occupation)
poe'na, poe'nae, f., *penalty, punishment* (penal)
prōvin'cia, prōvin'ciae, f., *province* (provincial)
pug'na, pug'nae, f., *fight, battle* (pugnacity, pugnacious)
pug'nō, pugnā're, [pugnā'vī, pugnā'tus], *fight* (repugnant)
ser'vō, servā're, [servā'vī, servā'tus], *save, guard* (conservation)
victō'ria, victō'riae, f., *victory* (victorious)

64. English Word Studies

1. Explain *curator, reservoir, incite, conservation.* From what Latin words are *vitamin, vitality, injury, commemoration* derived?

2. Latin phrases in English:

persona non grata, *an unacceptable person.*
Nova Scotia, *New Scotland,* a province in Canada.
ad nauseam, *to* [the point of] *seasickness* or *disgust.*
aqua vitae, *water of life,* formerly applied to alcohol.

51

Lesson IX

65. CORNĒLIA NAUTAM SERVAT

MĀTER[1]: Fīliae, fīliae, paene[2] quīnta hōra est. Portāte aquam ad casam[3] et cibum parāte. Anna, ubi est soror[4] tua Cornēlia?

ANNA: Aquam portābō, māter. Cornēlia in arēnā[5] est. Undās spectat.

MĀTER: Puella ignāva[6] est! Anna, nūntiā Cornēliae cūram meam.

        (Nunc quīnta hōra est.)   5

VOX[7] CORNĒLIAE: Māter! Pater![8] Adiuvāte![9]

MĀTER: Eheu! Eheu![10] Est vox Cornēliae. Fīlia mea exclāmat.[11] Festīnāte![12]

    (Māter et pater et Anna ad arēnam festīnant.)

CORNĒLIA: Spectāte—in undīs! Nauta est! Rēmum[13] longum prēnsat[14] 10 sed saucius[15] est!

PATER: Ubi est nauta, Cornēlia? Mōnstrā eum.[16]

    (Cornēlia nautam saucium monstrat.)

CORNĒLIA ET ANNA: Festīnā, pater! Servā eum!

MĀTER: Pater tuus ad nautam natat.[17] Eum servābit.   15

ANNA: Spectāte! Pater nautam et rēmum prēnsat. Nunc eōs[18] ad arēnam reportābit.[19]

CORNĒLIA: Strāgulum[20] parābō. (Cornēlia ad casam festīnat.)

    (Nunc decima[21] hōra est. Cornēlia et Anna cibum parant.)

NAUTA: Fortūna mea bona erat et grātia mea magna est. Semper   20 familiam tuam laudābō.

PATER: Aliquandō[22] fīlia mea Cornēlia ignāva est, sed nōn hodiē.[23] Mactē,[24] Cornēlia!

QUESTIONS

1. Why was Cornelia's mother angry?
2. How was the sailor saved?

[1] *Mother*   [2] *almost*   [3] *house*   [4] *sister*   [5] *beach*   [6] *lazy*
[7] *voice*   [8] *Father*   [9] *help*   [10] *Alas!*   [11] *is shouting*   [12] *hurry*
[13] *oar*   [14] *is clutching*   [15] *hurt*   [16] *him*   [17] *is swimming*   [18] *them*
[19] *will carry back*   [20] *blanket*   [21] *tenth*   [22] *sometimes*   [23] *today*
[24] *Well done!*

66. Summary of First and Second Declensions

	ENDINGS				USE
	FIRST DECLENSION		SECOND DECLENSION		
	SING.	PLUR.	SING.	PLUR.	
Nom.	–a	–ae	–us	–ī	Subject; Pred. Nom.
Gen.	–ae	–ārum	–ī	–ōrum	Possessive, etc.
Dat.	–ae	–īs	–ō	–īs	Indirect Object
Acc.	–am	–ās	–um	–ōs	Direct Object
Abl.	–ā	–īs	–ō	–īs	Means, etc.

	FIRST DECLENSION		SECOND DECLENSION	
	SINGULAR	PLURAL	SINGULAR	PLURAL
Nom.	via nova	viae novae	equus meus	equī meī
Gen.	viae novae	viārum novārum	equī meī	equōrum meōrum
Dat.	viae novae	viīs novīs	equō meō	equīs meīs
Acc.	viam novam	viās novās	equum meum	equōs meōs
Abl.	viā novā	viīs novīs	equō meō	equīs meīs

	FIRST AND SECOND DECLENSIONS	
	SINGULAR	PLURAL
Nom.	nauta bonus	nautae bonī
Gen.	nautae bonī	nautārum bonōrum
Dat.	nautae bonō	nautīs bonīs
Acc.	nautam bonum	nautās bonōs
Abl.	nautā bonō	nautīs bonīs

Note carefully which endings are the same. For example, in the first declension the genitive singular, the dative singular, and the nominative plural all end in **–ae.** Find all the rest. In a Latin sentence, how do you know which case is indicated? By deciding which of the various possibilities makes the best sense in that sentence. The secret of rapid reading is to know the endings so well that the decision becomes almost automatic.

Caution. In the first declension, short **–a** (nominative singular) and long **–ā** (ablative singular) are *not* the same ending.

Because of the frequency of **–a** in its endings, the first declension is also called the *A-Declension.* Similarly, the second declension is the *O-Declension* (in the nominative and accusative singular the **–o** changed to **–u**).

67. Stem

Notice in the final section of the chart above that *nauta,* because it is a masculine noun, requires its modifiers to be masculine also. Clearly, the agreement of nouns and adjectives is *not* based upon the use of identical endings. Even for apparent exceptions like *agricola* and *nauta,* this kind of agreement is based upon case, number, and gender.

68. Declension

To *decline* a noun or adjective is to give all its case forms, singular and plural. From this meaning of *decline* the noun *declension* is derived.

Practice

Decline together in all cases, singular and plural, **amīcus meus, numerus magnus, victōria parva, nauta malus.**

69. Present Imperative

The verbs you have studied so far have been either in the *infinitive* form or in the *indicative mood.* The indicative mood is used to make statements or ask questions.

Commands are expressed in both Latin and English by the *imperative mood.*

In Latin, the present imperative singular is the same as the present stem of the verb **(26),** as in **portā,** *carry.* The plural is formed with the ending **–te: portāte,** *carry.* An imperative usually stands at or near the beginning of the sentence.

Practice

Form the singular imperative of *fight, praise, report;* the plural imperative of *give, sail, save.*

70. Exercises

    A. 1. Mōnstrāte viam amīcīs.
         2. Nunc quīnta hōra est; nāvigābimus.
         3. Amā fīliam tuam et fīlia tua tē (*you*) amābit.
         4. Servā pecūniam tuam et pecūnia tua tē (*you*) servābit.
         5. Nautae vītam servōrum laudant et servī vītam nautārum laudant.

    B. 1. (*Show*) puellīs litterās meās.
         2. (*Arouse*) servum et pugnābit.
         3. Puellae, (*look at*) equōs magnōs.
         4. (*Entrust*) fāmam tuam fortūnae.
         5. Nunc, nautae, ad prōvinciam (*sail*).

C. 1. Laudā___, amīcī, fīliās bon___.
2. Laudā___ (*imper. plur.*) fīliās.
3. Dōnā pecūniam tuam amīc___ (*sing.*).
4. Occupā___ (*imper. plur.*) prōvinci___ (*sing.*).
5. Servā___ (*imper. plur.*) vītam puellae cib___.

71. Vocabulary

fī′lia, fī′liae, f. *daughter*	(filial)
hō′ra, hō′rae, f., *hour*	(hour)
me′us, me′a, *my, mine*	
quīn′tus, quīn′ta, *fifth*	(quintet, quintuple)
tu′us, tu′a, *your* (referring to one person)	

72. Latin Words in the Romance Languages

The Romance languages, which are derived from Latin, have received many words from it with little or no change. Compare the following list:

"Good," isn't it?

FRENCH	SPANISH	PORTUGUESE	ITALIAN
aimer	amar	amar	amare
ami	amigo	amigo	amico
bon	bueno	bom	buono
char	carro	carro	carro
famille	familia	familia	famiglia
forme	forma	forma	forma
heure	hora	hora	ora
lettre	letra	letra	lettera
province	provincia	provincia	provincia
terre	tierra	terra	terra

Judging from the Latin, what does each of these French, Spanish, Portuguese, and Italian words mean? Make a parallel column of English words, so far as possible.

Glimpses of Roman Life

73. THE ETERNAL CITY

Although modern archeology shows that men had lived on the site of Rome many centuries earlier, the Romans put the founding of their city in 753 B.C. The first settlement was on the Palatine Hill, named after Pales, the goddess of shepherds. This was natural because the first settlers were shepherds. As the city grew, it spread to the nearby hills and the valleys between them. In time it came to be known as the "City of the Seven Hills." These hills are neither high nor extensive. The Palatine is only 142 feet above the level of the Tiber River—about the height of a ten-story building.

Below the Palatine Hill was the valley which came to be known as the Forum. At first a marshy district, it became the market place of Rome, then the chief shopping and business district, and finally the civic center. Some of our cities have developed in a similar fashion.

Too often, ruins give only a glimpse of the original structure. These three columns are the only substantial remains of the Temple of Castor in the Roman Forum. But the Romans have left us both "pictures" of their buildings on, for example, ancient coins and references to them in their literature. With these helps and by studying the ruins themselves, scholars are often able to reconstruct the buildings. See page 161 for a reconstruction of this temple.

Joseph A. DiChello, Jr.

In its final development the Forum was a rectangular paved space surrounded by temples, law courts, senate house, and other public buildings. At one end was a speakers' platform called the *rostra* because it was ornamented with the beaks of ships (**rōstrum** = beak) captured in a war fought in the fourth century B.C.[1]

The Palatine, because of its nearness to the Forum, became the residential district for statesmen and wealthy people. That is why the first emperors had their homes there. Eventually the whole imperial administration was centered on this hill, and the emperor's buildings covered it completely. So the hill which had been named for the protecting goddess of the shepherds who built their rude huts there came to be the site of *palatial* buildings. Thus it happens that our word *palace* is derived from the name of the hill.

Another hill near the Forum, the Capitoline, got its name from the famous temple of Jupiter known as the Capitolium, because it was the "head" **(caput),** or chief temple of that god. From this the Capitol at Washington, or any other capitol building, gets its name. The Capitoline also had on it the temple of Juno Moneta. Why the goddess Juno was called Moneta is not certain. In connection with the temple a mint for coining money was later established, and thus from the word **monēta** we get our words *money* and *mint*. The others of the seven hills were the Aventine, Caelian, Esquiline, Viminal, and Quirinal. In the valley between the Palatine and the Aventine lay the Circus Maximus, a racecourse for chariots.

To the northwest of the Forum, in a bend of the Tiber River, stretched the Campus Martius, which in part enclosed a park and drill ground, in part was covered with temples, theaters, public baths, and other buildings. In the Middle Ages this was the most densely populated district in Rome, as we can still see from its many narrow, twisting streets. In modern times Rome expanded to the north, but recently it has grown in all directions.

The streets of Rome were narrow and crooked. In the early days they were unpaved. Only during the last part of the first century B.C. was there a program to beautify the city.

In the early days the people of Rome got their water from wells, springs, and the Tiber River, which winds its way along one side of the city in the shape of the letter S. In 312 B.C. Appius Claudius (also responsible for the Appian Way; see **36**) built the first aqueduct, which brought pure water from springs about seven miles east of the

---

[1] The fourth century B.C. (before Christ) covers 400–301 B.C.; the first, 100–1 B.C. Then comes the first century A.D., 1–100 A.D., etc.

city. Later, other aqueducts were built, some having their sources nearly forty miles away. There were many street fountains (pp. 24, 223), and eventually running water was piped into the public baths and many private houses.

For better administration the Emperor Augustus divided the city into fourteen regions, or wards. One feature of this arrangement was the reorganization and extension of the police and fire department (**vigilēs,** *watchmen*). Earlier fire protection had been so poor that private fire companies were organized. These even bought burning houses at bargain prices before they extinguished the fire.

In early days a wall known as the Servian wall was built around the city; parts of this wall may still be seen in the busy modern city, for example, near the railroad station (see below). But Rome soon outgrew this wall. In the third century A.D. the Emperor Aurelian built a new one, which is still standing.

The old Servian Wall of the fourth century B.C. stands in front of the ultramodern railroad station (completed 1950) in Rome. Here the wall stands in the midst of dense traffic. The stones have been "squared" and carefully fitted. The sign in front says, "Don't trample (the grass)."

Fototeca

Albert Moldvay

For centuries it has been known that an ancient cemetery lies below the Church of St. Peter in Rome, but excavations of the site were not begun until 1939. Roman tombs, coins, epigraphs, bricks, and remains of furnishings have been discovered. (See also page 280.)

At its height, ancient Rome had a population of more than a million. The modern city has been growing rapidly in recent years, and has nearly tripled this figure. By 1988, it had over 2,830,000 people, once again the largest city in Italy.

Rome has been an important city for a longer time than any other city in the world. For hundreds of years it was the capital of the great Roman Empire, then it continued its importance as the seat of the Pope, and in recent generations it has become also the capital of one of the leading nations of modern Europe. The name given it in ancient times—"Eternal City" **(urbs aeterna)**—has been justified.

DISCUSSION QUESTIONS

1. What is a civic center? Describe a modern one that you have visited and contrast it with that of ancient Rome.
2. Compare the development of Rome and that of Washington, D.C., or some other large city.
3. What factors cause a community to grow until it reaches the status of a city? A megalopolis?

UNIT II REVIEW

Lessons V–IX

74. ENGLISH WORD STUDIES

Give the nominative, genitive, gender, and meaning of the Latin noun suggested by each of the following derivatives:

copious, curate, informal, injure, literature, memorable, pecuniary, penalize, predatory, undulating, pugnacity, vitamin.

75. "To" Expressions

Tell whether the infinitive, the dative case, or **ad** with the accusative will be needed to express the *to* idea in the following:

I hurried home. My brother showed *me* his new motorbike, and gave *me* permission *to ride* it *to the garage*. But I was not able *to stop* in time, and broke the headlight. I'll have *to go to work* for weeks to pay *him* the money for it.

76. VOCABULARY

NOUNS			
1. amīcus	6. fōrma	12. numerus	18. rēgīna
2. cibus	7. hōra	13. pecūnia	19. unda
3. cōpia	8. iniūria	14. poena	20. victōria
4. cūra	9. littera	15. praeda	
5. fīlia	10. memoria	16. prōvincia	
	11. nauta	17. pugna	

ADJECTIVES			
21. clārus	22. grātus	24. plānus	26. tuus
	23. meus	25. quīntus	

VERBS			
27. dōnō	29. mandō	32. nūntiō	35. pugnō
28. incitō	30. mōnstrō	33. occupō	36. servō
	31. nāvigō	34. probō	

ADVERB
37. tum

PREPOSITION
38. ad

77. VOCABULARY (English Meanings)

NOUNS			
1. *friend*	6. *shape*	12. *number*	18. *queen*
2. *food*	7. *hour*	13. *money*	19. *wave*
3. *supply*	8. *wrong*	14. *punishment*	20. *victory*
4. *care*	9. *letter*	15. *loot*	
5. *daughter*	10. *memory*	16. *province*	
	11. *sailor*	17. *battle*	

ADJECTIVES			
21. *clear*	22. *pleasing*	24. *level*	26. *your*
	23. *my, mine*	25. *fifth*	

VERBS			
27. *give*	29. *entrust*	32. *report*	35. *fight*
28. *urge on*	30. *point out*	33. *seize*	36. *save*
	31. *sail*	34. *test*	

ADVERB
37. *then*

PREPOSITION
38. *to*

78. GRAMMAR SUMMARIES

A. Case Names

In Latin	In English
1. Nominative.	1. Nominative.
2. Genitive.	2. Possessive.
3. Accusative.	3. Objective.

B. Case Uses

	In Latin	In English
SUBJECT	1. Nominative.	1. Nominative.
DIRECT OBJECT	2. Accusative.	2. Objective.
INDIRECT OBJECT	3. Dative.	3. Objective with *to*.
POSSESSION, etc.	4. Genitive.	4. Possessive.
VARIOUS USES	5. Ablative with or without preposition.	5. Objective with various prepositions.

Parvi Romani. Two lifelike statues
in the Capitoline Museum in Rome.

C. Tense

In Latin	In English
Tense is usually indicated by endings **(Portābit).**	Tense is often indicated by an additional verb (*He **will** carry; He **has** carried*).

79. UNIT PRACTICE AND EXERCISES

Exercises

A. Decline **vīta mea, nauta malus.**

B. State the case required and then give in Latin:
1. *level land* (direct object)
2. *your daughter* (possessive)
3. *little girls* (indirect object)
4. *my wagons* (means)
5. *large horses* (direct object)

C. This is a rapid-fire drill. Answer as quickly as you can.
1. Translate: **occupābō, mōnstrās, dōnā, amīcōrum, pecūniā, laudābunt, servāre, nāvigātis, incitant.**
2. Translate: *of the victory, with money, we report, he will entrust, you (sing.) will be showing, they give, he fights.*
3. Tell the form of: **iniūriīs, numerō, undās, pugnābunt, grātam, spectātis, bonō, tua, mandās.**

UNIT III

LATIN AND THE ROMANS

The marble Arch of Septimius Severus, in the Roman Forum, is so large it contains several internal chambers and an internal staircase. It was erected in 203 A.D. in honor of the emperor whose name it bears. The monument was constructed to celebrate the military victories of Septimius Severus and his sons in Mesopotamia and Assyria. Through the arch, we can see two additional triumphal arches, the Arch of Titus, and further in the distance, the Arch of Constantine.

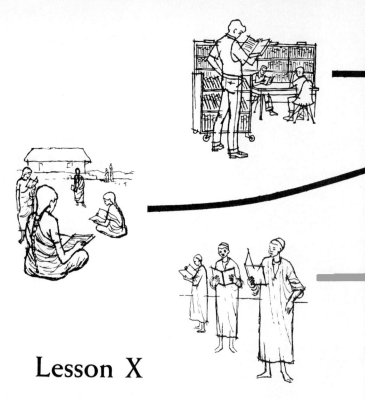

Lesson X

80. LINGUA LATĪNA

Lingua Rōmānōrum Latīna erat. Lingua patriae nostrae [1] nōn Latīna est, sed Anglica.[2] Linguā Latīnā scientiam [3] nostrae linguae augēmus. Lingua Latīna prīmō [4] nōbīs [5] nova erat, sed nunc nōn terret. Disciplīna nōs [6] nōn terret, quod magistrum [7] bonum habēmus.
5 Linguam Latīnam semper in memoriā habēbimus. In Britanniā, in Italiā, in Galliā, in Americīs, in multīs terrīs et prōvinciīs multī magistrī linguam Latīnam nunc docent et semper docēbunt. In patriā nostrā lingua Latīna magnam fāmam habet. Magistrī magnum numerum discipulōrum [8] docent. Disciplīna semper scientiam nostram [1]
10 augēbit. Magistrī nōs probābunt, sī [9] cūram habēbimus. Patria nōs probābit et laudābit, sī scientiam et fāmam bonam parābimus.

QUESTIONS

1. Where is Latin taught?
2. Do many pupils study Latin?
3. Do you agree that the study of Latin helps your knowledge of English? Count the number of different Latin words in this passage from which an English word you know is derived.

[1] *our.*   [2] *English.*   [3] *knowledge.*   [4] *at first.*   [5] *to us.*   [6] *us.*
[7] *teacher.* If the teacher is a woman read **magistram bonam** instead. Why?
[8] *pupils.*   [9] *if.*

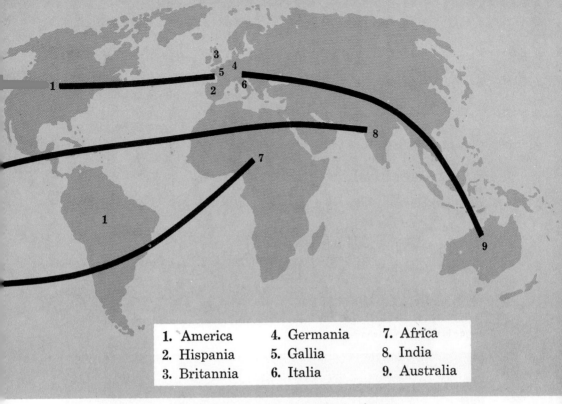

1. America	4. Germania	7. Africa
2. Hispania	5. Gallia	8. India
3. Britannia	6. Italia	9. Australia

In multis terris magistri linguam Latinam docent.

81. Second Conjugation: Present and Future Tenses

The verbs that have occurred in previous lessons contain the stem vowel –ā– and belong to the first conjugation. All verbs which show the stem vowel –ē– in the present and future tenses belong to the *second conjugation*. The only difference from the first conjugation is in the stem vowel and in the present first singular, which keeps the stem vowel, though shortened: **doceō.**

PRESENT

SINGULAR	PLURAL
doceō, *I teach, am teaching, do teach*	docēmus, *we teach, are teaching, do teach*
docēs, *you teach,* etc.	docētis, *you teach,* etc.
docet, *he, she, it teaches,* etc.	docent, *they teach,* etc.

FUTURE

docēbō, *I shall teach, shall be teaching*	docēbimus, *we shall teach,* etc.
docēbis, *you will teach,* etc.	docēbitis, *you will teach,* etc.
docēbit, *he, she, it will teach,* etc.	docēbunt, *they will teach,* etc.

82. Practice

1. Conjugate **habeō** in the present tense and **augeō** in the future; then translate.
2. Give the singular imperative of *fight, teach;* give the plural imperative of *have, scare.*
3. Translate: *they will have, he increases, we show, he will teach, you* (plur.) *scare.*

83. Exercises

A. 1. Anna, docē linguās.
2. Multās linguās nōn docēbō.
3. Magnae undae servōs terrēbunt.
4. Magnae undae cūrās nautārum augent.

Looking toward the water basin in a Roman bath in Pompeii. Romans used to meet here for bathing and conversation. This is one of the first baths uncovered after excavations began in the late eighteenth century.

5. Victōria numerum servōrum nōn augēbit.
6. Pecūniam servāre est fortūnam augēre.
7. Prōvinciīs magnam victōriam patriae nūntiābimus.
8. Amīcus meus magnam pecūniam et parvam disciplīnam habet.

B. 1. Fīlia linguās (*will teach*).
2. Nautae Annam (*are scaring*).
3. (*Love*) linguam patriae tuae.
4. Cibum multum nōn (*we do have*).
5. (*Increase*) fortūnam tuam disciplīnā.
6. Memoriam Rōmae linguā Latīnā (*we shall preserve*).
7. Patriam (*to seize*) et familiam meam (*to scare*) parābunt.

84. Vocabulary

au′geō, augē′re, [au′xī, auc′tus],[10] *increase* (augment)
disciplī′na, –ae,[11] f., *training, instruction* (disciplinary)
do′ceō, docē′re, [do′cuī, doc′tus], *teach* (docile)
ha′beō, habē′re, [ha′buī, ha′bitus], *have, hold* (habit)
lin′gua, –ae, f., *tongue, language* (bilingual, linguistic)
pa′tria, –ae, f., *fatherland, country* (expatriate)
sem′per, adv., *always* (sempiternal)
ter′reō, terrē′re, [ter′ruī, ter′ritus], *scare* (terrific)

85. English Word Studies

1. From what Latin words are *accurate, doctrine, document* derived? When is the word *doctor* used to mean one who teaches? What is a *linguist?* What does our word *discipline* usually mean? What was its original meaning?

2. Which one of these words does not belong with the others? Why?

terrible   *subterranean*   *deter*   *terrified*

3. A number of Latin verb forms are preserved as English words. First conjugation: *veto, habitat, ignoramus, mandamus.* Second conjugation: *tenet.* For their meaning, see the dictionary.

The Latin ablative of the first declension is preserved in English in the word *via:* "I am going to Toronto *via* (by way of) New York." The ablative plural is found in *gratis,* a shortened form of **grātiīs:** "He is giving this *gratis*" (for thanks, i.e., for nothing).

---

[10] Note that the last two *principal parts* of second conjugation verbs are not quite so regular as those of the first conjugation.
[11] From now on the genitive ending only will be given.

Lesson XI

86. BRITANNIA

Magna īnsula Britannia in amīcitiā Galliae manet. Caesar in Galliā pugnat et amīcitiam Britanniae et Galliae videt. Ibi māteriam et cibum parat et ad Britanniam nāvigat. Ibi amīcōs Gallōrum pugnīs terret sed in Britanniā nōn manet. Īnsulam videt, nōn occupat, sed
5 glōriam suam [1] auget. Semper prō [2] patriā et prō glōriā suā [1] labōrat. Caesar grātiam et amīcitiam Rōmānōrum meret,[3] quod magnae sunt victōriae. Multīs litterīs Rōmae victōriās nūntiat. Magna est grātia patriae quod Caesar patriam auget. Multam praedam carrīs et equīs ad patriam portat. Nunc Caesar magnam glōriam habet.

QUESTIONS

1. What did Caesar do in Britain?
2. Why did Caesar win the gratitude of his countrymen?

87. Prepositions of Place: In

In the preceding lessons the various uses of the prepositions *with, of, to, for, by* with nouns have been expressed in Latin by means of case endings without prepositions. But some English expressions require the use of corresponding prepositions in Latin.

In with the ablative = *in* or *on:*

in silvā, *in a forest.*
in viīs, *on the streets.*

88. Sentence Analysis

Before writing the translation of an English sentence into Latin, you may find it helpful to place above every noun the case and number required in the Latin sentence, as follows:

    Nom. S.   Acc. S.   Dat. S.
1. The *man* gave a *book* to the *boy.*

    Gen. S. Nom. S.   Acc. S. Abl. S.
2. My *friend's* *son* saved his *life* by *flight.*

---

[1] *his.* [2] *for.* [3] *wins.*

70

Great detail and shading can be achieved with mosaic, as this representation of a sea god shows. Why might this mosaic be described as symmetrical?

Photo Precision Ltd., St. Albans, England

89. Practice

Why not amicus tui (friend "of you")

See * p. 74

1. Decline **amīcus tuus, vīta longa,** and **agricola clārus.**
2. Give in Latin: *good friendship* in the acc., sing. and plur.; *good food* in the gen., sing. and plur.; *a small number* in the abl., sing. and plur.; *a famous language* in the dat., sing. and plur.

90. Exercises

A. 1. Laudāte amīcitiam.
2. Magna erat grātia puellārum.
3. In silvīs māteriam vidēbis.
4. Nautae in terrā nōn manēbunt.
5. In viīs multōs servōs nōn videō.
6. Multās hōrās nōn habētis. Labōrāte!
7. Disciplīnā glōriam patriae augēbimus.
8. In patriā magnam pecūniam nunc habēmus.

B. 1. (*On the streets*) carrōs vidēmus.
2. Multa māteria (*in the forest*) est.
3. Equī (*on the island*) nōn manēbunt.
4. (*In the provinces*) multōs servōs vidēbimus.
5. (*In my country*) magnum numerum amīcōrum habeō.

C. Translate into Latin.
1. Remain and see my friends.
2. They will remain on the island.
3. I shall see your daughter on the street.
4. By friendship you will increase your influence.
5. Through (by) injustice they will seize the land of the province.

91. Vocabulary

amīci′tia, –ae, f., *friendship*   **[amō]**
glō′ria, –ae, f., *glory*   (glorify, glorious)
grā′tia, –ae, f., *gratitude, influence*   **[grātus]**
i′bi, adv., *there*
in, prep. with abl., *in, on*
ma′neō, manē′re, [mān′sī, mānsū′rus],[4] *remain*   (mansion)
māte′ria, –ae, f., *matter, timber*   (material, materialize)
vi′deō, vidē′re, [vī′dī, vī′sus], *see*   (provide)

92. Latin Forms of English Names

1. Many English names of boys and girls are derived from Latin words: *a.* unchanged, or *b.* changed:

a. Alma, *kindly;* Clara, *clear, bright;* Leo, *lion;* Stella, *star;* Sylvester, *belonging to the woods.*

b. Mabel, from **amābilis,** *lovable;* Belle, from **bella,** *beautiful;* Florence, from **flōrentia,** *flourishing;* Grace, from **grātia,** *grace;* Margaret, from **margarīta,** *pearl;* Rose, from **rosa,** *rose.*

2. These names were in common use among the Romans:
August, Augustus, *venerable;* Rufus, *red-haired;* Victor, *conqueror;* Vincent **(vincēns),** *conquering.*

3. Other Roman names still used in English include:
Emil and Emily **(Aemilius, Aemilia);** Cecilia **(Caecilia);** Claudia; Cornelius, Cornelia; Horace **(Horātius);** Julius, Julia; Lavinia; Mark **(Mārcus);** Marcia; Paul **(Paulus).**

How many older brothers and sisters should a boy named Quintus have?

Do any members of your class have Latin names not included here?

---

[4] This form in **–ūrus** instead of **–us** will be explained later.

Servus laborat. A Roman wine shop. The slave carrying in the wine jars has hitched up his tunic, much as we "roll up our sleeves" for action (see section 206). As glass was expensive, clay jars of various sizes were used for liquids. From a relief sculpture in marble.

Lesson XII

93. PUERĪ RŌMĀNĪ

Lūcius, puer [1] Rōmānus, in Viā Altā amīcum Mārcum videt.

Lūcius: Ubi est socius tuus Quīntus?
Mārcus: Ad īnsulam nāvigāvit.
Lūcius: Cūr [2] ad īnsulam nāvigāvit?
Mārcus: Īnsulam amat. Ibi in aquā diū [3] manet; in silvā altā [5] ambulat.[4] In īnsulā multōs amīcōs habet.
Lūcius: Cūr nōn cum [5] sociō tuō ad īnsulam nāvigāvistī? Cūr hīc [6] mānsistī?
Mārcus: In casā labōrāre dēbeō,[7] quod servōs līberāvimus.

---

[1] *boy.*   [2] *why.*   [3] *a long time.*   [4] *walks.*   [5] *with.*
[6] *here.*   [7] *I have to.*

10   Lūcius: Magnum numerum servōrum habēmus et semper habuimus. In casā, in viā, in silvā labōrant, māteriam portant, agricolae
sunt. Servī grātiam nostram meruērunt, sed eōs[8] tenēbimus.

    Mārcus: Quod servī nostrī agricolae bonī erant et semper
15 labōrāvērunt eōs nōn tenuimus sed līberāvimus. Nunc amīcī et sociī
sunt et amīcitiam eōrum[9] semper memoriā tenēbō.

QUESTIONS

  1. Where is Quintus?
  2. Why isn't Marcus there?
  3. Whose slaves have been freed?

94. Perfect Tense

  In English, the *past* tense refers to an action that is completed:
He went yesterday.

  The *present perfect* refers to an action that is completed, but
from the point of view of the present: *He has just gone.* One does
not say *He has gone yesterday.*

  In Latin, the *perfect* tense is used like both the past and the
present perfect of English, though it more often corresponds to the
past.

95. Perfect Stem and Perfect Tense

  Verbs of the first conjugation studied so far form the perfect stem
by adding **–v** to the present stem: **līberā–, līberāv–.** Many verbs of
the second conjugation form the perfect stem like **doceō** below, but
no rules can be given for the others. Drop the **–ī** of the perfect first
person singular, which is the third principal part (**27,** n. 6), and you
have the perfect stem.

  The endings of the perfect tense, added to the perfect stem, are
used in no other tenses:

ENDINGS	FIRST CONJUGATION	SECOND CONJUGATION
–ī	portāvī, *I carried, I have car-ried, I did carry*	docuī, *I taught, I have taught, I did teach*
–istī	portāvistī, *you carried, etc.*	docuistī, *you taught, etc.*
–it	portāvit, *he carried, etc.*	docuit, *he taught, etc.*
–imus	portāvimus, *we carried, etc.*	docuimus, *we taught, etc.*
–istis	portāvistis, *you carried, etc.*	docuistis, *you taught, etc.*
–ērunt	portāvērunt, *they carried, etc.*	docuērunt, *they taught, etc.*

[8] *them.*   [9] *their.*

74

Practice

1. Conjugate the following in the perfect tense: **labōrō (labōrāv–), teneō (tenu–), mereō (meru–), maneō (māns–), mōnstrō (mōnstrāv–), augeō (aux–), habeō (habu–), videō (vīd–).**
2. Translate: *he has praised, we entrusted, they scared, we shall teach, I saw.*

96. Exercises

A. 1. Servō litterās mandāvī.
2. Multōs sociōs habuistis.
3. Agricola in terrā labōrābit.
4. Undae altae puellās terruērunt.
5. Cōpiam aquae clārae parāvistī.
6. Multōs servōs in casā vīdimus.
7. Agricolae, grātiam patriae meruistis.
8. Amīcus meus in prōvinciā nōn mānsit.

B. 1. The slave held the horses.
2. We saw a large number of horses.
3. The farmers have got the food ready.
4. The girls will carry the food to the house.
5. My comrade has deserved my friendship.

97. Vocabulary

al′tus, al′ta, *high*	(altitude, altimeter)
ca′sa, –ae, f., *house*	
lī′berō, līberā′re, līberā′vī,[10] **[līberā′tus],** *free*	(liberator)
me′reō, merē′re, me′ruī, [me′ritus], *deserve, earn*	(merit)
so′cius, so′cī,[11] m., *comrade, ally*	(associate)
te′neō, tenē′re, te′nuī, [ten′tus], *hold, keep*	(retention)

98. English Word Studies

From their meanings tell which of the following words come from **servāre** and which from **servus:** *serf, conserve, serve, servant, reserve.* What is an *equestrian*? A *copious* portion? A *nautical* mile? What does the derivation tell us about the meaning of *social, social service, social security, socialism*?

The Latin perfect tense of the first conjugation is preserved in English *affidavit.*

---

[10] Now that the perfect tense has been studied, the third principal part will hereafter be given without a bracket.

[11] Nouns (not adjectives) that end in **–ius** usually shorten **–iī** to **–ī** in the genitive singular: **so′ciī** becomes **so′cī,** and the accent is not changed. The nominative plural always ends in **–iī: sociī.**

Below: Roman strainer from Verulamium.
Right: Wine jar with "(b)ibe," "drink," on
it, from the same place; third century A.D.
Facing page: A lamp, also from Roman Britain. The wick, inserted in the small hole, was
fed with olive oil or animal fat.

Photo Precision Ltd.,
St. Albans, England

Below: The Roman amphitheater at Arles in southern France. Outdoor drama was a
favorite pastime. Everywhere the Romans carried with them their ideas of what a city
should have: a forum for business, baths for cleanliness and social gatherings, and amphitheaters for public entertainment.

French Government Tourist Office

Photo Precision Ltd.,
St. Albans, England

Lesson XIII

99. SERVĪ

Servī Rōmānī erant captīvī. Rōmānī multīs pugnīs singulās terrās occupāvērunt, et magnus erat numerus captīvōrum. Captīvōs ē Graeciā, ē Galliā, ex Asiā, ex Āfricā in [1] Italiam mōvērunt. In familiā Rōmānā erant multī servī, bonī et malī.

Servī aquam in casās portāvērunt; medicī [2] et agricolae erant; dē 5 vītā, dē glōriā, dē amīcitiā docuērunt. Multī clārī Graecī erant servī et amīcī Rōmānōrum. Litterae [3] Rōmānōrum memoriam servōrum *see mss* servāvērunt. Poena servī malī magna erat. Servōs bonōs multī Rōmānī *#2139* līberāvērunt.

In quādam [4] casā Rōmānā Maximus servōs vocāvit: "Mārce et 10 Stātī,[5] hōra quīnta est; portāte singulī māteriam dē silvā; Cornēlī, vocā socium tuum et movēte carrum ā viā et equōs ab aquā. Tum parāte cēnam; amīcōs meōs in Altā Viā vīdī et ad cēnam vocāvī." Servī māteriam portāvērunt, carrum et equōs mōvērunt. Tum cibum parāvērunt et ad mēnsam [6] portāvērunt. Post [7] cēnam amīcī mānsē- 15 runt, et Maximus amīcīs pictūrās mōnstrāvit. Interim [8] servī in culīnā [9] labōrāvērunt. Tum amīcī Maximī servōs laudāvērunt et eīs [10] pecūniam dōnāvērunt. Maximō singulī "valē" [11] dīxērunt.[12]

QUESTIONS

1. How and where did the Romans get their slaves?
2. Name four things that the slaves did.
3. To how many slaves does Maximus refer?

100. Vocative Case

In Latin as in English, the *vocative* case, used in addressing a person, has the same form as the nominative, except that the vocative singular of **–us** nouns and adjectives of the second declension ends in **–e** (in **–ius** nouns, **–ie** becomes **–ī**):

[1] *into.*   [2] *doctors.*   [3] *literature.*   [4] *a certain.*
[5] *Statius (Stā'shius).*   [6] *table.*   [7] *after.*   [8] *in the meantime.*
[9] *kitchen.*   [10] *to them.*   [11] *good-by.*   [12] *said.*

77

Relief of a food shop at Ostia showing chickens, apples (?), caged rabbits (lower right). The monkeys seem to be there just to attract customers.

Spectāte undās, parve Lūcī et parva Claudia, *Look at the waves, little Lucius and little Claudia.*

Līberā captīvōs, amīce Mārce, *Free the captives, friend Marcus.*

Unless emphatic, the vocative does not stand first in the sentence.

101. Exercises

A. 1. Vocā, Mārce, servōs ē casā.
   2. Sociī equōs ē Viā Quīntā movēbunt.
   3. In malā fortūnā bonōs amīcōs habuimus.
   4. Movē, Cornēlī, carrōs singulōs dē silvā altā.
   5. Portāte, captīvī, māteriam dē silvīs ad aquam.
   6. Servī malī multam praedam ab īnsulīs portāvērunt.

B. 1. We have called the girls to dinner.
   2. My daughter had a large number of friends.
   3. Brutus, move the prisoners from the island.
   4. One-at-a-time [13] they sailed from the island to the new land.

102. Vocabulary

ā, ab, [14] prep. with abl., *from*
captī′vus, –ī, m., *prisoner* (captivate, captivity)
cē′na, –ae, f., *dinner*
dē, prep. with abl., *down from, from, about*
ē, ex, [14] prep. with abl., *out of, from*
mo′veō, movē′re, mō′vī, [mō′tus], *move* (movement)
sin′gulī, –ae, plur., *one at a time* (single, singular)
vo′cō, vocā′re, vocā′vī, [vocā′tus], *call* (evoke, vocation)

[13] Words connected by hyphens are to be expressed by one word in Latin.
[14] The shorter forms **ā** and **ē** are used only before words beginning with a consonant (except *h*), **ab** and **ex** before vowels and sometimes before consonants.

103. Prepositions of Place Ab, Dē, Ex

$$\left.\begin{array}{l} \text{ā, ab} \\ \text{dē} \\ \text{ē, ex} \end{array}\right\} \text{ used with the ablative} = \textit{from}$$

Examples: ā viā, (*away*) *from the road.*
dē silvā, (*down*) *from the forest.*
ex aquā, (*out*) *from the water.*

Ā viā.　　　　Dē silvā.　　　　Ex aquā.

Although all three prepositions mean *from*, **ab** *means away from the outside;* **ex,** *out from the inside;* **dē,** merely *from* when it is not important to distinguish. Sometimes **dē** means *down from*.

104. Latin and English Word Formation

A great many Latin words are formed by joining prefixes (**prae** = *in front;* **fīxus** = *attached*) to root words. These same prefixes, most of which are prepositions, are those chiefly used in English. With these prefixes we are continually forming new words.

Examples of the prefixes **ab–, dē–** and **ex–** are:

ab– (abs–, ā–): *a-vocation, ab-undance, abs-tain.*
dē–: *de-fame, de-form, de-ter, de-viate, de-portation.*
ex– (ē–, ef–): *ex-alt, ex-patriation, ex-pect* (from **spectō**), *e-voke, ex-president.*

Define the words above according to prefix and root. For root words, see earlier vocabularies. Distinguish the meanings of *vocation* and *avocation*.

The following are other examples of the prefix **ex–** in English: *ex-cuse, e-dict, ex-empt, ef-fect, e-gress, ex-it.*

You will find it helpful to keep a list of prefixes in your notebook and to add examples of their use in English words.

Alexander the Great (356–323 B.C.) was the son of Philip II of Macedon. Even as a young boy, Alexander was a skilled horseman, a talented musician, and an avid reader. He was taught by the Greek philosopher Aristotle until called to duty at his father's side at age sixteen. When his father was murdered, Alexander became king. One of his most famous victories was the Battle of Issus in Asia Minor (333 B.C.) in which King Darius of Persia was put to flight. Later, Alexander succeeded in conquering all of Egypt and Persia.

Art Resource

Lesson XIV

105. ARISTOTELĒS ET ALEXANDER

Aristotelēs [1] magister bonus multōrum virōrum erat. Philosophiam et scientiam nātūrālem docuit. Quod clārus et bonus magister erat Aristotelēs, Philippus, rēx Macedoniae,[2] Aristotelem [3] probāvit.

Philippus fīlium habuit, Alexandrum, puerum bonum et amīcum.
5 Philippus puerum Alexandrum clārō magistrō Aristotelī [4] mandāvit: "Docē fīlium meum, philosophe."

Aristotelēs semper amīcus Alexandrō erat, et Alexandrum nōn terruit. Aristotelēs Alexandrum dē philosophiā et dē Homērō,[5] poētā clārō, docuit. Alexander Homērum amāvit et laudāvit, sed philosophia
10 erat disciplīna dūra et longa.

In agrō Alexander equum novum habuit. Alexander agrum et equum spectāvit, et Aristotelī [4] nūntiāvit:

---

[1] *Aristotle* (nominative).   [2] *king of Macedonia.*   [3] Accusative.
[4] Dative.   [5] *Homer.*

"Vidē, magister, agrum grātum. Casam tuam nōn amō. Docē mē in agrō. Puer sum,[6] nōn vir. Puer līber sum, fīlius Philippī, nōn captīvus tuus. In agrō Homērum et glōriam virī magnī Achillis [7] memoriae 15 mandābō."

Aristotelēs in agrō Alexandrum docēre parat. Sed ubi est puer Alexander? Alexander ad silvam equum incitat. Līber est!

Magna erat īra [8] Philippī, sed in philosophō amīcō nōn erat īra. Philippō Aristotelēs nūntiat: 20

"Puer nōn malus est. Puerī nostrī sacrī sunt; puellae nostrae sacrae sunt. Puerīs nostrīs magnam reverentiam dēbēmus.[9] Alexander bonus est, magnus erit." [10]

Et erat Alexander magnus. Multās terrās occupāvit. Semper fāmam Achillis [7] memoriā tenuit. 25

QUESTIONS

1. What did Aristotle teach?
2. What promise did Alexander make to Aristotle? Did he keep it?

[6] *I am.* [7] Genitive: *Achilles,* hero of Homer's *Iliad.* [8] *anger.*
[9] *owe.* [10] *he will be.*

Classical themes were particularly popular during the Renaissance. The great Dutch artist Rembrandt painted this picture "Aristotle Contemplating the Bust of Homer" in 1653, showing Aristotle in the costume of that time but Homer in ancient garb. For centuries the ancients regarded Homer's poetry with the same sort of reverence later ages have paid the Bible.

Metropolitan Museum of Art, Purchased with special funds and gifts of friends of the Museum, 1961 (61.198)

106. Second Declension: Nouns and Adjectives in –r

Nouns and adjectives of the second declension whose stem ends in –r omit the ending –us in the nominative singular. Such words therefore end in –er or –r in the nominative. The genitive singular shows whether –e– is retained before –r in the other forms. Examples are:

	SINGULAR		PLURAL	
Nom.	ager	noster	agrī	nostrī
Gen.	agrī	nostrī	agrōrum	nostrōrum
Dat.	agrō	nostrō	agrīs	nostrīs
Acc.	agrum	nostrum	agrōs	nostrōs
Abl.	agrō	nostrō	agrīs	nostrīs
	Stem: agr– nostr–			

In memorizing vocabularies, always note carefully: the *nominative,* the *genitive,* the *gender* of every noun.

1. Nouns and adjectives like **puer** and **līber** have the –e– throughout; those like **ager** and **noster** have it only in the nominative singular, while **vir** has no –e– at all. Most –er words are like **ager;** no others are like **vir.**

2. The English derivative will usually show whether –e– is retained or not; for example, *pu·e·rile, lib·e·ral, mis·e·rable;* but *agriculture, sacred, magistrate.*

3. Adjectives agree with their nouns in gender, number, and case, but not always in endings: *puer bonus, nauta līber.*

Reconstruction of the Stoa (i.e., portico) of Attalus in the Agora, or forum, of Athens. It was excavated by the American School of Classical Studies in Athens as part of an important project, the excavation of the entire Agora. The Stoa has been rebuilt and houses a museum containing the objects found in the Agora. The Acropolis is at the right.

Practice

1. Decline **magister novus, vir līber.**
2. Tell the form of **equīs, agrum, virō, nostrī, līberōs, sacrā, plānōrum, singulī, casārum.**

107. Exercises

A. 1. Incitā, Mārce, equum ad agrum.
2. Magister noster linguam clāram docet.
3. Memoria clārōrum nostrōrum virōrum sacra est.
4. Magister tuus puerō malō pecūniam nōn dōnāvit.
5. In Americā magnōs agrōs et virōs līberōs vidēbitis.
6. Virī nostrī agrōs sociōrum amīcōrum nōn occupāvērunt.

B. 1. Give Anna the boy's money.
2. Our country is free and sacred.
3. A friend of my son teaches boys.
4. I saw many horses in the fields of our friends.
5. The men moved the timber out of the forest with horses.

108. Vocabulary

a′ger, a′grī, m., *field*	[*agricola*]
amī′cus, –a, *friendly*	[*amō*]
fī′lius, fī′lī, m., *son*	[*fīlia*]
lī′ber, lī′bera, *free*	[*līberō*]
magis′ter, magis′trī, m., *teacher*	(Mr., master)
nos′ter, nos′tra, *our*	(nostrum)
pu′er, pu′erī, m., *boy*	(puerile)
sa′cer, sa′cra, *sacred*	(consecrate)
vir, vi′rī, m.. *man*	(virile)

109. English Word Studies

1. Several Latin words of the **–er** type are used in English.

Nouns: *arbiter, cancer, minister, vesper.*
Adjectives: *integer, miser, neuter, sinister* (the first two are used as nouns in English).

2. **Assimilation.** Some prefixes change their final consonants to make them like the initial consonants of the words to which they are attached. This is called *assimilation* (**ad** = *to;* **similis** = *like*).

The prefix **ad–** is generally assimilated. Define the following words—all of them formed from Latin words in the earlier vocabularies: *ac-curate, af-filiate, al-literation, an-nounce, ap-paratus, a-spect, as-sociate, ad-vocate.*

Additional examples are: *ab-breviate, af-fect, ag-gressive, ac-quire, ar-rogant, at-tend,* and the word *as-similation* itself.

Albert Moldvay

The Marcellus Theater, on the left, was begun by Julius Caesar and completed in 12 B.C. At various times the theater was converted into a fortress, and later a palace, before being restored in the twentieth century. The theater was semi-circular in shape and held 20,000 spectators. It served as a model for the more famous Colosseum.

Lesson XV

110. COLŌNĪ RŌMĀNĪ

Puer Rōmānus sum. Fīlius sum agricolae. Colōnī sumus et in prōvinciā Galliā habitāmus. Ex Italiā in prōvinciam migrāvimus. In prōvinciā sunt agrī novī et magnī. Agrī nostrī sunt bonī, sed casa nostra parva est. In agrīs multās hōrās labōrāmus. Līberī sumus, sed
5 labōrāmus; multōs servōs nōn tenēmus. Pecūniam nōn habēmus. Vīta agricolārum dūra est, sed agricolae et colōnī magnum animum habent.

Multī agricolae ad urbem [1] Rōmam migrāvērunt, sed familia mea ad urbem nōn migrābit. Rōmam vīdī, sed ibi nōn mānsī. Agricolae in urbem equīs et carrīs māteriam et frūmentum [2] portant, sed ibi nōn

---

[1] *city* (accusative).   [2] *grain.*

84

manent. Multī virī in viīs Rōmae sunt, agricolae, colōnī, nautae, 10
magistrī, captīvī, servī.

Es colōnus, puer? Ubi habitās? Ad urbem migrāvistī? Vīta dūra in
agrīs tē [3] terruit? Animum agricolae nōn habēs.

QUESTIONS

1. Why do the settlers move to the province?
2. Why do many other farmers migrate to Rome?
3. In what ways are people in cities today dependent on the
   farmers?

111. Present of Sum

The verb *to be* is irregularly formed in English and Latin, as well
as in other languages, and so does not belong to one of the "regular"
conjugations. The present infinitive of **sum** is **esse.** The present indicative is conjugated as follows:

sum,	*I am*	sumus,	*we are*
es,	*you are*	estis,	*you are*
est,	*he, she, it is*	sunt,	*they are*

[3] *you* (accusative).

This obelisk, or pointed pillar,
is ancient Roman in construction, though Egyptian in style.
The names of the Roman Emperors Vespasian, Titus, and
Domitian are inscribed on it in
hieroglyphics. The four colos-
sal statues are by Bernini
(1598–1680) and represent
rivers from the four corners
of the world.

Art Resource

Sum is a linking verb **(10)** and does not have a direct object. Give the Latin in the proper case for the underlined words, telling which is a predicate nominative, and which is a direct object:

1. They are sailors.
2. We are settlers.
3. They move the prisoners.

4. He is a slave.
5. I teach my friend.
6. You are boys.

Italian stamps showing the Arch of Constantine and the Basilica of Maxentius. They were issued in honor of the Olympic Games of 1960, which were held in Rome.

112. Exercises

A. 1. Animus virōrum est magnus.
2. Servī estis et in agrīs labōrātis.
3. Colōnī ex Eurōpā migrāvērunt.
4. Ad līberam Americam nāvigāvērunt.
5. Multī līberī virī in īnsulā magnā habitant.
6. Sociī nostrī in īnsulam captīvōs mōvērunt.
7. Carrīs dē silvīs ad aquam māteriam portābitis.

B. 1. Give the loot to the settlers.
2. Are you the sons of settlers?
3. The teacher's horse is in our field.
4. The prisoners will carry the timber into the fields.
5. The settlers will depart from the island and live in the province.

113. Vocabulary

a'nimus, –ī, m., *mind, courage* (unanimous)
colō'nus, –ī, m., *settler* (colonize)
ha'bitō, habitā're, habitā'vī, [habitā'tus], *live* (habitation)
in, prep. with acc., *into;* with abl., *in, on*
mi'grō, migrā're, migrā'vī, [migrātū'rus],[4] *depart* (migration)
sum, es'se, fu'ī, [futū'rus],[4] *be* (essence)

114. Prepositions of Place: Ad, In

1. **ad** with acc. = (*up*) *to*   2. **in** with acc. = *into*

[4] This form will be explained later.

Ad aquam.   In aquam.

Carrōs $\left\{ \begin{array}{l} \textbf{ad} \\ \textbf{in} \end{array} \right\}$ **aquam movent,** *They move the carts* $\left\{ \begin{array}{l} to \\ into \end{array} \right\}$ *the water.*

In a way, **ad** is the opposite of **ab**, and **in** of **ex (103).**

    1. **in** with acc. = *into*   2. **in** with abl. = *in* or *on*

In aquam.   In aquā.

115. English Word Studies

The preposition **in,** used as a prefix, is very common in English derivatives. Define the following, formed from words found in recent vocabularies: *in-gratiate, in-habitant, in-spect, in-undate, in-voke, in-form.*

The prefix **in–** is often assimilated **(109).** Define the following words: *im-migrant, im-port.* Other examples of assimilation are *il-lusion, ir-rigate.* Words that have come into English through French often have **en–** or **em–** for **in–** or **im–:** *enchant, inquire* or *enquire.* Our word *envy* comes from Latin **in-vidia** (from **in-videō,** *look into* or *against, look askance at*).

What is meant by a *colonial* period of a nation's history? What is a *magnanimous* person? What is the difference between *immigration* and *emigration?*

Minerva, a goddess who favored the Greeks, helps them build the wooden horse. A popular subject in ancient art, the wooden horse appears here on a Greek drinking cup of the fifth century B.C.

Archeological Museum, Florence

Lesson XVI

116. TROIA

Graecī et Troiānī [1] ad Troiam [2] pugnāvērunt. Troiānī barbarī erant, quī [3] in Asiā habitāvērunt. Troiānī et Graecī annōs IX pugnāvērunt. Decimō [4] annō Ulixēs,[5] clārus Graecus, cōnsilium novum in animō habuit. Graecōs signō ēvocāvit et eīs [6] cōnsilium mandāvit:
5 "Multam māteriam ex silvā ad castra portāte. Ex māteriā equum altum parāte. Barbarīs praemium novum dōnābimus."

Graecī equum parāvērunt et in equum virī singulī ascendērunt. In equō scrīpsērunt: [7] "Graecī Minervae [8] praemium dōnant." Tum ad Troiānōs equum mōvērunt. Ad īnsulam parvam nāvigāvērunt et
10 frūmentum parāvērunt. Barbarī equum et castra dēserta [9] Graecōrum vīdērunt. Equum vocāvērunt signum sacrum et in oppidum [10] mōvērunt. Nocte [11] Graecī ab īnsulā revertērunt [12] et ūnus ex Graecīs [13] signō ex equō virōs ēvocāvit. In oppidum sociōs vocāvērunt. Graecī Troiam occupāvērunt. Fortūna Troiānōrum mala erat.

---

[1] *the Trojans.* [2] *Troy.* [3] *who.* [4] *tenth.* [5] *Ulys'sēs.*
[6] *to them.* [7] *wrote.* [8] *Minerva,* a goddess who favored the Greeks.
[9] *deserted.* [10] *town.* [11] *at night.* [12] *returned.* [13] *one of the Greeks.*

1. From what material did the Greeks build the horse?
2. Why did the Trojans take the horse within their walls?
3. How did the Greeks inside the horse know when to come out?
4. Give an example of a modern "Trojan Horse" trick.

117. Neuters of the Second Declension

The second declension contains, in addition to masculine nouns ending in **–us (–ius)**, **–er**, and **–r**, neuter nouns ending in **–um (–ium)**. The only other difference between the neuter and the masculine nouns of the second declension is in the nominative and accusative plural, which both end in short **–a**.

Adjectives too have neuter forms. Thus the full nominative form of an adjective like **barbarus** is **barbarus** (m.), **–a** (f.), **–um** (n.). This is the way adjectives will appear in the vocabularies from now on.

A wall painting from Pompeii shows a wooden horse being brought into Troy. Thousands of paintings have been found at Pompeii. In earlier years, they were taken to the Naples Museum; now they are being left in place. They are mostly watercolors. Painted while the plaster was damp, they dried in with the plaster. Paintings done this way are known as frescoes.

Erich Lessing/PhotoEdit

	SINGULAR		PLURAL	
Nom.	signum	parvum	signa	parva
Gen.	signī	parvī	signōrum	parvōrum
Dat.	signō	parvō	signīs	parvīs
Acc.	signum	parvum	signa	parva
Abl.	signō	parvō	signīs	parvīs

Stem: sign– parv–

Practice

1. Decline **frūmentum bonum** and **praemium grātum.**
2. Give in Latin: *a new standard* in the acc., sing. and plur.; *a famous reward* in the abl., sing. and plur.; *a great plan* in the gen., sing. and plur.; *a small camp* in the dat.

118. Exercises

A. 1. Amīcus meus multa praemia merēbit.
2. Fabī, nūntiā signō victōriam amīcīs tuīs.
3. Litterīs ad castra virōs barbarōs ēvocāvit.
4. Cōnsiliō bonō vītam amīcī nostrī servābimus.
5. Castra sociōrum nostrōrum in magnā īnsulā sunt.
6. Agricolae ex agrīs in castra frūmentum portāvērunt.
7. Captīvī singulī virīs nostrīs cōnsilium nūntiāvērunt.

B. 1. We shall give our friends great rewards.
2. The colonists will sail from Europe to America.
3. The new year will increase the supply of grain.
4. The settlers then moved the grain with horse and wagon.
5. The strange shape of the horse did not scare the prisoners.

119. Vocabulary

an′nus, –ī, m., *year* (annual, biennial)
bar′barus (m.), **–a** (f.), **–um** (n.), *foreign;* as noun,
  foreigner, barbarian (barbarous)
cas′tra, –ō′rum, n. (plur. in form; sing in meaning), *camp*
  (Lancaster)
cōnsi′lium, cōnsi′lī,[14] n., *plan, advice* (counsel)
ē′vocō, ēvocā′re, ēvocā′vī, [ēvocā′tus], *call out, summon* **[vocō]**
frūmen′tum, –ī, n., *grain* (fruit)
prae′mium, prae′mī, n., *reward* (premium)
sig′num, –ī, n., *sign, standard, signal* (sign, significant)

---

[14] Nouns (not adjectives) that end in **–ium** usually shorten **iī** to **ī** in the genitive singular: **cōnsi′liī** becomes **cōnsi′lī,** but the accent is not changed.

This model of the Pantheon is in the Metropolitan Museum, New York. The temple, originally built by Agrippa during the reign of Augustus, was rebuilt later by the Emperor Hadrian (see pp. 118, 296). The inscription says: M(arcus) Agrippa, son of L(ucius), when consul for the third time, built (this).

120. English Word Studies

1. The following are Latin words of the **–um** and **–ium** type preserved in their original form in English:

SINGULAR	PLURAL	SINGULAR	PLURAL
addendum	addenda	delirium	deliria (or –ums)
	agenda	dictum	dicta (or –ums)
bacterium	bacteria	maximum	maxima (or –ums)
candelabrum	candelabra (or –ums)	memorandum	memoranda (or –ums)
curriculum	curricula (or –ums)	minimum	minima (or –ums)
datum	data (remember to say "**these** data")	spectrum	spectra (or –ums)
		stratum	strata (or –ums)

2. What is a *signatory* to a treaty? How did **barbarus,** meaning *foreigner,* come to mean *barbarian?* Are all foreigners barbarians? Are we considered barbarians by other nations?

3. More than twenty-five states have towns named *Troy;* South Dakota has both a *Troy* and a *Trojan.* There is a town called *Roma* in Texas and ten towns named *Rome* in other states. *Gallia* is in Ohio.

91

20°   10°   0°   10°

O C E A N U S   A T L A N T I C U S

MARE
GERMANICUM
(North Sea)

MARE SUEVICUM
(Baltic Sea)

HIBERNIA

Eboracum
(York)

BRITANNIA

Londinium

Saxones

GERMANIA

Albis
(Elbe)

Vistu

50°

Belgae

GERMANIA

Rhenus
(Rhine)

Remi

Lutetia
(Paris)

Sequana
(Seine)

Matrona (Marne)

G A L L I A

Liger
(Loire)

Celtae (Galli)

Genua

RAETIA

NORICUM

PANNONIA

Lugdunum
(Lyons)

Helvetii

Rhodanus
(Rhone)

(Rhone)

A L P E S

Mediolanum
(Milan)

AQUITANIA

Garunna
(Garonne)

Narbo

Padus
(Po)

Genua

Rubico

ILLYRICUM

40°

Numantia

Hiberus
(Ebro)

P Y R E N A E I

Massilia
(Marseilles)

I T A L I A

HISPANIA

Tagus

Tarraco

CORSICA

Roma

Dyrrachium

LUSITANIA

Saguntum

Ostia

Cannae

Anas
(Guadiana)

Corduba

Neapolis

Tarentum

Gades
(Cadiz)

BALEARES

SARDINIA

Pompeii

MARE

Nova Carthago
(Cartagena)

M A U R E T A N I A

Utica

Carthago

SICILIA

Aetna

ATLAS

NUMIDIA

Zama

AFRICA

Syracusae

MELITA
(MALTA)

M E

Thapsus

Leptis Magna

⌇⌇⌇⌇⌇⌇ Roman Walls

Roman Territory 264 B.C. *Before Punic Wars*

30°

Added   "   "   238-201 B.C. *After First and Second Punic Wars*

"   "   133 B.C.

"   "   44 B.C. *Death of Caesar*

"   "   14 A.D. *Death of Augustus*

"   "   Second Century A.D.

0°   10°   Longitude   East

Glimpses of Roman Life

121. SLAVES

In the earliest days the Romans had few slaves, but as prosperity increased they came to depend on them more and more. Slaves did much of the work on the farms and in the industries; but of course the industries were not nearly so highly developed as today. Many slaves were prisoners of war, obtained by the conquest of foreign nations. Some of those who came from more primitive countries may actually have profited from their exposure to Roman culture. But many from Greece and the Near East were superior to their masters as a result of their background and early education. They became teachers, doctors, musicians, actors, bookkeepers, and so on. Although the better slaves were given much personal freedom, they were still the master's property, and could be bought and sold. A highly educated one might cost as much as $12,000 at today's prices, a trained farm worker slightly more than $1,000, a common laborer much less. The slave was generally of the same race as his master.

Wealthy Romans kept large numbers of slaves, many of whom had specialized tasks in the household **(familia).** One might be in charge of polishing the silver, another of writing letters, another of announcing the guests or the hour of the day, and the like. Great landholders sometimes had hundreds of slaves on their estates, where they tended herds and did the work of growing grapes, olives, wheat, and so on.

The lot of the slave was not always so hard as we might imagine, though he was often enough mistreated by a cruel master or by a foreman who might himself be a slave. Disobedient slaves were punished in various ways. The master had the legal right to kill a slave, but naturally he was not often inclined to do so, as he would be destroying his own property. Flogging was a common punishment. Another was to send a city slave to the farm, where the work was harder. Runaway slaves when caught were branded on the forehead with the letter *F,* for **fugitivus.** In 73–71 B.C. a slave named Spartacus led a mass revolt that seriously disturbed the peace of Italy until it was ruthlessly suppressed (see Lesson XVIII).

On the other hand, some slaves and their masters became very close friends. A fine example of the close relationship between master and slave is that of Cicero and his secretary Tiro, a brilliant man who invented a system of shorthand. Many of Cicero's letters show the greatest affection for Tiro.

Above: Actors in a Roman comedy. They wore masks that indicated the type of part being played. Men played women's roles. Most actors were slaves or freedmen.

Left: Tombstone of Q. Fabius Diogenes and his wife, Fabia Primigenia, who lived 47 years with him at Cumae. It was set up by his freedmen, freedwomen, and slaves (familia). Obviously, these freedmen and slaves thought highly of their former master and mistress.

Metropolitan Museum of Art

95

Rich color and elaborate design are typical of later Roman art. Here we see a wall painting from the House of Lucrezio Frontone at Pompeii.

Most slaves were given an allowance, and the thrifty slave could hope to save enough in the course of years to buy his own freedom. Masters often granted freedom out of gratitude for services rendered, many from a genuine feeling that slavery was an evil thing. Others freed their slaves in their wills and left them a sum of money.

Many of these freedmen became very rich and influential. From the time of the Emperor Augustus in the first century A.D. more and more of them took over highly important secretaryships, almost cabinet posts, in the imperial administration. Narcissus, the freedman secretary of the Emperor Claudius, made a tremendous fortune. He was even sent to hasten the Roman invasion of Britain in 48 A.D.

QUESTION

What differences are there between Roman slavery and that which once existed in the New World?

UNIT III REVIEW

Lessons X–XVI

122. VOCABULARY

NOUNS
1. ager
2. amīcitia
3. animus
4. annus
5. captīvus
6. casa
7. castra
8. cēna
9. colōnus
10. cōnsilium
11. disciplīna
12. fīlius
13. frūmentum
14. glōria
15. grātia
16. lingua
17. magister
18. māteria
19. patria
20. praemium
21. puer
22. signum
23. socius
24. vir

ADJECTIVES
25. altus
26. amīcus
27. barbarus
28. līber
29. noster
30. sacer
31. singulī

VERBS
32. augeō
33. doceō
34. ēvocō
35. habeō
36. habitō
37. līberō
38. maneō
39. mereō
40. migrō
41. moveō
42. sum
43. teneō
44. terreō
45. videō
46. vocō

ADVERBS
47. ibi
48. semper

PREPOSITIONS
49. ā, ab
50. dē
51. ē, ex
52. in

123. ENGLISH WORD STUDIES

1. Give and define three English nouns that retain Latin nominative forms, singular and plural, of the first declension; three nouns of the second declension, masculine; and three nouns of the second declension, neuter.

2. Give prefix and Latin root word from which the following words are derived, and define:

defame, approve, advocate, invocation, immigrant, emigrant, avocation, vocation, deter

3. Choose the word in parentheses which in your opinion most nearly gives the meaning of the italicized word. Tell why you select it.

a. *amicable* relations (friendly, social, free, hostile)
b. a *puerile* act (poor, childish, manly, effeminate)
c. a *docile* creature (wild, untamed, stubborn, easily taught)
d. an animal's *habitat* (habit, appearance, living place, color)
e. a *migratory* bird (singing, wandering, tame, nocturnal)

124. VOCABULARY *(English Meanings)*

NOUNS
1. field
2. friendship
3. mind
4. year
5. prisoner
6. house
7. camp
8. dinner
9. settler
10. plan
11. training
12. son
13. grain
14. glory
15. gratitude
16. tongue
17. teacher
18. matter, timber
19. fatherland
20. reward
21. boy
22. sign
23. comrade
24. man

ADJECTIVES
25. high, deep
26. friendly
27. foreign
28. free
29. our
30. sacred
31. one at a time

VERBS
32. increase
33. teach
34. call out
35. have
36. live
37. free
38. remain
39. deserve
40. depart
41. move
42. be
43. hold
44. scare
45. see
46. call

ADVERBS
47. there
48. always

PREPOSITIONS
49. from
50. from, about
51. out of, from
52. in, on; into

125. GRAMMAR SUMMARIES

A. The Genitive Shows the Declension

FIRST DECLENSION		SECOND DECLENSION	
Nom.	–a	–us ⎫ –er ⎬ *Masculine* –r ⎭ –um *Neuter*	
Gen.	–ae	–ī	

B. Case Uses

	In Latin	*In English*
PLACE	1. **In** with ablative.	1. *In* with objective.
ADDRESS	2. Vocative (differs from nominative only in **–us** nouns).	2. Nominative.

C. Tenses

In Latin	In English
Perfect	Past
	Present Perfect

D. Agreement of Adjectives and Nouns

An adjective in Latin must agree with its noun in gender, number, and case. In order, therefore, to modify nouns of different genders, every adjective studied so far has a threefold declension; for example:

magnus, magna, magnum, etc. (For full declension see **553.**)

Caution. Since **nauta** and **agricola** are masculine—although they belong to the first declension—to agree with either, an adjective must have the second declension forms, as **nauta bonus, nautae bonī,** etc.

126. UNIT PRACTICE AND EXERCISES

Practice

1. Decline **līber, barbarus.**
2. Decline **socius noster, agricola novus, signum nostrum.**
3. Conjugate in full and translate: **migrō** in the present, **maneō** in the perfect, **doceō** in the future.
4. What forms are: **tenent, socī, tenuistis, fīliī, docēbitis, linguīs, fīlī, habēbis, habitāre, amīce?**
5. Translate: *he increases, they have, we have lived, he taught, I shall remain, they are calling, you* (sing.) *deserve, we work, you* (plur.) *will see, call out* (sing.), *remain* (plur.).

Exercises

A. Choose the right words in the parentheses to complete the sentences correctly. Give your reason for each choice and translate.
1. Agrī sunt (magnī, magnōs).
2. Agricola (agrōs, agrī) habet.
3. Agricolae (in agrōs, in agrīs) labōrant.
4. In īnsulā (multī colōnī, multōs colōnōs) vidēbō.
5. In patriā nostrā (multās, multōs) agricolās habēmus.

B. Fill in the blanks and then translate the sentences.
1. Agricola est bon___.
2. Serv___, portā aquam.
3. Colōnī multōs servōs habu___.
4. Amīcī meī sunt mult___ et bon___.

UNIT IV

ROMAN LIFE

This is the house of Poseidon and Amphitrite in Herculaneum, a town which was covered by lava and destroyed by the eruption of Vesuvius in 79 A.D. From this view we see the front portion of the house called the *atrium*. Here guests were received and meals were often served. It was common for people to recline on benches covered with pillows. A table with food would be set in the center of the room. In the back wall is the *lararium*, or shrine, where statuettes of the Lares, or household gods, were kept.

Lesson XVII

127. RŌMULUS, NUMA, ET TULLUS

Prīmus rex[1] Rōmae Rōmulus fuit. Armīs et consiliīs bonīs glōriam
Rōmae auxit. Virī et fēminae[2] Rōmulum amāvērunt quod multīs familiīs
asȳlum[3] dōnāvit et ad victōriam sociōs incitāvit. "Rōma magna erit,"
inquit[4] Rōmulus. "Clārī eritis."

5   Secundus[5] rex Rōmae fuit Numa Pompilius. Numa bellum nōn
amāvit. Deam[6] Ēgeriam amāvit. Ēgeria Numam dē cūrīs sacrīs docuit.
Tum rex Rōmānōs docēre mātūrāvit. "Deī[7] amīcī Rōmae erunt," inquit
Numa, "sī[8] bonī et grātī erimus. Multam grātiam deīs habēre dēbēmus."

Tertius[9] rex Rōmae fuit Tullus Hostīlius. Concordiam nōn amāvit et
10 reverentiam[10] parvam habuit. Tullus multa bella mōvit. Officia[11] sacra
nōn complēvit.[12] In extrēmīs,[13] Tullus inquit, "Bonus vir et rex erō." Sed
Iuppiter nōn probāvit et vītam Tullī occupāvit.

QUESTIONS

1. Why was Romulus a popular king?
2. How did Numa learn so much about the gods?
3. What did King Tullus neglect?

✓ 128. Future and Perfect of Sum

Review the present tense of the verb **sum (111).** The future tense
of **sum** also is slightly irregular.

erō, *I shall be*	**erimus,** *we shall be*
eris, *you will be*	**eritis,** *you will be*
erit, *he, she, it will be*	**erunt,** *they will be*

129. Infinitive Used as Subject

1. Since the infinitive is a form of the verb used as a noun, it may
be used as the subject of a verb; as

Amīcōs habēre est grātum, *To have friends is pleasing.*
Errāre est hūmānum, *To err is human.*

[1] *king*   [2] *women*   [3] *refuge, asylum*   [4] *said*   [5] *second*   [6] *goddess*
[7] *The gods*   [8] *if*   [9] *third*   [10] *reverence*   [11] *duties*
[12] *he did not fulfil*   [13] *in his final hours*

Note. Though the infinitive is used as a noun, it is not declined. Its gender is neuter. Therefore the predicate adjective must also be neuter, as **grātum** in the example above.

2. The infinitive may be used as a predicate nominative; as

Vidēre est crēdere, *To see is to believe.*

130. Infinitive Used as Object

With many verbs the infinitive may be used as direct object, like other nouns; as

Servōs līberāre parat, *He prepares to free the slaves.*

Foto F. Micheletti, Brescia, Italy

Victoria. *Right:* A fine Roman statue of the goddess of Victory in Brescia, northern Italy. She is often shown with wings. *Below:* An Italian stamp showing a Roman victory parade, called a triumph (see p. 382).

131. Exercises

A. 1. Puellae cēnam bonam parāre dēbent.
2. Multōs equōs in agrīs vidēre grātum fuit.
3. Pecūniam habēre est multās cūrās habēre.
4. Puerō praemium nostrum mōnstrāre mātūrāmus.
5. Bonum erit [3] concordiam et auxilium in bellō habēre.
6. Nūntiī praemiīs animōs nautārum incitāre parābunt.
7. Sociī signa et arma ad terram novam portāre mātūrāvērunt.

B. 1. Es (*my friend*).
2. Erit (*a farmer*).
3. Erat (*a sailor*).
4. Fuimus (*comrades*).
5. Erunt (*our friends*).

C. 1. It [3] is bad to owe money.
2. Farmers, hasten to increase the supply of grain.
3. We ought to report the plan of war to the men.
4. It [3] was pleasing to see the courage and harmony of the colonists.
5. The messenger will hasten to report the victory to the fatherland.

132. Vocabulary

ar′ma, –ō′rum, n., plur., *arms, weapons*	(armor)
auxi′lium, auxi′lī, n., *aid*	(auxiliary)
bel′lum, –ī, n., *war*	(belligerent)
concor′dia, –ae, f., *harmony*	(concord)
dē′beō, dēbē′re, dē′buī, [dē′bitus], *owe, ought*	(debt)
mātū′rō, mātūrā′re, mātūrā′vī, [mātūrā′tus], *hasten*	(maturity)
nūn′tius, nūn′tī, m., *messenger*	**[nūntiō]**

133. English Word Studies

1. What is meant by large *armaments?* When is a person called *bellicose?* What is an *auxiliary* engine on a sailing ship? What is a *debenture?* a *debit?* a *premature* judgment?

2. Latin phrases in English:

multum in parvo, *much in little.*

de novo, *anew,* literally, *from a new* (start).

in memoriam, *to the memory* (*of*). Tennyson used this as a title for a poem.

---

[3] In English we add *it;* in Latin no such word is used.

Tomas D. W. Friedmann/Photo Researchers, Inc.

Seating 50,000 people, the Colosseum was used for a variety of public entertainment, including gladiatorial contests between Roman slaves who had been trained to fight. Spartacus was one of the most famous Roman gladiators. In the foreground are columns of the Temple of Venus and Rome.

Lesson XVIII

134. SPARTACUS

Spartacus fuit clārus servus, captīvus Rōmānōrum. Sociōs ēvocāvit et ad bellum incitāvit: "Ō sociī, Rōmānī nōn sunt aequī. Puer eram in oppidō meō, et vīta grāta semper erat. Magna erat concordia in patriā nostrā. Populus aequus erat. Silvās magnās et agrōs lātōs amāvī. Dominum nōn habuī; līber ibi fuī. Vērum amīcum habuī, 5 puerum bonum et grātum. Sed Rōmānī patriam meam occupāvērunt; mē et amīcum meum ex patriā portāvērunt. Nunc post [1] multōs annōs vir sum et in arēnā pūblicā pugnō. Hodiē [2] in hōc [3] oppidō virum quem [4] nōn cognōvī [5] occīdī [6]—et erat amīcus meus! Estisne virī? Populum Rōmānum et dominōs malōs nōn amātis. Iniūriās nōn 10

[1] *after.*   [2] *today.*   [3] *this.*   [4] *whom.*
[5] Perf. of **cognōscō,** *recognize.*   [6] *I killed.*

105

merēmus. Causa nostra est aequa. Nōnne nunc hōra est? Ad arma!
Pugnāte! Animum vestrum mōnstrāte! Vocāte sociōs vestrōs ad
auxilium! Servōs līberābimus, līberī erimus, ad patriam nostram
sacram migrāre mātūrābimus et ibi in agrīs nostrīs labōrābimus et
15 in concordiā habitābimus."

QUESTIONS

1. What happened to Spartacus and his boyhood friend?
2. How did the friend die?

135. Asking Questions

In Latin a question is usually introduced by an interrogative word
—either a pronoun (**quis**, *who?* **quid**, *what?*), adverb (**ubi**, *where?*
etc.), or the syllable **–ne**. This last is therefore a kind of question
mark at the beginning of a sentence and cannot be translated. It is
never used alone but is always attached to the first word in the sentence. Since it becomes part of the word, the word accent may shift:
īnsulam'ne. [7]

When **nōn** is used in a question, it is put first and **–ne** is attached
to it: **nōnne.** Such a question expects the answer "Yes."

136. Conversation: A Geography Lesson

M. = Magister, *teacher*   **D. = Discipulī,** *pupils*

M: Spectāte, discipulī. D: Spectāmus, magister.

M: Ubi est Italia? D: In Eurōpā Italia est.

M: Estne Italia lāta? D: Italia longa sed nōn lāta est.

M: Īnsulamne vidētis? D: Corsicam vidēmus.

5   M: Estne Corsica magna īnsula? D: Parva, nōn magna īnsula est
Corsica.

M: Quid in Siciliā vidētis? D: Aetnam vidēmus.

M: Magnam īnsulam mōnstrō; Britannia est. Colōnī ex Britanniā
ad Americam et ad Austrāliam migrāvērunt.

10   M: Fuitne Gallia prōvincia? D: Gallia fuit prōvincia imperī [8]
Rōmānī.

---

[7] There was a tendency to avoid attaching **–ne** to a word ending in a short vowel if
the next to the last syllable was also short (see **518**). Thus **Corsi'cane** would not be
used but **–ne** would be attached to some other word in the sentence.

[8] *Empire.*

Roman shops as shown in a model. The vegetable stall in the center is deserted
while the lady (left) looks at jewelry and the men (right) patronize the bar.

M: Nōnne magna fuit glōria Galliae? **D:** Magna fuit glōria Galliae.[10]
M: Discipulī, quis oculōs bonōs habet? **Lūcius:** Ego.[11]
M: Mōnstrā discipulīs Rōmam. **Lūcius:** Rōma in Italiā est.

Note. Ask questions and make statements similar to those above, using
the map on pages 92–93 or a large wall map.

137. Questions

Answer in Latin.
1. Eurōpane est in Italiā?
2. Estne Italia īnsula?
3. Ubi est Rōma?
4. Estne Italia prōvincia?

138. Vocabulary

ae′quus, –a, –um, *even, just, calm*	(equality, equate)
cau′sa, –ae, f., *cause, reason, case*	(causal, because)
do′minus, –ī, m., *master*	(dominate, dominion)
lā′tus, –a, –um, *wide*	(latitude)
op′pidum, –ī, n., *town*	
po′pulus, –ī, m., *people*	(popular, populace)
pū′blicus, –a, –um, *public*	(publish)
vē′rus, –a, –um, *true*	(verify)
ves′ter, ves′tra, ves′trum, *your*	(referring to two or more persons)

139. English Word Studies

1. What is *popular* government? Use *depopulate* in a sentence.
What is meant by the sentence: "I listened to his attacks with
equanimity"? Give three more derivatives of **aequus.**

2. Give three derivatives apiece from **nūntiō, portō, spectō,** and
vocō by attaching one of the prefixes **ad–, dē–, ex–,** or **in–.**

---

[10] This whole sentence can be translated very simply: *Yes.*
[11] *I.*

Lesson XIX

140. PATRŌNUS ET CLIENTĒS[1]

In ātriō[2] multī clientēs exspectant. Patrōnus, vir clārus, mox aderit.[3] Interim[4] clientēs dē officiīs agunt. Patrōnum laudant quod amīcus et generōsus est.

CLIENS PRĪMUS: Salvē, amīce! Vīdistīne patrōnum nostrum?

5   CLIENS SECUNDUS: Minimē.[5] Multa officia habet et in tablīnō[6] labōrat.

CLIENS PRĪMUS: Parvum ōtium[7] habet quod prō aliīs[8] vītam agit. Cūrae aliōrum virōrum semper eum[9] movent.

CLIENS SECUNDUS: Ab officiīs novīs et dūrīs numquam[10] cēdit. Nōnne 10 saepe[11] auxilium ad familiās nostrās mīsit?

CLIENS PRĪMUS: Ita.[12] Ergo[13] grātum est eum laudāre et grātiā nostrā fāmam eius[14] augēre.

Nunc patrōnus accedīt et virōs in ātrio salūtat.[15] Sportulās[16] portat. In sportulīs cibum et pecūniam posuit. Sportulae sunt praemia. Quod 15 clientēs fīdī[17] fuērunt, patrōnus sportulās ad familiās mittit.

Aliquandō[18] clientēs patrōnum spectant dum[19] causās in Forō agit. Aliquandō patrōnus clientēs[20] dēfendit. Aliquandō ad cēnam clientēs vocat. Nōn servī sunt, sed patrōnus paene[21] dominus est. ''Manus manum lavat.''[22]

QUESTIONS

1. What do the clients take home from the visit to their patron?
2. In what other way did Roman patrons provide for their clients?

---

[1] a patron and his clients   [2] entrance hall   [3] soon he will be present
[4] meanwhile   [5] no   [6] the study   [7] leisure   [8] for others   [9] him
[10] never   [11] often   [12] yes   [13] therefore   [14] his   [15] greets
[16] gift-baskets, sportulae   [17] faithful   [18] sometimes   [19] while
[20] accusative   [21] almost   [22] "One hand washes the other."

This artist's reconstruction of an ancient house is based on existing remains in Pompeii. The view looks through the atrium (note its basin) and the owner's office into the peristyle. At right is a balcony leading into second-story rooms. The lower portions of some columns are painted red to hide fingermarks—a wise precaution against small boys.

141. Third Conjugation

1. Verbs of the *third conjugation* have the stem vowel –ě–. Note the difference of stem vowel in:

1st Conj. (Long-A Verbs): Pres. stem **portā–** (from infin. **portāre**)
2d Conj. (Long-E Verbs): Pres. stem **docē–** (from infin. **docēre**)
3d Conj. (Short-E Verbs): Pres. stem **pōně–** (from infin. **pōněre**)

2. In the present tense, the short vowel –ě– of the third conjugation changes to –ǐ–, except in:

a. the first person singular, where it disappears before –ō,
b. the third person plural, where it becomes –u–, and
c. the second person singular of the imperative, where it remains –ě–.

	pōnō, *I place,* etc.	pōnimus
PRES. TENSE:	pōnis	pōnitis
	pōnit	pōnunt
PRES. IMPER.:	pōne	pōnite

Law and Medicine. *Left:* The Vatican stamp honors the International Juridical Congress in 1934, just 1400 years after the Code was accepted by Justinian. *Right:* An Italian stamp for an international health congress. Shown are the snake and rod of Aesculapius, Roman god of healing. Physicians today use a modified form of this. At the bottom of this stamp, St. Peter's and the Colosseum.

3. The endings of the perfect tense are the same as in the first and second conjugations.

posu**ī**, *I placed*, etc.	posu**imus**
posu**istī**	posu**istis**
posu**it**	posu**ērunt**

Practice

1. Conjugate **agō** and **dēfendō** in the present and perfect tenses.
2. Form the present imperative, singular and plural, of the above verbs, and of **vocō** and **videō**.
3. Give the Latin for *he departs, he moves, he hastens, we are defending, you* (plur.) *approach.*

142. Apposition

1. **Dominum meum, Lūcium Cornēlium, exspectō,** *I am waiting for my master, Lucius Cornelius.*
2. **Nautīs, amīcīs nostrīs, pecūniam dōnāvimus,** *We gave money to the sailors, our friends.*

Observe that **Lūcium Cornēlium** (1) identifies the object **dominum** and stands in direct relation to it, and is therefore, like **dominum,** in the accusative. **Amīcīs nostrīs** (2) identifies **nautīs,** the indirect object, and is therefore likewise in the dative. No verb is involved. This construction is called *apposition* (**ad** + **pōnō,** *place next to*). A noun in apposition with another noun (or pronoun) is in the same case as the other noun (or pronoun).

Practice

Give the Latin for the words in italics: I saw John, my *friend.* Have you heard the story of Spartacus, the *slave?* We lived in England, a large *island.* I told it to Mr. Jones, *my teacher.*

143. Exercises

A. 1. Litterāsne ad amīcōs vērōs mīsistī?
2. Semper, puerī, agite vītam bonam.
3. Equōsne tuōs, Cornēlī, in aquam agis?
4. Ubi praedam pōnitis? In viā praedam pōnimus.
5. In Americā, patriā nostrā, semper habitābimus.
6. Ad īnsulam cessimus et castra dēfendere parāvimus.

B. 1. Is he not living a long life?
2. Send aid to our allies, the Roman people.
3. It is the duty of the prisoner to work in the fields.
4. Ought we not to increase the number of settlers in the province?
5. The slave, a prisoner of the Romans, is-getting-ready to put the grain into the wagon.

144. Vocabulary

a′gō, a′gere, ē′gī, [āc′tus], *drive, do, discuss, live or spend* (time) (agent)

cē′dō, cē′dere, ces′sī, [cessū′rus], *move, retreat, yield* (cede)

accē′dō, accē′dere, acces′sī, [accessū′rus], *approach* (with **ad**)

excē′dō, excē′dere, exces′sī, [excessū′rus], *depart*

dēfen′dō, dēfen′dere, dēfen′dī, [dēfēn′sus], *defend* (defendant)

exspec′tō, exspectā′re, exspectā′vī, [exspectā′tus], *look out for, await* [*spectō*]

mit′tō, mit′tere, mī′sī, [mis′sus], *let go, send* (admittance)

offi′cium, offi′cī, n., *duty* (official, officiate)

pō′nō, pō′nere, po′suī, [po′situs], *put, place* (postpone)

145. English Word Studies

We have seen that many English nouns and adjectives have preserved their original Latin forms. A great many more have preserved the base of the Latin word. Others again consist of the Latin stem plus silent –e. The same is true of verbs. The following are examples:

stem: *defend, form, laud, public, sign;* stem plus –e: *cause, cede, fortune, fame, cure*

The same rules are illustrated in the following words in which changes in the base have taken place:

stem: *letter* (**littera**), *number* (**numerus**), *car* (**carrus**), *clear* (**clārus**); stem plus –e: *evoke* (**ēvocō**), *single* (**singulī**)

Give ten other examples from nouns, adjectives, and verbs already studied.

Lesson XX

146. RŌMĀNĪ

Quondam [1] Rōma, oppidum Italiae, parva erat. Rōmānī, populus firmus, oppidum mūnīvērunt quod arma capere et patriam dēfendere parāvērunt. Victōriīs magnīs patriam servāvērunt et auxērunt. Ex multīs terrīs praedam ēgērunt. Deīs grātiās ēgērunt et templa magna
5 et alta fēcērunt. Magna praemia Rōmānī meruērunt et accēpērunt, quod officium fēcērunt. Magnum numerum colōnōrum in aliās [2] terrās mīsērunt. Multās terrās barbarās cēpērunt, prōvinciās fēcērunt et aequē [3] rēxērunt. Barbarī linguam Latīnam accēpērunt. Rōmānī frūmentum ex aliīs [2] terrīs in Italiam portāvērunt. Ad Britanniam,
10 Hispāniam, Āfricam, Graeciam, Asiam nāvigāvērunt et oppida mūnī-vērunt. Rōma multōs annōs multōs populōs rēxit.

Nunc Rōma magna et pulchra est. Multī ad Italiam veniunt et viās antīquās et templa pulchra inveniunt. Mātūrābisne in Italiam venīre et ruīnās Rōmānās invenīre?

QUESTIONS

1. Why were the Romans rewarded?
2. What do visitors to Italy see?

147. Present of Third (–iō) and Fourth Conjugation Verbs

In a few important verbs of the third conjugation, short –ĭ– is inserted before the stem vowel in the first person singular and in the third person plural of the present tense. They are often called "–iō verbs" of the third conjugation.

But most verbs ending in –iō belong to the *fourth conjugation* and have the stem vowel long –ī–. They retain this long –ī– throughout their conjugation except where long vowels are regularly shortened (**25,** 4).

---

[1] *once.* [2] *other.* [3] *justly.*

112

In the Forum of Julius Caesar we see the three columns of the Temple of Venus Genetrix. In the background are the arched remains of the numerous shops which prospered during Roman times. The Forum of Julius Caesar is located a short distance from the Roman Forum.

Larry Lee/West Light

THIRD CONJUGATION (*I take*, etc.)		FOURTH CONJUGATION (*I fortify*, etc.)	
capiō	capimus	mūniō	mūnīmus
capis	capitis	mūnīs	mūnītis
capit	capiunt	mūnit	mūniunt

The imperative shows similar differences: **cape, capite;** [4] **mūnī, mūnīte.**

The endings of the perfect tense are the same as in the other conjugations: **cēpī, mūnīvī,** etc. (see **141, 569–570**).

Practice

Conjugate and give all possible meanings of the present and perfect tenses of **accēdō, inveniō, faciō.**

---

[4] The imperative singular of **faciō** is **fac.**

Coin of Queen Elizabeth of England issued in 1953. The Latin inscription reads: "Elizabeth II Dei gra(tia) Britt(anniarum) omn(ium) regina f(idei) d(efensor)," "Elizabeth II by the grace of God queen of all the Britains, defender of the faith." The spelling with two *tt's* in *Britt* is a sign of the plural, as we abbreviate *pages* by *pp*.

Wide World

148. Hints for Developing "Word Sense"

Few words in any language, except prepositions, etc., have exactly the same meaning at all times. While words usually have one general meaning, they may have several *shades of meaning,* which depend entirely upon their context, or surroundings. In translating a Latin word, therefore, it is necessary to get its exact meaning (as opposed to its general or "vocabulary" meaning) from its context or setting; for example,

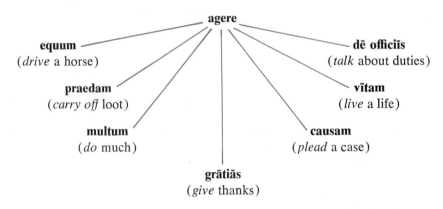

agere

equum
(*drive* a horse)

praedam
(*carry off* loot)

multum
(*do* much)

grātiās
(*give* thanks)

dē officiīs
(*talk* about duties)

vītam
(*live* a life)

causam
(*plead* a case)

The above are only a few of the meanings of **agō.** When translating do not stick to the meanings given to words in the vocabulary, but figure out one best suited to the context. In this way you will learn to express yourself in good English.

149. Exercises

A. 1. Castra mūniunt et virōs ēvocant.
2. Ubi estis, puerī et puellae? Venīmus, magister.
3. Nōnne aequum est semper amīcōs dēfendere?
4. In agrīs frūmentum, magnum auxilium, invenīmus.
5. Virī singulī praemia accipiunt, quod officium fēcērunt.
6. Mārcus multum agit. In agrīs equōs agit, in bellō praedam agit, in forō causās agit, amīcō prō [5] cēnā grātiās agit, cum [6] amīcīs dē officiīs agit. Vītam bonam agit.

B. 1. We are fortifying the camp.
2. It is pleasing to find money.
3. We do not find our friend Marcus.
4. Marcus is not receiving a reward because he did not come.
5. A beautiful queen rules the people.

150. Vocabulary

ca′piō, ca′pere, cē′pī, [cap′tus], *take, seize* [*captīvus*]
   acci′piō, acci′pere, accē′pī, [accep′tus], *receive*
fa′ciō, fa′cere, fē′cī, [fac′tus], *do, make* (efficient)
mū′niō, mūnī′re, mūnī′vī, [mūnī′tus], *fortify* (munitions)
pul′cher, –chra, –chrum, *beautiful* (pulchritude)
re′gō, re′gere, rē′xī, [rēc′tus], *guide, rule* (regent)
tem′plum, –ī, n., *temple* (Templar)
ve′niō, venī′re, vē′nī, [ventū′rus], *come* (convene)
   inve′niō, invenī′re, invē′nī, [inven′tus], *come upon, find*

151. Latin and English Word Formation: Vowel Changes

When a Latin word is compounded with a prefix, short –ă– or short –ĕ– in the root is usually "weakened" to short –ĭ– before a single consonant except –r–. The English derivatives show the same change. Long –ā– and long –ē– are not affected. Study these examples:

From **agō,** Latin **ex-igō, ab-igō, red-igō,** etc.; English *exigency.*
From **habeō,** Latin **pro-hibeō, ex-hibeō,** etc.; English *prohibit, exhibit.*
From **teneō,** Latin **con-tineō, re-tineō,** etc.; English *continent, retinue.*

(But **veniō** and its compounds do not follow this rule; English *convene.*)

Illustrate the rule further by compounding **capiō** and **faciō** with **ad–, dē–, ex–,** and **in–,** giving English derivatives where possible.

[5] *for.* [6] *with.*

Lesson XXI

152. AMĪCITIA

Mārcus, amīcus meus, fīlius est vīcīnī[1] nostrī. Nōn in oppidō sed in agrīs habitāmus. Causam amīcitiae nostrae nārrābō.

Mārcus praemium accēpit: equum et carrum. Carrus parvus est et pretium carrī nōn magnum erat. Prīmō[2] equus carrum dūcere nōn 5 voluit.[3] Sed Mārcus equum docuit et disciplīnā multum effēcit. Nunc Mārcus equum dūcit et equus carrum dūcit.

Quōdam diē[4] Mārcus ad casam nostram vēnit et vocāvit: "Ad terminum agrōrum māteriam carrō portābō. Auxilium tuum rogō. Venī."

10 Māteriam in carrō posuimus. Prīmō[2] in viā plānā, tum ad locum altum, terminum agrōrum, Mārcus equum agere mātūrāvit. Ibi puer malus dē locō nōn cessit et equum terruit et ego[5] ex carrō paene[6] cecidī.[7] Sed aequus erat animus Mārcī, quī[8] equum tenuit et mē[9] servāvit. Ad terminum vītae meae nōn vēnī. Nōnne Mārcō, vērō 15 amīcō, grātus esse dēbeō et praemium dōnāre? Perīculum semper amīcōs firmōs efficit.

QUESTIONS

1. Why did the wagon cost little?
2. Why is the speaker grateful to Marcus?

153. Word Order

We have seen that the words in a Latin sentence show their connection with one another by means of endings, regardless of position (unlike English). They may therefore be shifted rather freely without obscuring the relationship. The more or less normal order is:

SUBJECT	PREDICATE
noun—*adjective* (*gen., appositive*)	*abl.*—indir. obj.—dir. obj.—*adverb*—**verb**

---

[1] *neighbor.* [2] *at first.* [3] *did not want.* [4] *one day.* [5] *I.*
[6] *almost.* [7] *fell.* [8] *who.* [9] Accusative of **ego.**

1. *Remember,* therefore, that:

a. Adjectives usually follow their nouns, but adjectives indicating quantity and size usually precede: **virī bonī; multī virī.**

b. Possessive adjectives (**meus, tuus,** etc.) follow their nouns, unless emphatic.

c. A genitive often follows its noun.

d. An indirect object often stands before a direct object.

e. A word used to ask a question usually stands first, as in English.

f. The verb generally stands last. Forms of the linking verb are often placed in the middle of a sentence, as in English.

g. **Nōnne** is put first in the sentence **(135).**

2. *But this normal order is far less regular in Latin than the normal order in English.* The shifted order serves to bring out varying shades of emphasis. This is done also in English, though to a less degree, largely in imitation of the Latin. Emphasis is gained in Latin particularly by:

a. Putting the emphatic words *first* in the sentence: **Magna est glōria Dominī,** also common in English: *Great is the glory of the Lord!*

b. *Separating* the emphatic word from the word to which it belongs: **Magnās puer amīcō grātiās ēgit,** *The boy thanked his friend very much.*

154. Exercises

A. 1. Magnum fuit pretium victōriae.

2. Invēnī in viā pecūniam, nōn cēpī.

3. Ubi est terminus agrōrum Mārcī, amīcī nostrī?

4. Virōs ad arma vocā, Mārce, et mūnī loca plāna.

5. Ad locum altum vēnērunt et magnam silvam vīdērunt.

6. Multōs habēre dēbēmus equōs, sed magnum est pretium.

7. Magister tuus concordiam nōn efficit, quod malī sunt puerī.

Albert Moldvay

The Pantheon, begun in 27 B.C., is famous for the way in which the great weight on its brick and concrete dome is supported. The distance from the skylight to the pavement is the same as the inner diameter of the building. The Pantheon was a temple dedicated to many dieties, particularly to Mars and Venus. Located in the center of Rome, it is one of the best preserved ancient monuments in the world.

Victoria, the capital of British Columbia, has a parliament building in the Roman style, like the Capitol in Washington (p. 148) and many state capitols (pp. 149, 170).

National Film Board, Ottawa

B. 1. Great is the fame of our teacher.
2. Have you seen many famous places?
3. Are you coming to our friend's dinner?
4. They are hastening to lead the horses to water.
5. The price of instruction is small, but the rewards are great.

155. Vocabulary

dū′cō, dū′cere,[10] **dū′xī, [duc′tus],** *lead, draw* (reduce)
effi′ciō, effi′cere, effē′cī, [effec′tus], *make (out), bring about*
[*faciō*]
lo′cus, –ī, m., *place;* plur., **lo′ca,** n.[11] (local)
pre′tium, pre′tī, n., *price* (precious, appreciate)
ter′minus, –ī, m., *end, boundary* (term, terminal)

156. English Word Studies

1. Explain by derivation: *admit, equity, demote, location, efficiency, terminate, invention.*

2. Latin phrases in English:

ex animo, *from the heart* (sincerely).
Experientia docet, *Experience teaches.*
ad infinitum, *to infinity,* i.e., without limit.
ad astra per aspera, *to the stars through difficulties* (used by Kansas as its state motto).

---

[10] The imperative sing. is **dūc.**   [11] Note that **locus** changes gender in the plural.

Glimpses of Roman Life

157. SIGNS OF THE TIMES

Perhaps nothing gives us quite so intimate a glimpse of a civilization as its signs and posters on walls, in windows, on posts, and the like. We are fortunate in being able to catch such a glimpse of the everyday life of an ancient city through the signs found at Pompeii, a city near Naples which was buried by a shower of volcanic ash from Mt. Vesuvius in 79 A.D. For more than two hundred years digging has been going on in the ruins, and hundreds of notices painted or scratched on house walls have been uncovered. Among them are the scribblings of small boys, who over and over practiced writing the alphabet. Sometimes they started a fable, as "Once upon a time a mouse. . . ." Sometimes they quoted lines from Virgil and other poets. They (and adults, too) wrote their names over and over again. A kind of "pig Latin" is represented by **anumurb** for **urbānum,** like "eesay" for "see." There are messages to sweethearts; in one, greetings are sent

Election posters and notices of gladiatorial shows on a house front in Pompeii. Lucretius Satrius furnishes 20 pairs of gladiators and his son 10 pairs.

Traces of election posters are still visible on this Pompeian house, which was uncovered in 1917. But fifty years' exposure to the weather has faded the paint and now even the stucco must be braced to the wall. The posters tell us that the house belonged to one Marcus Epidius Hymenaeus.

to a girl whom the lover calls his little fish. Another girl is called the queen of Pompeii, evidently meaning the beauty queen. To another, who is unnamed, there is merely the message **Venus es.** Several run like this: **Helena amātur ā Rūfō,** "Helen is loved by Rufus." But another tells about a girl who cannot stand a certain boy. Some of the messages are not very complimentary: "thief" occurs several times. One reads: **Stronnius nīl scit,** "Stronnius knows nothing." In another, one person says hello to another and adds: **Quid agit tibi dexter ocellus?** "How is your right eye?"—apparently having some fun about a black eye. The owners of houses tried to keep away idlers by such signs as this: **Ōtiōsīs locus hic nōn est. Discēde, morātor,** "This is no place for idlers. Go away, loafer." Sometimes there are New Year's greetings or "Christmas" greetings (**Iō Sāturnālia**). In some cases record is kept of special events, as a birthday or the arrival of the emperor. One writer indicates that he has a cold. One says he (or she) baked bread on April 19; another that he put up olives on October 16; another tells of setting a hen on April 30. One wall lists daily expenditures, as for cheese, bread, oil, and wine. What appears to be a laundry list mentions a tunic [shirt] and a cloak on April 20, underwear on May 7, two tunics on May 8. No wonder that some unknown wrote: "Wall, I wonder that you have not collapsed from having to bear the tiresome stuff of so many writers."

These Italian farmers are baking bread in a wood heated oven. This custom of baking bread by hand is similar to the way bread was baked in Roman times. The round loaves were creased to make them easier to break into pieces.

Gianni Tortoli/Photo Researchers, Inc.

When we come to formal notices, we find that election posters play a prominent part. These ask support for this man or that because he is deserving or respectable or honest or because he delivers good bread, etc. The supporters include teamsters, tailors, barbers, dyers, and many other groups. One inscription advocates giving away the money in the public treasury.

Another group of notices advertises the shows of gladiators, similar to our prize fights. Besides mentioning the number of matches, they often name other attractions, such as awnings to keep the sun off, sprinklers to keep the dust down, animal fights, athletic contests.

Hotels advertised frequently. One offers a dining room with three couches and all conveniences (**commodīs**). In an apartment house (**īnsula**) shops on the ground floor are offered from July 1, and luxurious (**equestria,** suitable for a rich man) upstairs apartments; "see agent of the owner."

Signs offer rewards for return of lost or stolen articles. On one sign a man says that he found a horse on November 25 and asks the owner to claim it on a farm near the bridge.

UNIT IV REVIEW

Lessons XVII–XXI

158. ENGLISH AND LATIN WORD STUDIES

1. Give prefix and Latin root word from which the following are derived: **excipiō, adigō, ērigō, afficiō;** *allocation, depopulate, exigency, efficient, accessory.*

2. Make Latin words out of **ad–** and **capiō, in–** and **pōnō, ad–** and **teneō, dē–** and **mereō.**

3. The first word in each of the following lines is a Latin word. Pick the correct derivative from the English words which follow it.

pōnō	pone	pony	exponent	put
mittēmus	mitten	meet	send	remit
populus	poplar	population	pope	pop
capit	cap	cape	decapitate	recipient
dūcō	conduct	paint	duck	deuce
aequum	equestrian	equine	equity	equip

159. VOCABULARY

NOUNS			
1. **arma**	4. **causa**	8. **nūntius**	12. **pretium**
2. **auxilium**	5. **concordia**	9. **officium**	13. **templum**
3. **bellum**	6. **dominus**	10. **oppidum**	14. **terminus**
	7. **locus**	11. **populus**	

ADJECTIVES			
15. **aequus**	16. **lātus**	18. **pulcher**	20. **vester**
	17. **pūblicus**	19. **vērus**	

VERBS			
21. **accēdō**	25. **cēdō**	30. **excēdō**	35. **mittō**
22. **accipiō**	26. **dēbeō**	31. **exspectō**	36. **mūniō**
23. **agō**	27. **dēfendō**	32. **faciō**	37. **pōnō**
24. **capiō**	28. **dūcō**	33. **inveniō**	38. **regō**
	29. **efficiō**	34. **mātūrō**	39. **veniō**

160. VOCABULARY (English Meanings)

NOUNS
1. arms
2. aid
3. war
4. cause
5. harmony
6. master
7. place
8. messenger
9. duty
10. town
11. people
12. price
13. temple
14. end

ADJECTIVES
15. even, just
16. wide
17. public
18. beautiful
19. true
20. your

VERBS
21. approach
22. receive
23. drive, do
24. take
25. move, yield
26. owe, ought
27. defend
28. lead
29. bring about
30. depart
31. await
32. do, make
33. come upon
34. hasten
35. send
36. fortify
37. put
38. rule
39. come

161. GRAMMAR SUMMARIES

A. Conjugations

The four conjugations are distinguished by the stem vowel, easily found by detaching the **–re** ending of the infinitive. They may be called the Ā, Ē, Ĕ, and Ī conjugations.

First conj.:	portĀre
Second conj.:	docĒre
Third conj.:	pōnĔre
Third conj. (**–iō** verbs):	capĔre
Fourth conj.:	mūnĪre

B. Questions

In Latin	*In English*
1. Interrogative pronoun or adverb at beginning.	1. Interrogative pronoun or adverb at beginning; or interrogative form of verb (*Did you go?*).
2. **–ne** attached to first word.	2. Interrogative form of verb.

C. Word Order

In Latin	In English
1. Comparatively free.	1. Used to show relation of words.
2. Adjectives, except those indicating quantity or size, more often follow.	2. Adjectives precede.
3. Verb is usually at end.	3. Verb is after subject.
4. Objects are usually before verb.	4. Objects follow verb.

162. UNIT PRACTICE AND EXERCISES

Noun and Adjective Drill

1. Decline **multum auxilium, populus clārus, concordia vēra.**
2. Give in Latin the singular and plural of the following in the case indicated:

nom.: *my duty*   acc.: *a small price*   abl.: *our friend*

dat.: *a good place*   gen.: *a sacred land*   nom.: *a just man*

Verb Drill

A. Decide which form of **sum** translates the English in the first column:

they were	fuimus	sunt	erant	sumus
you will be	erō	eris	estis	fuistis
you are	eris	fuistī	fuistis	es
he was	erant	erat	erit	fuērunt
we are	sunt	sumus	estis	erimus
they will be	erunt	erant	erit	sunt
we were	erant	erimus	sumus	fuimus

B. Give the third plural of the following verbs in the present, future, and perfect: **sum, exspectō, dēbeō, mātūrō, ēvocō.**

C. 1. Give tense, person, and number, and translate: **regunt, pōnit, erunt, mātūrātis, mīsit, fuit, fēcistī, es, exspectābimus, eris, dūxērunt, invenīmus, veniunt, accēdit, laudābunt.**

2. Give in Latin: *he will be; I fortified; they approached; you* (sing.) *await; we are; they do; they received; you* (plur.) *came; we shall be; they will hasten; they will be; he leads; we are defending; he departed; he takes.*

UNIT V

FAMOUS STORIES

Roman theaters were typically semi-circular, just as the earlier Greek theaters were. This Roman theater at Orange, France has been restored. The seating is contemporary, but follows the Greek and Roman style. The oval area immediately in front of the stage is called the orchestra, or "dancing ground."

Lesson XXII

163. CERĒS ET PRŌSERPINA

Cerēs, dea frūmentī, et fīlia Prōserpina [1] in Siciliā habitāvērunt. Quondam [2] Prōserpina et aliae puellae in agrīs erant. Locum commodum invēnērunt et flōrēs [3] variōs lēgērunt. Ōtium grātum erat; magnum erat studium puellārum.

5 Plūtō, deus īnferōrum, [4] Prōserpinam vīdit et amāvit. Equōs incitāvit et ad locum ubi puellae erant accessit. Puellae fūgērunt. Prōserpina fugere mātūrāvit, sed Plūtō valuit et eam [5] cēpit, in carrō posuit, ad īnferōs dūxit.

Cerēs nocte [6] ex agrīs vēnit. Fīliam exspectāvit, sed Prōserpina 10 nōn vēnit. Magna erat cūra deae. Ad multa loca, ad terminōs terrae Cerēs accessit. Ōtium nōn invēnit.

Quod Cerēs Prōserpinam nōn invēnit, in agrīs nōn labōrāvit. Flōrēs nōn erant, frūmentum in agrīs nōn erat. Populus vītam dūram ēgit et deam accūsāvit quod pretium cibī magnum erat. Multī agri- 15 colae dīxērunt:

"Quid [7] agēmus? In agrīs labōrāmus sed frūmentum nōn habēmus. Nōn valēmus. Deī nōn aequī sunt; officium nōn faciunt."

Iuppiter, quī deōs et virōs regit, iniūriās populī vīdit et deae agrōrum nūntiāvit:

20 "Prōserpina valet sed Plūtō eam habet. Mercurium nūntium ad īnferōs mittam. Mercurius fīliam tuam ad tē [8] dūcet. Sed nōn semper in terrā Prōserpina manēbit. Ita commodum erit: partem [9] annī in terrā, partem sub terrā aget."

Ita Iuppiter concordiam effēcit. Cerēs fīliam accēpit. Prōserpina 25 partem annī in terrā, partem sub terrā ēgit. Cum [10] lībera in terrā

---

[1] *Proser'pina.* [2] *once.*
[3] *flowers.* [4] *those below,* i.e., the ghosts of the dead in Hades.
[5] *her.* [6] *at night.*
[7] *what.* [8] *you.*
[9] Accusative sing. of **pars.** [10] *whenever.*

Metropolitan Museum of Art, Rogers Fund, 1922

Proserpina being carried off by Pluto. From two old woodcuts, the larger from an edition of Ovid printed in 1501, the smaller from a 1539 edition.

Dick Fund, 1931

est, multōs flōrēs et magnam cōpiam frūmentī vidēmus, quod Cerēs grāta in agrīs est et magnum est studium deae. Sed cum Prōserpina ad īnferōs excēdit, Cerēs trīstis [11] est, et flōrēs variī nōn sunt.

QUESTIONS

1. What was Proserpina doing when Pluto came?
2. What happened to the flowers after Proserpina left?
3. On what terms did Proserpina go back to her mother?

164. Third Conjugation: Future

The future sign of verbs of the first and second conjugations is **–bi– (49)**. The future sign of verbs of the third and fourth conjugations, however, is long **–ē–**. The **–ō** verbs of the third conjugation substitute this long **–ē–** for the stem vowel **–ĕ–**, except in the first singular **(–am)**.

I shall place, etc.	
pōnam	pōnēmus
pōnēs	pōnētis
pōnet [12]	pōnent [12]

[11] *sad.* [2] The third singular and plural have **–ĕ–**, according to rule **(25, 4)**.

129

Practice

1. Give the present of **mittō,** the future of **cēdō,** and the perfect of **dēfendō.**
2. Tell the form of **fūgit, valēbis, efficit, dūcēmus, docēmus, accipitis, mūniunt, migrāvit, agent.**

165. Exercises

A.
  1. Cēdētisne puerīs malīs?
  2. Valēsne, fīlia mea? Valeō.
  3. Captīvī ab oppidō in silvās lātās fugiunt.
  4. Litterās ad Mārcum, amīcum meum, mittam.
  5. Puerī bonī ex studiīs magnam fāmam accipiunt.
  6. Virī ex oppidō nōn excēdent sed puellās dēfendent.
  7. Multās hōrās in ōtiō nōn agēmus sed semper labōrābimus.

B.
  1. They fortify the camp.
  2. They will rule the province.
  3. Did you approve the shape of the wagon?
  4. It is not convenient to send a letter.
  5. We shall remain in the town and send a messenger.

166. Vocabulary

com′modus, –a, –um, *suitable, convenient*   (commodious)
de′us, –ī, m., *god*   (deity)
fu′giō, fu′gere, fū′gī, [fugitū′rus], *run away, flee*   (fugitive)
i′ta, adv., *so*
ō′tium, ō′tī, n., *leisure*   (otiose)
stu′dium, stu′dī, n., *eagerness, interest;* plur., *studies*   (studious)
va′leō, valē′re, va′luī, [valitū′rus], *be strong, be well*   (valid)
va′rius, –a, –um, *changing, varying*   (variable, variety)

167. English Word Studies

1. What are *commodities* and why are they so called? Why does a good student "pursue" his *studies*? Can you explain the word *cereal?* Give three more derivatives of **varius.**

2. Latin phrases in English:

auxilio ab alto, *by aid from* (*on*) *high.*
victoria, non praeda, *victory, not loot.*
Montani semper liberi, *Mountaineers* (*are*) *always free* (motto of the state of West Virginia).
ex officio, *out of* (*as a result of*) *one's duty* or *office;* for example, a president of an organization may be a member of a committee *ex officio* (pronounced "offishio" in English) as a result of his office as president.

Albert Moldvay

The Arch of Constantine was the last triumphal arch built in Rome. It celebrates the victory of Constantine, the first Christian emperor, over Maxentius in 312 A.D. Many of the sculptures on the arch were taken from older buildings. The Colosseum is in the background.

Lesson XXIII

168. LŪCIUS ET MĀRCUS

Rōmānī cum Germānīs, populō firmō et dūrō, bella perpetua gessērunt. Ōtium semper bellō cēdit, et nunc quoque [1] bella perpetua gerimus. Variae sunt bellōrum causae.

Quondam [2] Rōmānī et Aquītānī, sociī Rōmānōrum, cum Germānīs pugnābant.[3] Germānī pugnam nōn aequē incipiunt, et Rōmānī cum 5 sociīs lātē fugiunt. Lūcius, clārus Aquītānus, ex equō virōs Rōmānōs et Aquītānōs in Germānōs incitāvit. Servus Lūciō clārē nūntiāvit: "Germānī frātrem [4] tuum Mārcum capiunt!" Lūcius frātrem amāvit. Perīculum Mārcī Lūcium magnā cūrā affēcit. Lūcius equum incitāvit, armīs Germānōs terruit, frātrem servāvit, fūgit. Sed equus nōn valuit: 10 Lūcius frātrem sōlum [5] in equō posuit et ad castra Aquītānōrum et Rōmānōrum equum incitāvit. Tum sōlus Germānōs exspectāvit. Multī Germānī accessērunt. Lūcius firmus cēdere incipit, auxilium exspectat—sed auxilium nōn venit—ē vītā excēdit. Mārcus vīdit et equum in Germānōs incitāvit et vītam āmīsit.[6] 15

Varia et dūra est fortūna bellī et variē virōs afficit, sed glōriam semper laudāmus.

---

[1] *too.* [2] *once.* [3] *were fighting.* [4] *brother.* [5] *alone.* [6] *lost.*

1. Who was Marcus' brother?
2. Who was killed?

169. Formation of Adverbs

In English, adverbs are usually formed from adjectives by adding the suffix *–ly:* adj., *clear;* adv., *clearly.*

In Latin, adverbs are usually formed from first and second declension adjectives by adding **–ē** to the base:

adj., **clārus**	**līber**
adv., **clārē**	**līberē**

Practice

Form adverbs from **pūblicus, grātus, commodus, aequus.** Give the Latin for *harshly, truly, firmly.*

170. Ablative of Accompaniment

As you already know, the means *with which* something is done is expressed by the ablative without a preposition **(61):** *They fought with arms,* **Armīs pugnāvērunt.** When, however, *with* means *together with* or *along with,* the preposition **cum** is used with the ablative. This expresses *accompaniment:* **Cum servō venit,** *He is coming with the slave.*

Caution. Do not use **cum** (*with*), unless the *with* means accompaniment or association. In the following English sentences decide when **cum** should be used and when it should be omitted:

1. Come *with me.*
2. Play *with us,* Jane.
3. John writes *with ink.*
4. Anna is *with the teacher.*
5. George fights *with inkwells.*
6. Play *with these toys,* Grace.

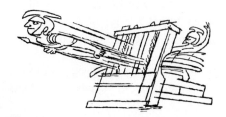

Virō pugnat.

(The man is used as a weapon.)

Cum virō pugnat.

Equi carros ducunt. Relief on a sarcophagus (stone coffin) in Rome.

171. Exercises

A. 1. Nautae, pūblicē līberāte captīvōs.

2. Nautae terram firmam clārē vidēre incipiunt.

3. Cum populō barbarō bellum perpetuum gerēmus.

4. Armīs templa dēfendent et cum sociīs pugnābunt.

5. Magister dūrus poenā puerōs malōs aequē afficit.

6. In amīcitiā firmā et perpetuā cum sociīs nostrīs manēbimus.

7. Servus cum magnā cōpiā pecūniae fūgit; nōn ōtium sed cūrās invēnit.

B. 1. We shall send the slave with food.

2. They will defend the island with arms.

3. It is not just to carry on war with friends.

4. A bad boy afflicts the family with constant care.

5. The settlers are beginning to flee with (their) families.

172. Vocabulary

affi′ciō, affi′cere, affē′cī, [affec′tus], *affect, afflict with*　　[*faciō*]

cum, prep. with abl., *with*

fir′mus, –a, –um, *strong, firm*　　(firmness, affirm)

ge′rō, ge′rere, ges′sī, [ges′tus], *carry on*　　(belligerent)

inci′piō, inci′pere, incē′pī, [incep′tus], *take to, begin*　　[*capiō*]

perpe′tuus, –a, –um, *constant*　　(perpetuity)

173. Latin and English Word Formation

The preposition **cum** is often used as a prefix in Latin and English but always in the assimilated forms **com–, con–, col–, cor–, co–**. In compounds it usually means *together* rather than *with*.

Define the following words, all formed from verbs which you have studied: *convoke, collaborate, commotion, convene*. What is a political *convention*?

Give five other English words formed by attaching this prefix to Latin verbs, nouns, or adjectives already studied.

133

Lesson XXIV

174. PLĀGŌSUS ORBILIUS

Multa [1] dē clārīs Rōmānīs ā magistrō tuō audiēs et ex librīs trahēs. Venīte, puerī et puellae! Nunc audiētis fābulam novam dē magistrō Orbiliō et dē discipulō eius [2] Quīntō.

Orbilius grammaticus [3] dūrus erat; saepe [4] discipulōs tardōs poenā
5 afficiēbat. Quīntus saepe tardus erat, quod in viīs Rōmānīs pater eius [2] multa [1] dē vītā mōnstrābat.

In scholā [5] Orbilius discipulīs nūntiāvit: "Librī vestrī multa adiec-tīva [6] continent, quae litterīs –ōsus fīniuntur.[7] Litterae –ōsus sunt signum plēnitūdinis.[8] Spectāte, mōnstrāre incipiam:

10 "Verbum—verb-ōsus. Liber multa verba continet. Liber plēnus est verbōrum. Liber verbōsus est. Spectāte:

"Glōria—glōri-ōsus. Patria magnam glōriam accipiet. Patria plēna glōriae erit. Patria glōriōsa erit. Spectāte:

"Iniūria—iniūri-ōsus. Bellum plēnum iniūriārum est. Bellum iniūriō-
15 sum est.

"Sed ubi est Quīntus Horātius? Tardusne est? Nōnne est semper tardus? Studiōsus nōn est—ōtiōsus est. Poenā Quīntum afficiam—multās plāgās [9] dōnābō."

Et poenā nōn grātā miserum [10] Quīntum affēcit. Sed nunc Orbilius
20 famōsus est. Cur? Quod tardus discipulus Quīntus erat Quīntus Horā-tius Flaccus, clārus poēta Rōmānus. Posteā [11] Horātius poēta magis-trum Orbilium "plāgōsum Orbilium" in librō appellāvit, quod Orbilius plēnus plāgārum fuerat.[12] Quod Horātius verbum novum "plāgōsum" invēnit, multī discipulī plāgōsum Orbilium memoriā tenuērunt et
25 semper tenēbunt.

QUESTIONS

1. What would be a good name for Orbilius today?
2. What English derivatives can you form by adding **–ōsus** to **victōria, cōpia, cūra?**

---

[1] *many things.* [2] *his.* [3] *schoolteacher.*
[4] *often.* [5] *school.* [6] *adjectives.*
[7] *which end with the letters –ōsus.* [8] *of fullness.* [9] *whacks* (with a stick or whip).
[10] *poor.* [11] *afterward.* [12] *had been.*

134

Bettmann Archive

Magister discipulum tardum terret. While two other boys begin to read from their rolls, the teacher rebukes a latecomer. From a sculptured relief now in Treves, Germany.

175. Future of Third (–iō) and Fourth Conjugation Verbs

Verbs of the fourth conjugation form the future by adding –ē– (–a– in the first person singular) and the personal endings directly to the present stem. Long –ī– of the stem is shortened, however, since it precedes another vowel (**512, 1**). The future of verbs of the third conjugation ending in –iō is the same as that of fourth conjugation verbs, because of the insertion of –ĭ– (**147**).

THIRD CONJUGATION (–iō)		FOURTH CONJUGATION	
(*I shall take*, etc.)		(*I shall fortify*, etc.)	
capiam	capiēmus	mūniam	mūniēmus
capiēs	capiētis	mūniēs	mūniētis
capiet	capient	mūniet	mūnient

Practice

1. Give the future tense of **incipiō** and **audiō.**
2. Give the Latin for *they will affect, we shall hear, you* (plur.) *will receive, they will draw, it will contain.*
3. Tell the form of **inveniētis, audīs, faciam, vidēbunt, parāvistī.**

135

Left: Stamp of Lebanon, on the eastern Mediterranean, showing an ancient Roman temple at Baalbek (see p. 206).
Above: Roman theater at Leptis Magna in Libya, North Africa, on an Italian stamp; Italy once ruled that region.

176. Exercises

A. 1. Equī carrōs agricolārum tardē trāxērunt.
2. Carrī magnam cōpiam frūmentī continent.
3. Equōs in locō lātō et commodō continēbimus.
4. Magister tardōs puerōs poenā pūblicē afficiet.
5. Nautae nostrī ex aquā virōs trahent et servābunt.
6. Colōnī ex agrīs frūmentum portābunt et magnam pecūniam accipient.

B. 1. Will you come to my house?
2. We shall save the people with food.
3. Anna, a friendly girl, will receive a book.
4. The late boys will not hear the words of the famous man.
5. The boys will not receive a reward, because they are late.

177. Vocabulary

au′diō, audī′re, audī′vī, [audī′tus], *hear* (audience)
conti′neō, continē′re, conti′nuī, [conten′tus], *hold (together),*
  contain **[teneō]**
li′ber, li′brī, m., *book* (library)
tar′dus, –a, –um, *slow, late* (retard)
tra′hō, tra′here, trā′xī, [trāc′tus], *draw, drag* (attraction)
ver′bum, –ī, n., *word* (verbal)

178. Latin and English Word Formation

Most prefixes are also used as prepositions, but a few are not. **Re–** is used only as a prefix in both Latin and English; it means *back* or *again*. It sometimes has the form **red–**, especially before vowels. Examples: **retineō,** *hold back;* **reficiō,** *make again;* **redigō,** *drive back.*

In English, **re–** is freely used with all sorts of words: *remake, revisit, rehash, refill.*

Give seven examples of the prefix **re–** in English words derived from Latin. Explain *revoke, incipient, refugee, audition.*

Aeneas patrem portat et filium parvum
ducit. Sculpture on a Roman tomb.

Lesson XXV

179. AENĒĀS

[The Trojan War was fought more than three thousand years ago at
Troy, in Asia Minor near the Dardanelles in what is now Turkey. The story
of the war is told by the Greek poet Homer in the *Iliad*. Virgil, the Roman
poet, tells part of the story in his *Aeneid* and goes on to tell of the Trojan
Aeneas, said to be the son of the goddess Venus. After the fall of Troy
Aeneas eventually reached Italy and, according to the story, he and his
companions were the ancestors of the Romans.]

Troiānī cum Graecīs multōs annōs bellum gessērunt. Graecī Troiam
occupāvērunt. Aenēās Troiānus arma cēpit et cum multīs virīs
oppidum dēfendere mātūrāvit. Sed Venus dea, māter Aenēae,[1] eum [2]
in mediō oppidō invēnit et verba fēcit:

"Audī sententiam meam. Tenē memoriā familiam tuam. Convocā 5
familiam et amīcōs firmōs et fuge. Novam patriam inveniēs. Cēde
fortūnae. Deī Troiānōs poenā dūrā afficient."

Cōnsilium Aenēās nōn grātē audīvit sed officium fēcit. Virōs redūxit
et amīcōs convocāvit. Amīcī convēnērunt et excēdere parāvērunt. Tum
Aenēās ex oppidō patrem [3] portāvit et fīlium parvum dūxit. Cum 10

---

[1] Genitive singular. [2] *him.* [3] Accusative singular of **pater.**

Mosaic showing the Roman poet Virgil holding a papyrus roll on which is written one of the opening lines of the "Aeneid": "Musa mihi causas memora. . . ." On either side are two of the nine Muses, goddesses associated with the arts. Why are the Muses shown in this mosaic?

Bettmann Archive

multīs servīs et sociīs fūgit. Singulī in locum commodum convēnērunt et ibi castra posuērunt. Māteriam ex silvā portāvērunt et nāvēs [4] parāvērunt. Tum nāvēs in aquam trāxērunt et undīs mandāvērunt et migrāvērunt. Ad multās īnsulās et terrās novās vēnērunt sed patriam
15 novam nōn invēnērunt. Vītam dūram ēgērunt. Īra Iūnōnis,[5] rēgīnae deōrum, hoc [6] effēcit.

In īnsulā Crētā castra posuērunt. Tum in mediō somnō Aenēās Penātēs [7] vīdit et sententiam audīvit:

"Crēta patria vestra nōn erit. Excēdite, Troiānī. Locus est quem [8]
20 Graecī Hesperiam, aliī Italiam vocant. Ibi terminum cūrārum perpetuārum inveniētis. Ibi in ōtiō et concordiā habitābitis et magnum oppidum pōnētis et mūniētis."

Ita Troiānī cōnsilium novum cēpērunt. Castra mōvērunt et ad Italiam nāvigāvērunt.

QUESTIONS

1. What did Venus tell Aeneas to do?
2. Whom does Aeneas take with him from Troy?
3. Why didn't Aeneas stay in Crete?

[4] Accusative plural of **nāvis.**   [5] *of Juno.*   [6] *this.*
[7] Accusative plural.   [8] *which* (accusative).

180. Idioms

Every language has expressions whose real meanings are lost when they are translated word for word into another language. The French for "How do you do?" literally means "How do you go?" which doesn't sound right to us. Come to think of it, "How do you do?" sounds peculiar to us too when we look at the separate words. It doesn't mean "In what way are you doing something?" And of course a Frenchman considers our expression just as strange as we consider his.

Such expressions are called *idioms.* Every language has hundreds of them. The following are some of the common ones in Latin. Memorize them and put them in your notebook under the heading "Idioms."

1. **grātiās agō,** *thank,* with dat. (literally, *act gratitude*)
2. **grātiam habeō,** *feel grateful,* with dat. (lit., *have gratitude*)
3. **vītam agō,** *live a life* (lit., *act life*)
4. **bellum gerō,** *wage* or *carry on war*
5. **castra pōnō,** *pitch camp* (lit., *place camp*)
6. **viam mūniō,** *build a road* (lit., *fortify a road;* roads were built like walls)
7. **verba faciō,** *speak, make a speech* (lit., *make words*)
8. **memoriā teneō,** *remember* (lit., *hold in memory*)
9. **cōnsilium capiō,** *adopt a plan* (lit., *take a plan*)

181. Exercises

A. 1. Puerōs ex mediā silvā in oppidum redūcam.
2. Virī ex multīs terrīs convenient et verba facient.
3. Rōmānī multās longās viās in Italiā mūnīvērunt.
4. Puerōs singulōs convocābimus et sententiās audiēmus.
5. Pōnite castra, puerī, in agrīs et ibi agite līberam vītam.
6. Magistrō nostrō grātiam habēmus et līberē grātiās agēmus.

B. 1. The boys will find water and pitch camp.
2. We ought to feel grateful to your friends.
3. The girls feel grateful and will thank the teacher.
4. We shall remember the teacher's words about duty.
5. You will not lead your comrades back to your fatherland.

Italian stamp for refugees, based on a painting by Raphael, who took the detail from the story of Aeneas and Anchises. Compare page 137.

182. Vocabulary

conve'niō, convenī're, convē'nī, [conventū'rus], *come together*
[*veniō*]

con'vocō, convocā're, convocā'vī, [convocā'tus], *call together*
[*vocō*]

me'dius, –a, –um, *middle, middle of* (mediator)

redū'cō, redū'cere, redū'xī, [reduc'tus], *lead back* [*dūcō*]

senten'tia, –ae, f., *feeling, opinion, motto* (sentence)

183. English Word Studies

Often a careful *inspection* of a familiar English word will reveal an *unexpected aspect* of meaning. A "sentence" in grammar is a single complete *opinion* or expression. A judicial "sentence" is a judge's *opinion*. A "convention" *comes together* in an "auditorium" to *hear* the speaker. A "mediator" settles disputes by taking a *middle* position. A spiritualistic "medium" is supposed to take a *middle* position between the unseen spirit and the "audience" who *hear*. A "studious" person is one who is *eager* to learn. An "alarm" is a call *to arms* (**ad arma**). To "repatriate" a person is to bring him *back* to his *fatherland*.

Mediator and belligerents.

What is a *convocation? Verbosity?* An *audition?*

In the United States there are towns named Aeneas, Virgil, Juno, Venus, and Crete.

Many firms dealing in women's clothes, cosmetics, etc., are called *Venus.* Why is this a popular name?

Lesson XXVI

184. POĒTA CLĀRUS

Quondam puer parvus Pūblius prope [1] Mantuam, oppidum Italiae, habitābat. Fīlius erat agricolae. In agrīs Pūblius nōn labōrābat, quod numquam valuit, sed agrōs, silvās, frūmentum, equōs amābat. In lūdō [2] multōs librōs legēbat, multās fābulās dē glōriā patriae et dē locīs clārīs Italiae audiēbat, verba sententiāsque magistrī memoriā 5 tenēbat.

Reliquī puerī in patriā mānsērunt, sed Pūblius, nunc vir, in urbe [3] Rōmā studia coluit.[4] In Forō Rōmānō verba numquam fēcit, quod timidus erat et populus eum [5] terrēbat. Bella armaque semper fugiēbat, concordiam ōtiumque amābat. Agrōs et casam familiae āmīsit,[6] sed 10 auxiliō amīcōrum recēpit. Magnam gratiam amīcīs semper habēbat. Amīcōs nōn multōs sed firmōs habēbat. Tum carmina [7] varia dē agrīs agricolīsque scrībere incēpit. Tardē scrībēbat multumque labōrābat, sed nōn multa carmina [7] effēcit. Posteā [8] magnum carmen [9] dē bellō Troiānōrum et dē glōriā Rōmae scrīpsit. 15

Audīvistisne dē Pūbliō, puerī puellaeque? Erat Pūblius Vergilius Marō,[10] poēta clārus Rōmānus, quī reliquōs poētās Rōmānōs superāvit. Lēgistis legētisque fābulam pulchram Vergilī dē Aenēā.

QUESTIONS

1. What did Virgil prefer to do as a boy?
2. Why did Virgil never become an orator?
3. What did Virgil write about?

185. Hints for Understanding Latin

As your eyes move across the page, following the order of words, separate the words into groups according to their sense and grammatical relation. Since this grammatical relation is shown by the

---

[1] *near.*   [2] *school.*   [3] *city.*   [4] *cultivated, carried on.*
[5] *him.*   [6] *lost.*   [7] *songs, poems* (accusative plural).
[8] *afterwards.* [9] Accusative singular. [10] Nominative singular.

word endings—not, as in English, by the word order—watch the endings carefully. Each word group, or phrase, should be read and understood as a unit. When you come to the end of the sentence translate in the English word order.

Here are the first four sentences of **Poëta Clārus** separated into groups of words according to their grammatical relation. Each division represents the words your eye should take in at each stop.

Quondam || puer parvus Pūblius || prope Mantuam, || oppidum Italiae, || habitābat. || Fīlius erat agricolae. || In agrīs || Pūblius || nōn labōrābat, || quod numquam valuit, || sed agrōs, silvās, frūmentum, equōs || amābat. || In lūdō || multōs librōs legēbat, || multās fābulās || dē glōriā patriae || et dē locīs clārīs Italiae || audiēbat, || verba sententiāsque magistrī || memoriā tenēbat.

186. Imperfect Tense

The Latin *imperfect* tense is called imperfect because it often represents incomplete acts. It is formed by adding the tense sign **–bā–** to the present stem and then attaching the personal endings, which you already know:

SINGULAR	PLURAL
portābam, *I was carrying, did carry, carried*	portābāmus, *we were carrying, etc.*
portābās, *you were carrying, etc.*	portābātis, *you were carrying, etc.*
portābat, *he, she, it was carrying, etc.*	portābant, *they were carrying, etc.*

Similarly **docēbam, pōnēbam, mūniēbam, capiēbam.** (For full conjugation see **567–570**.) For the imperfect of **sum** (**eram**, etc.) see **571**.

Vergilius carmina de agris agricolisque scripsit. A woodcut from an edition of Virgil printed in 1800.

Observe that the personal ending for the first person singular is **–m,** not **–ō** as in the present tense. For the short vowels see **25,** 4.

187. How the Perfect and Imperfect Differ

The imperfect tense always refers to action or being as *repeated, customary,* or *continuous,* like the English progressive past, and must be carefully distinguished from the perfect. In the following sentences the first group would be in the perfect in Latin, the second in the imperfect:

<table>
<tr><td align="center">PERFECT</td><td align="center">IMPERFECT</td></tr>
<tr><td>1. I saw John yesterday.</td><td>1. I saw John frequently.</td></tr>
<tr><td>2. I went to camp last year.</td><td>2. I used to go to camp every year.</td></tr>
<tr><td>3. Did you ever play football?</td><td>3. Did you play football long?</td></tr>
<tr><td>4. The alarm clock rang and I got up.</td><td>4. The alarm clock kept on ringing, but I did not get up.</td></tr>
</table>

Latin has two past tenses: perfect and imperfect; English has six ways of translating them: past, emphatic past, present perfect, progressive past, customary past, repeated past. Notice the difference in the following:

Vēnī, *I came* (past), or *I have come* (present perfect), or *I did come* (emphatic past).

The translation will depend on the context, but the first is much more common.

Veniēbam, *I was coming* (progressive past), or *I used to come* (customary past), or *I kept on coming* (repeated past).

Sometimes, however, the imperfect is best translated by the simple past; this is especially true of **sum.**

In Latin, the perfect is used much more often than the imperfect. In translating the English past into Latin, use the perfect unless there is a clear reason for using the imperfect.

Can you explain why each of the verbs in **184** is in the tense it is?

188. Exercises

A. 1. Multōsne librōs lēgistis?
2. Puellae puerīque litterās scrībēbant.
3. In casam veniēbam; ibi amīcum meum vīdī.
4. Mārcus amīcum vocābat sed amīcus nōn vēnit.
5. Multōs equōs in viīs vidēbāmus, sed nunc ubi sunt equī?
6. Multī virī in agrīs habitābant sed nunc ad oppida migrāvērunt.

B. 1. Have you never received letters?
2. We were leading the horses to water.
3. We kept-on-waiting but they did not come.
4. Marcus, did you read about the causes of the war?
5. Marcus came to dinner but the-rest-of the boys did not come.

189. Vocabulary

le′gō, le′gere, lē′gī, [lēc′tus], *gather, choose, read*   (legible)
num′quam, adv., *never*
poē′ta, –ae, m., *poet*   (poetry)
–que, conj., *and* (translated before the word to which it is joined)
re′liquus, –a, –um, *remaining, rest* (*of*)   (relic)
scrī′bō, scrī′bere, scrīp′sī, [scrī′ptus], *write*   (scribe)

190. English Word Studies

1. How did the *Mediterranean* Sea get its name?

The English word *deficit* preserves the third person singular present of Latin **dēficiō.**

2. Latin phrases in English:

magnum bonum, *great good.*
via media, *a middle way* or *course.*
amicus curiae, *friend of the court.*
consilio et armis, *by counsel and by arms.*

Deficit.

Ira Neptuni magna est. Neptune drives the winds away from the Trojan ships.
A sketch by the Flemish painter Rubens.

Lesson XXVII

191. AD ITALIAM

In magnīs undīs nāvēs [1] Troiānōrum volvuntur.[2] Sed Troiānī ex mediīs undīs servantur et ad Actium [3] properant; ibi inveniunt Helenum Troiānum, quī terram regēbat. Helenus Troiānōs convocat et verba pauca facit:

"Longa est via ad Italiam, ad quam [4] accēdere parātis. Accēdite 5 ad Siciliam et nāvigāte ab Siciliā ad Italiam fīnitimam. Dūrum est semper nāvigāre, sed Fāta viam invenient."

Sententia Helenī grātē accipitur, et Aenēās Helenō grātiās agit. Castra moventur nāvēsque [1] undīs committuntur. "Italiam, Italiam videō!" clāmat nauta et terram mōnstrat. In terrā equī clārē videntur. 10 "Signum proelī sunt equī," dīcit Anchīsēs; [5] "equīs bellum geritur. Proelium committere nōn dēbēmus." Nōn ibi manent sed ad Siciliam fīnitimam properant. Aetna eōs [6] terret et ab Siciliā fugiunt.

---

[1] Nominative plural.   [2] *are tossed.*   [3] *Actium (Ak'shium).*   [4] *which.*
[5] Father of Aeneas; pronounced *Ankī'sēs* in English.   [6] *them.*

Tum Iūnō, rēgīna deōrum, quae [7] Troiānōs nōn amāvit, ad Aeolum, 15 quī ventōs regit et continet, venit dīcitque:

"Sī ventī dūrī in nāvēs [8] Troiānōrum mittentur, magnam grātiam habēbō et magna praemia tibi [9] dōnābō."

Aeolus ventōs in nāvēs mittere mātūrat. Altīs undīs Troiānī terrentur. Arma virīque in undīs sunt. Tum Neptūnus, deus undārum, 20 ventōs audit et ad locum venit ubi nāvēs sunt. Īra Neptūnī magna est; ventī lātē fugiunt. Paucī Troiānī āmittuntur; reliquī ad terram fīnitimam veniunt et servantur. Sed in quā [10] terrā sunt? Nōn sciunt.[11] Sed castra pōnere nōn dubitāvērunt.

QUESTIONS

1. Where does Helenus tell the Trojans to go?
2. What does Juno ask Aeolus to do?
3. What does Neptune do?

192. Voice: Active and Passive

When the verb shows that the subject acts, i.e., is doing something, it is in the *active voice:*

Vir dūcet, *The man will lead.*

When the verb shows that the subject is acted upon, it is in the *passive voice:*

Vir dūcētur, *The man will be led.*

Observe that voice is shown in Latin by endings. The linking verb **sum** has no voice, for it merely indicates existence.

[7] *who.*   [8] Accusative plural.   [9] *to you.*   [10] *what.*   [11] *know.*

Three orders of classical architecture illustrated here, Doric, Ionic, and (center) Corinthian, are notably different in the capitals of their columns. The Doric is the simplest, the Corinthian the most ornate. The Ionic capital is distinguished by its rolled shape.

Models and photographs by Denoyer-Geppert Co.

Philip Gendreau

The Lincoln Memorial in Washington. The strength and simplicity of the Doric temple are especially appropriate for a building honoring a strong and simple man.

193. *Progressive and Passive Verb Forms in English*

Distinguish in English between active progressive forms and passive verb phrases, both of which use some form of the verb *to be.*

Active (progressive): *He is seeing* **(videt);** *They were calling* **(vocābant).**
Passive: *He is seen* **(vidētur);** *They were being called* **(vocābantur).**

In Latin it is not difficult to distinguish active and passive.

Active   *Passive*

He is kicking.   He is being kicked.

Practice

Tell which of these verbs are passive: *he called, we were cold, he was laughing, they were found, you are being beaten, he is fighting, they will be scolded, he will praise, you will be invited, it was being written, we were reading, she was sent.*

147

Courtesy Washington Convention and Visitors Bureau

The Capitol at Washington has a Roman dome and Corinthian columns.

194. Passive Voice of the Four Conjugations

In Latin the passive voice of all conjugations is formed by adding the passive personal endings to the present stem: [12]

ENDINGS		PRESENT	
–r	**–mur**	port**or**, *I am carried*	portā**mur**, *we are carried*
–ris	**–minī**	portā**ris**, *you are carried*	portā**minī**, *you are carried*
–tur	**–ntur**	portā**tur**, *he is carried*	porta**ntur**,[13] *they are carried*

Similarly **doceor, pōnor, mūnior, capior** (see **567–570**).

IMPERFECT	
portā**bar**, *I was being carried, was carried*	portā**bāmur**, *we were being carried, etc.*
portā**bāris**, *you were being carried, etc.*	portā**bāminī**, *you were being carried, etc.*
portā**bātur**, *he was being carried, etc.*	portā**bantur**, *they were being carried, etc.*

Similarly **docēbar, pōnēbar, mūniēbar, capiēbar** (see **567–570**).

---

[12] But in forms ending in **–ō** in the active (as **portō** and **portābō**), the passive ending **–r** is *added to,* not *substituted for,* the active ending. The **–ō–** becomes short (**512**, 2).　　[13] For the vowel shortened before **–ntur**, see **25**, 4.

Observe that **r** occurs in five of the six passive endings.

Practice

1. Conjugate **accipiō** in the present passive, **dēfendō** in the imperfect passive, **inveniō** in the future passive.
2. Translate: *we shall be called, he is being taught, it is not approved, they were being sent, it will be received, he will be heard, you* (sing.) *are moved, they are ruled, you* (plur.) *will be seen, we are awaited.*

---

[14] **Faciō** has no passive, though its compounds do.

The Virginia state capitol at Richmond, built in the eighteenth century, was modeled after a Roman temple in Nîmes, France. The columns are Ionic.

Virginia State Chamber

195. Exercises

A.
1. Amā fīnitimum tuum.
2. Litterae in ōtiō scrībuntur.
3. Reliquī nautae ad prōvinciam mittentur.
4. Rōmānī proelium cum barbarīs nunc committunt.
5. Paucī virī in fīnitimīs agrīs oppidīsque vidēbantur.
6. Multa praemia reliquīs puerīs puellīsque dōnābuntur.
7. Captīvī ad oppidum redūcentur et proelium committētur.

B.
1. Few books were being read in camp.
2. They will find food in the house.
3. Food will be found in the house.
4. The-rest-of the men will be sent to the island.
5. Are the-rest-of the boys working in the fields?

196. Vocabulary

commit′tō, commit′tere, commī′sī, [commis′sus], *join together, commit, entrust;* proe′lium commit′tō, *begin battle*   [*mittō*]

fīni′timus, –a, –um, *neighboring;* fīni′timus, –ī, m., *neighbor*

pau′cī, –ae, –a, *few*   (paucity)

proe′lium, proe′lī, n., *battle*

pro′perō, properā′re, properā′vī, [properātū′rus], *hasten*

197. Latin and English Word Formation

We have seen how Latin and English words are formed from others by the use of prefixes. There are other ways of forming new words. These we shall discuss later. For the present it is sufficient to recognize the roots that words have in common. Note the relationship and review the meanings of the following words which have occurred in earlier vocabularies:

1. **amīcus** and **amīcitia**
2. **nāvigō** and **nauta**
3. **nūntiō** and **nūntius**
4. **capiō** and **captīvus** (a "captive" is one who is *taken*)
5. **pugna** and **pugnō**
6. **puer** and **puella**
7. **habeō** and **habitō** (to "inhabit" a place is to keep on *having* it)

Try to associate new Latin words with those you have already studied, as well as with English derivatives which you find.

Towns named *Neptune* are in New Jersey and Tennessee; *Neptune Beach* is in Florida.

The four cities in the United States which have more firms named *Neptune* listed in their telephone directories than other cities are New York, Boston, Seattle, Los Angeles. Why is this name popular in these cities?

At the dinner Dido prepared, Aeneas told the story of the fall of Troy. Some of the people and events connected with the Trojan War are shown in this sixteenth-century enamel. Can you identify any?

The Metropolitan Museum of Art, Gift of Henry Walters, 1925

Lesson XXVIII

198. IN ĀFRICĀ AENĒĀS AUXILIUM ACCIPIT

Aenēās sociōs convocāvit et verba fēcit:

"In terrā nōn nōtā sumus. Sed deī praesidium nostrum sunt. Deīs vītam committite. Neque terra neque aqua nōs [1] terret. Inveniēmus viam aut faciēmus. Italia nostra erit. Ibi et terminus malōrum nostrōrum et ōtium perpetuum ā Troiānīs invenientur. Ibi patria erit et 5 nova Troia. Ē novā patriā numquam excēdēmus."

Tum Aenēās cum sociō ūnō ex castrīs excessit. Loca explōrāre mātūrāvit. Venus māter eum [2] vīdit et appellāvit. Nōmen oppidī, quod [3] appellātur Carthāgō et in Āfricā est, et nōmen rēgīnae, quae [4] est Dīdō, Aenēae [5] Venus nūntiat. Via ā deā Aenēae mōnstrātur; 10 Aenēās prōcessit et magnum oppidum vīdit. In mediō oppidō templum erat. Ad templum rēgīna Dīdō cum paucīs sociīs vēnit. Ibi erant reliquī Troiānī quōs [6] undae ab Aenēā [7] sēparāverant.[8]

[1] *us.*   [2] *him.*   [3] *which.*   [4] *who.*   [5] Dative.   [6] *whom.*
[7] Ablative.   [8] Use the English derivative in the past perfect tense (*had —*).

Memorial gate at the University of Pennsylvania in Philadelphia, with the Latin motto above: "Inveniemus viam aut faciemus."

Dīdō mala Troiānōrum audit et dīcit:

15   "Auxiliō meō aut in Italiam aut in Siciliam commodē veniētis, amīcī. Sed sī in nostrā patriā manēre grātum est, oppidum nostrum vestrum est, et praesidium habēbitis."

Tum magna cēna et cibī ēgregiī ā rēgīnā parantur. Aenēās nūntium ad fīlium, quī Iūlus [9] appellātur, mittit; nūntius dīcit:

20   "Properā ad oppidum, Iūle. Pater tē [10] exspectat."

Sed in locō Iūlī Venus deum Amōrem [11] mittit. Sed et Aenēās et reliquī Troiānī deum crēdunt esse Iūlum.[12] Tum Amor rēgīnam afficit, et Dīdō Aenēam amāre incipit.

QUESTIONS

1. How does Aeneas find out where he is?
2. Whom does he see at the temple?
3. What choice does Dido offer the Trojans?

---

[9] *Iulus* (*Īyū′lus*).   [10] *you.*   [11] *Love,* the Roman god Cupid.
[12] **deum . . . Iūlum:** *believe the god to be Iulus.*

199. Transitive and Intransitive Verbs

A transitive verb is one which tells what the subject does to the direct object:

Puer virum videt, *The boy sees the man.*

An intransitive verb is one which cannot have a direct object:

Puer excēdit, *The boy departs.*

In English, and generally in Latin, transitive verbs are the only verbs that are used in the passive voice. Some Latin verbs that are intransitive can be used transitively in English:

Anna labōrat, *Anna is working* (intransitive).
He works the brakes (transitive).

200. Ablative of Agent

Let us see what happens when the two sentences containing transitive verbs are turned around and the verb becomes passive:

Aqua ab Annā portātur, *The water is carried by Anna.*
Vir ā puerō vidētur, *The man is seen by the boy.*

Observe that in both English and Latin (*a*) the direct object of the active verb becomes the subject of the passive verb; (*b*) the subject of the active verb becomes the object of a preposition (**ā, ab,** *by*), indicating the *agent.*

Chicago's Museum of Science and Industry has a Roman dome and Ionic columns. Can you find another feature showing classical influence?

Chicago Museum of Science and Industry

Caution. Distinguish carefully between the ablative of agent and the ablative of means, both of which are often translated with *by*. Remember that *"means" refers to a thing*, while *"agent" refers to a person*.[13] Besides, the ablative of *means* is never used *with* a preposition, but the ablative of *agent* is never used *without* the preposition **ā (ab)**. This preposition means *by* only when used before nouns referring to persons and with passive verbs.

1. **Puella poenā terrētur**, *The girl is scared by punishment* **(means)**.
2. **Puella ā puerīs terrētur**, *The girl is scared by the boys* **(agent)**.

201. Practice

A. Tell which expresses means and which agent:
1. I was hit *by a stone*.
2. He was liked *by everybody*.
3. The game will be won *by our team*.
4. This book was bought *by me with my own money*.
5. John will be sent for *by messenger*, Mary *by letter*.
6. The note had been written *by hand* and not *with a typewriter*.

B. Change the following from active to passive, or from passive to active, and translate:
1. Vir librum videt.
2. Oppida ā populō reguntur.
3. Puerī verba tua exspectābant.
4. Reliqua pecūnia ab amīcō meō accipiētur.

C. Turn back to **176** and put into the passive **A.** 4, 5, 6.

202. Agreement

In both English and Latin, when two subjects are connected by *or* **(aut)**, *either . . . or* **(aut . . . aut)**, *neither . . . nor* **(neque . . . neque),** the verb agrees with the nearer subject: *Neither the boys nor the girl is in the forest*, **Neque puerī neque puella in silvā est.**

203. Exercises

A. 1. Aut puerī aut virī ad agrōs equōs redūcent.
2. Neque servus neque equus in viīs vidēbitur.
3. Equus puerum trahit; puer ab equō trahitur.
4. Mārcus amīcus [14] vērus ā multīs virīs appellābātur.

---

[13] Or occasionally an animal.

[14] Observe that the predicate nominative **(10)** may be used with verbs other than **sum.**

5. Neque praesidium neque auxilium ā sociīs nostrīs mittitur.
6. Multa praemia ā reliquīs puerīs puellīsque grātē accipientur.
7. Magister puerōs puellāsque docēbat; puerī puellaeque ā magistrō docēbantur.

B. 1. The letter was written by my friend.
2. The girls were scared by the bad boys.
3. The grain is being carried by wagon to the town.
4. The men see few houses; few houses are seen by the men.
5. Neither water nor grain is being carried by the-rest-of the settlers.

204. Vocabulary

appel′lō, appellā′re, appellā′vī, [appellā′tus], *call* (appellate)
aut, conj., *or;* aut . . . aut, *either . . . or*
et . . . et, conj., *both . . . and*
ne′que (or nec), conj. *and not, nor;* ne′que . . . ne′que, *neither . . . nor*
praesi′dium, praesi′dī, n., *guard, protection*

205. English Word Studies

1. What is meant by taking an *appeal* to a higher court? Why is such a court called an *appellate* court? What is meant by an *appellation? Carthage* is a town name in eleven states; *Cartago* is in California.

2. Latin phrases in English:

terra firma, *solid earth* (as opposed to water and air).
In Deo speramus, *In God we trust* (motto of Brown University).
pauci quos aequus amat Iuppiter, *the few whom fair-minded Jupiter loves.*
Explain **Elizabeth regina.**

Terra nōn firma.

Glimpses of Roman Life

206. DRESS

The most obvious difference between ancient and modern clothing was that civilized men did not in the old days wear trousers. These garments were worn only by barbarians. After the barbarians destroyed the Roman Empire, their dress became the fashion for all Europe. The same is true of the mustache (without beard). No Roman ever wore one, and it was just as much the mark of the barbarian as trousers were. Most Romans were smooth shaven, until the second century A.D., when beards and hair worn across the forehead came into fashion.

Over a sort of pair of trunks, Roman men wore as an outer garment a long shirt called a tunic, made of white wool. Senators and knights had crimson stripes down the front and back, the senators' stripes being broader than those of the knights. A belt was worn around this, and the upper part was bloused out over the belt. When a Roman was engaged in some active occupation, he pulled his tunic up to his knees. In the house, the tunic was usually clothing enough.

A Roman necklace of gold and amethyst beads in the Metropolitan Museum, New York. Even the catch looks modern.

Metropolitan Museum of Art, Rogers Fund, 1923

The fact that the ancient Roman matron in the modern-looking wicker chair has three hairdressers testifies to her wealth and position. The mirror shown was probably of highly polished bronze. The girl in the middle holds a jar of unguents. This relief is now in Treves, Germany.

Over the tunic the Roman citizen might wear a toga. This garment was the official dress of Roman citizens, and only citizens were allowed to wear it. It was made of white wool. The toga worn by boys and government officials had a crimson border. When boys grew up, they changed to the plain white toga. Important citizens always wore this garment when appearing in public, but the ordinary Roman wore it much less frequently.

The toga was really a sort of blanket which was thrown over the left shoulder, pulled across the back and under the right arm, and again thrown over the left shoulder. It was not fastened in any way, and it must have been quite a trick to learn to wear it.

Roman women also wore a tunic. Over this the married women wore a **stola,** a long dress with a protecting band sewn around the bottom. For street wear a shawl, called a **palla,** was added.

Wool was the chief material for clothing; next came linen. Silk was rare and expensive, cotton almost unknown.

In the house men and women wore sandals or slippers; outdoors they wore shoes. The shoes of officials were red. No stockings were worn, though in cold weather old and sickly people sometimes wound cloth around their legs.

Hats were rarely worn, except on journeys. Such as there were had broad brims and were flat. Women often wore ribbons and elaborate pins in their hair. Styles in hairdressing changed constantly as with us, but women did not cut their hair short.

The head is that of Julia, daughter of the Emperor Titus.

MUSEUM THOUGHTS
Portrait of a Lady (c. 75 A.D.)

Julia to the barber went
And got herself a permanent.
Since the perm was unsurpassed,
"Fine!" she said. "But will it *last?*"

(I approximate the sense
Of *"Estne vere permanens?"*)
Then the vehement coiffeur,
Warmly reassuring her,
Guaranteed with confidence
The permanence of permanents.

Rome is gone and all her pride,
Still the dainty curls abide;
Venus, Mars, and Jove are dead,
Still remains the lovely head.

Let a thousand years go by,
Let our gods and empires die,
Time will never set a term
To the life of Julia's perm.
Mundo semper erit gratus
Iste capitis ornatus.

—Morris Bishop [1]

QUESTIONS

1. What was the distinctive garment of Roman men? Of women?
2. When did the Romans begin to wear mustaches and trousers?

[1] Permission of the author. Copyright 1953 The New Yorker Magazine, Inc.

UNIT V REVIEW

The Story of Lucius

207. FORUM RŌMĀNUM

Quondam puer parvus Lūcius in Italiā habitābat. Dē glōriā patriae multa [1] audiēbat. Magister Lūciō reliquīsque puerīs loca clāra Rōmae mōnstrābat. In medium Forum Rōmānum cum puerīs properābat. In hunc [2] locum populus Rōmānus conveniēbat. Ibi virī amīcōs vidēbant et aedificia [3] pūblica templaque spectābant. Ibi nūntiī populum convocābant et magnās victōriās nūntiābant. Ibi virī clārī in rōstrīs [4] verba pūblicē faciēbant et sententiās dēfendēbant.

Magister multa dē patriā in Forō docēbat. Puerī magistrō magnam grātiam habuērunt, quod Forum amāvērunt. Ē Forō Lūcius reliquīque puerī cum magistrō in Sacram Viam properābant et tabernās [5] spectābant. Plūra [6] dē Lūciō audiētis.

QUESTIONS

1. Where did the Romans meet their friends?
2. Why were the boys grateful to their teacher?

---

[1] *many things.* [2] *this.* [3] *buildings.* [4] *the rostra* (speakers' platform).
[5] *shops.* [6] *more.*

The Roman Forum at night, seen from the House of the Vestals. The Vestal Virgins were responsible for keeping the sacred fire of Rome burning at all times.

Albert Moldvay

GRAMMAR SUMMARIES

208. Ablative Uses

	In Latin	In English
MEANS	1. Ablative without preposition.	1. Objective with preposition *with* or *by*.
ACCOMPANI-MENT	2. Ablative with **cum.**	2. Objective with preposition *with*.
AGENT	3. Ablative with **ab.**	3. Objective with *by*.

209. Past Tenses

In Latin	In English
1. Perfect (**vēnī**).	1. *a.* Past (*I came*).
	b. Present Perfect (*I have come*).
2. Imperfect (**veniēbam**).	2. *a.* Progressive past (*I was coming*).
	b. Customary past (*I used to come*).
	c. Repeated past (*I kept on coming*).

The **Plymouth Rock Monument,** commemorating the **300th** anniversary of the landing of the Pilgrims at Plymouth, Massachusetts, in **1620,** is in classical style.

Compliments, Town of Plymouth and Plymouth Area Chamber of Commerce

The Forum as it was: Temples of Vesta and Castor, Basilica Julia; above, on the Capitoline Hill, Temple of Jupiter; at the end of the open Forum are the Rostra, other temples, and Tabularium behind; Arch of Severus at right.

210. VOCABULARY

NOUNS			
1. deus	3. ōtium	6. proelium	9. verbum
2. liber	4. poēta	7. sententia	
	5. praesidium	8. studium	

ADJECTIVES			
10. commodus	12. firmus	15. perpetuus	18. varius
11. fīnitimus	13. medius	16. reliquus	
	14. paucī	17. tardus	

VERBS			
19. afficiō	23. contineō	28. incipiō	33. trahō
20. appellō	24. conveniō	29. legō	34. valeō
21. audiō	25. convocō	30. properō	
22. committō	26. fugiō	31. redūcō	
	27. gerō	32. scrībō	

ADVERB	
	35. numquam

PREPOSITION	
	36. cum

CONJUNCTIONS			
37. aut	39. et . . . et	41. neque . . .	42. -que
38. aut . . . aut	40. neque	neque	

161

211. VOCABULARY (English Meanings)

NOUNS
1. god
2. book
3. leisure
4. poet
5. guard
6. battle
7. opinion
8. eagerness
9. word

ADJECTIVES
10. convenient
11. neighboring
12. strong
13. middle (of)
14. few
15. constant
16. remaining
17. slow
18. changing

VERBS
19. affect
20. call
21. hear
22. join together, entrust
23. contain
24. come together
25. call together
26. flee
27. carry on
28. begin
29. gather, read
30. hasten
31. lead back
32. write
33. draw
34. be strong

ADVERB
35. never

PREPOSITION
36. with

CONJUNCTIONS
37. or
38. either . . . or
39. both . . . and
40. nor
41. neither . . . nor
42. and

UNIT PRACTICE AND EXERCISES

212. Form Drill

1. Form and translate adverbs from **lātus, līber,** and **perpetuus.**
2. Conjugate **trahō, incipiō,** and **audiō** in the future, active and passive.
3. Translate: **gerit, geret, incipient, incipiunt, līberābō, fugiam, audīris, audiēris, afficiuntur, mittentur, convēnimus, continēbitur, convocābuntur, invenientur.**
4. Give in Latin: *they will hear, they will be heard, I shall see, I shall be seen, he will begin, she will be heard, we shall be called together, it will draw, they will be led back, he was being taught, you* (sing.) *will write, you* (plur.) *will be affected.*
5. Give the Latin for the following in the singular and plural in the case required: *great interest* (nom.), *a good price* (gen.), *varying opinion* (dat.), *a small guard* (acc.), *a neighboring place* (abl.).

Italian stamp for the Olympic Games, showing an ancient bronze statue of a resting boxer.

The Lee Mansion in Arlington, Virginia, has Doric columns. This style of American architecture is called Greek Revival, and is a blend of Greek, Roman, and American elements.

213. Sentence Drill

A. Complete and translate:
1. (*We are called*) amīcī bonī.
2. Rēgīna (*by many*) vidēbitur.
3. Patria ā puerīs (*will be saved*).
4. Verba magistrī ā paucīs (*are heard*).
5. Puer ex aquā ā virō (*will be dragged*).
6. Multa bella ā Rōmānīs (*were carried on*).

B. Translate:
1. Few find leisure.
2. The men will receive aid.
3. The boy scares the horses.
4. Many will read my words.
5. The teacher will praise the girls.

C. Change the above into the passive (the subject becomes the agent; the direct object becomes the subject) and translate.

214. ENGLISH WORD STUDIES

1. Define according to derivation: *relic, digest, Mr., doctor, libel, audio-visual, mediation, retardation.* Look up in the dictionary if necessary.

2. Give prefix and Latin root word from which the following are derived: **redigō, concipiō, attrahō, committō;** *respect, component, incorrigible, exhibit.*

UNIT VI

STORIES OF ROME

The poet Virgil (70–19 B.C.) is known as one of the world's greatest writers. His masterpiece was the *Aeneid*, an epic poem which tells of the wanderings of the Trojan Aeneas and his attempts to find a new home after the capture of Troy by the Greeks in the twelfth century B.C. It also describes Aeneas' arrival in Italy where his descendants were said to have founded Rome. In this painting by Guérin, we see Aeneas and Queen Dido in the palace in Carthage.

Scala/Art Resource

Above: Stamp issued by Italy in honor of Virgil, with a quotation from his most famous poem, the "Aeneid." *Left:* Another Italian stamp honoring Virgil. Aeneas is greeting the land promised him by the Fates, the land which is to be his home and his country.

Lesson XXIX

215. AENĒĀS ET DĪDŌ

Ad Annam sorōrem [1] Dīdō properāvit: "Anna soror," dīxit, "animus meus miser perīculīs terrētur; Aenēam amō. Quid [2] agam?"

Anna respondit: "Aenēās est bonus et amīcus vir. Prō Troiā pugnāvit sed patriam āmīsit; nunc prō nostrā patriā multōs annōs
5 pugnābit. Fīnitimī nōn sunt amīcī. Terminī nostrī ab Aenēā proeliīs dēfendentur."

Aenēās in Āfricā cum rēgīnā pulchrā mānsit. Dīdō Troiānum per medium oppidum dūxit et eī [3] oppidum mōnstrāvit.

Tum Iuppiter Mercurium nūntium ad Aenēam mīsit. "Annum in
10 hōc [4] locō ēgistī," Mercurius dīxit. "Verba deī memoriā nōn tenēs; properā in Italiam cum sociīs tuīs, ubi fīlius tuus reget. Ibi ōtium habēbis."

Aenēās sociōs convocāvit. Sociī frūmentum in nāvēs [5] portāvērunt. Dīdō Aenēam appellāvit:

15 "Cūr fugis? Dūrus es; iniūriam facis. Magnum est perīculum nostrum. Ā populīs fīnitimīs agrī nostrī occupābuntur, oppidum āmittētur. Praesidium nostrum esse dēbēs. In concordiā perpetuā habitābimus."

Aenēās respondit: "Deum Mercurium vīdī. Officium meum est ad
20 Italiam nāvigāre. Dūrum est, sed deus imperat."

---

[1] Accusative: *sister.*   [2] *what.*   [3] *to him.*   [4] *this.*   [5] Accusative plural.

Aenēās tardē excessit et ad nāvēs vēnit. Sociī convēnērunt et nāvēs in aquam trāxērunt. Tum nāvēs undīs ventīsque commīsērunt. Dīdō misera nāvēs vīdit et sē [6] interfēcit.[7]

Troiānī ad Italiam migrāvērunt et patriam novam invēnērunt. Dīdō vītam āmīsit, Aenēās patriam invēnit. Ita in librīs poētārum 25 scrībitur.

QUESTIONS

1. What does Mercury tell Aeneas to do?
2. What argument did Dido use to persuade Aeneas to stay in Carthage?

216. Words Used as Nouns

A *pronoun* is a word used instead of a noun, as *he* or *she*, which takes the place of the name of some person, or as *that*, which takes the place of the name of a thing.

We have seen that the infinitive form of the verb may be used as a noun, as subject or object **(129–130)**.

An adjective also may be used as a noun. In Latin the masculine and feminine adjectives refer to persons, the neuter to things. The

---

[6] *herself.*   [7] *killed.*

Mercury in modern style at Rockefeller Center, New York. He still has his familiar symbols: winged hat and winged staff with snakes (called caduceus).

Mercury, the messenger, is a familiar figure on postage stamps. Here he is on stamps of Greece, France, Australia, Tripolitania, South Africa, and Italy. Caduceus, winged hat, and winged feet are favorite symbols.

usage, although common in English, is limited to adjectives of certain meanings. Like English are:

1. **Bonī laudantur,** *The good* (i.e., *good men*) *are praised.*
2. **Multum facit,** *He does much.*

But Latin can use almost any adjective as a noun:

3. **Nostrī veniunt,** *Our* (*men*) *are coming.*
4. **Multa facit,** *He does many* (*things*).
5. **Fīnitimī nōn sunt amīcī,** *The neighboring* (*men, peoples*) *are not friendly* (*men, peoples*), or *The neighbors are not friends.*

217. Conversation

(See map of the Roman world on pp. 92–93.)

M = Magister   D = Discipulī

M: Spectāte, puerī et puellae. D: Spectāmus, magister.

M: Ubi oppida vidētis? D: In Āfricā et in Asiā et in Eurōpā multa oppida vidēmus.

M: In mediā terrā aquam vidētis. Illam [8] aquam "Medi-terrāneum
5 Mare" [9] appellāmus.

M: Ibi est Lūsitānia—vidētisne? D: Vidēmus.

M: Ubi est Hibernia? D: Hibernia est īnsula in Ōceanō Atlanticō.

M: Multī virī multōrum populōrum in Eurōpā habitant.

M: Ubi pugnābat Caesar? D: Caesar in Galliā pugnābat.

[8] *that.*   [9] *Sea.*

168

QUESTIONS

Answer in Latin.

1. Ubi habitāmus?
2. Ubi agricolae multum frūmentum parant?
3. Ubi loca nōn plāna vidētis?
4. Ubi est Londīnium? Rōma? Lutetia? Corduba?

218. Exercises

A. 1. Magna in proeliō fēcit.
2. Nōnne bonum facere dēbēmus?
3. Puer miser in viā librum āmīsit.
4. Vīta ā multīs in bellō āmittētur.
5. Nostrī prō patriā et familiīs patriae pugnābant.
6. Multōs annōs in perīculō ēgimus; nunc ōtium habēmus.

B. 1. Were the girls being scared by the horses?
2. The people will be called together by the queen.
3. I have entrusted the care of the money to the teacher.
4. The boys saw the danger clearly and fled to the woods.
5. By harsh discipline the master ruled the unhappy slaves.

A fine display of carving knives in a cutlery shop. This relief, now in the Vatican Museum, came from the tomb of the shop's owner, Lucius Cornelius Atimetus.

The Vatican

219. Vocabulary

āmit′tō, āmit′tere, āmī′sī, [āmis′sus], *let go, lose*   **[mittō]**
mi′ser, mi′sera, mi′serum, *unhappy, poor*   (misery)
perī′culum, –ī, n., *danger*   (perilous)
prō, prep. with abl., *in front of, before, for*

220. English Word Studies

1. As a prefix **prō–** has its prepositional meanings, with the additional one of *forward*. Define the following derivatives of words which you have already studied: *provoke, prospect, produce, proceed.*

What is an *annuity?* Tell which of the following are derived from **līber, lībrī,** and which from **līber, –a, –um:** *liberty, librarian, liberal, liberate.*

2. Latin phrases in English:

pro patria, *for (one's) country.*
pro forma, *for (as a matter of) form.*
pro bono publico, *for the public good.*

The old capitol at Frankfort, Kentucky, is classical in design. Its columns are Ionic.

The Sibyl, Aeneas, and Charon in a painting by the Dutch artist Van Dyck (1599–1641).

Kunsthistorisches Museum, Vienna

Lesson XXX

221. AENĒĀS AD ĪNFERŌS [1]

Aenēās fīlius Anchīsae [2] fuit, quī in Siciliā ē vītā excesserat. Tum Anchīsēs in somnō ad fīlium vēnerat et fīlium vocāverat: "Venī, fīlī, ad īnferōs, ubi sum. Sibylla [3] viam nōvit et tē [4] dūcet."

Ita Aenēās in Italiam prōcessit, ubi Sibylla habitābat. Cōnsilium Sibyllae erat: "Sī in silvā rāmum [5] aureum inveniēs, ad īnferōs tē 5 prōdūcam et sine perīculō redūcam, sed sine rāmō numquam tē prōdūcam." Ita Aenēās in silvam properāvit. Auxiliō Veneris [6] rāmum invēnit et cum Sibyllā ad īnferōs dēscendit. Ibi multa nova vīdit et nōvit.

Tum ad magnam silvam vēnērunt. Ibi erat Dīdō. Aenēās rēgīnam 10 vīdit et appellāvit: "Vērumne nūntius nūntiāvit? Vītamne āmīsistī? Causane fuī? Invītus [7] ex patriā tuā excessī, sed ita deus imperāvit." Sed rēgīna, nunc inimīca, verbīs lacrimīsque Aenēae nōn movētur. Neque Aenēam spectāvit neque respondit sed in silvam fūgit.

Aenēās tardē ex silvā excessit et locum vīdit ubi malī poenā affi- 15 ciēbantur. Tum Aenēās Sibyllaque in Ēlysium [8] prōcessērunt. Ibi animae [9] bonōrum in concordiā vītam agēbant. Iniūriae et pugnae

[1] *The Lower World* (cf. **163**, n. 4).
[2] *Anchises (Ankī'sēs;* gen.*).*
[3] *the Sibyl* (a prophetess).
[4] *you* (acc.).
[5] *branch.*
[6] Genitive of **Venus.**
[7] *unwillingly.*
[8] *Elȳ'sium,* Greek and Roman heaven.
[9] *souls.*

Mexico City's Memorial to Benito Juárez, the Abraham Lincoln of Mexico. What is the style of the columns?

aberant. Ibi Anchīsēs erat. Grātus fīlium accēpit et nūntiāvit: "Clārōs Rōmānōs quī posteā in terrā erunt et glōriam populī tuī mōnstrābō.
20 Rōmānī malōs superābunt et populōs aequē regent." Aenēās ab Anchīse nōn retinētur et ā Sibyllā in terram redūcitur. Tum loca commoda in Italiā occupāre mātūrāvit.

QUESTIONS

1. What did Aeneas need to go safely into the Lower World?
2. Whom did he see there?

222. Past Perfect Active

The *past perfect* tense (sometimes called pluperfect) refers to an action that was completed before a certain time in the past: *He had gone* (before something else happened).

In Latin, the past perfect is formed by adding the tense sign **–erā–** to the perfect stem, together with the personal endings of the imperfect. The tense signs and personal endings together are the same as the various forms of the imperfect tense of **sum: portāveram, docueram, fueram,** etc. (For full conjugation see **566–571.**)

172

Note. The *future perfect* tense refers to an action completed before a certain time in the future: *He will have gone* (before something else will happen). In Latin, it is formed by adding the tense sign **–eri–** to the perfect stem, together with the personal endings of the present: **portāverō, docuerō, fuerō,** etc. (cf. **566–571**).

The past perfect and the future perfect are found much less frequently than the perfect.

Practice

1. Conjugate in the perfect: **videō, legō, efficiō;** in the past perfect: **moveō, incipiō;** in the imperfect: **retineō, prōcēdō.**
2. Tell the form of **āfuimus, prōdūxerat, retinuistī, nōvērunt, prōcesserimus, āmīserātis, docēbās.**

223. Exercises

A.
1. Parvī puerī linguam retinēre dēbent.
2. Multī puerī aberant. Nōnne valēbant?
3. Carrī ex silvā vēnerant et ad oppidum tardē prōcēdēbant.
4. Agricolārum fīliī et fīliae multa dē agrīs et equīs nōvērunt.
5. Magister puerōs nōn retinuit, quod fōrmās verbōrum nōn nōverant.
6. Paucī labōrābant sed reliquī puerī in castrīs semper manēbant.
7. Magistrī fīlius multa dē librīs nōvit, sed agrī fīlium agricolae docent.

B.
1. We know much about many lands and peoples.
2. We shall read about strange towns and peoples.
3. Marius has fought in Gaul for (his) native land.
4. We are the sons of free (men) and love our native land.
5. The slave deserved a large reward, because he had saved the life of our son.

224. Vocabulary

ab′sum, abes′se, ā′fuī, [āfutū′rus], *be away, be absent*   [*sum*]

inimī′cus, –a, –um, *unfriendly;* as noun, *enemy*   [*amīcus*]

nōs′cō, nōs′cere, nō′vī, [nō′tus], *learn;* in perf. tense, "have learned" = *know*

prōcē′dō, prōcē′dere, prōces′sī, [prōcessū′rus], *go forward, advance*   [*cēdō*]

prōdū′cō, prōdū′cere, prōdū′xī, [prōduc′tus], *lead out*   [*dūcō*]

reti′neō, retinē′re, reti′nuī, [reten′tus], *hold* (*back*)*, keep*   [*teneō*]

si′ne, prep. with abl., *without*   (sinecure)

225. Latin and English Word Formation

We have seen that the preposition **in** is used as a prefix **(115).** There is another prefix **in–,** used chiefly with adjectives and nouns, which has an entirely different meaning and must be carefully distinguished from the former. It is a *negative* prefix, as in *injustice.* It is assimilated like the other prefix **in–,** as in *il-legal, im-moral, ir-regular.* Define the following derivatives of words which you have already studied:

immemorial, immaterial, inglorious, ingratitude, illiberal, illiteracy, infirm

Tell which of the two prefixes (preposition or negative) is used in each of the following:

inhabit, invalid, invoke, induce, invariable, inequality, inundate, immovable, impecunious

The prefix **dis–** in English and Latin means *apart,* but sometimes it is purely negative like **in–.** It is either assimilated or left unchanged, as follows:

dis-inter, dis-locate, dis-arm, dif-fuse, di-vert, di-stant, dis-similar

Define the first three of these words, derived from words in previous vocabularies.

The Town Hall (left) in Dunedin, New Zealand, is in the familiar Roman style. England, once a Roman colony herself, passed on Roman ways to her former colonies.

James Sawders

Beatrice Hohenegger

Stone masks were probably used as props in performing plays. (See p. 95)

Lesson XXXI

226. IN ITALIĀ AENĒĀS AUXILIUM ACCIPIT

Olim in Latiō erat oppidum appellātum Pallanteum. Rex[1] oppidī, Ēvander, cum multīs colōnīs ab Arcadiā mīgrāverat. In Italiā oppidum mūnīverant in locō ubi posteā[2] Rōmulus Rōmam mūnīvit. Cum fīnitimīs, populīs Latīnīs, bellum semper gerēbant.

Aenēās et colōnī Troiānī etiam[3] in Italiā habitābant et etiam cum 5
Latīnīs pugnābant. Quod sociōs cupiēbant, Aenēās et paucī virī ad Pallanteum accessērunt. Extrā[4] oppidum Troiānī fīlium Ēvandrī et paucōs Arcadiānōs invēnērunt.

PALLAS: Pallas sum, fīlius Ēvandrī. Ego et amīcī meī vōs salūtāmus.[5]
Quī[6] estis? Cur[7] tu et virī tuī ad Pallanteum vēnistis? 10

AENĒĀS: Appellor Aenēās. Ego et virī meī ad Italiam ā deīs ductī sumus. Nunc auxilium vestrum cupimus. Accipite nōs, quaesō,[8] et fābulam[9] nostram audīte.

PALLAS: Vōs nōn dīmittam. Multa dē vōbīs audīvī. Ad oppidum nōbīscum prōcēdite. 15

(Rex Ēvander grātē Aenēās accipit.)

ĒVANDER: Ubi[10] puer eram in Arcadiā, Aenēās, pater tuus ad patriam meam vēnit. Is mihi multa grāta dōnāvit. Virum grātē memoriā teneō. Tu etiam vidēris[11] vir bonus et pius.[12] Tē probō et tibi auxilium dōnābō.

AENĒĀS: Grātiās tibi agō, Ēvander. Firmī sociī erimus. 20

ĒVANDER: Quod ego nōn iam[13] iuvenis[14] sum, pūgnāre vōbiscum dubitō. Tibi, Aenēās, fīlium meum mandābō. Is integer est et prō mē

---

[1] *king* [2] *afterwards* [3] *also* [4] *outside* [5] *greet* [6] *who*
[7] *why* [8] *please* [9] *story* [10] *when* [11] *seem to be* [12] *loyal*
[13] *not now = no longer* [14] *young* [15] *bravely* [16] *alive* [17] *again*

pugnābit. Pallas, mī filī, tē cum Troiānīs nunc dīmittam. Tēcum prōdūce multōs virōs.

25   PALLAS: Valē, pater! Nōs fortiter[15] bellum gerēmus.

Et fortiter pugnāvit Pallas. Sed miser Ēvander numquam fīlium vīvum[16] iterum[17] vīdit.

QUESTIONS

1. What is particularly interesting about the site of Pallanteum?
2. What common enemy did the Trojans and the Arcadians have?
3. Why didn't Evander himself lead his men into battle alongside Aeneas?

227. How Personal Pronouns Are Used

In English, personal pronouns are used to show the person of the verb: *I am, you are.* In Latin, as we have seen **(22, 3)**, personal endings are used instead. When, however, emphasis or sharp contrast in subjects is desired, the Latin uses the personal pronouns **ego** (*I*) and **tū** (*you*). **Is** and **ea** serve as the personal pronouns of the third person (*he* and *she*). The full declension of these will be given later. Memorize the declensions of **ego** and **tū**:

	SINGULAR	PLURAL
Nom.	**ego,** *I*	**nōs,** *we*
Gen.	**meī,** *of me*	**nostrum,** *of us*
Dat.	**mihi,** *to* (*for*) *me*	**nōbīs,** *to* (*for*) *us*
Acc.	**mē,** *me*	**nōs,** *us*
Abl.	**mē,** *with* (*from,* etc.) *me*	**nōbīs,** *with* (*from,* etc.) *us*

	SINGULAR	PLURAL
Nom.	**tū,** *you*	**vōs,** *you*
Gen.	**tuī,** *of you*	**vestrum,** *of you*
Dat.	**tibi,** *to* (*for*) *you*	**vōbīs,** *to* (*for*) *you*
Acc.	**tē,** *you*	**vōs,** *you*
Abl.	**tē,** *with* (*from,* etc.) *you*	**vōbīs,** *with* (*from,* etc.) *you*

228. Possessive Adjectives

The possessive adjectives, **meus, noster, tuus,** and **vester,** are derived from the bases of their corresponding personal pronouns: **ego (me–), nōs (nostr–), tū (tu–),** and **vōs (vestr–).**

The possessive adjective follows its noun except when emphatic.

Italian stamp in honor of the 2000th anniversary in 1930 of Virgil's birth. It carries a quotation from Virgil saying how fortunate farmers are, if they would only realize their advantages.

Caution. To show possession, use the possessive adjectives **meus, tuus, noster,** and **vester,** *not* the genitives **meī, tuī, nostrum,** and **vestrum: amīcus meus,** *my friend,* not **amīcus meī.** Remember that an adjective agrees in gender, number, and case *with the noun it modifies.* A woman referring to a woman friend might comment **Est amīca mea;** a woman referring to her husband would say **Est vir meus.** In other words, the ending of the possessive adjective does not depend upon the possessor, but upon the thing possessed.

QUESTION

What is the difference between **tuus** and **vester?**

229. Personal Pronoun Test

Translate the italicized English words into the proper Latin forms.

1. I shall give *you* a present.
2. *I* criticize *you; you* criticize *me.*
3. She showed *us* beautiful flowers.
4. *She* is *my* friend; *he, my* enemy.
5. I shall show *you* (*sing.*) the house.
6. We'll treat *you* (*plur.*) if you'll treat *us.*
7. He came *to us* and showed *us* many pictures.
8. Come *with us* and we shall go *with you* (*plur.*).
9. *He* was mentioned *by me,* but *she* told *me* nothing.
10. *Your* daughter was seen *by us* with *you* (*sing.*) on the street.

230. Exercises

A. 1. Multa ā tē, amīce, accēpī.
2. Liber tuus ā mē nōn retinēbitur.
3. Cupitisne vidēre nōs, amīcōs vestrōs?
4. Ego sum amīcus tuus; is est inimīcus.
5. Ego sum miser sine tē; tū misera es quod tēcum nōn maneō.
6. Fīlius meus in perīculum mēcum properāre numquam dubitāverat.

B. 1. We are foreigners; you are Romans.
2. My words are not being heard by you.
3. I desire to present the reward to you (*sing.*).
4. They had not hesitated to free the prisoners.
5. Come (*plur.*) with us; we are your friends, not your enemies.

cu′piō, cu′pere, cupī′vī, [cupī′tus], *desire* (cupidity)

dīmit′tō, dīmit′tere, dīmī′sī, [dīmis′sus], *let go, send away* [*mittō*]

du′bitō, dubitā′re, dubitā′vī, [dubitā′tus], *hesitate, doubt*

(indubitable)

e′go, me′ī, *I* (egoist)

in′teger, –gra, –grum, *untouched, fresh* (integer, integrity)

is, *he, it;* [6] ea, *she, it*

tū, tu′ī, *you*

I...I...I....
..now let's talk about
me for awhile..

Egoist.

232. Latin and English Word Formation

We have seen that prefixes are so called because they are attached to the beginnings of words **(104)**. *Suffixes* are attached to the ends of words (**sub,** *under, after;* **fīxus,** *attached*). Like the Latin prefixes, the Latin suffixes play a very important part in the formation of English words.

The Latin suffix **–ia** usually has the form *–y* in English. Give the English forms of the following words found in the preceding vocabularies: **memoria, glōria, familia, iniūria, victōria, cōpia** (with change of meaning in English).

What must be the Latin words from which are derived *elegy, history, industry, infamy, Italy, luxury, misery, perfidy, philosophy, Troy?*

Some **–ia** nouns drop the **–ia** entirely in English: *concord, vigil, matter* (from **māteria**).

You will find it useful to list suffixes in your notebook, together with many examples of their use in English words.

---

[6] The word *it* is used to translate **is** and **ea** when the noun referred to is masculine or feminine in Latin but its English equivalent is neuter **(31).**

Left: Robert Aitken's modern statue of Jupiter, with thunderbolt, scepter, and eagle. *Right:* An ancient statue of Neptune with aplustre (an ornament for the stern of a ship), trident, and dolphin. Jupiter sits in great majesty; Neptune, resting his foot on the prow of a ship, seems to scan the sea wearily.

Lesson XXXII

233. Q. FABIUS MAXIMUS

Bellō [1] Pūnicō secundō Hannibal virōs cum Rōmānīs pugnāre iubēbat sed Q.[2] Fabius Maximus semper discēdēbat neque in ūnō locō manēbat. Sine victōriīs Hannibal Italiam in prōvinciam redigere nōn poterat.[3]

Maximus perpetuō labōre [4] etiam Tarentum, oppidum Italiae, 5 recēpit. Līvius [5] in hōc [6] oppidō fuerat sed oppidum āmīserat et ad arcem [7] virōs remōverat. Maximus ad portās oppidī virōs prōcēdere iussit et oppidum recēpit; tum is etiam ad arcem prōcessit. Ibi Līvius, superbus quod arcem retinuerat, Fabiō dīxit: "Meā operā [8] Tarentum

---

[1] Ablative: *in* ——. [2] **Q. = Quīntus.** [3] *was able.*
[4] Ablative. [5] The general in command of the town. [6] *this* (ablative).
[7] *citadel* (accusative). [8] *effort.*

10 recēpistī." Fabius respondit: "Vērum est, Līvī: ego recēpī oppidum quod [9] tū āmīsistī."

Statuās deōrum ex oppidō Tarentō Maximus nōn remōvit sed, quod deī inimīcī Tarentīnīs erant, Tarentīnōs in oppidō statuās retinēre iussit.

QUESTIONS

1. How did Maximus weaken Hannibal?
2. How did Livius help in recovering Tarentum?

234. Infinitive Object

1. *Virōs discēdere* **iussī,** *I ordered the men to go away.*
2. *Mē labōrāre* **nōn cupīvistī,** *You did not desire me to work.*

Observe that (1) with such English verbs as *order, teach* (also *wish, forbid,* etc.) the infinitive object is often used with a noun or pronoun in the accusative, which may be regarded as its *subject;* (2) in Latin, too, certain verbs of similar meaning have the infinitive with its subject in the accusative case. In sentence 1 above, the phrase **virōs discēdere** is the *object* of **iussī** and the word **virōs** is the *subject* of **discēdere.**

235. Exercises

A. 1. Māteria ā servīs removēbitur.
2. Deus nōs etiam inimīcōs amāre docet.
3. Librīne bonī, puerī, ab amīcīs vestrīs leguntur?
4. Fīliōs nostrōs bonōs librōs semper retinēre docēmus.
5. Magister nōs amīcōs nostrōs dīmittere et ā viā discēdere iussit.
6. Nōnne bonum est inimīcōs in amīcitiam et concordiam redigere?

B. 1. It was good to see our friends.
2. They had hesitated to remove the grain without wagons.
3. The sons of farmers are beginning to go away from the farms (*use* **ager**).
4. Lucius, order the boy to lead out fresh horses to the gates of the town.

[9] *which.*

Stamp of the republic of San Marino with Latin inscription: "Vox populi iubet."

These stones from Lavinium, a city south of Rome, are ancient sacrificial altars. They date from the sixth to the first century B.C. Aeneas is said to have founded the city, naming it after his wife Lavinia, daughter of King Latinus (see section 238).

236. Vocabulary

discē′dō, discē′dere, disces′sī, [discessū′rus], *go away, depart* [cēdō]

e′tiam, adv., *also, even*

iu′beō, iubē′re, ius′sī, [ius′sus], *order*

por′ta, –ae, f., *gate*   (portal)

reci′piō, reci′pere, recē′pī, [recep′tus], *take back, recover*   [capiō]

red′igō, redi′gere, redē′gī, [redāc′tus], *drive back, reduce*   [agō]

remo′veō, removē′re, remō′vī, [remō′tus], *remove*   [moveō]

237. Latin and English Word Formation

The Latin suffix **–ia** usually has the form **–y** in English, as we have seen **(232)**. When it is preceded by **–t–**, the combination **–tia** generally has the form **–ce** in English.

Give the English forms of the following words found in the preceding vocabularies: **grātia, sententia.**

What must be the Latin words from which are derived *science, diligence, prudence, absence?*

The *tarantula* (a spider) and the *tarantella* (a dance) both got their names from Tarentum. Look them up in the dictionary.

Fabius is the name of towns in three states. Missouri, New York, Ohio, and Wisconsin have towns named *Hannibal.* Pennsylvania has a *Tarentum.*

Lesson XXXIII

238. AENĒĀS ET TURNUS

Troia ā Graecīs capta erat et Aenēās cum paucīs Troiānīs ad Italiam vēnerat et per terrās barbarōrum virōs prōdūxerat. Sed Iūnō inimīca mānsit et contrā Aenēam miserum multōs barbarōs populōs Italiae incitāvit. Ā Turnō Lāvīnia, fīlia rēgis [1] Latīnī, amābātur sed
5 Aenēae [2] dōnāta est. Turnus bellum gerere nōn dubitāvit. Ab Aenēā bellum nōn grātē susceptum est; ad terminum vītae sub armīs esse nōn cupīvit. Sed causa Troiānōrum ā Fātīs suscepta erat. Aenēās etiam ā Graecīs quī in Italiā habitābant beneficium et auxilium accēpit, quod Turnō inimīcī erant. Per multōs diēs bellum gestum
10 est et multa ēgregia exempla virtūtis [3] in proeliīs clārīs prōposita sunt.

Tandem Turnus sōlus Aenēam sōlum ad pugnam ēvocāvit, quod reliquīs exemplum prōpōnere cupīvit. In locō commodō sub portīs oppidī pugnāvērunt. Nōn longa fuit pugna, quod Venus, māter Aenēae, fīliō ēgregia arma dōnāverat quae [4] deus Vulcānus fēcerat.
15 Fāta iusserant auxilium ad Turnum nōn mittī; [5] itaque Iūnō aberat. Turnī vīta fūgit et Aenēās ad terminum perīculōrum vēnit et ōtium invēnit.

QUESTIONS

1. Why did Turnus carry on war with the Trojans?
2. Why did Aeneas defeat Turnus?

239. Perfect Participle

A *participle* is that form of a verb which is used like an adjective.
The *past participle* in English usually ends in *–ed: carried*. The *perfect (passive) participle* in Latin is declined like the adjective

---

[1] Genitive singular of rēx: *King Latinus.*   [2] Dative.   [3] *of courage.*
[4] *which.*   [5] *to be sent.*

182

"Venus at the Forge of Vulcan," a painting by the Flemish artist Anthony Van Dyck (1599–1641).

magnus. In the first conjugation it is regularly formed by adding **–tus** to the present stem: **portā–tus.** It agrees, like an ordinary adjective, with a noun or pronoun in gender, number, and case: **litterae plicātae,** *the folded letter.* The perfect participle represents an act as having taken place before the time indicated by the main verb.

The perfect participle serves as the fourth principal part of the verb; from now on it will be given without brackets in the vocabularies.

240. Perfect Passive Tense

In English, the past passive tense is formed by using the past tense of *to be* (i.e., *was*) as an auxiliary (i.e., helping) verb with the past participle: *he was carried.*

In Latin, the perfect passive tense is formed by using the *present* tense of **sum** as an auxiliary with the perfect participle: **portātus est.** The participle really modifies the subject and therefore agrees with it in gender, number, and case.

	sum, *I was, have been carried*		sumus, *we were, have been carried*
portātus (–a, –um)	es, *you were, have been carried*	portātī (–ae, –a)	estis, *you were, have been carried*
	est, *he was, has been carried*		sunt, *they were, have been carried*

Similarly **doctus sum, positus sum, mūnītus sum, captus sum.**
(For full conjugation see **567–570.**)

241. Past Perfect and Future Perfect Passive

In English, the past perfect passive is formed by using the past perfect tense of *to be* (i.e., *had been*) as an auxiliary with the past participle: *he had been carried.*

In Latin, the past perfect passive is formed by using the *imperfect* tense of **sum** (i.e., **eram**) as an auxiliary with the perfect participle: **portātus erat.** (For full conjugation see **566–570.**) The future perfect passive is formed by using the *future* tense of **sum** with the perfect participle: **portātus erit.** (For full conjugation see **566–570.**)

Practice

1. Conjugate in the perfect passive: **trahō, –ere, trāxī, trāctus; videō, –ēre, vīdī, vīsus;** in the past perfect passive: **moveō, –ēre, mōvī, mōtus; agō, –ere, ēgī, āctus.**
2. Translate: *they have been seen; I had been dragged; you have been moved; driven; having been driven.*

242. Exercises

A. 1. Arma carrīs ad castra portāta erant.
2. Causam populī suscipere est officium bonōrum.
3. Equī ab agricolā per silvam ad aquam āctī sunt.
4. Ēgregiumne exemplum amīcitiae memoriā tenētis?
5. Ēgregium exemplum beneficī ā magistrō vestrō prōpositum est.
6. Vir ā puerō sub aquam trāctus erat, sed et vir et puer servātī [6] sunt.

B. 1. He knew much about horses.
2. He was taught by good teachers.
3. The farmer's son had seen few towns.
4. An excellent example was presented to my son.
5. The rest of the books had been removed by the teacher.

[6] Note that the participle is plural because it refers to both **vir** and **puer.**

243. Vocabulary

benefi′cium, benefi′cī, n., *kindness*   **[*faciō*]**
ēgre′gius, –a, –um, *distinguished, excellent*   (egregious)
exem′plum, –ī, n., *example*   (sample, exemplify)
per, prep. with acc., *through*
prōpō′nō, prōpō′nere, prōpo′suī, prōpo′situs, *put forward,*
     offer   **[*pōnō*]**
sub, prep., *under, close to;* with acc. after verbs of motion; with
     abl. after verbs of rest
susci′piō, susci′pere, suscē′pī, suscep′tus, *undertake*   **[*capiō*]**

244. Latin and English Word Formation

The preposition **sub,** used as a prefix in Latin and English, means *under, up from under:* **sus-tineō** *hold up;* **suc-cēdō,** *come up.* It is regularly assimilated before certain consonants: *suc-ceed, sus-ceptible, suf-fer, sug-gest, sus-pend, sup-port, sur-rogate, sus-tenance,* but *sub-mit, sub-trahend.* We use it freely in English to form new words: *sub-lease, sub-let, sub-orbital.*

Per usually remains unchanged when used as a prefix.

Explain by derivation the meaning of *permanent, permit, sustain, suspect.* What is meant by being *susceptible* to colds?

Why are iron and steel mills named after *Vulcan?* Why is the name *Vulcan* so often given to firms located in Pittsburgh, Birmingham, Chicago, Detroit, and New York?

A view of the remains of a Roman villa at Chedworth, Gloucestershire, England.

British Crown Copyright Reserved—Royal Air Force Photograph

Ancient statue of a daughter of Niobe fleeing from certain death. It is in a museum in Florence, Italy.

Lesson XXXIV

245. NIOBĒ

Niobē,[1] rēgīna superba, in Graeciā habitābat. Avus erat Iuppiter, quī deōs virōsque rēxit, et hoc[2] superbiam rēgīnae auxit. Niobē erat superba etiam quod septem fīliōs et septem fīliās habuit.

Apollō deus erat fīlius deae Lātōnae, et Diāna erat fīlia. Aliōs
5 līberōs Lātōna nōn habuit.

Sacra[3] Lātōnae ā populō suscipiēbantur. Superba Niobē adfuit et rogāvit:

"Cūr mātrī[4] duōrum līberōrum sacra suscipitis? Hoc[5] nōn permittam. Etiam Niobē dea est; XIV, nōn duōs, līberōs habet. Lātōna
10 glōriam nōn meret—Niobē esse prīma dēbet. Vōbīs līberīsque vestrīs

---

[1] *Nī'obē.*   [2] *this* (nom.).   [3] *sacred rites.*   [4] *for the mother.*   [5] *this* (accusative).

exemplum ēgregium prōpōnō. Sī sententia mea ā vōbīs nōn probata erit, poenā afficiēminī."

Superba verba rēgīnae ā Lātōnā audīta sunt. Novum cōnsilium cēpit: fīlium vocāvit et officium permīsit:

"Tē iubeō septem fīliōs Niobae interficere." 15

Prīmus fīlius adfuit et interfectus est, tum reliquī. Niobē septem fīliōs nunc per linguam superbam āmīserat, tamen remānsit superba quod fīliae remānsērunt. Itaque Lātōna iussit etiam fīliās septem ēdūcī et ā Diānā interficī. Singulae fīliae ē vitā discessērunt, et Niobē misera in saxum dūrum mūtāta est. Poenā magnā affecta erat. Niobae 20 exemplum memoriā tenēre dēbēmus.

QUESTIONS

1. Give three reasons for Niobe's pride.
2. Who was Diana's brother?
3. Why were Niobe's children killed?

246. How to Study a Latin Paragraph

Do not turn at once to the vocabulary at the end of the book for a word you do not know. Try to read an entire paragraph before you look up a word. There are three good ways to find the meaning of a word without looking it up:

1. English derivatives. Nearly every Latin word has at least one English derivative.
2. Related Latin words. If you know the meaning of re– and **dūcō,** you know the meaning of **redūcō.**
3. Sensible guessing from the context.

Do not become a slave to the vocabulary at the end of the book.

247. Developing "Word Sense"

And do not become a slave to a single meaning for a word. Choose English equivalents that sound natural. Give a different translation for **incitat** in each of the following sentences:

1. Agricola equōs incitat.
2. Caesar animōs sociōrum incitat.
3. Dominus servum tardum incitat.
4. Concordia ōtium incitat.
5. Magister bonus discipulōs ad studia incitat.
6. Memoria poētam incitat.

187

The illumination of the Colosseum at night shows the grace and power of the most famous monument of the Romans.

Marcello Bertinetti/Photo Researchers, Inc.

248. Practice

1. Conjugate in the perfect passive: **āmittō, –ere, āmīsī, āmissus; retineō, –ēre, retinuī, retentus; redigō, –ere, redēgī, redāctus; cupiō, –ere, cupīvī, cupītus;** in the past perfect passive: **iubeō, –ēre, iussī, iussus; nōscō, –ere, nōvī, nōtus.**

2. Tell the form and translate: **ēductī sumus, susceptum erat, permissum erit, trāctī estis, mōtus es, āctī erant, vīsae estis, iussae sunt, portātus erō, prōpositum est.**

249. Present Infinitive Passive

In English, the present infinitive passive is formed by using the auxiliary *to be* with the past participle: *to be seen, to be heard.*

Active: portāre, *to carry*   docēre, *to teach*   mūnīre, *to fortify*
Passive: portārī, *to be carried* docērī, *to be taught* mūnīrī, *to be fortified*

In the third conjugation, final **–ĕre** is changed to long **–ī.**

Active: pōnere, *to place*   capere, *to take*
Passive: pōnī, *to be placed*   capī, *to be taken*

Practice

Form and translate the present passive infinitive of **videō, agō, trahō, suscipiō, ēdūcō, moveō, appellō,** and **inveniō.**

250. Exercises

A. 1. Nōnne dūrum est sub aquā remanēre?
2. Equī ex oppidō per agrōs lātōs ēductī erunt.
3. Pecūnia merērī et servārī ā puerīs puellīsque dēbet.
4. Puerī adfuērunt prīmī, quod puellae tardae fuērunt.
5. Tibi vītam līberōrum meōrum permittere nōn dubitāvī.
6. Verbīs bonōrum virōrum semper incitārī et regī dēbēmus.

B. 1. We have ordered the boys to be dismissed.
2. The boys are absent, but the girls are present.
3. The men had been ordered to seize the fortified town.
4. The children ought to be called together by the teacher.

251. Vocabulary

ad'sum, ades'se, ad'fuī, adfutū'rus,[6] *be near, be present*   **[sum]**
ēdū'cō, ēdū'cere, ēdū'xī, educ'tus, *lead out*   **[dūcō]**
interfi'ciō, interfi'cere, interfē'cī, interfec'tus, *kill*   **[faciō]**
lī'berī, –ō'rum, m., *children*   **[līber]**
permit'tō, permit'tere, permī'sī, permis'sus, *let go through, allow, entrust* (with dat.)   **[mittō]**
prī'mus, –a, –um, *first*   (primitive, primary)
rema'neō, remanē're, remān'sī, remānsū'rus,[6] *remain*   **[maneō]**

252. English Word Studies

1. What is a *primary* school? A political *primary?*

The word *education* is often wrongly said to be derived from **ēdūcere.** As you can see, the derivative of **ēdūcere** would be *eduction.* *Education* comes from a related word, **ēducāre,** *to bring up.* According to derivation, if you are well educated you are well brought up.

2. Latin phrases in English:

Deo gratias, *thanks to God.*
per annum, *by* (*through*) *the year.*
sub rosa, *under the rose,* i.e., *in concealment.*
Dei gratia, *by the grace of God* (seen on Canadian coins).
sic semper tyrannis, *thus always to tyrants* (motto of the state of Virginia).

---

[6] A few verbs lack the perfect participle; some of these have the future active participle in –**ūrus,** which then is used as the fourth principal part.

Glimpses of Roman Life

253. ROMAN SCHOOLS

Even before they went to school, some Roman children learned the alphabet by playing with letters cut out of ivory—as modern children do from their blocks. They started to school at about the same age as our children. The schools were quite different, however. They were very small private schools, usually run by slaves for small fees. Work began early in the morning. The children were taken to and from school by slaves called **paedagōgī,** a Greek word which means those who "lead (take) children." They did no teaching but merely kept their children in order. The English term *pedagogue* is derived from this word.

In the elementary school, called the **lūdus litterārum,** the three *R*'s formed the basis of the curriculum, which, like the teaching, was fairly unimaginative. For reading the Romans had to depend at first on

Tablet with Greek spelling exercises, styli, inkwell, and wax tablets.

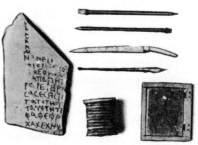

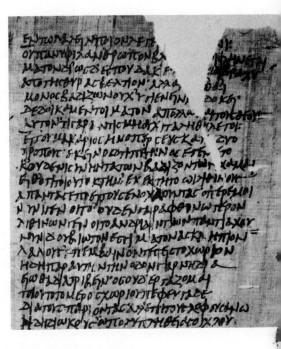

Papyrus sheet showing part of the "Dyskolos," a Greek comedy by Menander, discovered in recent years. One can see clearly the grain of the papyrus and the width of some of the strips.

the Twelve Tables of the law, the first set of laws that the Romans put in writing. In the third century B.C. a schoolteacher translated the *Odyssey* from Greek for the use of his pupils. Later, other works of literature were used.

The pupils wrote on wax tablets that consisted of wooden boards covered with a thin layer of wax. They wrote by scratching the wax with a pointed stylus made of metal or bone. The other end of this was flat for erasing, or rather, smoothing over the wax.

The Romans also wrote with pen and ink on papyrus, a kind of paper made of thin strips of a reed which grew in Egypt. Most books were made by hand out of rolls of this material. But it was expensive, and school children used only the backs of old books and loose sheets for their "scratch paper." For tablets, parchment came to be used instead of wax-covered wood. Eventually a number of these were put together to form a book of the kind familiar to us, and the papyrus roll went out of fashion.

Arithmetic was complicated by the fact that the Romans did not have the Arabic system of numerals, with its zero, that we use. Multiplication and division were impossible. The Romans had two helps in their arithmetic: an elaborate system of finger counting and the abacus, or counting board, similar to those used as toys by children today and those which you sometimes see in Chinese laundries.

191

More advanced education prepared boys for the one respected profession in ancient Rome, that of law and public life. Hence the secondary school, called the **schola grammaticī** (*school of the grammarian*), specialized in language, composition, rhetoric, and public speaking. But the course was also a broadly cultural one and included literature, both Greek and Latin. Most educated Romans learned to speak and write Greek fluently.

The college course in the **schola rhētoricī** (*school of the rhetorician*) was still more technical in preparation for a career in which public speaking, whether in a law court or a legislative body, played a very important role. For graduate work students could go to such university centers as Athens or Rhodes and listen to lectures by famous philosophers and professors of rhetoric.

Although the aim of the schools beyond the elementary stage was the relatively narrow one of preparing citizens for public service, the practical Romans felt that a liberal training in literature and philosophy was the best system for their needs.

QUESTIONS

1. What educational advantages do you have that a Roman boy did not have?
2. Compare books and writing material then and now.
3. What sort of education should our government officials have?

The Temple of Caelestis in the Roman city of Dougga, Tunisia, northern Africa.

Gian Berto Vanni/Art Resource

UNIT VI REVIEW

Lessons XXIX–XXXIV

The Story of Lucius (cont.)

254. LŪDUS

Lūciumne in memoriā habētis? Lūcius reliquīque puerī Rōmānī
ā magistrō in pulchrum Forum Rōmānum ēductī erant. Nunc iterum
dē Lūciō audiētis. Dē lūdō Lūcī nunc agēmus. Lūdus est locus ubi
magister puerōs puellāsque docet. Prīmus lūdus vocātus est "lūdus
litterārum." In Lūcī lūdō puellae nōn erant, et paucī puerī. Rōmānī 5
līberōs in pūblicum lūdum nōn mīsērunt quod lūdī pūblicī nōn erant.
Sed tamen [1] pretium disciplīnae erat parvum. Puerī pecūniam et
praemia ad magistrum portābant. Servī puerōs ad lūdum ante lūcem [2]
dūcēbant et lanternam librōsque portābant. Nōnne dūrum erat multās
hōrās in lūdō agere? Servī in lūdō manēbant et puerōs ad familiās 10
redūcēbant.

WHAT ROMAN BOYS STUDIED

Etiam magister servus erat. Litterās et verba et numerōs docuit.
Lingua lūdī erat Latīna, quod puerī Rōmānī erant. Numerōs Lūcius
nōn amāvit. Magister puerīs fōrmās litterārum mōnstrābat. Tum
digitōs puerōrum tenēbat, et litterās faciēbant. Sententiae [3] puerīs ā 15
magistrō mōnstrātae sunt. Exemplum sententiae est: "Ibi semper est
victōria ubi concordia est." Sententiās pulchrās semper amābat Lūcius
et in memoriā tenēbat. Dīligentiā et studiō praemia merēbat.

QUESTIONS

1. Name some duties of the slaves toward the Roman schoolboys.
2. How did Lucius feel about his studies?
3. What differences are there between your school and that of
   Lucius?

---

[1] *nevertheless.*   [2] *before dawn.*   [3] *mottoes.*

255. WORDS USED AS NOUNS

1. Pronouns

Ego (in place of a person's name), **tū,** etc.

2. Infinitives

a. *As subject:* **Cēdere nōn est grātum,** *To yield is not pleasant.*
b. *As object:* **Viam novam** *mūnīre* **dēbēmus,** *We ought to build a new road.*

3. Adjectives

a. **Miser** (nom. sing. masc.) **terrētur,** *The unhappy (man) is scared.*
b. **Aequae** (nom. plur. fem.) **praemia merent,** *The just (women) deserve rewards.*
c. **Multum** (acc. sing. neut.) **facimus,** *We do much.*
d. **Multa** (acc. plur. neut.) **facimus,** *We do many (things).*

256. GRAMMAR SUMMARY

First Conjugation: Principal Parts

Verbs of the first conjugation generally form the perfect stem by adding –v– to the present stem and form the perfect participle by adding –tus to the present stem. Review the following verbs, whose principal parts are regular.

The capitol in Caracas, Venezuela, is classical in design.

Standard Oil Company (New Jersey)

Henle from Monkmeyer

Modern schoolgirls walk past the ancient Roman temple in Evora, Portugal.

amō, appellō, convocō, dōnō, dubitō, ēvocō, exspectō, habitō, incitō, labōrō, laudō, līberō, mandō, mōnstrō, nāvigō, nūntiō, occupō, parō, portō, probō, pugnō, servō, spectō, vocō.

257. VOCABULARY

NOUNS		
1. beneficium	2. exemplum	4. perīculum
	3. līberī	5. porta

ADJECTIVES		
6. ēgregius	7. inimīcus	9. miser
	8. integer	10. prīmus

PRONOUNS			
	11. ego	12. is, ea	13. tū

VERBS			
14. absum	19. discēdō	25. permittō	31. remaneō
15. adsum	20. dubitō	26. prōcēdō	32. removeō
16. āmittō	21. ēdūcō	27. prōdūcō	33. retineō
17. cupiō	22. interficiō	28. prōpōnō	34. suscipiō
18. dīmittō	23. iubeō	29. recipiō	
	24. nōscō	30. redigō	

ADVERB		
	35. etiam	

PREPOSITIONS		
36. per	37. prō	39. sub
	38. sine	

258. VOCABULARY (English Meanings)

NOUNS		
	2. *example*	4. *danger*
1. *kindness*	3. *children*	5. *gate*

ADJECTIVES		
	7. *unfriendly*	9. *unhappy*
6. *distinguished*	8. *untouched*	10. *first*

PRONOUNS	11. *I*	12. *he, she*	13. *you*

VERBS	19. *depart*	25. *entrust*	31. *remain*
14. *be away*	20. *hesitate*	26. *go forward*	32. *remove*
15. *be present*	21. *lead out*	27. *lead out*	33. *hold back*
16. *lose*	22. *kill*	28. *offer*	34. *undertake*
17. *desire*	23. *order*	29. *take back*	
18. *send away*	24. *learn*	30. *reduce*	

ADVERB	35. *also*

PREPOSITIONS	37. *for*	39. *under*
36. *through*	38. *without*	

259. UNIT PRACTICE AND EXERCISES

Form Drill

A. Give the Latin for *I, me, we, us, with me, with us, you* (as sing. subject and object), *you* (as plur. subject and object), *of you* (sing. and plur.), *with you* (sing. and plur.).

B. Give in Latin the singular and plural of *great danger* and *my son* used as subject, used as direct object, and used as indirect object.

C. 1. Give the present passive infinitive of **appellō, āmittō, removeō,** and **audiō.**
2. Translate *to undertake, to be undertaken; to order, to be ordered; to lead out, to be led out.*

D. Give in six tenses, translating each tense form: 1. the active first singular of **iubeō,** and 2. the passive third plural of **permittō.**

E. 1. Translate **fuerant, fuistī, iusserāmus, discessit, remōvī, retinuistis, cupīvimus, ēdūxit, prōpositum est, remōtī sunt, dubitāverō.**
2. Give in Latin *he had been, she has been seen, it has been presented, he has remained, undertaken, it will be entrusted, they have been, we had been sent away.*

Vincenzo Carcavallo, Naples

A street in ancient Herculaneum, a city near Naples, destroyed in 79 A.D. by the eruption of the volcano Vesuvius. Notice the narrowness of the street. The house on the left has a balcony.

260. ENGLISH WORD STUDIES

1. Find and use in sentences as many English derivatives as possible from **servō, moveō, dūcō, capiō.** For example: from **servō** is derived *conservation,* used as follows: *The conservation of our soil and of our forests is a necessity.*

2. Pick out from **257** the Latin words from which each of the following is derived: *primitive, permission, beneficiary, exemplary, proposition, librarian, inimical, integration, commiserate, retention, reproduce.*

A Latin Play

261. POST BELLUM

Persōnae

Lūcīlia ⎫	**Gāius,** *frāter Lūcīliae*
Valeria ⎬ *Rōmānae*	**Philippus,** *servus*
Zōē, *serva* ⎭	

Locus: *In ātriō Lūcīliōrum.* (*Accēdunt Lūcīlia et Valeria.*)

VALERIA: Victōria est nostra! Multa oppida, multa castra nostrī occupāvērunt.

LŪCĪLIA: Deī bonī sunt!

VALERIA: Caecilius tuus aderit—et meus vir pactus,[1] Arrius.

5 LŪCĪLIA: Zōē! Zōē! (*Accēdit Zōē.*) Zōē, nova mea ōrnāmenta! (*Exit Zōē.*)

VALERIA: Nova est serva.

LŪCĪLIA: Captīva est. Ea cum praedā praemissa est.

VALERIA: Parva′ est—et trīstis.[2] Lacrimās in oculīs vīdī. (*Zōē* 10 *accēdit. Ōrnāmenta et vestēs pulchrās portat. Lūcīlia et Valeria eam nōn vident.*)

LŪCĪLIA: Bellum dūrum est. Zōē patriam et familiam āmīsit. Misera est.

VALERIA: Serva est.

15 LŪCĪLIA: Serva nunc est—sed puella misera. Amīca mea erit. Eam amō.

VALERIA: Bah! (*Lūcīlia servam videt.*)

LŪCĪLIA: Ōh, Zōē! (*Zōē ōrnāmenta et vestēs Lūcīliae dat.*) Ecce,[3] Valeria! (*Lūcīlia ōrnāmenta et vestēs Valeriae mōnstrat.*)

20 VALERIA: Pulcherrima [4] sunt! Et tū es pulcherrima.

LŪCĪLIA: Nōn pulchra sum, Valeria. Ecce, lenticulās [5] habeō, multās lenticulās!

VALERIA: Quod flāva [6] es lenticulae adsunt. Sed tū es pulchra.

LŪCĪLIA: Nōn pulchra, sed misera sum. Caecilius mē nōn amābit.

25 VALERIA: Nūgae! [7] Tē amābit. (*Accēdit Gāius.*)

GĀIUS: Arrius adest, Valeria.

VALERIA: Quid?

GĀIUS: Arrius, vir pactus tuus, domum vēnit.

VALERIA: Quis eum [8] vīdit?

---

[1] *fiancé.*   [2] *sad.*   [3] *see!*   [4] *very beautiful.*
[5] *freckles.*   [6] *blonde.*   [7] *nonsense.*   [8] *him.*

Roman soldiers shown on the Column of Trajan in Rome. The many reliefs on this column depict the Emperor's conquests in Dacia, which became a Roman province.

GĀIUS: Ego eum vīdī. 30

VALERIA: Ōh, valē, Lūcīlia! Valē! (*Exit cum Gāiō.*)

LŪCĪLIA: Beāta [9] est Valeria.

ZŌĒ: Et tū beāta eris, domina.

LŪCĪLIA: Quid dīcis?

ZŌĒ: Serva sum, domina; sed tū amīca mihi es. Lenticulās cūrābō. 35

LŪCĪLIA: Cūrābisne?

ZŌĒ: Remediō mihi nōtō.

LŪCĪLIA: Vērumne dīcis?

ZŌĒ: Ego multās lenticulās habēbam; nunc absunt.

LŪCĪLIA: Ōh, Zōē! Sī lenticulās cūrābis, Caecilius mē amābit! 40

ZŌĒ: Tē amābit. (*Accēdit Gāius.*)

GĀIUS: Lūcīlia! Novus servus adest—meus.

LŪCĪLIA: Novusne servus?

GĀIUS: Puer est—captīvus. Is praemissus est. Iam [10] accessit. Appellātur Philippus. 45

ZŌĒ: Philippus?

GĀIUS: Ecce! (*Ad iānuam [11] properat. Accēdit Philippus.*)

ZŌĒ: Philippus est—frāter meus!

PHILIPPUS: Zōē est—soror mea! (*Lacrimant.*)

ZŌĒ: Ō domina, beāta sum. Deī bonī sunt. 50

LŪCĪLIA: Familia nostra beātissima Rōmae [12] erit.

---

[9] *happy.*   [10] *already.*   [11] *door.*   [12] *the happiest in Rome.*

UNIT VII

GAMES AND GODS

The Roman Colosseum is constructed of limestone blocks called travertine. It was built between 72 and 80 A.D. The arena is 83 yards by 50 yards. The Colosseum was built for large-scale gladiatorial combats, fights with wild animals, and naval battles for which it could be flooded. The capacity of the Colosseum was 50,000. The seats were divided into three tiers. The lowest tier was for the senators, vestals, and ambassadors; the second tier for the wealthy citizens; and the upper tier for the general public.

In this photo, we can see the subterranean passages which were used for keeping wild animals, and through which scenery and props were brought into the arena for the spectacles. Over the centuries, nearly two-thirds of the Colosseum was removed for use in the construction of various other Roman buildings.

Marcel Eskenazy/PhotoEdit

Lesson XXXV

262. LŪDĪ RŌMĀNĪ ET NOSTRĪ

Inter lūdōs Rōmānōs et nostrōs similitūdō [1] nōn magna est. In lūdīs Rōmānīs inter puerōs erant nūllae puellae, in nostrīs sunt multae; puerī Rōmānī ad lūdum ā servīs ductī sunt, nōs sōlī aut in carrīs venīmus; magistrī Rōmānī servī erant, nostrī līberī sunt; lingua
5 lūdōrum Rōmānōrum erat Latīna, lingua lūdōrum nostrōrum est Anglica. Lūdī Rōmānī nōn erant pūblicī. Ob dīligentiam et studium puerīs Rōmānīs praemia pulchra data sunt, nunc puerī ob dīligentiam "A" merent. Malī discipulī Rōmānī poenā affectī sunt, sed malī discipulī poenā semper afficiuntur. Ob variās causās vīta discipulōrum
10 nostrōrum grāta est, sed etiam puerī Rōmānī lūdum librōsque amāvērunt. Magna pecūnia lūdīs nóstrīs datur et beneficia disciplīnae pūblicae omnēs [2] puerī puellaeque accipiunt. Nōnne est officium pūblicum pecūniam dare et lūdīs auxilium submittere? Rōmānī lūdīs auxilium nōn submīsērunt, neque beneficia disciplīnae pūblicae puerī
15 Rōmānī accēpērunt. Lūdus Rōmānōrum prīmus "lūdus litterārum" appellātus est quod ibi magistrī litterās docēbant. Etiam nostrī lūdī sunt lūdī litterārum.

QUESTIONS

1. How do our schools resemble Roman schools?
2. How did the boys get to school?

263. Conversation: School

MAGISTER: Discipulōs appellābō. Anna. ANNA: Adsum.

M: Marīa. MARĪA: Adsum.

M: Mārcus. DISCIPULĪ: Abest.

M: Ubi est Mārcus? D: Ad lūdum nōn vēnit. (Etc.)

5 M: Grātane erat vīta puerōrum Rōmānōrum? D: Nōn grāta erat vīta puerōrum Rōmānōrum, quod puerī Rōmānī ante lūcem in lūdum dūcēbantur.

---

[1] *likeness* (nominative feminine).   [2] *all.*

A teacher poses with his pupils, perhaps members of a chorus. This mosaic of about 300 A.D. with its stiff poses and serious eyes, shares the mood of some present-day class photographs.

M: Ubi puerī Rōmānī labōrābant? D: In lūdō puerī Rōmānī labōrābant.

M: Multīne puerī in lūdō fuērunt? D: Paucī puerī in lūdō fuērunt. 10

QUESTIONS

Answer in Latin.

1. Ubi nunc estis?
2. Pecūniamne tuam āmīsistī?
3. Estne grātum in lūdō esse?
4. Tardusne in lūdum vēnistī?
5. Semperne tardus in lūdum veniēs?
6. Ubi librum tuum Latīnum āmīsistī?

264. Principal Parts

The principal parts of the model verbs of the four conjugations and of **sum** are as follows:

CONJUGATION	PRES. INDIC.	PRES. INFIN.	PERF. INDIC.	PERF. PART.
I	portō	portāre	portāvī	portātus
II	doceō	docēre	docuī	doctus
III	(*a*) pōnō	pōnere	posuī	positus
	(*b*) capiō	capere	cēpī	captus
IV	mūniō	mūnīre	mūnīvī	mūnītus
Irregular Verb	sum	esse	fuī	futūrus

Fototeca

Above: The baths at the fashionable Roman winter resort of Baiae, north of Naples. *Right:* Hadrian's Villa (see p. 48), showing a temple of Serapis, an Egyptian god. The statues were found in 1951.

265. Tense Stems

The many different forms of every Latin verb are built upon only *three stems*. These are obtained from the principal parts as follows:

1. To find the *present stem*, drop **–re** from the present infinitive active; **portā–,** etc.

2. To find the *perfect stem*, drop **–ī** from the perfect indicative active: **portāv–,** etc.

3. To find the *participial stem,* drop **–us** from the perfect participle: **portāt–,** etc.

QUESTION

What tenses are formed (*a*) upon the present stem, (*b*) upon the perfect stem, (*c*) with the perfect participle?

266. Exercises

A. 1. Puerōs poenā afficī iussimus.
2. Ob amīcitiam auxilium submīsimus.
3. Castra in locō plānō inter oppidum et silvam erant.
4. Ob multās causās concordia inter līberōs esse dēbet.
5. Officium pūblicum est puerīs puellīsque disciplīnam dare.

B. 1. The fields had been seized by the slaves.
2. He has been aroused by the messenger's harsh words.
3. We have furnished reinforcements to the scared provinces.
4. On-account-of the danger we did not desire to sail to Europe.

267. Vocabulary

dīligen′tia, –ae, f., *diligence* (diligent)
dō,[3] da′re, de′dī, da′tus, *give* (dative, data)
in′ter, prep. with acc., *between, among*
lū′dus, –ī, m., *school*
ob, prep. with acc., (*toward*), *on account of, for*
submit′tō, –mit′tere, –mī′sī, –mis′sus, *let down, furnish* [*mittō*]

268. Latin and English Word Formation

As a prefix in Latin and English, **inter–** has its usual meanings. It is rarely assimilated. It is used rather freely in English to form new words: *inter-class, inter-state, inter-scholastic,* etc.

As a prefix **ob–** has the meaning *towards* or *against*. It is regularly assimilated before certain consonants: *oc-cur, of-ficial, o-mission, opponent;* but *ob-tain, ob-serve, ob-durate, ob-vious.*

Opponents.

Explain by derivation the meaning of *intercede, opponent, intervene, obvious.* What are *data?*

---

[3] **Dō** is irregular: it has perfect **dedī,** and short ă in all forms except the present tense, second person singular (**dās**), the imperative singular (**dā**), and the present participle (**dāns**) (to be studied later):

Pulchra templa deorum. A Roman temple at Baalbek, Lebanon (see p. 136).

Lesson XXXVI

269. TEMPLA DEŌRUM

Silvae erant prīma templa deōrum. Prīmō [1] virī in agrīs habitābant et Nātūram colēbant. Posteā virī quī in oppidīs habitābant templa pulchra in altīs locīs ad glōriam deōrum pōnēbant. Templa saepe in locīs altīs posita sunt. Cūr? Quod haec [2] loca caelō fīnitima erant, in 5 quō deī habitābant.

"Nātūra est pulchra," hominēs [3] dīxērunt. "Etiam loca sacra ad quae convenīmus et in quibus deōrum beneficia petimus pulchra esse dēbent. Deī nōbīs fortūnam bonam dedērunt. Deīs grātiam habēmus ob frūmentum quō vītam sustinēmus et ob auxilium perpetuum quod 10 nōbīs submīsērunt."

Itaque Graecī et Rōmānī ob beneficia deōrum magna et pulchra templa faciēbant quae deīs erant grāta. Statua aut deī aut deae semper in templō pōnēbātur.

In Graeciā et in Italiā ruīnae templōrum multōrum et pulchrōrum 15 videntur. Templum clārum Athēnae, appellātum Parthenōn, ob fōr-

[1] *at first.*   [2] *these.*   [3] *men.*

206

mam pulchram semper laudātum est. Nōnne fuērunt multa templa Rōmāna inter pictūrās quās vīdistī? Cūr pictūrās templōrum et Graecōrum et Rōmānōrum, quae in multīs librīs inveniuntur, nōn spectātis? Etiam in actīs diurnīs [4] pictūrās templōrum antīquōrum invenietis.

In templīs virī auxilium deōrum petēbant. Virī malī quōrum vīta [5] 20 in perīculō erat saepe ad templa fugiēbant, quod neque ex templīs removēbantur neque ibi poenam sustinēbant.

QUESTIONS

1. Where were the first temples? Why?
2. How can we find out what the ancient temples looked like?

270. The Relative Pronoun Quī

The English pronouns *who, which, what,* and *that* are called *relative* pronouns because they *relate* or refer to some preceding word, called the *antecedent: The boy who lives next door collects stamps.* The word *boy* is the antecedent of *who.*

In Latin there is only one relative pronoun. It is declined as follows:

| | SINGULAR | | | PLURAL | | |
	M.	F.	N.	M.	F.	N.
Nom.	quī	quae	quod	quī	quae	quae
Gen.	cuius	cuius	cuius	quōrum	quārum	quōrum
Dat.	cui	cui	cui	quibus	quibus	quibus
Acc.	quem	quam	quod	quōs	quās	quae
Abl.	quō	quā	quō	quibus	quibus	quibus

| **English Meanings in Singular and Plural** | |
M., F.	N.
Nom.	who, which, that	which, that, what
Gen.	of whom, whose, of which	of which, whose
Dat.	to (for) whom, which	to (for) which
Acc.	whom, which, that	which, that, what
Abl.	by, etc., whom, which	by, etc., which

Note carefully which forms are alike.

[4] *newspapers.* [5] We use the plural in English; **vītae** (plural) means *biographies.*

2. the accusative singular, masculine and feminine, ends in **–m,** as in English *whom;*

3. the nominative singular feminine is like the nominative plural feminine and neuter.

271. Relative Pronouns as Used in English

That as a relative can be used to refer to both persons and things, but *who* always refers to persons and *which* to things. In other words, *which* is the neuter of *who. Which* and *that* do not change form to indicate case, while *who* does:

Nom. *who*   Poss. *whose*   Obj. (Acc.) *whom*

272. The Relative Pronoun as Used in Latin

When a sentence contains two or more subjects and predicates, the separate parts are called *clauses*. A *relative clause* is introduced by a relative pronoun.

In the following sentences the antecedent and relative are underlined. Give the number and gender of each.

1. **Vīdī rēgīnam quae Britanniam regit,** I saw the queen who rules Great Britain.
2. **Puer cuius librum habeō est amīcus noster,** The boy whose book I have is our friend.
3. **Virum cui librum dedī vīdistī,** You saw the man to whom I gave the book.
4. **Oppidum quod vīdit erat parvum,** The town which he saw was small.
5. **Lūdī ex quibus vēnimus erant magnī,** The schools from which we came were large.

Now compare the case of the relative pronoun and its antecedent in these same sentences. You will see that the relative pronoun agrees with its antecedent in gender and number, but that its case depends upon its use in its own clause.

Finally, check each one of the sentences once more. What function does the relative clause serve? What does it do for its antecedent? To what part of speech would you compare the relative clause?

Give in Latin the proper form of the italicized English words:

1. That is not *what* I mean.
2. The boy *whom* I visited is my cousin.
3. I saw the horses *that* were on the road.
4. I know the town *in which* the president was born.

5. Have you seen the girl *to whom* I gave the books?
6. The man *by whom* we were robbed has been arrested.
7. The land *from which* our parents came is beautiful.
8. Have you seen the islands *to which* we sailed two years ago?
9. All the men *to whom* we spoke were pleased by your action.
10. All the girls (*whom*) [1] I have invited have accepted, but one girl *whose* mother is sick may not be able to come.

274. Exercises

A.
1. Via quā vēnimus pulchra erat.
2. Librōs quī dē fāmā et fortūnā agunt puerī amant.
3. Vir cui pecūniam permīsī amīcus meus vērus erat.
4. Cūr pecūniam puerō vīsō ā tē in Viā Quīntā nōn dedistī?
5. Cūr nōn fortūnam quam Nātūra vōbīs dedit sustinētis?
6. Patria nostra ob iniūriās quās accēperat bellum suscipere nōn dubitāvit.

B.
1. I saw the boy whose book I lost.
2. The friendly boy whom I saw in the woods is approaching.
3. He endured constant dangers on-account-of (his) enemies.
4. I departed from the province on-account-of the unhappy life which I led there.

275. Vocabulary

cūr, interrog. adv., *why*
nātū′ra, –ae, f., *nature* (natural, naturalize)
pe′tō, pe′tere, petī′vī, petī′tus, *seek, ask* (compete, petition)
quī, quae, quod, *who, which, that*
susti′neō, sustinē′re, –ti′nuī, –ten′tus, *hold up, maintain, endure*
[*teneō*]

276. Word Study: Intensive Prefixes

Most of the Latin prepositions which are used as prefixes in Latin and English may have intensive force, especially **con–, ex–, ob–, per–.** They are then best translated either by an English intensive, as *up* or *out,* or by an adverb, as *completely, thoroughly, deeply.* Thus **commoveō** means to *move greatly,* **permagnus,** *very great,* **obtineō,** to *hold on to,* **concitō,** to *rouse up,* **excipiō,** to *catch, receive;* **cōnservō,** to *save up, preserve;* **complicō,** to *fold up.*

Explain *component, confirmation, evident, elaborate.* What is meant by *conservation* of natural resources? What is a political *conservative?* What is a *contract?*

---

[1] The relative pronoun may be omitted in English but never in Latin: *The man* (*whom*) I saw, **Vir** *quem* **vīdī.**

Lesson XXXVII

277. COLOSSĒUM

Lūdōs et pompās populus Rōmānus magnō studiō spectābat. In
Italiā, in Āfricā, in Galliā cōnservantur theātra et amphitheātra
Rōmānōrum, in quibus lūdī etiam nunc habentur. Nātūra virōrum
varia est sed paucī lūdōs nōn amant.

5 Captīvī et servī malī quōs dominī in amphitheātrum mīserant in
mediā arēnā pugnāre cōgēbantur. Populus Rōmānus studium lūdōrum
numquam intermīsit. Multī captīvī cum magnō animō pugnābant et
lībertātem¹ obtinēbant. Multī malī virī etiam prō vītā² pugnābant
et poenam in arēnā sustinēbant.

10 Quondam duo gladiātōrēs¹ in arēnā Rōmānā pugnābant. Tum
inter gladiātōrēs vēnit sine armīs vir bonus aequusque, quī petīvit:
"Cūr pugnātis? Proelium intermittite, nam amīcī estis. Malum exemplum prōpōnitis." Gladiātōrēs verbīs nōn permōtī sunt sed virum
bonum interfēcērunt. Servī virum ex arēnā trahere incipiēbant. Tum
15 populus īrā permōtus est, quod vir erat Tēlemachus, quī amīcus
miserīs semper fuerat et magnam fāmam obtinuerat. Numquam posteā
gladiātōrēs in Colossēō pugnāvērunt, et Colossēum cum cūrā cōn-
servātum est.

Scrīptum est:

20 "Quamdiū³ stat Colisaeus,⁴ stat et⁵ Rōma. Quandō⁶ cadet Colisaeus, cadet et Rōma. Quandō cadet Rōma, cadet et mundus."⁷

QUESTIONS

1. To what use are some ancient theaters put today?
2. What two classes of people fought in the amphitheaters?
3. How long will the world last?

---

¹ Use the English derivative. ² See **269**, note 5. ³ *as long as.* ⁴ = **Colossēum.**
⁵ *also.* ⁶ *when.* ⁷ *world.*

Italian Government Travel Office

This symbol of the Eternal City, the Colosseum, has been damaged at various times by fires and earthquakes. Much of the missing stone was used to build palaces in Rome.

278. Second Conjugation: Principal Parts

These are verbs already studied, here given with their principal parts for review:

habeō	habēre	habuī	habitus
teneō	tenēre	tenuī	tentus
contineō	continēre	continuī	contentus
sustineō	sustinēre	sustinuī	sustentus
augeō	augēre	auxī	auctus
iubeō	iubēre	iussī	iussus
maneō	manēre	mānsī	mānsūrus
moveō	movēre	mōvī	mōtus
videō	vidēre	vīdī	vīsus

Note. No general rule can be given for forming the perfect and participial stems of verbs of the second conjugation. There are three general types, as can be seen above. **Habeō** represents the most common type. Like it are **dēbeō, doceō, mereō, terreō, valeō** (participle, **valitūrus**). **Retineō** is like **contineō; removeō,** like **moveō.**

Practice

Give the first singular of **augeō** and the third plural of **videō** in all tenses of the active voice.

211

The Roman theater at Trieste, Italy, was built in the second century A.D. The semi-circular area is called the orchestra (originally, "dancing ground"). The actors performed on the rectangular platform shown at the bottom of the picture (see p. 254).

279. Ablative of Manner

In English, the manner of an action is expressed by an adverb or by a phrase (i.e., a group of words) answering the question *How?* When a phrase is used, a preposition, such as *with*, introduces it.

In Latin, manner is similarly expressed:

1. **Cum studiō labōrat,** *He labors with eagerness* (*eagerly*).
2. **(Cum) magnō studiō labōrat,** *He labors with great eagerness* (*very eagerly*).

When an adjective is used, **cum** may be omitted.

Be careful to distinguish this latest use of "with" from the "with" studied in **170.** Distinguish the three different uses of "with" in the following sentences:

1. *I shall go with him with the greatest pleasure.*
2. *We can work with greater success with this equipment.*
3. *With my car I can cover the distance with you with ease.*

280. Exercises

    A. 1. Magnā cūrā silvās nostrās cōnservābimus.
         2. Cibō et pecūniā colōnōs miserōs līberē sustinuimus.
         3. Multī puerī ob bellum studia intermīsērunt.

4. Magnā iniūriā tum populus miser regēbātur.
5. Puer quī prīmum locum obtinuerat cum magnā cūrā studiōque labōrāverat.
6. Amīcus noster nōn permōtus est sed firmō animō ad casam nostram prōcēdere mātūrāvit.

B. 1. He has been deeply-moved by my words.
2. The teacher carefully taught the boys to save money.
3. Why did you give a reward to the boy who was absent?
4. The bad boy very carefully removed the teacher's books.

281. Vocabulary

cōnser'vō, –ā're, –ā'vī, –ā'tus, *save, preserve* **[servō]**
intermit'tō, intermit'tere, –mī'sī, –mis'sus, *let go, stop,*
 interrupt **[mittō]**
obti'neō, obtinē're, obti'nuī, obten'tus, *hold, obtain* **[teneō]**
permo'veō, permovē're, –mō'vī, –mō'tus, *move* (*deeply*) **[moveō]**

282. Interesting English Words

Many ordinary English words have very interesting stories locked up within them. The key to these stories is Latin.

The "efficient" person is the one who *accomplishes* **(efficiō)** something—remember this when you hear people talk about "efficiency." A "traction" company is engaged in *drawing* or *hauling* vehicles. What is a "tractor"? What sort of person is a "tractable" person? Politicians should remember that a public "office" is a *duty*. An "office" is also a place where one does his *duty* or *daily work*.

Find the stories in *petition, competition, promotion, demotion, condone, conservative.*

Competition.

The English form of **Colosseum** is *Coliseum*. There are several well-known modern coliseums. How many can you name?

The Roman Forum was the political, religious, and social center of Roman life. This is where the politicians met in the Senate House, or *Curia*. The Vestal Virgins guarded the sacred fire in the Temple of Vesta. Surrounding the Forum were commercial buildings where people bought and sold their products. After the fall of the Roman Empire (5th–6th century A.D.), the Forum slowly became covered with earth until by the Middle Ages it was transformed into a large field where cattle and sheep grazed. At the beginning of the nineteenth century archaeologists began excavating and restoring the Forum. Here we see, on the left, the Temple of Vespasian. Across the street is the Arch of Septimius Severus and, behind it, the *Curia*. In the foreground, we can see the eight columns of the Temple of Saturn, one of the oldest temples in Rome.

After six centuries of use, the Roman Forum became too crowded, and several emperors, including Julius Caesar, built other fora as monuments to themselves. In the Forum of Julius Caesar stood the Temple of Venus Genetrix, the mythical ancestor of Caesar's family who, as one of the oldest families in Rome, claimed to be descended from Ascanius, the son of Aeneas, and grandson of Venus.

The statue below shows Julius Caesar (100–44 B.C.), the general and statesman whose dictatorship led to Rome's transition from republic to empire. After a long and brilliant career, Caesar was murdered by Brutus, Cassius, and other conspirators on the Ides of March, 44 B.C.

Albert Moldvay

The Samnites, a people who lived in central Italy, were known for their bravery and love of freedom. They warred against Rome from 343 B.C. until finally defeated in 290 B.C., in the consulship of Dentatus. The armor tells that these warriors are Samnites; they are from a tomb painting of the third century B.C.

Lesson XXXVIII

283. VĒRUS RŌMĀNUS

Audīvistīne dē Dentātō? "Quis fuit et quid fēcit?" rogās. Quod Dentātum nōn nōvistī aut memoriā nōn tenēs, tē monēbō.

Dentātus fuit Rōmānus clārus quī patriam dēfendit et variīs modīs inimīca oppida castraque cēpit. Modus eius [1] vītae et ab amīcīs et ab
5 inimīcīs probābātur ac laudābātur, nam Rōmānus bonus erat. Cum [2] officia pūblica intermittēbat, agricola erat atque in agrīs labōrābat.

Samnītēs,[3] quōs Dentātus cēdere coēgerat, magnam pecūniam ad virum clārum mīsērunt et nūntiāvērunt: "Pecūnia quam coēgimus est tua. Auxilium tuum atque amīcitiam petimus." Tum Dentātus per-
10 mōtus eōs [4] monuit: "Quod aurum mihi datis? Cōnservāte aurum vestrum. Nam vērus Rōmānus pecūniam obtinēre nōn cupit sed eōs [4] quī aurum habent superāre."

QUESTIONS

1. What did Dentatus do when he was not in public service?
2. What is the point of Dentatus' answer to the Samnites?

---

[1] *his.*   [2] *whenever.*   [3] *the Sam'nītes.*   [4] *them.*

284. Interrogatives

Interrogative pronouns and adjectives are used to ask questions.

1. **Pronoun.** In English, the interrogative pronoun *who* refers only to persons, *what* refers only to things.

In Latin, the interrogative pronoun corresponding to *who* and *what* is **quis, quid,** declined as follows:

	SINGULAR		PLURAL		
	M., F.	N.	M.	F.	N.
Nom.	**quis,** *who?*	**quid,** *what?*	**quī**	**quae**	**quae**
Gen.	**cuius,** *whose?*	**cuius,** *of what?*	**quōrum**	**quārum**	**quōrum**
Dat.	**cui,** *to whom?*	**cui,** *to what?*	**quibus**	**quibus**	**quibus**
Acc.	**quem,** *whom?*	**quid,** *what?*	**quōs**	**quās**	**quae**
Abl.	**quō,** *by whom?*	**quō,** *by what?*	**quibus**	**quibus**	**quibus**

The plural is translated like the singular.

2. **Adjective.** In English, the interrogative pronoun *who* is not used as an adjective; we cannot say, *who man?* But *what* may be used as an adjective, referring to either persons or things: *What man? What thing?*

In Latin, the interrogative adjective is **quī, quae, quod,** declined like the relative pronoun (270). Compare the interrogative **quis** with the relative **quī** and note the differences in the singular.

Lapsūs Linguae (*"Slips of the Tongue"*). Have you ever said, *Who did you see?* Why is *who* incorrect? Give the correct form and translate the sentence into Latin.

285. Practice

    A. Decline *what comrade? what price?*

    B. Decide whether the words in italics are pronouns or adjectives, then give the proper Latin form:

        1. *What* girls came?
        2. *What* did he say?
        3. *Whose* book is that?
        4. To *whom* shall I go?
        5. *Who* were those men?
        6. *What* boys do you mean?
        7. To *whom* shall I give this?
        8. *What* towns were destroyed?
        9. By *whom* (sing.) was he seen?

286. Exercises

A. 1. Quis mē petit?
2. Quō modō sociī praedam coēgērunt?
3. Quī puer verbīs bonī virī nōn permōtus est?
4. Cui puerō, cui puellae, Nātūra nōn vītam grātam dedit?
5. Ā quō vōs puerī magnā cūrā dē perīculīs monitī erātis?
6. Quid amīcī tuī fēcērunt atque quod praemium accipient?
7. Quod cōnsilium, puellae, ā magistrō vestrō vōbīs datum est?

B. 1. Whom did you seek?
2. To whom shall we give the books?
3. By what street did you girls come?
4. In what manner did you obtain the money?
5. In what place is he preparing to make a speech?

287. Vocabulary

at′que (ac), conj., *and*
cō′gō, –ere, coē′gī, coāc′tus, (*drive together*), *collect, compel* **[agō]**
mo′dus, –ī, m., *manner*   (mood, mode)
mo′neō –ē′re, mo′nuī, mo′nitus, *remind, warn*   (monitor)
nam, conj., *for* (in the sense of "because," introducing a verb)
quis, quid, *who, what*

288. English Word Studies

1. What is a *cogent* reason for doing something? What is an *intermission* in a play? Explain the meaning of *modal, model, admonition.*
2. Latin phrases in English:

inter nos, *between us.*
in absentia, *in absence.*
Pax vobiscum, *Peace (be) with you!*
in perpetuum, (*into perpetuity*) *forever.*
sine qua non, *a necessity* (*lit., without which* [*condition it is*] *not* [*possible*]).
cui bono? (*lit., to whom for a good?*) *for whose benefit is it? What good is it?*
Ilium fuit, *Ilium has been* (i.e., *no longer exists*), said of Troy **(Ilium)** after its destruction; now applied to anything that is past and gone.

The Pont du Gard, a Roman
aqueduct, on a French stamp.

This Roman arch and tomb near Saint-Remy in southern France date from the first century A.D. The top of the tomb has the form of a round Roman temple.

Erich Lessing/PhotoEdit

Lesson XXXIX

289. PŪBLIUS MĀRCŌ SAL.[1]

[A letter that a young Roman with Caesar's forces in Gaul in 55 B.C. might have sent to a friend in Rome.]

Sī valēs, bene est; ego valeō. Magnō studiō litterās tuās lēgī quae cum cūrā scrīptae et plicātae erant.

Dē Galliā rogās ac dē nōbīs cognōscere cupis. Vīta nostra nōn dūra est. Magnus numerus captīvōrum in castrīs iam coāctus est. Caesar multās pugnās iam pugnāvit et multa oppida mūnīta cēpit, 5 quae praesidiīs tenet. Mox erit dominus Galliae; Gallia in prōvinciam redigētur et viae novae mūnientur. Sed dominus aequus erit. Tum virōs nostrōs trāns Rhēnum ēdūcet et Germānōs terrēbit. Iam eōs [2] monuit. Modum quō bellum gerit probō. Sententia eius [3] est: "Veniō, videō, vincō." Magnus et ēgregius vir est. Fortasse trāns aquam in 10 Britanniam prōcēdēmus, quae est magna īnsula dē quā nōn ante lēgī aut cognōvī.

Quid Quīntus noster agit? Quae nova officia suscēpit? Cūr nōn ante scrīpsit? Litterās tuās cum studiō exspectābō. Valē.[4]

---

[1] For **salūtem dīcit**: *Publius pays his respects to Marcus,* the usual form of greeting in a letter.

[2] *them.*   [3] *his.*   [4] *farewell.*

QUESTIONS

1. Did Publius have an easy time in Gaul?
2. Has Publius seen Germany yet? Britain?

290. Third Conjugation: Principal Parts

Review the principal parts of the following verbs of the third conjugation already studied. No rule can be given for the formation of the third and fourth parts, but in the commonest type the perfect ends in **–sī**. The participle regularly ends in **–tus** or **–sus**:

1. **cēdō**	**cēdere**	**cessī**	**cessūrus**
(Similarly **accēdō, discēdō, excēdō, prōcēdō**)			
dūcō	**dūcere**	**dūxī**	**ductus**
(Similarly **ēdūcō, prōdūcō, redūcō**)			
gerō	**gerere**	**gessī**	**gestus**
mittō	**mittere**	**mīsī**	**missus**
(Similarly **āmittō, committō, dīmittō, intermittō, permittō, submittō**)			
regō	**regere**	**rēxī**	**rēctus**
scrībō	**scrībere**	**scrīpsī**	**scrīptus**
trahō	**trahere**	**trāxī**	**trāctus**
agō	**agere**	**ēgī**	**āctus**
cōgō	**cōgere**	**coēgī**	**coāctus**
redigō	**redigere**	**redēgī**	**redāctus**
legō	**legere**	**lēgī**	**lēctus**
nōscō	**nōscere**	**nōvī**	**nōtus**
petō	**petere**	**petīvī**	**petītus**
pōnō	**pōnere**	**posuī**	**positus**
(Similarly **prōpōnō**)			
2. **capiō**	**capere**	**cēpī**	**captus**
accipiō	**accipere**	**accēpī**	**acceptus**
incipiō	**incipere**	**incēpī**	**inceptus**
suscipiō	**suscipere**	**suscēpī**	**susceptus**
cupiō	**cupere**	**cupīvī**	**cupītus**
faciō	**facere**	**fēcī**	**factus**
afficiō	**afficere**	**affēcī**	**affectus**
efficiō	**efficere**	**effēcī**	**effectus**
fugiō	**fugere**	**fūgī**	**fugitūrus**

A Roman relief sculpture showing a circus race. The driver at the top right has just turned the corner of the wall which runs down the center of the track.

Note. The change or lengthening of the vowel in the perfect and participial stems may be compared with the change of vowel in English: *sing, sang, sung; drink, drank, drunk,* etc.

Practice

Give the third singular of **committō** and the first plural of **accipiō** in all tenses of the passive voice.

291. Exercises

A. 1. Quid sub aquā scrībit?
2. Bella trāns Ōceanum cum victōriā gessimus.
3. Litterae ā tē scrīptae cum cūrā plicātae erant.
4. Captīvī, quī ante portam positī erant, līberātī sunt.
5. Litterās quās scrīpsī plicābō et ad familiam meam mittam.
6. Bonus est dominus noster, quod populum cum concordiā regit.
7. Linguam Latīnam cum studiō legere incipimus; nova verba iam cognōvimus.

B. 1. The new words ought always to be learned.
2. Marcus, who wrote the letter which you are reading?
3. The poor prisoners had been dragged across the fields.
4. I do not know the small boy who lives across the street.

292. Vocabulary

an′te, adv. and prep. with acc., *before* (of time or place)
cognōs′cō, cognōs′cere, cognō′vī, cog′nitus, *learn;* perf. tense, "have learned" = *know*   [*nōscō*]
iam, adv., *already*
pli′cō, –ā′re, –ā′vī, –ā′tus, *fold*   (pleat, application)
trāns, prep. with acc., *across*

221

Another colorful painting from the wall of a house in Pompeii. Everything is neatly balanced and intended to draw attention to the center picture, with its background of Pompeian red. There are smaller pictures at top and bottom.

293. Latin and English Word Formation

Ante– has its regular meaning and form when used as a prefix. **Trāns–** (or **trā–,** as in **trā-dūcō**) means *through* or *across*.

Importance of the Verb. The most important part of speech in Latin for English derivation is the verb, and the most important part of the verb is the *perfect participle*. This form is also the most important for Latin word formation. Therefore *learn carefully* the principal parts of every verb.

By associating Latin word and English derivative, you can make the English help you in your Latin, and *vice versa*. You can often tell the conjugation or the perfect participle of a Latin verb by the help of an English derivative. The English word *mandate* shows that **mandō** has **mandātus** as its perfect participle and is therefore of the first conjugation. Similarly *migrate, donation, spectator,* etc. The word *vision* helps one remember that the perfect participle of **video** is **vīsus.** Similarly *motion* from **mōtus,** *missive* from **missus,** *active* from **āctus.** Give the derivatives from **lēctus, nōtus, ductus.** Explain *election, deposit, complication, domineer.*

In compounds short **–a–** becomes short **–e–** before two consonants (cf. **151**): **captus, acceptus.** Give two examples each from compounds of **capiō** and **faciō.**

Glimpses of Roman Life

294. FOOD AND MEALS

The easiest way to give an idea of Roman foods is by listing some important foods which were unknown to the Romans: potatoes, tomatoes, bananas, oranges, sugar, coffee, tea. Butter was rarely used, except externally as a sort of salve or cold cream, but milk and cheese were common foods. Instead of sugar, honey served for sweetening. The extensive use of honey made beekeeping a very important occupation. Wheat bread baked in round loaves (see picture on page 122) was the "staff of life." Cabbage, onions, beans were among the

Food shop in Pompeii. This reconstruction is based on actual remains. Even the public corner fountain has a gay floral decoration.

chief vegetables. Apples, pears, grapes, and olives were the chief fruits. The **mālum Persicum** (from which our word *peach* is derived) was, as its name shows, originally brought from Persia.

Canning and freezing were unknown, but salted fish and fish sauces were put up in earthenware jars. This practice led to a wider consumption of fish. The lack of refrigeration restricted the importation and preservation of many foods except those that could be preserved by drying, such as grapes and figs. Ice (in the form of snow) was a great luxury.

Much use was made of salads of various kinds, as is still true in Italy today. This is one reason for the importance of olive oil, which was used also in cooking instead of butter, and besides was burned in lamps.

The favorite meat was pork; beef was less important than mutton. Various kinds of fowl and birds were eaten, even peacocks by the wealthy classes. Fish and oysters became extremely popular.

Besides milk and water the chief drink of the Romans was wine. There were many grades of native and imported wines. They were usually mixed with water when drunk at meals.

Breakfast was a simple meal, chiefly of bread. In the country, dinner (**cēna**) was at noon, but in the city this was postponed till early evening. Instead there was a luncheon (**prandium**) at midday or somewhat earlier.

Marble-covered counter, or bar, in an inn at ancient Herculaneum, near Naples. Travelers could buy here wine, bread, cheese, fruit, and other foods.

The Mildenhall Treasure; some of the 34 Roman silver spoons, bowls, etc., of the fourth century A.D. found in ploughing a field near Mildenhall, England. Tableware this valuable and elaborate was an ancient status symbol.

The dinner consisted of a course of relishes (lettuce, onions, eggs, oysters, asparagus, etc.), called the **gustus** (*taste*), followed by the chief course (meat, fish, or fowl and vegetables), then the dessert, called the **secunda mēnsa** (*second table*), of fruit, nuts, and sweets. The Latin expression **ab ōvō usque ad māla,** *from eggs to apples,* meaning from beginning to end, shows what the usual relishes and desserts were; cf. English *from soup to nuts.* Wine was served with the meal. Tobacco was unknown.

The guests reclined on couches instead of sitting on chairs. The couches were placed along the three sides of the rectangular table, each with room for three people. As the guests reclined on their left elbows, only their right hands were free. Forks were rarely used; food was taken up with the fingers or with spoons. Meat was cut up before being served. Though much use was made of the fingers, we may well imagine that people of culture ate quite as daintily as we do who have forks to help us. They had finger bowls and napkins.

QUESTIONS

1. Where did we originally get the important foods which the Romans knew nothing about?
2. Name the order of meals and describe a Roman dinner.
3. How would you arrange a Roman banquet in your Latin club or school?

Aeneas meets his mother Venus when he lands on African soil. From a beautiful
tapestry woven in the seventeenth century, now in the Cleveland Museum of Art.

*The Cleveland Museum of Art, Gift of Mrs. Francis F. Prentiss in Memory of Dr. Dudley P.
Allen, 15.79.*

UNIT VII REVIEW

Lessons XXXV–XXXIX

The Story of Lucius (cont.)

295. FORTŪNA MALA

Magister lūdī in quō Lūcius docēbātur erat dūrus. Tardī discipulī poenā affectī sunt, sed Lūcius semper prīmus vēnit, quod ad lūdum properāvit neque in viīs remānsit. Sed fortūna mala vēnit. Pecūnia quae Lūciō permissa erat ad magistrum portābātur. In viā pecūniam āmīsit et tardus fuit. Magister puerōs appellāverat, et reliquī puerī 5 responderant, "Adsum!" Tum magister Lūcium appellāvit. Puerī respondērunt, "Abest!" Tum vēnit Lūcius sine pecūniā et magister puerīque dē pecūniā āmissā audīvērunt. Magister dūrus Lūcium miserum ā puerīs sublevārī [1] iussit et poenā eum [2] affēcit, quod pecūniam āmīserat et tardus fuerat. 10

Magister discipulōs dīmīsit et singulī excessērunt. Lūcius cum servō discessit et pecūniam quam āmīserat in viā sub carrō invēnit. Ad lūdum properāvit et magistrō pecūniam dōnāvit. Magister grātiās puerō ēgit, sed ā Lūciō poena semper memoriā tenēbātur.

QUESTIONS

1. What was found?
2. What did the teacher say?

296. VOCABULARY

NOUNS	2. lūdus	4. nātūra	
1. dīligentia	3. modus		
PRONOUNS	5. quī	6. quis	
VERBS	10. dō	14. permoveō	18. sustineō
7. cognōscō	11. intermittō	15. petō	
8. cōgō	12. moneō	16. plicō	
9. cōnservō	13. obtineō	17. submittō	
ADVERBS	19. cūr	20. iam	
PREPOSITIONS	22. inter	24. trāns	
21. ante	23. ob		
CONJUNCTIONS	25. atque, ac	26. nam	

[1] *to be lifted up.*   [2] *him.*

297. VOCABULARY (English Meanings)

NOUNS	2. *game, school*	4. *nature*
1. *diligence*	3. *manner*	

PRONOUNS	5. *who*	6. *who?*

VERBS	10. *give*	14. *move deeply*	18. *maintain*
7. *learn*	11. *stop*	15. *seek*	
8. *collect, compel*	12. *remind, warn*	16. *fold*	
9. *save*	13. *hold, obtain*	17. *furnish*	

ADVERBS	19. *why*	20. *already*

PREPOSITIONS	22. *between, among*	24. *across*
21. *before*	23. *on account of*	

CONJUNCTIONS	25. *and*	26. *for*

A duck in a Roman mosaic floor. The Romans were fond of representing birds, animals, and fish on their floors.

University Museum, Philadelphia

Girl with a puppy. A bronze statuette (several inches high) of the first century A.D. in the Metropolitan Museum in New York. The little Roman girl is evidently calling to someone.

298. UNIT PRACTICE AND EXERCISES

Principal Parts

1. Give the four principal parts of the following verbs: **committō, cēdō, dūcō, agō, efficiō.**
2. Give in Latin the principal parts of the following verbs: *defend, flee, have, be, see, remain, increase, learn.*

Form Drill

1. Give in all tenses the second singular active of **moveō;** the third singular passive of **agō;** the third plural passive of **accipiō.**
2. Decline **quae nātūra, quod signum, quī dominus.**
3. Supply the missing words in the right form and translate:
   a. (*Whom*) petis?
   b. (*What*) librōs lēgistī?
   c. (*Who*) litterās scrīpsit?
   d. (*To whom*) librum dabō?
   e. (*By whom*) litterae scrīptae sunt?

"With" Ablatives

Review **61, 170, 279,** and then decide whether the "with" phrase in each of the following sentences expresses *a.* means, *b.* manner, or *c.* accompaniment:

1. Say it *with flowers.*
2. My uncle farms *with a mule.*
3. I spent the evening *with friends.*
4. The soloist sang *with deep feeling.*
5. We shall talk over matters *with him.*
6. All supported the cause *with enthusiasm* and *money.*

299. ENGLISH WORD STUDIES

1. Find and use in sentences as many English derivatives as possible from **vocō, videō, mittō,** and **faciō.** Remember the importance of the perfect participle.

2. The first word, printed in boldface type, in each of the following lines is a Latin word. From among the last five words in each line pick the one which is an English derivative of the first word.

dō	dough	dote	do	dot	dative
moneō	month	remain	admonition	moan	remind
cōgō	cog	incognito	cognate	cogency	concoct
petō	pet	compete	petal	petite	impede
legō	leg	log	collect	lag	lick

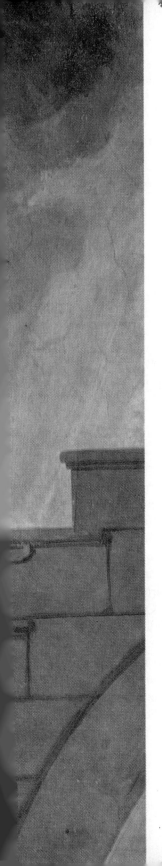

UNIT VIII

TRAVEL AND ADVENTURE

Homer's *Odyssey* was popular among the Romans, either in the original Greek or translated into Latin as an elementary school reader. This epic poem tells the story of Ulysses, King of Ithaca, and his many adventures as he attempts to return to his homeland after the Trojan War. In this painting by Stradano, we see Ulysses descending into the Underworld where he will learn news of his wife, Penelope, and his homeland, from his deceased mother. You may recall a similar episode from Virgil's epic, the *Aneid* in which Aeneas goes to the Lower World (see p. 171). Virgil imitated many other episodes from Homer's *Odyssey*.

Ulixes sub ove ligatus ex spelunca excessit. From a Greek vase of about 475 B.C. This type of vase painting is called red-figured because the subjects were left in the natural red color of the clay, and a black background was painted in around them.

Courtesy, Museum of Fine Arts, Boston
Anonymous gift in memory of L. D. Caskey

Lesson XL

300. ULIXĒS

[Ulysses (or Odysseus) was a Greek who fought in the Trojan War. His many wanderings before he returned home to Ithaca, an island west of Greece, are described by the Greek poet Homer in the *Odyssey*.]

Ulixēs, dux Graecus quī in bellō Troiānō pugnāverat, post pācem ad Ithacam, in quā īnsulā habitāverat, properāvit. Sed multa mala miser sustinuit nec salūtem invēnit. Cūrīs dūrīs pressus decem annōs in multīs terrīs ēgit.

5 Post pācem ā Troiā cum multīs mīlitibus Ulixēs migrāverat. Ad terram Lōtophagōrum[1] accessit. Paucī mīlitēs Graecī lōtum ēdērunt[2] et amāvērunt; et ducem et sociōs nōn memoriā tenuērunt. Ulixēs mīlitēs ad nāvēs redūxit, quās undīs commīsit.

Tum ad Siciliam ventīs āctus est. In Siciliā habitāvērunt Cyclōpēs,[3] 10 hominēs altī et dūrī quī singulōs oculōs[4] habuērunt. Neque deōrum neque hominum lēgēs timuērunt. Ulixēs cum paucīs nautīs in hōc[5] locō frūmentum petīvit. Magna spēlunca[6] inventa est quae magnam cōpiam frūmentī continuit. Tum vēnit Cyclōps[7] quī appellātus est Polyphēmus. Ovēs[8] in spēluncam ēgit. Polyphēmus Graecōs vīdit et 15 clāmāvit: "Ā quō locō venītis? Quī hominēs estis? Quid petitis?" Ulixēs respondit: "Nōs Graecī sumus. Ego Nēmō[9] appellor. Auxilium tuum petimus."

Polyphēmus duōs hominēs cēpit et ēdit;[10] tum somnum cēpit. Reliquī Graecī sude[11] oculum Polyphēmī pressērunt, quī clāmāvit et 20 sociōs ēvocāvit. "Quid est?" rogant. "Quis tē vulnerāvit?" Polyphēmus respondet: "Nēmō mē vulnerāvit." Itaque reliquī Cyclōpēs discessērunt. Polyphēmus Graecōs petīvit sed nōn invēnit quod sub

[1] *Lotus-eaters.*   [2] *ate the lotus.*   [3] *Cȳclō'pēs.*   [4] *one eye apiece.*
[5] *this.*   [6] *cave.*   [7] *Cȳclŏps.*   [8] *sheep.*
[9] *No-man.*   [10] *ate.*   [11] *with a stake.*

ovibus ligātī ex spēluncā excessērunt. Līberātī ad nāvēs properā-
vērunt atque ibi salūtem invēnērunt.

QUESTIONS

1. How long did it take Ulysses to reach home?
2. Why did not the other Cyclopes help Polyphemus?
3. What does the term "lotus-eater" mean when applied to anyone today?

301. Third Declension: Masculine and Feminine Nouns

In nouns of the *third declension* the genitive singular ends in **–is;**
the base is obtained by dropping this ending. All three genders occur
in nouns of the third declension; no general rule for gender can be
given. The gender, as well as the nominative and genitive singular,
must therefore be learned from the vocabulary. Masculine and
feminine nouns are declined alike:

	ENDINGS		EXAMPLES			
	SING.	PLUR.	SING.	PLUR.	SING.	PLUR.
Nom.	— [12]	– ēs	mīles	mīlit ēs	lēx	lēg ēs
Gen.	– is	– um	mīlit is	mīlit um	lēg is	lēg um
Dat.	– ī	– ibus	mīlit ī	mīlit ibus	lēg ī	lēg ibus
Acc.	– em	– ēs	mīlit em	mīlit ēs	lēg em	lēg ēs
Abl.	– e	– ibus	mīlit e	mīlit ibus	lēg e	lēg ibus

The dative and ablative plural are alike, as is true in all declensions.
The nominative and accusative plural also are alike in the third
declension.

Practice

1. Decline **homō magnus, pāx aequa.**
2. Tell the form of **salūtem, ducum, modum, māteriā, mīlitibus, lēgī, nātūrae, ducem, mīlite.**

---

[12] The ending of the nominative singular varies. When not omitted, it is usually
–s; c or **g** of the base combines with **–s** to form **–x.**

Ulysses and his companion escaping from Polyphemus. From a painting by Tibaldi.

Finnish postage stamp with the word Pax
on it, issued at the end of the war with
Russia.

302. Exercises

A. 1. Sine pāce vīta dūra est.
2. Dux mīlitēs ad pugnam prōdūxit.
3. Ibi valet populus ubi lēgēs valent.
4. Salūs patriae in armīs mīlitum nostrōrum pōnitur.
5. Sine bellō pācem et ōtium et salūtem obtinēre cupimus.
6. Magna est glōria mīlitum quī bellō pressī nōn cessērunt.

B. 1. Which boys were absent?
2. "Safety first!" is a good motto on the roads.
3. The general ordered the soldiers to be called-together.
4. Many books sent by boys and girls were received by the soldiers.

303. Vocabulary

clā′mō, –ā′re, –ā′vī, –ā′tus, *shout, cry out*   (claim, clamor)
dux, du′cis, m., *leader, general*   **[dūcō]**
ho′mō, ho′minis, m., *man, human being*   (homicide)
lēx, lē′gis, f., *law*   (legal, legislator)
mī′les, mī′litis, m., *soldier*   (military)
pāx, pā′cis, f., *peace*   (pacifist, Pacific)
pre′mō, –ere, pres′sī, pres′sus, *press, press hard*   (pressure)
sa′lūs, salū′tis, f., *health, safety*   (salutary)

304. English Word Studies

1. Explain *illegal, impressive, depression, ducal, militant.* To *salute* a person is to wish him *health,* as we say "*good* morning," not "*bad* morning." To *pay* a person is to *pacify* him. What is a *pacifist?*

Four states have towns named *Ithaca,* best-known being that in New York. Four states have towns named *Ulysses.* Why do you think that iron and steel works in San Francisco, Oakland, and Pittsburgh have the name *Cyclops?*

2. Latin phrases in English:

lex scripta, *the written law.*
pax in bello, *peace in* (*the midst of*) *war.*
novus homo, *a new man* (in politics); hence, *an upstart.*
Dux femina facti, *A woman* (*was*) *leader in* (*of*) *the deed.*

235

Lesson XLI

305. COLŌNĪ

Dē colōnīs quī ē Britanniā ad Americam vēnērunt multa fortasse nōvistī. Patriam relīquērunt et terram novam petīvērunt. Multī antecessērunt, reliquī posteā ad terram petītam trānsportātī sunt. In locīs altīs stetērunt et terram novam grātē spectāvērunt. Etiam puerī 5 puellaeque Rōmānae dē "colōnīs" cognōvērunt.

Mīlitēs ā Rōmānīs in Britanniam trānsportātī sunt et bella ibi gessērunt. Vālla fēcērunt atque viās mūnīvērunt. Tum colōnōs trādūxērunt et colōnīs agrōs captōs et oppida occupāta dedērunt. Per colōnōs in Britanniam trāductōs lingua Latīna et lēgēs Rōmānae 10 Britanniae datae sunt. Semper mīlitēs antecēdunt, tum colōnī veniunt et in pāce salūteque vīvunt.

Rōmānī oppida in Britanniā mūnīvērunt—Londīnium, Eborācum, Lindum; nunc appellantur London, York, Lincoln. Multae ruīnae Rōmānae etiam nunc in Britanniā stant. Quis nōn cupit ad Britan- 15 niam nāvigāre et ibi ruīnās relīctās vidēre?

QUESTIONS

1. How did the Roman colonists get farms?
2. Compare the reasons for Roman and British colonization.

306. Fourth Conjugation: Principal Parts

Review the principal parts of these verbs, which have occurred in previous lessons:

audiō	**audīre**	**audīvī**	**audītus**
veniō	**venīre**	**vēnī**	**ventūrus**
conveniō	**convenīre**	**convēnī**	**conventūrus**
inveniō	**invenīre**	**invēnī**	**inventus**

236

A Roman fort as it appears today in Richborough, England (see section 310).

307. Numerals

Ūnus [1] puer et ūnus puer sunt **duo** puerī; duo ducēs et ūnus dux
sunt **trēs** ducēs; duo equī et duo equī sunt **quattuor** equī; trēs carrī
et duo carrī sunt **quīnque** carrī; quattuor oppida et duo oppida sunt
sex oppida; sex mīlitēs et ūnus mīles sunt **septem** mīlitēs; quīnque nautae
et trēs nautae sunt **octō** nautae; septem hominēs et duo hominēs sunt [5]
novem hominēs; sex puellae et quattuor puellae sunt **decem** puellae.

Summary: **ūnus, duo, trēs, quattuor, quīnque, sex, septem, octō,
novem, decem.**

TRICK QUESTION

Quīnque mīlitēs et trēs rēgīnae sunt octō hominēs. Quot [2] virī sunt
trēs dominī et quattuor dominae?

308. Exercises

A. 1. Ubi pecūnia quam āmīserās inventa est?
2. Ob quās causās hominēs agrōs relīquērunt?
3. Servī trāns agrōs equōs territōs trādūxērunt.
4. Multī mīlitēs in Eurōpam iam trānsportātī sunt.

[1] one.   [2] how many.

5. Nūntium mīsimus ad Marium, quī sine auxiliīs antecesserat.
6. Cum cūrā carrum age; tua fortasse erit vīta quam cōn-
servābis.

B. 1. We ought to work with eagerness.
2. How did you hear about your friend's health?
3. Marius ordered our soldiers to be led-across.
4. Why do you stand in the middle (of the) street?

309. Vocabulary

antecē′dō, –ere, –ces′sī, –cessū′rus, *go before* [*cēdō*]
fortas′se, adv., *perhaps*
relin′quō, –ere, relī′quī, relīc′tus, *leave* (*behind*), *abandon*
(relinquish)
stō, stā′re, ste′tī, stātū′rus, *stand* (station)
trādū′cō, –ere, –dū′xī, –duc′tus, *lead across* [*dūcō*]
trānsportō, –ā′re, –ā′vī, –ā′tus, *transport* [*portō*]

310. The Latin Influence upon English

Latin words have been coming into English continuously from the beginning of our language to the present moment. Julius Caesar twice invaded Britain, and a century later the Romans conquered the island. For the next four hundred years the Romans ruled Britain, and the language, at least in the towns, came to be Latin. When the Angles and Saxons invaded Britain in the fifth century and gave their name (*Angle-land, Eng-land*) and language to the island, they adopted a number of Latin words. Even before that they had come into contact with the Romans in northern Germany and borrowed some Latin words. So you might say that Latin affected English even before English existed as a separate language. Among such early borrowings probably are *wine* from **vīnum,** *cheese* from **cāseus,** and *pound* from **pondus.**

As the Romans in Britain found it necessary to build many mili-tary camps, which developed into towns, the word **castra** is to be found in a number of town names, many of which have been used elsewhere also. So *Chester* (Pa.), *Ro-chester* (N. Y., Minn., Australia), *Man-chester* (N. H., Ia., N. C.), *Wor-cester* (South Africa, Mass., pronounced Wŏoster and so spelled in Ohio), *Lan-caster* (Pa.). What other names with these endings can you give?

We have seen a similar evolution in North America where frontier forts, erected originally as defenses against the Indians, became trad-ing posts, out of which have grown such cities as Fort Dodge (Ia.), Fort Scott (Kan.), and Fort Worth (Tex.). Similarly in Canada, Fort Frances, etc.

Part of the inscription that once stood on the baths Pliny gave to his home town of Como. Most of the inscription has been lost; it originally listed the offices Pliny held and the gifts he made to the people, including a public library. "Imp(erator) Caesar Nerva," in the fourth line, is part of the name of the Emperor Trajan, who made Pliny governor of a province.

Rostagni, "Storia della letteratura latina" (UTET, Torino)

Lesson XLII

311. PLĪNIUS ET PUER

Plīnius,[1] cuius facta bona vōbīs fortasse iam ante nōta fuērunt, multās litterās scrīpsit quās etiam nunc legere possumus. Audīte factum pulchrum Plīnī. Quondam ad oppidum parvum in quō nātus[2] erat vēnit. Ibi inter multōs hominēs stābat et dē salūte familiārum rogābat. Tum amīcum nōtum cum fīliō cernit. Plīnius puerum rogāvit: "Dis- 5 cipulusne es?" Puer respondit: "Discipulus Mediōlānī[3] sum." Plīnius commōtus quod puer patriam relīquerat, rogāvit: "Cur nōn hīc?[4] Cūr patriam relīquistī?" Puer respondit: "Nōn possum hīc manēre, nam magistrōs nōn habēmus." Tum Plīnius verba fēcit: "Verbīs puerī commōtus sum. Certē lūdum hīc habēre potestis atque dēbētis. 10 Cognōscite cōnsilium meum. Ego nōn līberōs habeō sed tertiam partem pecūniae quam dabitis parātus sum dare. Vōsne parātī estis reliquam partem dare, sī ego tertiam partem dabō?"

QUESTIONS

1. Where did Pliny see his friend?
2. Why did the boy go to school in another town?
3. What was Pliny's offer?

---

[1] *Pliny.* [2] *born.* [3] *at Milan.* [4] *here.*

312. Participles Used as Adjectives and Nouns

Perfect participles of many verbs came to be used as simple adjectives just as in English: **parātus,** "prepared," *ready;* **nōtus,** "known," *familiar.* A participle, like any adjective, may be used as a noun: **factum,** "having been done," *deed.*

313. Conjugation of Possum

Possum is a compound of **sum** and is therefore irregular. It has no passive voice. Review the conjugation of **sum. Possum = pot(e) + sum. Pot–** becomes **pos–** before all forms of **sum** which begin with **s–.** The perfect tenses are regular.

PRESENT

possum, *I can, am able*   **possumus,** *we can, are able*
potes, *you can, are able*   **potestis,** *you can, are able*
potest, *he can, is able*   **possunt,** *they can, are able*

Imperfect **poteram,** etc.,   Future **poterō,** etc.,
   I could, was able   *I shall be able*

(For full conjugation see **571.**)

Practice

1. Give the form and the meaning of **potuerās, poterātis, potuērunt, possunt, poterit, posse.**
2. Translate *you could, they had been able, we shall be able, he can, they could.*

314. Exercises

A. 1. Amīcus certus in malā fortūnā cernitur.
2. "Facta, nōn verba" sententia nostra esse dēbet.
3. Linguam Latīnam et legere et scrībere possum.
4. Perīcula vītae bonum hominem commovēre nōn poterunt.
5. Facta virōrum clārōrum semper nōta erunt et laudābuntur.
6. Ante bellum patria nostra nōn parāta erat, nam paucōs mīlitēs habēbāmus.

B. 1. Few men can neither read nor write.
2. My motto is: "Always ready." Is it yours? I ask you.
3. They had not been able to come on-account-of the bad streets.
4. We came across the level fields, because the road was not familiar.

315. *Vocabulary*

cer′nō, –ere, crē′vī, crē′tus, (*separate*), *discern, see*   (discretion)
cer′tus, –a, –um, *fixed, sure*   **[cernō]**
commo′veō, –ē′re, –mō′vī, –mō′tus, *disturb*   **[moveō]**
fac′tum, –ī, n., *deed*   **[faciō]**
nō′tus, –a, –um, *known, familiar*   **[nōscō]**
parā′tus, –a, –um, *prepared, ready*   **[parō]**
pos′sum, pos′se, po′tuī, —, *can, be able* (with infinitive)   **[sum]**
ro′gō, –ā′re, –ā′vī, –ā′tus, *ask*   (interrogate)
ter′tius, –a, –um, *third*   (tertiary)

316. *English Word Studies*

1. Explain *commotion, certificate, notorious, tertiary.*
2. Latin words and phrases in English:

erratum (plur. **errata**), *error.*

terra incognita, *an unknown land.*

Te Deum, *Thee, God* (*we praise*); the name of a hymn.

Et tu, Brute, *you too, Brutus* (said by Caesar on receiving the death-blow from his friend, Brutus).

de facto, *from* or *according to fact, actual;* as a **de facto** government, one which is actually in operation, even if not recognized as legal.

Translate **ante bellum.**

Cars and buses pass under the arches of the Roman Aqueduct in downtown Segovia, Spain. The aqueduct is still used to bring water from the mountains nearby. Spain became Roman very early (see map, pp. 92–93).

PhotoEdit

A wall painting from Pompeii showing Roman writing materials: wax tablets, inkwells, papyrus rolls, etc. At upper right is a cylindrical box containing a number of papyrus rolls. The box has a hinged cover and straps for carrying.

Lesson XLIII

317. MĀRCUS PŪBLIŌ SAL.[1]

[An answer to the letter in **289**.]

Adductus litterīs ā tē, Pūblī, in Galliā scrīptīs, respondēbō, nam multa rogāvistī. Multa nova sunt. Quid putās? Quīntus noster fīliam tertiam Rūfī in mātrimōnium dūxit! Ego nōn potuī hoc [2] prōvidēre; Quīntus mē nōn cōnsuluit. Tūne hoc prōvīdistī? Tenēsne memoriā
5 puellam, parvam ac timidam? Nōn iam timida est; nunc pulchra est, ā multīs amāta.

Dē Caesaris ducis ēgregiīs victōriīs scrīpsistī. Cum magnō studiō litterās tuās lēgī, nam ultima Gallia semper fuit terra nova et nōn mihi nōta. Paucī nūntiī dē Galliā vēnērunt, quī fugam Gallōrum
10 nūntiāvērunt. Caesar victōriīs suīs glōriam et fāmam armōrum Rōmānōrum auxit et pācem effēcit. Caesarī grātiam habēmus quod prō salūte nostrā pugnāvit. Gallōs in fugam datōs nōn iam timēbimus. Alpēs, quae inter nōs et Gallōs stant, nunc Rōmam ā perīculō dē-

---

[1] See **289**.   [2] *this.*

fendunt, nam Gallī timidī trāns Alpēs mīlitēs nōn trānsportābunt. Mīlitēs trāductōs removēre dūrum erit. 15

Sī Caesar mē cōnsulit, librum "Dē Bellō Gallicō" scrībere dēbet. Sī liber ab eō[3] scrībētur, ā multīs hominibus legētur; etiam post spatium multōrum annōrum cum cūrā et dīligentiā legētur.

Litterae tuae nōn longae erant. Cūr longās litterās nōn scrībis? Multa nova in terrīs ultimīs vīdistī atque vidēbis. Valē.[4] 20

QUESTIONS

1. What girl was pretty?
2. Where did Caesar win victories?

318. *Participles Used as Clauses*

The participle, although not much used in English, is very common in Latin. It often is best translated by a subordinate clause, introduced in English by *who,* etc., *when* or *after, since* or *because,*

[3] *him.*   [4] *farewell.*

A round temple of the first century B.C. standing in the Forum Boarium, the ancient cattle market of Rome. The roof is modern.

although, and *if;* at other times, by a coördinate clause, i.e., one connected with the preceding by *and.* The meaning of the Latin sentence as a whole will always show the exact meaning of the participle. Think of the participle's literal meaning before trying to expand it into a clause. The various translations in the following sentences show the flexibility of the Latin participle:

Relative	1.	**Pecūniam** *amissam* **invēnit,** *He found the money which had been lost* (literally, *the lost money*).
Temporal (time)	2.	*Convocātī* **puerī verba magistrī audient,** *After they have been called together, the boys will hear the words of the teacher* (literally, *having been called together*).
Causal	3.	*Territī* **nōn prōcessērunt,** *Because they were scared, they did not advance* (literally, *having been scared*).
Coördinate	4.	**Librum** *lēctum* **tibi dabō,** *I shall read the book and give it to you* (literally, *the book read*).

Observe that (a) the *perfect* participle denotes time *before* that of the leading verb; (b) it agrees like an adjective with a noun or pronoun (sometimes not expressed) in gender, number, and case.

319. Exercises

A. 1. Perīculum prōvīsum nōs nōn terruit.
  2. Rōmānī multa oppida occupāta relīquērunt.
  3. Monitī vōs dē perīculō cōnsulere nōn poterāmus.
  4. Pecūnia, ā mē in viā āmissa, ab amīcō meō inventa est.
  5. Malus puer, ab amīcīs monitus, verbīs addūcī nōn iam potest.

B. Substitute a participle for the words within parentheses:
  1. Quattuor librōs (*after reading them*) accēpī.
  2. Liber bonus (*if read*) semper amīcus vērus erit.
  3. Numerus librōrum (*which I consulted*) magnus fuit.
  4. Multōs librōs lēgī (*because I had been influenced*) ā magistrīs meīs.
  5. Nōnne magnum est pretium ultimae casae (*which was shown to me by you*)?

C. 1. I have read the letter written by my son.
  2. I saw the girl who had been scared by you. (*Express in two ways.*)
  3. The boys read the book because they had been influenced by the teacher's words.

Above: Stamp of Chile with Latin words.
Right: Italian stamp with a quotation from Virgil's "Aeneid" in which Jupiter prophesies the greatness of the Romans.

320. Vocabulary

addū′cō, –ere, addū′xī, adduc′tus, *lead to, influence*	**[dūcō]**
cōn′sulō, –ere, –su′luī, –sul′tus, *consult*	(consultation)
fu′ga, –ae, f., *flight;* **in fu′gam dō,** *put to flight*	**[fugiō]**
nōn iam, adv., *no longer*	
prōvi′deō, –ē′re, –vī′dī, –vī′sus, *foresee*	**[video]**
spa′tium, spa′tī, n., *space, time*	(spacious)
ti′midus, –a, –um, *timid*	(timidity)
ul′timus, –a, –um, *farthest*	(ultimate)

321. The Latin Influence upon English (Cont.)

In an earlier lesson **(310)** we saw that a number of Latin words came into English as result of the Roman occupation of Britain. Other examples are *wall* (from **vāllum**), together with place names like *Walton* (*Walltown*); *port* (from **portus,** *harbor*), together with place names like *Portsmouth; street* (from **strāta**); *Lincoln* (from **colōnia,** *colony*); cf. *Cologne,* the name of a German city which was an ancient Roman colony.

A century and a half after the Angles and Saxons settled in England, Pope Gregory sent missionaries to convert the island to Christianity. Since the missionaries spoke Latin, they introduced a number of new Latin words into English, especially words dealing with the Church, as *temple* **(templum),** *disciple* **(discipulus),** *bishop* **(episcopus).**

Explain *cologne, Stratford, antecedent, relic, providence.*

Ultima Thūlē was a phrase the Romans used for the "Farthest North." This explains why the American base on Greenland was named Thule. Columbus was inspired by a prophecy of the Roman poet Seneca that new worlds **(novōs orbēs)** would be discovered and Thule would no longer be **Ultima Thūlē.**

Lesson XLIV

322. CIRCĒ

Siciliā relīctā, Ulixēs ad rēgnum Aeolī, rēgis ventōrum, nāvigāvit, quī Ulixī ventōs malōs in saccō ligātōs dedit et dīxit: "Malīs ventīs ligātīs, nōn iam impediēris et in patriā tuā salūtem inveniēs."

Itaque multōs diēs [1] Graecī sine impedīmentō et sine cūrā nāvi-
5 gāvērunt, ūnō amīcō ventō āctī, reliquīs ligātīs. Iam Ithacam clārē cernunt. Sed nautae dē saccō cūrā affectī sunt quod dē ventīs quī in saccō erant nihil audīverant. "Praemia et pecūnia in saccō sunt," nauta dīxit. "Rēx Ulixēs nautīs quī mala sustinuērunt pecūniam dare dēbet." Itaque, saccō apertō,[2] ventī expedītī Graecōs ad rēgnum
10 Aeolī redēgērunt. Sed nōn iam Aeolus auxilium dat. Ūnam nāvem Graecī nunc habent, reliquīs āmissīs.

Nunc, impedīmentīs relīctīs, ad īnsulam veniunt quam Circē pulchra regēbat. Vīgintī hominēs, ab Ulixe ad rēgīnam missī, pācem praesidiumque lēgum petīvērunt. Ab Eurylochō [3] duce per silvam
15 ad rēgīnam pedibus ductī sunt, quae eōs [4] in animālia [5] vertit. Eurylochus sōlus in animal nōn versus ad nāvem fūgit et Ulixī omnia [6] dē sociīs impedītīs nūntiāvit. Ulixēs commōtus cum reliquīs auxilium sociīs pressīs dare mātūrāvit. In viā Mercurium deum vīsum cōnsuluit. Mercurius eum [7] monuit et herbam eī [8] dedit. "Hāc [9] herbā,"
20 inquit, "vītam tuam servāre et mīlitēs tuōs expedīre poteris." Ulixēs rēgīnam iussit sociōs in hominēs vertere. Circē Ulixis verbīs et factīs territa animālia in hominēs vertit. Rēgīna, quae nōn iam inimīca fuit, magnam cēnam ac cibōs bonōs parāvit; ita concordiam amīcitiamque redūxit. Sociīs expedītīs, annum ibi Ulixēs mānsit et vītam grātam ēgit.
25 Tum ā sociīs adductus discessit.

QUESTIONS

1. What caused the storm that prevented Ulysses from reaching Ithaca?
2. How did Ulysses find out what Circe had done to his men?
3. By what means did he rescue them?

---

[1] Accusative plural. [2] Participle of **aperiō**, *open*. [3] *Eurylochus* (Ūril′okus).
[4] *them.* [5] Accusative plural: *animals.* [6] *everything.*
[7] *him.* [8] *to him.* [9] *with this.*

From Lester M. Prindle's "Mythology in Prints"

Circe turns some of Ulysses' men into pigs. From an engraving made in 1619. The picture, like many of this period with classical themes, combines details of the time of the artist with some from ancient times. Similarly, modern plays dealing with an earlier period are sometimes given in contemporary dress.

323. Ablative Absolute

In English, we sometimes say, *Such being the case, there is nothing I can do.* Because such phrases as "Such being the case" are used loosely and have no direct connection with either the subject or the predicate of the sentence, they are said to be in the *nominative absolute,* i.e., they are *absolutely free* in a grammatical sense from the rest of the sentence. The phrase quoted above is equivalent to an adverbial clause: *Since such is the case.*

247

In Latin, this loose construction is very common, with this difference: the *ablative* is used instead of the nominative. This independent use of the participial phrase is therefore known as the *ablative absolute*. The perfect participle is most frequently used in this construction. Occasionally a noun, adjective, or present participle is used (examples below).

Consider the participle's *literal* meaning before attempting to expand it into a clause beginning with *when, since, after, because, if, although* (see **318**) or an active participle.

1. *Officiō factō* (lit., *the duty having been done*), **dominus discessit,** *After doing his duty, the master departed.*

2. **Puer,** *litterīs nōn missīs* (lit., *the letter not having been sent*), **pecūniam nōn accēpit,** *Because he did not send the letter, the boy did not receive the money.*

3. **Dux,** *signō datō* (lit., *the signal having been given*), **prōcessit,** *Having given the signal, the general advanced.*

4. *Oppidīs nostrīs captīs* (lit., *our towns captured*), **bellum gerēmus,** *If our towns are captured, we shall wage war.*

In the first three of these sentences, a natural English translation is achieved by converting from the Latin perfect *passive* participle to the English perfect *active* participle (which Latin does not have). The ablative absolute is quite simple if you take the words in order and think of the literal meaning of the participle before rendering it freely into English.

When forms other than the perfect passive participle are used in the ablative absolute, the conversion to English is even simpler. Often you must supply a form of the verb *to be*.

1. *Numā rēge,* **pācem habuimus,** *(When) Numa (was) king, we had peace.*

2. *Populō līberō,* **vīta grāta erit,** *(If) the people (are) free, life will be pleasant.*

When the participle can agree with a noun or pronoun in the main sentence, it does so, and the ablative absolute is not used. Compare the following sentences:

1. **Servus** *monitus* **territus est,** *The slave, having been warned, was terrified.*

2. **Dominus servum** *monitum* **terruit,** *The master terrified the slave he warned* (lit., *the having-been-warned slave*).

But with the ablative absolute,

3. *Servō monitō et territō,* **dominus familiam dīmīsit,** *Having warned and terrified the slave* (lit., *the slave having been warned and terrified*), *the master dismissed the household.*

324. Exercises

    A. In translating the following sentences, be careful to distinguish the ablative absolute from other uses of the participle.
1. Librō āmissō, puella legere nōn potuit.
2. Dux servōrum, signō datō, equōs ēdūcī iussit.
3. Expedītī ex perīculō Deō grātiam habēre dēbēmus.
4. Rōmānī, castrīs positīs, Gallōs in fugam vertērunt.
5. Captīvī miserī, tractī ad pedēs rēgis, pācem timidē petēbant.
6. Impedīmentīs in oppidō relīctīs, mīlitēs salūtem petīverant.
7. Librīs lēctīs, puerī magistrum aequō animō exspectāvērunt.
8. Hominēs, praedā armīsque impedītī, properāre nōn poterant.

A cartoon from the fourth century B.C. The sorceress Circe tries to drug the weary Ulysses. Her loom is at the right.

Department of Antiquities, Ashmolean Museum

B. Translate the words in italics by participles:
1. This boy, *sent* to visit his aunt, lost his way.
2. The boy *having been freed,* everyone was happy.
3. *Having read* the books, we returned them to the library.
4. *After putting* the prisoner in jail, the policeman went home.
5. *After* the money *was given,* the boy was returned to his parents.
6. The boys *having been compelled* to stop fighting, the principal went back to his office.

C. 1. Having written good letters, the boys will receive rewards.
2. Hindered by bad roads, we have not been able to come on foot.
3. The advice of the teacher having been heard, we shall read the book.
4. After sending a messenger, the king shouted: "My kingdom for **(prō)** a horse!"

325. Vocabulary

li′gō, –ā′re, –ā′vī, –ā′tus, *bind* (ligature, ligament)
pēs, pe′dis, m., *foot* (pedal, pedestrian)
  expe′diō, –ī′re, expedī′vī, expedī′tus, (lit., *make the foot free*), *set free*
  impedīmen′tum, –ī, n., *hindrance;* plur., *baggage*
  impe′diō, –ī′re, impedī′vī, impedī′tus, (lit., *entangle the feet*), *hinder*
rēx, rē′gis, m., *king* (regal, royal)
  rēg′num, –ī, n., *royal power, kingdom*
ver′tō, –ere, ver′tī, ver′sus, *turn* (version, vertigo)

Porta San Sebastiano marks the beginning of the Appian Way as it leaves Rome going toward southern Italy.

Alan Oddie/PhotoEdit

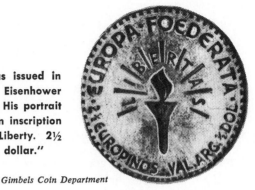

This commemorative coin was issued in 1952 in honor of Dwight D. Eisenhower when he was chief of NATO. His portrait is on the other side. The Latin inscription reads: "Federated Europe. Liberty. 2½ Europinos; value in silver, ½ dollar."

Gimbels Coin Department

326. Latin and English Word Studies

Latin words should not always be studied individually but can often be grouped together by *families,* so to speak. This is much easier, much more useful, and much more interesting. For example, there is the word **pēs,** the father of its family. From it are derived many other words in Latin and in English. **Im-pediō** means to *entangle the feet.* An "impediment" is a *tangle,* something in the way. Transportation is still a big problem with an army; it is no wonder that the Romans, without railroads, aircraft, or motor trucks, called the baggage train of the army **impedīmenta. Ex-pediō** means to get the *foot out* of the tangle; therefore in English an "expedient" is a means of solving a difficulty. To "expedite" matters is to hurry them along by removing obstacles.

Speech impediment.

You have already become acquainted with several other "families" of words **(197).** Other words which should be studied in groups are **regō, rēgnum,** and **rēx; dō** and **dōnō; dūcō** and **dux; ager** and **agricola; cōnsulō** and **cōnsilium.** Show how the members of these families are related.

What is the meaning of *ligature, ligament, obligation, pedestrian*? Why was *Aeolus* chosen as the name of a company dealing in ventilators? What do you really mean when you say "I am much *obliged*"?

327. AMUSEMENTS AND SPORTS

Roman children had as good times as our children have in playing games. Even the babies had their rattles. Girls had dolls; boys played various kinds of marble games with nuts. The phrase **rēlinquere nucēs** (*to give up nuts*) meant to grow up, but grown men, even the Emperor Augustus, sometimes played such games. Vacation was the time for marble games. The poet Martial says: "Sadly the boy leaves his marbles and is called back to school by the teacher—the Saturnalia [Christmas] vacation is all over."

Other amusements included spinning tops, walking on stilts, flying kites, rolling hoops (p. 417), playing with toy wagons (p. 276) and toy soldiers. Among Roman children's games were also blindman's buff, hide and seek, leapfrog, jacks. Ball games, some like today's tennis and handball, were favorites, especially for men who played at the large public baths.

Bowling with walnuts. The boy in the center bends to throw at walnut "castles" built up on the ground. He has already knocked two piles down, and a fight is breaking out behind him. The girls at the left play a gentler game.

The Vatican

For indoor amusement the Romans had a board game which was something like chess and checkers, and another like the many games we have in which the throwing of dice controls the number of moves made on a board.

Roman boys and men had their sports—swimming, fishing, hunting (p. 14), as well as athletic contests: running, jumping, throwing the discus, boxing, wrestling, fencing.

The chief amusements for the people as a whole were the circus, the gladiatorial shows, and the theater. The oldest and most popular was the circus with its races, more fully described in the "Story of Lucius" in **328** (see also pictures, pp. 257–259). The races were the main thing; gradually various side shows and acrobatic exhibitions were added to fill in the time between races. The modern circus is a revival of the ancient, but the chariot races no longer have the same prominence. Even the circus parade which precedes the performance today is borrowed from the Romans, who called it a **pompa.**

Roman lamp showing men playing a game. The man at the left has just thrown the dice. Found at Tabessa, Algeria.

The Arena and Amphitheater in Arles, France. The arena was used by the Romans for various athletic contests and games. The amphitheater was for plays and public readings.

The circus games were held at public expense on holidays. They took place in the valley between the Palatine and Aventine hills. Originally the people sat on the hillsides; later, magnificent stands seating as many as 200,000 people were built. Other circuses were built in Rome and elsewhere, but the original Circus Maximus remained the chief one.

The games created as much interest as our baseball, football, soccer, and hockey. There were various racing clubs, distinguished by their colors, like those in modern schools and colleges; we are reminded also of the Red Sox and White Sox of baseball. Drivers were popular heroes and often became rich. Their records and those of the horses were carefully kept. One man is said to have won 3559 races. This is much like the attention we give to the number of home runs made by famous baseball players.

The theater was another important place for outdoor amusement. In imitation of Greek custom, Roman theaters were semicircular. The actors usually wore masks that indicated what kind of part the actor was playing. Women's parts were played by men. Both comedies and tragedies were given. The most famous Roman writers of comedies were Plautus and Terence, whose plays are not only still being performed but have even been turned into Broadway hits—*The Boys from Syracuse* and *A Funny Thing Happened on the Way to the Forum.*

The gladiatorial contests were rather late importations from Etruria, the region to the north of Rome. At first they consisted of sword fights between two men, curiously enough, at funerals. Later on they became very popular. Fights between men and animals (like the Spanish bullfights) were added, as well as fights between animals. Sometimes very elaborate shows were put on in open-air amphitheaters. The famous Colosseum at Rome **(277),** which had room for 50,000 people, was not built until 80 A.D.

QUESTIONS

1. What modern sports compare with the circus games of the Romans in popular appeal?
2. In what ways did the Roman theater differ from ours?
3. What were good and bad features of the gladiatorial contests?

255

UNIT VIII REVIEW

Lessons XL–XLIV

The Story of Lucius (cont.)

328. CIRCUS

Dē "lūdō" in quō magister docēbat lēgistis. Sed erat etiam "lūdus" [1] in quō ōtium agēbātur; nam puerī Rōmānī nōn semper labōrābant sed etiam lūdēbant. Dictum est: "Puerī puerī erunt."

"THE PARADE'S COMING"

Fēriae [2] erant. Lūcius, amīcus noster parvus, ad lūdōs pūblicōs
5 in Circō factōs ā servō adductus est. Multī hominēs ad Circum con-
veniēbant; nam populus lūdōs probābat amābatque. Nōn paucī ante
lūcem [3] vēnerant. Locīs commodīs beneficiō amīcī inventīs, Lūcius
et servus exspectāvērunt. Sed quid audiunt? Servus clāmat: "Pompa
venit! Pompa venit!" Pompa per Forum et Sacram Viam ad Circum
10 prōcesserat et nunc per portam in Circum prōcēdēbat. In pompā
fuērunt deōrum fōrmae, virī, puerī, equī, quadrīgae,[4] aurīgae.[5]

THE CHARIOT RACE: "THEY'RE OFF!"

Pompā per Circum ēductā, Lūcius cum studiō exspectāvit. Tum sex
quadrīgae, ad portam redāctae, signum exspectāvērunt. Signō datō,
equī ā portā missī sunt.

15   Inter aurīgās fuit Pūblius, quī magnam fāmam ob multās victōriās
habuit. Erat amīcus firmus familiae Lūcī nostrī, et Lūcius multa dē
Circō ā Pūbliō cognōverat. Nunc Lūcius cum reliquīs Pūblium magnō
studiō spectābat.

---

[1] See Vocabulary.   [2] *holidays.*   [3] **From lūx.**
[4] *four-horse chariots.*   [5] *charioteers.*

256

Air view of the Circus Maximus in Rome, in a valley between the Aventine (above) and Palatine hills. Modern buildings above, ruins of the ancient imperial palace below.

Fototeca

PUBLIUS HANDICAPPED AT THE START

Sed Pūblius habuit ūnum equum quī erat novus et timidus et tardus; reliquae quadrīgae antecessērunt. Lūcius magnā cūrā affectus, 20 fortūnam malam amīcī prōvīderat. Sed victōria nōn āmissa erat; nam septem spatia erant.

TWO CHARIOTS OUT OF THE RACE

In mediō Circō erat longa spīna.[6] Terminī spīnae "mētae" appellātī sunt. Magnum erat perīculum aurīgārum ad mētās. Itaque in prīmō spatiō nec prīmus nec secundus aurīga quadrīgās ā mētīs 25 regere potuit. Ēiectī [7] per [8] terram equīs tractī sunt atque iniūriās accēpērunt. Servī virōs ad spīnam portāvērunt et auxilium dedērunt.

PUBLIUS STILL LAST

Nunc erant quattuor quadrīgae. Sex spatia restābant, sed Pūblius antecēdere nōn poterat. Quīnque, quattuor spatia restābant. Pūblius ultimus erat. Duo spatia restābant; populus clāmābat et cōnsilium 30 multum Pūbliō dabat sed nōn audiēbātur. Pūblius magnā cūrā equōs regēbat et etiam retinēbat, sed populus nōn cognōverat. Ūnum spatium restābat; Lūcius commōtus lacrimās retinēre nōn potuit. Fortūna inimīca erat.

[6] *wall.*   [7] *thrown out.*   [8] *over.*

Chariot race from the motion picture "Ben Hur." The leading racers are rounding the sharp, dangerous curve, where many spills took place in the seven-lap races. The wall in the center was called a "spina," "spine."

"AND THE LAST SHALL BE FIRST!"

35 Sed quid vidēmus? Pūblius antecēdit! Nōn iam equōs retinet sed incitat. Ūnus equus, "Parātus" appellātus (nam semper parātus erat), integer fuit et properāre incipit. Nōn iam Pūblius erat ultimus; iam tertium, iam secundum locum tenet. Ūnus aurīga ante Pūblium restat. Aequī sunt—deī sunt bonī!—prīmus ad mētam ultimam Pūblius venit
40 et victōriae praemia quae meruit accipit! Et Lūcius—quid faciēbat? Clāmābāt: "Iō! Iō! Pūblius! Parātus! Clāra victōria!"

QUESTIONS

1. What was the route of the parade?
2. How many laps were there in the race?
3. How many chariots took part?
4. What kept Publius from being in the lead at the start?
5. What helped him win?

258

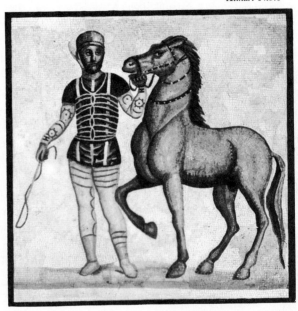

A charioteer with favorite horse and whip, shown in a mosaic.

Alinari Photo

329. VOCABULARY

NOUNS			
1. dux	4. homō	8. pāx	12. salūs
2. factum	5. impedīmentum	9. pēs	13. spatium
3. fuga	6. lēx	10. rēgnum	
	7. mīles	11. rēx	

ADJECTIVES			
14. certus	15. nōtus	17. tertius	19. ultimus
	16. parātus	18. timidus	

VERBS			
20. addūcō	24. commoveō	29. possum	34. stō
21. antecēdō	25. cōnsulō	30. premō	35. trādūcō
22. cernō	26. expediō	31. prōvideō	36. trānsportō
23. clāmō	27. impediō	32. relinquō	37. vertō
	28. ligō	33. rogō	

ADVERBS		
	38. fortasse	39. nōn iam

259

330. VOCABULARY (English Meanings)

NOUNS
1. leader
2. deed
3. flight
4. man
5. hindrance
6. law
7. soldier
8. peace
9. foot
10. kingdom
11. king
12. health, safety
13. space

ADJECTIVES
14. sure
15. known
16. prepared
17. third
18. timid
19. farthest

VERBS
20. influence
21. go before
22. discern
23. cry out
24. disturb
25. consult
26. set free
27. hinder
28. bind
29. can
30. press
31. foresee
32. leave behind
33. ask
34. stand
35. lead across
36. transport
37. turn

ADVERBS
38. perhaps
39. no longer

331. GRAMMAR SUMMARY

Absolute Construction

In Latin	In English
1. Ablative.	1. Nominative.
2. Perfect passive participle usually.	2. Present or past active or passive participle.
3. Construction very common.	3. Construction much less common.

332. UNIT PRACTICE AND EXERCISES

Participle Drill

A. Substitute a Latin participle in the right gender, number, and case for the words in italics:
1. Perīcula (*if foreseen*) mē nōn terrent.
2. Librum (*after I had read it*) amīcō dōnāvī.
3. Puerī (*although they were called*)nōn vēnērunt.
4. Puellae (*because they had been scared*) fūgērunt.
5. Auxilium (*which had been furnished*) ā sociīs nostrīs patriam cōnservāvit.

B. Translate the ablative absolute in each of the following sentences into good English:
1. **Litterīs scrīptīs,** I took a walk.
2. **Rēgnō āmissō,** he was still king.
3. **Auxiliō missō,** they can still win.
4. **Agrīs occupātīs,** the people were starving.

260

Form Drill

1. Decline **rēx magnus, lēx bona.**
2. What is the case of **ducum, hominī, mīlitibus, disciplīnae, pācem?**
3. Give in all tenses the third plural of **possum,** translating each tense form.
4. Give the principal parts of **commoveō, dō, expediō, submittō, absum, prōpōnō, premō.**

Numerals Drill

1. The teacher assigns a number—"Ūnus," "Duo," "Trēs," etc., to each of ten pupils. The following questions and others like them should be answered by the pupil whose number furnishes the correct answer.

   MAGISTER: Quot (*how many*) sunt trēs et quattuor?
   DISCIPULUS "SEPTEM": Trēs et quattuor sunt septem.
   M.: Quot sunt quattuor et quīnque?
   D. "NOVEM": Quattuor et quīnque sunt novem.
   (A competitive game can be made by having two sets of ten or less and scoring one for the side whose representative answers first.)

2. Give the Latin word for the missing numeral represented by the question mark:

   a. III + V = ? *c.* IV + ? = X *e.* X − ? = VIII
   b. XII ÷ III = ? *d.* II × V = ? *f.* VI − I = ?

333. ENGLISH WORD STUDIES

1. Make a sketch map of England (not including Scotland) and indicate on it all the names you can of towns derived from Latin **castra.** Then see how many of these town names are found either in the United States and in how many states, or, if you prefer, in some other country.

2. The first word in each of the following lines is a Latin word. From among the last five words in each line pick the one which is an English derivative of the first word.

stāre	status	stair	stare	star	stay
hominī	homely	home	hominy	homicide	hum
mīles	mile	militant	mill	millinery	million
premō	supreme	premises	premonition	express	prime
clāmō	clam	clamp	clammy	inclement	exclaim
pāx	pace	packs	Pacific	impact	pass

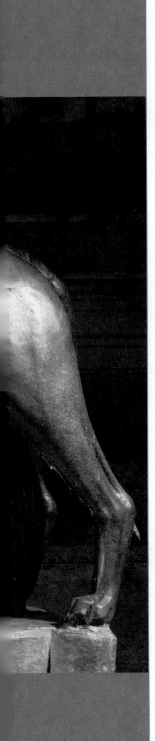

UNIT IX

MYTH AND HISTORY

According to legend, Romulus and Remus were the twin sons of Mars and the Vestal virgin Rhea Silvia. When the babies were thrown into the Tiber River, they were miraculously saved by a she-wolf, who nursed them until they were found later by shepherds. Upon reaching adulthood, Romulus killed his brother in a quarrel and became the founder of Rome. This famous bronze of the wolf dates from the Etruscan times (c. fifth century B.C.).

Scala/Art Resource

A Roman mosaic from Cherchel, Algeria, showing Ulysses in his ship, with the two Sirens, half women, half birds, at each end, along with playful dolphins.

Lesson XLV

334. SĪRĒNĒS ET PHAEĀCIA

Annō in īnsulā quam Circē rēxit āctō, Ulixēs ad Sīrēnēs [1] vēnit. Sīrēnēs corpora avium [2] et capita puellārum habuērunt. Carmina pulchra canēbant, quibus nautae mōtī nāvēs ad saxa vertēbant. Hōc [3] modō vītam āmittēbant.

5 Sed Ulixēs dē Sīrēnibus ā Circē [4] monitus erat. Perīculō prōvīsō, aurēs [5] sociōrum cērā [6] clausit, sed nōn suās. Iussit manūs [7] pedēsque suōs ad nāvem ligārī. Hōc modō carmina Sīrēnum clārē audīvit neque vītam āmīsit.

Posteā sociī Ulixis interfectī sunt et Ulixēs sōlus ad īnsulam 10 parvam āctus est in quā habitābat rēgīna pulchra cui [8] nōmen erat Calypsō. Rēgīna Ulixem nōn dīmīsit. Itaque Ulixēs ibi octō annōs— longum temporis spatium—remānsit. Sed tum Iuppiter rēgīnam iussit Ulixī nāvem parāre. Hōc factō, Ulixēs expedītus rēgīnam relīquit.

Sed nāvis undīs frācta est ad īnsulam cui [8] nōmen erat Phaeācia. [9] 15 Vulneribus impedītus homō miser vix potuit corpus in silvam fīniti- mam ad flūmen trahere, ubi somnum cēpit.

Interim Nausicaa, [10] rēgis Phaeāciae fīlia, cum aliīs puellīs carrō ad flūmen prōcēdēbat, quod in flūmine vestēs lavāre cupīvit; nam tempus mātrimōnī Nausicaae aderat. Ubi vestēs in flūmine lāvērunt, 20 labōre intermissō, Nausicaa pilam [11] ad reliquās puellās in ōrdine iaciēbat. Sed puella quaedam [12] in flūmen pilam iēcit. Clāmōribus puellārum ab Ulixe audītīs, Ulixēs nōn dubitāvit sed pilam ex aquā servāvit. Puellae timidae fugere incipiunt, quod is ob mala atque vulnera quae sustinuerat nōn iam pulcher erat. Sed Nausicaa nōn

---

[1] the Sī′rens.   [2] of birds.   [3] this (ablative).   [4] Ablative.
[5] ears.   [6] wax.   [7] hands.   [8] whose.
[9] Phaeacia (Fēā′shia).   [10] Nausic′āa.   [11] ball.   [12] one girl.

territa ante Ulixem stetit et eī[13] grātiās ēgit. Vestibus plicātīs, ad 25
oppidum in ōrdine prōcessērunt. Ulixēs ab rēge Alcinoō[14] acceptus
est, cui factīs clārīs nōtus fuit. Paucōs diēs Ulixēs in Phaeāciā mānsit.
Tum Alcinous Ulixem ad patriam Ithacam mīsit. Itaque post vīgintī
annōs Ulixēs sōlus sine sociīs ad patriam vēnit.

Ulixe in Ithacā vīsō, Neptūnus nāvem in quā Ulixēs trānsportātus 30
erat ante portum Phaeāciae in saxum vertit. Portus īnsulae hōc[15]
impedīmentō clausus est neque posteā Alcinous et hominēs īnsulae
nāvigāre potuērunt.

QUESTIONS

1. How did Ulysses manage to hear the Sirens without danger?
2. Why did Nausicaa go to the river?
3. With how many comrades did Ulysses return?

335. Third Declension: Neuter Nouns

	ENDINGS		EXAMPLE	
	SINGULAR	PLURAL	SINGULAR	PLURAL
Nom.	—	–a	corpus	corpora
Gen.	–is	–um	corporis	corporum
Dat.	–ī	–ibus	corporī	corporibus
Acc.	—	–a	corpus	corpora
Abl.	–e	–ibus	corpore	corporibus

In the third declension, as in the second, the nominative and accusative singular of neuter nouns are alike. The nominative and accusative
plural both end in **–a.**

[13] *to him.* [14]*Alcinous (Alsin'o-us).* [15] *this.*

**The ship of the Phaeacians that brought Ulysses home was turned into a rocky
island—and here it is, so they say, near the island of Corfu in the Adriatic.**

Puellae timidae fugere incipiunt. The helmeted goddess Minerva watches Ulysses come out of the water. Nausicaa looks ready to run (section 334).

Practice

1. Decline **nōmen clārum.**
2. Tell the form of **flūminum, capita, tempus, lēgēs, vulnerī, nōmine, rēgibus.**

336. Exercises

A. 1. Quae nōmina flūminum Galliae cognōvistis?
2. Corpore hominis inventō, mīles ducem vocāvit.
3. Pāce factā, ōrdō certus in Eurōpā nōn reductus est.
4. Ob tempus annī frūmentum trānsportāre nōn poterāmus.
5. Litterae quās fīlia mea scrīpsit nec caput nec pedem habent.
6. Rēx, victōriā barbarōrum territus, mīlitēs trāns flūmen trādūxit.

B. 1. The river which you see is wide.
2. Horses have large bodies but small heads.
3. (There) were many wounds on the farmer's body.
4. Since the river is closed, grain can no longer be transported.

337. Vocabulary

ca′put, ca′pitis, n., *head*	(capital, chief)
clau′dō, –ere, clau′sī, clau′sus, *close*	(clause, include)
cor′pus, cor′poris, n., *body*	(corporation, corpse)
flū′men, flū′minis, n., *river*	(fluid)
nō′men, nō′minis, n., *name*	(nominate, nominative)
ōr′dō, ōr′dinis, m., *order, rank*	(ordinary)
tem′pus, tem′poris, n., *time*	(temporal, temporary)
vul′nus, vul′neris, n., *wound*	(vulnerable)

338. English Word Studies

1. Many English words preserve the original Latin forms of the third declension:

SINGULAR	PLURAL	SINGULAR	PLURAL
amanuen- sis	amanuenses	insigne (sing- ular rare)	insignia
apex	apexes or apices	stamen	stamens or stamina (with
appendix	appendixes or appendices		difference of meaning)
genus	genera	vertex	vertexes or vertices
index	indexes or indices		viscera (singular rare)

Nouns with their plurals in **–s** are *consul, ratio,* and many nouns in **–or:** *doctor, actor, factor, labor, victor,* etc.

Decapitate.

2. Explain *contemporary, invulnerable, decapitate, capitalism, capital punishment.* What is a *corporation?* What is meant by *incorporated?* State two ways in which *siren* is used today.

3. There is a town named *Calypso* in North Carolina.

Lesson XLVI

339. PĒNELOPĒ

Ulixēs, nāvī et sociīs āmissīs, corpore vulneribus cōnfectō, in patriam pervēnerat. Ad fīnem itineris sed nōn labōrum perpetuōrum vēnerat. Et cīvēs et hostēs crēdidērunt Ulixem nōn iam vīvum esse.

Prīmus quī Ulixem vīdit sed nōn cognōvit erat pāstor cuius nōmen
5 erat Eumaeus. Ab Eumaeō Ulixēs nōn pauca dē uxōre Pēnelopē et fīliō Tēlemachō audīvit. Tēlemachus ab īnsulā tum aberat, quod Pēnelopē eum [1] trāns mare ad ultima rēgna cīvitātēsque Graeciae mīserat, in quibus locīs itinera faciēbat et Ulixem petēbat. Per multōs annōs nūllam fāmam dē Ulixe Pēnelopē accēperat. Interim multī ducēs
10 rēgēsque cupiditāte rēgnī Ulixis adductī dē montibus Ithacae et ē fīnitimīs īnsulīs convēnerant et rēgīnam in mātrimōnium petēbant. Cīvēs hōs [2] hostēs ē fīnibus Ithacae sine auxiliō ad montēs redigere nōn poterant. Itaque Pēnelopē, capite submissō, dīxit:

"Ubi vestem quam faciō cōnfēcerō, nōn iam dubitābō in mātri-
15 mōnium darī."

Itaque exspectāvērunt. Sed cōnsilium Pēnelopae fuit tempus tra-here. Itaque nocte retexēbat [3] vestem quam multā dīligentiā texuerat. Post trēs annōs hominēs cōnsilium Pēnelopae cognōvērunt, et Pēne-lopē vestem cōnficere coācta est.

20 Hōc [4] tempore Ulixēs nāvī ad īnsulam Ithacam trānsportātus est. Eōdem [5] tempore Tēlemachus ā Minervā monitus in patriam prope-rāvit. Ibi ad mare ab Ulixe vīsus atque cognitus est. Ulixēs Tēle-machum ad oppidum antecēdere iussit. Ab Ulixe monitus Tēlemachus neque mātrī neque aliīs dē patre nūntiāvit.

QUESTIONS

1. Who was Telemachus' father?
2. Why was Telemachus away when Ulysses arrived in Ithaca?
3. How did Penelope deceive the suitors?

---

[1] *him.*   [2] *these.*   [3] *unwove.*   [4] *at this.*   [5] *at the same.*

Penelope, as imagined by the sixteenth-century Italian architect-painter Peruzzi.

Alinari Photo

340. Third Declension: I-Stem Nouns

The group of nouns which have **–ium** instead of **–um** in the genitive plural are called *i–stem nouns*. In addition to this difference, neuters ending in **–e** have **–ī** instead of **–e** in the ablative singular, and **–ia** in the nominative and accusative plural. The classes of masculine and feminine **i**–stem nouns are:

1. Nouns ending in **–is** having no more syllables in the genitive than in the nominative: **cīvis.**
2. Nouns of *one* syllable whose base ends in two consonants: **pars** (gen. **part–is**), **nox** (gen. **noct–is**).

	SINGULAR	PLURAL		SINGULAR	PLURAL
Nom.	cīvis	cīvēs	mare	maria
Gen.	cīvis	cīvium	maris	marium
Dat.	cīvī	cīvibus	marī	maribus
Acc.	cīvem	cīvēs [6]	mare	maria
Abl.	cīve	cīvibus	marī	maribus

[6] Occasionally **–īs** is used in the accusative plural.

Like Penelope waiting for Ulysses, this woman carries out her household duties with her maid. A red-figured vase of about 465 B.C.

Courtesy, Museum of Fine Arts, Boston, Gift of Dr. Lloyd E. Hawes

Practice

1. Decline **nāvis pulchra, iter longum.**
2. Give the singular and plural in Latin in the case required: *high mountain* (gen.), *level sea* (acc.), *small mountains* (dat.), *neighboring enemy* (abl.), *our end* (nom.).

341. Exercises

A. 1. Ad fīnem itineris longī vēnērunt.
2. Altōs montēs et flūmina alta [7] in Eurōpā vīdī.
3. Bonī cīvēs officia pūblica suscipere nōn dubitant.
4. Parvā nāvī colōnī trāns mare lātum ad prōvinciam migrāvērunt.
5. Ob numerum hostium quī in montibus erant cīvēs in castrīs remānsērunt.

B. 1. By whom was a ship seen on a mountain?
2. We have made a long journey but can now see the end.
3. A large number of citizens was called together by the leader.
4. If [8] the sea is closed, the enemy's ships will not be able to transport soldiers.

---

[7] *deep,* when applied to a river, sea, etc.   [8] Use ablative absolute.

342. Vocabulary

*cī′vis, cī′vis,[9] **cī′vium,** m., *citizen* (civic, civil)

cōnfi′ciō, –ere, –fē′cī, –fec′tus, (*do thoroughly*), *complete, exhaust* (cf. "do up") **[faciō]**

*fī′nis, fī′nis, fī′nium, m., *end;* plur., *borders, territory* (final, finite)

*hos′tis, hos′tis, hos′tium, m., *enemy,* [10] usually plur. (hostile)

i′ter, iti′neris, n., *journey, road, march* (itinerary)

*ma′re, ma′ris, ma′rium, n., *sea* (marine, submarine)

*mōns, mon′tis, mon′tium, m., *mountain* (mount, montane)

*nā′vis, nā′vis,[11] **nā′vium,** f., *ship* (navy, naviform)

343. English Word Studies

1. Many Latin ī–stem nouns ending in **–is** are preserved in their original form in English. The original plural in **–es** is pronounced like "ease": *axis, axes; basis, bases.*

Distinguish *axēs* from *axĕs* (plural of *ax*), *basēs* from *basĕs* (plural of *base*).

2. Latin phrases in English:

Tempus fugit, *Time flies.*

per capita, *by heads* or *individuals.*

me iudice, *in my judgment* (lit., *I being judge*).

Fata viam invenient, *The Fates will find a way.*

pro tem. (pro tempore), *for the time, temporarily.*

de jure, *according to right,* as a **de jure** government; cf. **de facto (316).**

---

[9] Nouns marked with an asterisk (*) are **i**–stem nouns. The genitive plural of such nouns is always given in the lesson vocabularies.

[10] *national enemy,* differing from **inimīcus,** personal enemy.

[11] The ablative singular ends in **–ī.** A few other masculine and feminine nouns sometimes have this ending.

Foto Soprintendenza alle Gallerie delle Campania

Canis tamen Ulixis dominum cognovit. A relief from a second century A.D. Roman sarcophagus, now in a Naples Museum.

Lesson XLVII

344. FĪNIS LABŌRUM

Ulixēs, rēx fortis Ithacae, ad portās oppidī quod rēxerat stābat, ā multīs cīvibus vīsus, sed nōn cognitus, quod vestēs sordidās gerēbat. In oppidum facilī itinere prōcessit. Multōs servōs vīdit ā quibus nōn cognitus est. Canis tamen Ulixis dominum cognōvit et gaudiō [1] affectus
5 ē vītā excessit. Ubi Ulixēs ad rēgīnam adductus est, omnēs procī [2] eum [3] hostem appellāvērunt et discēdere iussērunt. Sed tamen Pēnelopē, quae eum nōn cognōverat, vestibus sordidīs permōta eum manēre iussit et eī [4] cibum dedit.

Pēnelopē vestem cōnfēcerat et nunc tempus aderat quō iūs erat
10 marītum dēligere. Iussit magnum arcum [5] pōnī ante procōs [2] quem

---

[1] *joy.*   [2] *suitors.*   [3] *him.*   [4] *to him.*   [5] *bow.*

Ulixēs clārus ante vīgintī annōs tetenderat. Tum nūntiāvit:

"Homō quī arcum Ulixis fortis tendere poterit marītus meus erit; marītus novus pār Ulixī esse dēbet. Ita iūs est."

Itaque singulī in ōrdine arcum cēpērunt sed tendere nōn potuērunt quod Ulixī parēs nōn fuērunt. Tum Ulixēs arcum petīvit. Omnēs 15 rīsērunt,[6] sed Pēnelopē iussit arcum Ulixī darī, nam iūs erat. Id [7] quod reliquī nōn facere poterant—arcum tendere—Ulixī facile erat. Tum in procōs arcum tendit, quōs in fugam dedit. Tēlemachus et Eumaeus auxilium dedērunt. Ulixēs omnēs portās oppidī claudī iusserat, ob quam causam procī ex oppidō ad montēs fugere nōn potuērunt. Salūte 20 petītā, nōn inventā, omnēs interfectī sunt. Hōc [8] modō rēgnum et uxōrem Ulixēs recēpit et in lībertāte pāceque vītam ēgit. Nōn iam nāvibus itinera trāns maria faciēbat.

QUESTIONS

1. Why was Ulysses not recognized?
2. Why did everyone laugh when Ulysses asked for the bow?
3. Why did Ulysses not reveal his identity immediately?

[6] From **rīdeō.**   [7] *that.*   [8] *this.*

Penelope is often pictured in an attitude of mourning. This small Greek relief was once a decoration attached to furniture. It shows Ulysses gesturing to Penelope. Behind her is Telemachus.

The Metropolitan Museum of Art, Fletcher Fund, 1930

345. Adjectives of the Third Declension

The adjectives so far studied, such as **magnus, –a, –um** and **sacer, –cra, –crum,** have been declined like nouns of the first and second declensions. Many adjectives, however, belong to the third declension. With the exception of one important class, which will be studied later, almost all adjectives of the third declension are **i**–stems. They are divided into classes according to the number of forms which are used in the nominative singular to show gender, as follows:

1. **Two endings** [9]—masculine and feminine in **–is,** neuter in **–e: fortis, forte.**
2. **One ending**—one form for all genders: **pār.**

Adjectives of the third declension have **–ī** in the ablative singular, **–ium** in the genitive plural, and **–ia** in the neuter nominative and accusative plural. Note particularly that the ablative singular, unlike that of most **i**–stem *nouns,* ends in **–ī.**

	SINGULAR		PLURAL	
	M., F.	N.	M., F.	N.
Nom.	fortis	forte	fortēs	fortia
Gen.	fortis	fortis	fortium	fortium
Dat.	fortī	fortī	fortibus	fortibus
Acc.	fortem	forte	fortēs [10]	fortia
Abl.	fortī	fortī	fortibus	fortibus
Nom.	pār	pār	parēs	paria
Gen.	paris	paris	parium	parium
Dat.	parī	parī	paribus	paribus
Acc.	parem	pār	parēs [10]	paria
Abl.	parī	parī	paribus	paribus

Practice

1. Decline **lībertās pār, iter facile.**
2. Give in Latin: *brave boys* (acc.), *brave citizen* (abl.), *all towns* (gen.), *equal right* (acc.), *few enemies* (dat.).

[9] A few adjectives in **–er** have *three endings* in the nominative singular, one for each gender: **celer, celeris, celere.**
[10] Occasionally **–īs** is used instead of **–ēs** (**340,** footnote 6).

Below: Libertas. The Statue of Liberty in New York harbor, once used as a lighthouse. She is dressed in Roman garb.

UPI/Bettmann Newsphotos

Above: Roman coin showing lighthouse at Messina, Sicily, with statue of Neptune.

Above: Ancient lighthouse at Dover, England, restored.

346. Exercises

A. 1. Quid est pretium lībertātis?
2. Servus fortibus factīs lībertātem obtinuit.
3. Omnia maria nāvibus hostium clausa erant.
4. In nostrā patriā omnēs cīvēs sunt līberī et parēs.
5. Nōvistīne, amīce bone, hominem quem in nāvī vīdimus?
6. Facilī itinere inventō, dux omnēs mīlitēs dē montibus dūcere mātūrāvit.

B. 1. All free men love peace.
2. Nature has given us many beautiful (things).
3. We ought not to undertake a long journey now.
4. It will not be easy to defend the freedom of our country on the sea.

347. Vocabulary

fa′cilis, fa′cile, (lit., "do-able"), *easy*	**[faciō]**
for′tis, for′te, *strong, brave*	(fort, fortitude)
iūs, iū′ris, n., *right*	(jury, justice)
līber′tās,[11] **lībertā′tis,** f., *freedom*	**[līber]**
om′nis, om′ne, *all, every*	(omniscient)
pār, gen. **pa′ris,** *equal*	(parity, peer)
ta′men, adv., *nevertheless*	
ten′dō, –ere, teten′dī, ten′tus, *stretch*	(tendon, intent)

348. English Word Studies

A number of English nouns and adjectives preserve the nominative singular, and a few the nominative plural of Latin adjectives of the third declension: *par, pauper, simplex, duplex,* etc.; *September,* etc.; *amanuensis.* Neuter forms occur in *simile, facsimile, insignia* (singular rare), *regalia* (singular rare), *forte* (singular only). The dative plural is seen in *omnibus* (a vehicle *for all*); in the common shortened form *bus* only the ending is left.

---

[11] All nouns ending in –tās are feminine.

Roman toys now in the Toronto Museum.

Faustulus Romulum et Remum invenit. A painting by the artist Rubens (1577–1640). Stories of babies nourished by wolves and other animals are still heard occasionally.

Alinari Photo

Lesson XLVIII

349. RŌMULUS ET REMUS

Silvius Proca, rēx fortis Albānōrum,[1] Numitōrem et Amūlium fīliōs habuit. Numitōrī rēgnum relīquit, sed Amūlius, Numitōre ē cīvitāte pulsō, rēxit. Rhēa Silvia, fīlia Numitōris, geminōs [2] Rōmulum et Remum habuit. Geminōrum pater deus Mārs erat; itaque Mārs auctor populī Rōmānī appellābātur. Amūlius puerōs in Tiberī flūmine pōnī 5 iussit. Sed aqua geminōs in siccō [3] relīquit. Lupa [4] accessit et puerōs aluit.[5] Posteā Faustulus, pāstor rēgis, puerōs invēnit. Post multōs annōs Rōmulō et Remō dīxit: "Numitor est avus vester." Adductī pāstōris verbīs, geminī Amūlium interfēcērunt et Numitōrī, quem Amūlius ē cīvitāte pepulerat, rēgnum mandāvērunt. 10

Posteā oppidum mūnīvērunt in locō in quō inventī erant, quod dē nōmine Rōmulī Rōmam appellāvērunt.

Rōmulus Remusque parēs erant, sed tamen Rōmulō nōn facile erat Remō cēdere. Remō interfectō, Rōmulus sōlus Rōmānōs rēxit et omnibus iūra dedit. 15

QUESTIONS

1. How was Amulius related to Numitor?
2. To Rhea Silvia?
3. To Remus?

---

[1] *the Albans.*   [2] *twins.*   [3] *on dry ground.*   [4] *wolf.*   [5] *fed.*

277

350. Developing "Word Sense"

By now it should be clear that a Latin word may have many shades of meaning, which are suggested by the context. In translating, therefore, do not stick to the "vocabulary" meaning of the word, but use the one required in good English. Note the varying translation of **magnus** when used with the following nouns:

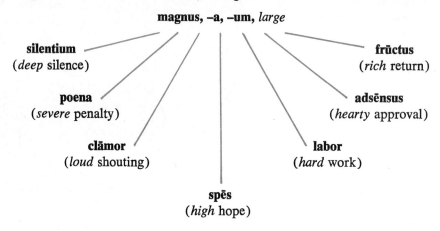

magnus, –a, –um, *large*

silentium
(*deep* silence)

poena
(*severe* penalty)

clāmor
(*loud* shouting)

spēs
(*high* hope)

frūctus
(*rich* return)

adsēnsus
(*hearty* approval)

labor
(*hard* work)

Practice

1. Combine **magnus** with each of the following nouns already studied and translate freely: **perīculum, studium, pecūnia, pretium.**
2. How does **altus** differ when applied to rivers and mountains?
3. Translate **puella pulchra** and **homō pulcher.**

Roman ruins at Sabratha, Libya, in northern Africa.

James Sawders

A later copy of the famous she-wolf, symbol of Rome, mounted on an Ionic column in Rome. Beneath her are the twins Romulus and Remus.

Anthony Paccione

351. Exercises

A. 1. Ego aut viam inveniam aut faciam.
2. Dēbēmusne, pāce factā, numerum nāvium augēre?
3. Flūmina omnia Italiae ex montibus ad mare tendunt.
4. Auctōrēs librōrum nōn semper magnam pecūniam merent.
5. Poteruntne hostēs, montibus occupātīs, posteā iter facere?
6. Post multōs annōs Rōmānī iūra cīvitātis omnibus dedērunt.
7. Post oppidum erat mōns altus, in quō fortēs mīlitēs hostium pulsī erant.

B. 1. Is it not pleasing to all men to see friends?
2. The road stretches through the mountains.
3. Equal rights of citizenship were given to many Gauls.
4. My father made many journeys across high mountains and deep seas.
5. After a long journey my friend is approaching **(ad)** the end of life.

352. Vocabulary

auc′tor, auctō′ris, m., *maker, author*	(authorize)
cī′vitās, cīvitā′tis, f., *citizenship, state*	**[cīvis]**
pa′ter, pa′tris, m., *father*	(paternal)
pel′lō, –ere, pe′pulī, pul′sus, *drive, defeat*	(repulsive)
post, prep. with acc., *behind* (of place); *after* (of time)	
post′eā, adv., *afterwards*	

A pagan tomb below the Church of St. Peter in Rome; its discovery caused a sensation. Modern Rome rests on ancient Rome, literally and figuratively. This may be seen everywhere but nowhere more strikingly than here. (See also p. 60.)

353. English Word Studies

1. The suffix –tās is usually found in nouns formed from adjectives. Its English form is –ty, which is to be distinguished from –y **(232).**

What must be the Latin words from which are derived *commodity, integrity, liberty, publicity, timidity, variety?* Note that the letter preceding the ending is usually –i–.

2. Latin phrases in English:

ad fin. (ad finem), *near the end* (of the page).
P.S. (post scriptum), *written after* (at the end of a letter).

What is the sense behind the motto of the University of Texas: **Disciplina praesidium civitatis?** The inscription **in libris libertas** on the Los Angeles Public Library?

Lesson XLIX

354. CĪNEĀS ET PYRRHUS

Pyrrhus erat rēx Ēpīrī. Cīneās,[1] quī erat lēgātus in Pyrrhī castrīs et reliquōs lēgātōs auctōritāte et virtūte superābat, cōnsiliīs Pyrrhī nōn probātīs, multā cum lībertāte [2] rēgem monēbat. Quondam Pyrrhus Cīneae familiārī dīxit: "In Italiam prōcēdere et cīvitātem Rōmānam cum celeritāte superāre parō." 5

Cīneās, "Superātīs Rōmānīs," rogat, "quid est tibi in animō [2] facere, rēx fortis?"

"Italiae fīnitima est īnsula Sicilia," inquit rēx, "quam facile erit armīs occupāre."

Tum Cīneās, "Occupātā Siciliā," rogat, "quid posteā faciēs?" 10

Pyrrhus tum respondit: "Posteā trāns mare in Āfricam mīlitēs meōs celerēs trānsportābō et hostēs, quī celeritāte et virtūte mīlitibus meīs nōn parēs sunt, pellam."

Cīneās, "Pulsīs hostibus," rogat, "quid tum faciēs?" "Post haec [3] bella, Cīneā," [4] inquit Pyrrhus, "pāce cōnfirmātā, vītam in ōtiō agam." 15

Celer Cīneās respondit: "Familiāris meus es. Cūr nōn etiam nunc pācem cōnfirmāre potes atque mēcum in ōtiō vītam agere? Quid tē impedit?"

[1] *Cineas* (*Sin'eas*).
[2] = **cum multā lībertāte;** the **cum** in the ablative of manner often stands between the adjective and the noun.   [3] **quid . . . animō,** *what do you intend?*
[4] *these.*   [5] Vocative.

The ancient tomb of Eurysaces, a Roman baker, stands near the Roman gate Porta Maggiore. The holes represent the mouths of ovens; above them is a relief illustrating breadmaking. Roman tombs often bore sculpture portraying the former occupations of those buried inside.

Gian Berto Vanni/Art Resource

Albert Moldvay

A mosaic showing the twin masks of Tragedy and Comedy. Many of the traditions in our modern theater go back to the Romans, and before that to the Greeks (see p. 255).

QUESTIONS

1. What were Pyrrhus' plans?
2. What did Cineas want Pyrrhus to do?
3. What are some of the causes of war?

355. Ablative of Respect

Notice the use of the ablative in the following sentences:

1. **Equī et hominēs nōn sunt parēs celeritāte,** *Horses and men are not equal in swiftness.*
2. **Puer erat vir factīs,** *The boy was a man in deeds.*
3. **Numerō, nōn animō superāmur,** *We are surpassed in number, not in courage.*

Observe the following points:

1. The ablative expresses the respect in which the meaning of an adjective, a noun, or a verb is true.
2. No preposition is used in Latin, but in English we use a preposition, chiefly *in.*

282

356. Exercises

A. 1. Omnēs hostēs ē fīnibus nostrīs certē pellēmus.
2. Servī cum magnā celeritāte ad flūmen fūgērunt.
3. Nōn omnēs puerī dīligentiā et celeritāte parēs sunt.
4. Puer erat celer pede sed studiīs ab omnibus superābātur.
5. Sex familiāribus vīsīs, ad oppidum fīnitimum iter fēcimus.
6. Colōnī ex patriā migrant et in variīs terrīs cīvitātem petunt.
7. Pāx et amīcitia cum cīvitātibus fīnitimīs ā Rōmānīs cōnfirmātae sunt.

B. 1. We cannot all be swift of foot.
2. Does a horse excel a boy in swiftness?
3. He was king in name; nevertheless he did not have a kingdom.
4. (Now that) peace has been established,[5] free citizens will maintain the state.

357. Vocabulary

auctō′ritās, auctōritā′tis, f., *authority, influence* [*auctor*]
ce′ler, ce′leris, ce′lere, *swift* (celerity)
  cele′ritās, celeritā′tis, f., *swiftness*
cōnfir′mō, –ā′re, –ā′vī, –ā′tus, *make firm, encourage, establish* [*firmus*]
familiā′ris, –e, *of the family, friendly;* as noun, m., *friend* [*familia*]
respon′deō, –ē′re, respon′dī, respōn′sus, *answer* (response)
su′perō, –ā′re, –ā′vī, –ā′tus, *overcome, excel* (insuperable)
vir′tūs, virtū′tis, f., *manliness, courage* [*vir*]

358. Latin Phrases in English

in omnia paratus, *prepared for all things.*
Dominus providebit, *The Lord will provide.*
Fortes Fortuna adiuvat, *Fortune aids the brave.*
extempore, *without preparation* (lit., *from the moment*).
Arma non servant modum, *Armies do not show* (preserve) *restraint.*
Virtute et armis, *By courage and by arms* (motto of the state of Mississippi).
Vanitas vanitatum et omnia vanitas, *Vanity of vanities, and all* (*is*) *vanity* (from the Vulgate, or Latin translation of the Bible, *Ecclesiastes, I, 2*).
Ense petit placidam sub libertate quietem, *With the sword she seeks quiet peace under liberty* (motto of the state of Massachusetts).

---

[5] See **323.**

"The Frightened Woman" is one of a series of fine paintings found in the Villa of the Mysteries in Pompeii. The woman is afraid because she sees a companion being whipped. The series shows the initiation of women into the mysteries, or secret society, of Bacchus. The man sitting down is Silenus (see p. 305).

Glimpses of Roman Life

359. THE HOUSE AND ITS FURNITURE

The Pompeian town house was different from ours, more like the kind one finds in southern Europe and Latin America today. It was usually built of concrete covered with stucco. For privacy and security, and because glass was expensive, there were few windows on the street. The typical house consisted of two parts, front and rear. The front contained a large room, called the **ātrium,** surrounded by small bedrooms. The atrium had an opening in the roof for light and air. The roof sloped down to the opening. Below the opening there was a basin into which the rain fell. This cistern **(impluvium)** furnished the soft water for washing, so necessary in a country where most of the water is hard. At the corners of the basin there were often columns extending to the roof.

Since the house was built directly on the street, it had no front yard. The heavy front door opened into a hall leading into the atrium. On one side of the hall there might be a small shop, usually rented out to people who did not live in the house. On the other side there was the room of the doorkeeper **(iānitor).** Very often there was a place for a watchdog. Sometimes a fierce dog was painted on the wall or depicted in mosaic on the floor of the hall.

A floor mosaic from Pompeii. That the Romans were fond of birds is shown by the frequency with which they put them in wall paintings and floor mosaics. Roman literature too tells of pet birds.

Restoration of the atrium of a Roman house, based on remains in Pompeii.

Opposite the entrance was the study or office **(tablīnum)** of the master of the house, placed so that he could keep an eye on what was going on. Here he kept his safe. Often there were also upstairs rooms.

The rear of the house surrounded a garden. Because of the columns which ran all around the garden this part was called the peristyle (which means "columns around"); today we might call it a colonnade. It was often very pretty. Charming fountains and statuary were usually to be seen in the garden. Kitchen, bathroom, and dining rooms were in this part of the house. There were often two dining rooms, one on the shady side for summer, the other on the sunny side for winter use.

The walls were covered with elaborate paintings (p. 25, etc.). Rugs and draperies were in common use. The floors were usually made of tile or flagstone, as in Italy today, instead of wood. Chairs were few, and many of them were without backs. On the other hand, there were many couches, used like easy chairs, not only for reading and resting but also at the dinner table (p. 76). There were many kinds of tables and stands, often beautifully made. Many small lamps of bronze or clay were placed everywhere, some on stands, some on large, elaborate candelabra. These burned olive oil. Glass chimneys were unknown. The light was so poor that people went to bed early and got up early. Candles were also used. Portable charcoal heaters were common. In northern Italy central heating was sometimes used.

Modern wooden shutters in a Pompeian window. The ashes which covered the originals left a perfect cast, which made this restoration easy.

Kitchen utensils and dishes were made of bronze, silver, or earthenware. Those made of earthenware were chiefly red in color and were decorated with engraved lines.

The size of the population and the scarcity and cost of land within Rome's city limits prevented all but the very wealthy from living in houses such as these from Pompeii. Instead, the Romans expanded vertically and lived in apartment houses, called **insulae** because they were "islands" surrounded by the narrow streets. Often they were five or six stories high, and in design remarkably like apartment houses today (p. 374). In fact, in exterior decoration and the imaginative use of varied building materials (concrete, brick, stone, stucco, wood) they were probably more interesting. But in safety and convenience they left a good deal to be desired; many were flimsily built by speculators during the period of Rome's greatest growth (100 B.C. to 100 A.D.) and stood in constant danger of fire or collapse. Unlike the Pompeian house, the apartment dwelling did not have rooms designed for specific functions; they were just spaces for the tenant to use as he chose. The filth, smoke, and noise must often have been nearly intolerable.

Many of the rich and socially prominent, and those who wanted to be, lived in individual houses or luxurious ground-floor apartments on or near the Palatine Hill, a sort of ancient Beverly Hills that was eventually reserved for the imperial family. The wealthy also had country houses **(villae)** in other parts of Italy, which they used to escape the heat and bustle of the city, or as places to stop overnight when traveling.

DISCUSSION QUESTIONS

1. In what ways did Roman houses differ from ours?
2. How did the poor lighting facilities affect the daily life of the people?
3. How does climate affect the types of houses?

Iuppiter, rex deorum.

UNIT IX REVIEW

Lessons XLV–XLIX

The Story of Lucius (cont.)

360. DEĪ

Rōmānī multōs deōs quōrum officia erant varia habuērunt. Deōs in omnibus locīs vīdērunt—in terrā, in agrīs, in frūmentō, in montibus, in silvīs, in undīs maris, in aquā flūminum, in omnī nātūrā. Nōn omnēs parēs auctōritāte erant, nam magnī deī erant et parvī deī, deī
5 deaeque. Inter magnōs deōs prīmus auctōritāte erat Iuppiter, rēx atque pater deōrum hominumque, quī in caelō habitābat et fulmine malōs terrēbat. Iūnō erat uxor Iovis [1] et rēgīna deōrum. Venus erat pulchra dea amōris. Mārs, deus bellī, arma pugnāsque amābat. Auctor populī Rōmānī vocābātur, et fortasse ob hanc [2] causam
10 Rōmānī semper bella gerēbant. Mercurius, celer nūntius deōrum, omnēs celeritāte superābat. Neptūnus erat deus maris, quī equōs in undīs regēbat. Reliquī magnī deī erant Cerēs, dea frūmentī, Minerva, dea sapientiae, Diāna, dea silvārum, Vulcānus, deus ignis, Apollō, quī omnia prōvidēbat et quem hominēs cōnsulēbant, Bacchus, deus
15 vīnī. Lūcius noster nōmina omnium magnōrum deōrum et multōrum parvōrum cognōverat—quod nōn facile erat, nam magnus erat numerus deōrum deārumque. Etiam "terminus agrōrum" deus erat.

---

[1] Genitive singular of **Iuppiter.**   [2] *this.*

361. VOCABULARY

NOUNS			
1. auctor	6. cīvitās	12. iūs	18. ōrdō
2. auctōritās	7. corpus	13. lībertās	19. pater
3. caput	8. fīnis	14. mare	20. tempus
4. celeritās	9. flūmen	15. mōns	21. virtūs
5. cīvis	10. hostis	16. nāvis	22. vulnus
	11. iter	17. nōmen	

ADJECTIVES			
23. celer	24. facilis	26. fortis	28. pār
	25. familiāris	27. omnis	

VERBS			
29. claudō	30. cōnficiō	32. pellō	34. superō
	31. cōnfirmō	33. respondeō	35. tendō

ADVERBS		
	36. posteā	37. tamen

PREPOSITION	
	38. post

Pompeian wall painting depicting a fight in the amphitheater, not between gladiators, but between Pompeians and visitors from the nearby town of Nuceria. Feelings ran high in the crowds, and riots were as common then as today.

362. VOCABULARY (English Meanings)

NOUNS			
1. author	6. state	12. right	18. order
2. authority	7. body	13. freedom	19. father
3. head	8. end	14. sea	20. time
4. swiftness	9. river	15. mountain	21. courage
5. citizen	10. enemy	16. ship	22. wound
	11. journey	17. name	

ADJECTIVES			
23. swift	24. easy	26. strong, brave	28. equal
	25. friendly	27. all	

VERBS			
29. close	30. complete	32. drive	34. overcome
	31. make firm	33. answer	35. stretch

ADVERBS		
	36. afterwards	37. nevertheless

PREPOSITION	
	38. after

363. GRAMMAR SUMMARY

Ablative Uses

The ablative case really is a combination of three cases and that is why it has so many different uses.

When an ablative is always used with a preposition we generally do not need a special name for it. One exception is the ablative of agent. The reason is that the preposition **ab** with this ablative cannot be translated in its usual sense of *from* (see **103**). We also use a name ("accompaniment") for the ablative with **cum.** This is to distinguish it from the ablative of means, since both are expressed by *with* in English (see **170**).

This altar in the Roman Forum is associated with a water nymph, Juturna, and the twin gods Castor and Pollux, who were "seen" to water their horses at the nearby spring after a famous battle in 496 B.C. In the central panel are the Gemini (twins) and their sister Helen, on the ends their parents, Jupiter and Leda.

Fototeca Unione

Pay particular attention to the ablatives used without a preposition because the construction differs from English. What are the three ablatives of this class that you have studied?

What ablative have you studied with which a preposition is sometimes used, sometimes not?

What prepositions are used with the ablative?

364. UNIT PRACTICE AND EXERCISE

Form Drill

1. Decline **dux fortis, lībertās nostra, omnis mīles, rēx magnus.**
2. Give the following in Latin: *a small ship,* in the nom., sing. and plur.; *an easy journey,* in the gen., sing. and plur.; *a good citizen,* in the dat., sing. and plur.; *a brave enemy,* in the acc., sing. and plur.; *the deep sea,* in the abl., sing. and plur.
3. Give the genitive and the accusative, singular and plural, of **tempus, casa, mōns, corpus, fīnis, celeritās, mare, ōrdō, flūmen.**
4. Give in all tenses the third plural active of **impediō;** the first plural passive of **claudō;** the third singular active of **līberō;** the second plural passive of **teneō;** the second singular active of **cōnficiō.**

365. ENGLISH WORD STUDIES

1. Give the Latin noun suggested by each of the following: *civil, finish, submarine, navigate, corpulent, legislate, nominal, decapitate.*

Corpulent.

2. Give the Latin verb suggested by each of the following: *expedite, press, verse, attention, repellent.*

3. Give the Latin adjective suggested by each of the following: *omnipresent, celerity, facilitate, disparity, fortitude.*

4. Find and use in sentences as many English derivatives as possible from **parō, teneō, agō,** and **scrībō.**

5. Make a sketch map of your state and indicate on it all the names you can of towns with classical names.

291

UNIT X

GODS AND HISTORY

The area of the Roman Forum was originally a marsh. At the peak of the Roman Republic this same location was the center of Roman religious, political, and social life. By the time of Julius Caesar, 100–44 B.C., Rome had grown so large that much of the political and social activity had to be moved elsewhere in the city. After the fall of the Roman Empire, the Forum gradually became covered by earth and by the Middle Ages, it was not much more than a "cattle pasture." This is the condition of the Roman Forum as seen in this painting by David Roberts (1796–1864).

At the top of this beautiful medal, Jupiter hurls a thunderbolt at the snake-legged Giants. The artist Pistrucci made it to celebrate the victory of the English over Napoleon at Waterloo. In the center, the triumphant generals Wellington and Blücher in classical armor are attended by Victory.

Lesson L

366. SĀTURNUS ET IUPPITER

Auctor et prīmus rēx deōrum Ūranus erat. Hunc fīlius Sāturnus ex rēgnō expulit. Ūranus hīs verbīs Sāturnum monuit: "Tempus auctōritātis tuae nōn longum erit; nam tū ā fīliō tuō expellēris." Hīs verbīs territus Sāturnus omnēs fīliōs in ōrdine dēvorābat. Sed māter
5 illum quem ante[1] reliquōs amābat servāvit. Hic fuit Iuppiter, ad īnsulam Crētam ā mātre missus. Post paucōs annōs hic patrem expulit et rēgnum illīus occupāvit. Sāturnus reliquōs fīliōs reddere coāctus est. Rēgiam[2] in monte Olympō Iuppiter posuit, ex quō in omnēs partēs spectāre poterat. Frātrēs convocāvit. Neptūnō maris
10 rēgnum, Plūtōnī rēgnum īnferōrum[3] permīsit.

Sed posteā Gigantēs,[4] fīliī Terrae, cum deīs bellum gessērunt. Illī ad Olympum praecipitēs cucurrērunt sed ā deīs proeliō superātī poenīs dūrīs affectī sunt. Posteā multa templa in terrā deīs ab hominibus posita sunt.

[1] *more than.*   [2] *palace.*   [3] *of those below*, i.e., the dead.   [4] *the Giants.*

1. Who was the father of Saturn?
2. Of Jupiter?
3. Who were the sons of Saturn?

367. The Demonstratives Hic and Ille

In English, *this* (plur., *these*) and *that* (plur., *those*) are called *demonstratives* because they "point out" persons or objects. They may be used as either adjectives or pronouns: *This man certainly did not write **that**; that could not have been done by **these** boys.*

In Latin, **hic** means *this* (*near* the speaker in place or thought), while **ille** means *that* (*more distant* from the speaker).

	SINGULAR				SINGULAR		
	M.	F.	N.		M.	F.	N.
Nom.	hic	haec	hoc	*Nom.*	ille	illa	illud
Gen.	huius	huius	huius	*Gen.*	illīus	illīus	illīus
Dat.	huic	huic	huic	*Dat.*	illī	illī	illī
Acc.	hunc	hanc	hoc	*Acc.*	illum	illam	illud
Abl.	hōc	hāc	hōc	*Abl.*	illō	illā	illō

Both **hic** and **ille** are declined regularly in the plural, like **bonus** (**hī,** etc., **illī,** etc.), with the exception of the nominative and accusative plural neuter of **hic,** i.e., **haec.** For full declension see **563.** Note that **hic** and **ille** resemble **quī** in the genitive singular.

From such expressions as *this man, that woman,* etc., the demonstrative adjectives **hic** and **ille** came to be used as a third person pronoun *he, she, it.* The personal pronoun, however, is usually not required in Latin.

368. Position of Demonstratives

Demonstrative adjectives regularly precede their nouns in English and Latin: *these boys,* **hī puerī;** *that girl,* **illa puella.** In English, when *that* precedes its noun, it is the demonstrative adjective **(ille);** when it follows, it is the relative pronoun **(quī),** equivalent to *who* or *which: The man **that** I saw was famous,* **Vir quem** (not **illum**) **vīdī clārus erat.**

369. Exercises

A. 1. Ille erat dux ducum.

2. Hunc cognōvī sed illum ante hoc tempus nōn vīdī.

3. Hī hominēs sunt patris meī amīcī; illī sunt inimīcī.

4. Haec est mea patria; nam ego cīvis in hōc locō sum.

5. Praeceps in illud flūmen cucurrī, quod illud nōn vīdī.

6. Māter mea huic hominī grātiam habet, quod hic patrem meum servāvit.

B. Supply the right forms of **hic** and **ille** and translate:

1. (*This*) flūmen altum est, (*that*) nōn altum est.

2. (*These*) hominēs laudō, (*those*) numquam probābō.

3. (*This*) puerī patrem et (*that*) puellae mātrem vīdī.

4. Studia ab (*this*) puerō intermissa sunt, nōn ab (*that*).

C. 1. This is my money; that is yours.

2. This boy excels that (one) in discipline.

3. What names did the mother give to the children?

4. When this prisoner has been bound,[6] I shall bind that (one).

[6] Use ablative absolute.

The Pantheon, in Rome, is a temple built in the time of Augustus to honor several gods. From this view of the main entrance, we see some of the sixteen columns, each one over 14 feet in circumference. For a view of the interior, see page 118.

M·AGRIPPA·L·F·COS·TERTIVM·FECIT

The Rotunda of the University of Virginia. Thomas Jefferson modeled it after the Pantheon. He was an excellent classical scholar, deeply interested in the ancient civilizations, and helped introduce classical architecture and other phases of ancient culture in our country.

James Sawders

370. Vocabulary

cur′rō, –ere, cucur′rī, cursū′rus, *run*	(current, course)
expel′lō, –ere, ex′pulī, expul′sus, *drive out*	[*pellō*]
hic, haec, hoc, *this*	
il′le, il′la, il′lud, *that*	
mā′ter, mā′tris, f., *mother*	(maternal, matron)
prae′ceps, gen. praeci′pitis, *headlong, steep*	(precipice)

371. English Word Studies: The Third Declension

The third declension is very important in Latin because so many words belong to it. More English words are derived from nouns and adjectives of this declension than from any other. The English word is usually derived from the stem, not from the nominative. It is therefore doubly important to memorize the genitive, from which the stem is obtained. It would be difficult to see that *itinerary* is derived from **iter** if one did not know that the genitive is **itineris.** See how many of the words of the third declension already studied have derivatives from the base. Note the help given for English spelling: *temporal, corporal, military, nominal,* etc.

On the other hand, the English derivative will help you remember the genitive. In the following list of words, a derivative is placed after each; give the genitive: **religiō** (*religion*), **sermō** (*sermon*), **latus** (*lateral*), **rādīx** (*radical*), **orīgō** (*original*), **ēruptiō** (*eruption*), **custōs** (*custody*), **dēns** (*dental*), **mōs** (*moral*).

Many towns are named after the Roman gods: *Jupiter, Juno, Mars, Mercury, Minerva, Bacchus, Ceres.* Many firms or their products are also named after them.

The planets too are named after Roman gods: *Mercury, Venus, Mars, Jupiter, Saturn, Neptune, Pluto. Uranus* is from the Greek.

Captured shields, spears, helmets, and other trophies of war are represented on the pedestal of Trajan's Column (see back cover and p. 199). In this pedestal were kept the emperor's ashes, housed in a golden urn.

Anthony Paccione

Lesson LI

372. CAEDICIUS FORTIS

Prīmō bellō Pūnicō hostēs locum nātūrā mūnītum occupāverant, et perīculum mīlitum Rōmānōrum magnum erat. Aestās erat, nam Rōmānī semper aestāte, nōn hieme, bella gerēbant. Dux nihil facere poterat. Rogat: "Quod cōnsilium capere dēbeō?" Tribūnus mīlitum
5 Rōmānus cui [1] nōmen Caedicius [2] erat, ad ducem hōc tempore vēnit et sententiam prōposuit, locō quōdam [3] mōnstrātō:

"Virōs tuōs servāre poteris sī ad illum locum CCCC mīlitēs currere iubēbis. Hostēs, ubi hōs mīlitēs vīderint, proelium committent et hōs omnēs interficient. Dum haec faciunt, facile erit reliquōs mīlitēs
10 ex hōc locō ēdūcere. Haec est sōla via salūtis."

"Bonum tuum cōnsilium probō," inquit dux, "sed tamen quis illōs praecipitēs in mortem certam dūcet?"

---

[1] *whose* (lit., *to whom*).   [2] *Caedicius* (*Sēdish'us*).   [3] *certain.*

"Cūr mē nōn mittis? Mors mē nōn terret," respondit tribūnus. Itaque dux tribūnō magnās grātiās ēgit et hunc cum CCCC mīlitibus contrā hostēs mīsit. Fortēs illī Rōmānī nihil timuērunt. Neque ces- 15 sērunt neque fūgērunt sed magnō numerō hostium superātī sunt. Omnēs aut vītam āmīsērunt aut vulnera accēpērunt. Interim reliquī mīlitēs Rōmānī integrī salūtem petīvērunt.

Deī praemium tribūnō ob ēgregium exemplum dōnāvērunt; nam vītam nōn āmīsit. Vulnera multa accēpit sed neque in capite neque 20 in corde. Illā aestāte hostēs expulsī sunt, et hieme Rōmānī hostēs nōn iam timuērunt.

QUESTIONS

1. What was Caedicius' suggestion?
2. What happened to Caedicius?

373. Ablative of Time When

In English, time is expressed with or without the prepositions *in, on,* etc.: *last summer, in winter, on Friday.*

In Latin, the "time when" something happens is expressed by the ablative, *usually without a preposition.*

1. **Illō annō in oppidō mānsimus,** *That year we remained in town.*
2. **Aestāte agrī sunt pulchrī,** *In summer the fields are beautiful.*

Note. Compare with the ablative of "place where" **(87).** When *at, in,* or *on* denotes *time* instead of *place,* no preposition is used.

374. Exercises

A. 1. Hic puer et aestāte et hieme in agrīs labōrat.
2. Mīlitēs nostrī, paucī numerō sed corde fortēs, prōvinciam illō tempore occupāvērunt.
3. Illā hieme decem librōs lēgī sed hāc aestāte nihil fēcī.
4. Quīntā hōrā omnēs servī cum magnā celeritāte fūgērunt.
5. Hōc annō nihil timēmus, quod cōpiam frūmentī habēmus.
6. Prō Deō et patriā! Haec clāra verba corda virōrum semper incitāvērunt.

B. 1. In summer the rivers are not deep.
2. In that year we had many ships on every sea.
3. Good citizens love God and do not fear an enemy.
4. Our country contains brave sons and beautiful daughters.
5. If [4] Marcus is our leader, nothing will scare us this winter.

---

[4] Use ablative absolute, omitting *is.*

375. Vocabulary

aes′tās, aestā′tis, f., *summer*
cor, cor′dis, n., *heart* (cordial, record)
hi′ems, hi′emis, f., *winter*
*****mors, mor′tis, mor′tium,** f., *death* (mortal)
ni′hil, *nothing* (annihilate, nil)
ti′meō, –ē′re, ti′muī, —,[5] *fear, be afraid* (timid)

376. English Word Studies

1. An *excursion* is a little *run out of* town. What is a *current* of water? *Cursive* writing? A *recurrent* illness? *Concurrent* powers of the federal government and the states? *Discord* is *hearts apart; concord, hearts together.* What is a *cordial* welcome? An apple *core*?

2. Latin phrases in English:

primus inter pares, *first among his equals.*
A.D. (anno Domini), *in the year of our Lord.*
aut Caesar aut nihil, *either Caesar or nothing.*
Alma Mater, *kindly mother,* applied to a school or college.
iustitia omnibus, *justice for all* (motto of the District of Columbia).
Pater Noster, *Our Father,* i.e., the Lord's Prayer, which begins with these words.

---

[5] Neither perfect nor future participle used.

The ships in this pavement mosaic remind us that the city of Ostia was the main seaport for Rome. It served as the base for Roman overseas expeditions and later developed into a major commercial trading center.

Albert Moldvay

The Arch of Diocletian at now-deserted Sbeitla in northern Africa. After the utter destruction of Carthage in 146 B.C., Africa became a Roman province. Roman colonists later built a new Carthage, which became a flourishing provincial capital and educational center. Sbeitla, about 30 miles away, was in a fertile area important for the production of grain and olive oil.

Tunisian Trade Office

Lesson LII

377. CĪVITĀS RŌMĀNA

Duae partēs cīvitātis Rōmānae, Troiānī et Latīnī, contrā perīcula commūnia pugnāvērunt. Ubi cīvitās nova concordiā aucta est, rēgēs populīque fīnitimī praedae cupiditāte adductī partem agrōrum Rōmānōrum occupābant. Paucī ex amīcīs [1] auxilium Rōmānīs submittēbant quod perīculīs territī sunt. Sed Rōmānī properābant, parā- 5 bant, cum hostibus proelia committēbant, lībertātem patriamque commūnem armīs dēfendēbant, mortem nōn timēbant. Dum pāx incerta est,[2] dum eī nē spīrāre quidem [3] sine perīculō possunt,[2] cūram perpetuam nōn remittēbant.

Dum haec geruntur,[2] eī Rōmānī quōrum corpora ob annōs nōn iam 10 firma erant sed quī bonō cōnsiliō valēbant dē rē pūblicā [4] cōnsulē-bantur; ob aetātem patrēs aut senātōrēs appellābantur.

Prīmō rēgēs erant, quī lībertātem cōnservābant et rem pūblicam augēbant, sed posteā, quod eōrum rēgum duo ex Etrūriā superbī fuērunt, Rōmānī rēgēs pepulērunt et fēcērunt duo cōnsulēs. Eī cōnsulēs appellābantur quod senātōrēs dē rē pūblicā cōnsulēbant.

---

[1] **ex amīcīs = amīcōrum.**   [2] Use the past tense.   [3] **nē . . . quidem,** *not even.*
[4] Translate by the English derivative of this compound noun.   [5] Accusative.

Eō tempore corda omnium Rōmānōrum glōriam spērāvērunt. Virī fortēs bella amābant, in castrīs aestāte atque hieme labōrābant, nihil timēbant: virtūs vēra eōrum omnia superāverat. Itaque populus Rōmānus magnum hostium numerum paucīs mīlitibus in fugam dabat, 20 oppida nātūrā mūnīta pugnīs capiēbat. Hostibus superātīs et perīculō remōtō, Rōmānī aequē regēbant. Iūra bellī pācisque cōnservābant; hōc modō auctōritās eōrum cōnfirmāta est. In ultimās partēs mīlitēs colōnīque eōrum missī sunt. Lingua Latīna in omnibus terrīs docēbātur. Post tertium Pūnicum bellum Rōmānī fuērunt dominī omnium terrā- 25 rum mariumque. Nunc sine cūrā spīrāre et animōs remittere potuērunt.

Sed tum fortūna, semper incerta, eōs superāvit. Hī pecūniam imperiumque, nōn iam glōriam spērāvērunt. Superbī, nōn iam aequī fuērunt; iūra lēgēsque nōn iam cōnservāvērunt.

QUESTIONS

1. How did the old men serve the state?
2. After the expulsion of the kings, how was the power shared?
3. What caused the decay of Rome?

378. The Demonstrative Is

| | SINGULAR | | | PLURAL | | |
	M.	F.	N.	M.	F.	N.
Nom.	is	ea	id	eī (iī)	eae	ea
Gen.	eius	eius	eius	eōrum	eārum	eōrum
Dat.	eī	eī	eī	eīs (iīs)	eīs (iīs)	eīs (iīs)
Acc.	eum	eam	id	eōs	eās	ea
Abl.	eō	eā	eō	eīs (iīs)	eīs (iīs)	eīs (iīs)

Practice

Decline **ea pars, id longum iter, is vir.**

379. How Is *Is* Used

Instead of pointing out a particular person or thing, as **hic** and **ille** do, **is** usually refers less emphatically to somebody or something just mentioned. When used without a noun, it is usually translated as a personal pronoun, *he, she,* or *it;* therefore, the genitive **eius** may be translated *his, her, its,* while **eōrum** and **eārum** mean *their.* Is often serves as the antecedent of a relative clause; as **Is quī videt probat,** *He who sees approves.*

The Roman ruins in Dougga, Tunisia, are among the best in all Roman Africa. The Temple of Jupiter shown here dates from the second century A.D. The high platform is characteristic of Roman temples.

Corinthian columns, remains of the Roman theater at Mérida, in western Spain.

380. Exercises

A. 1. Dum spīrō spērō. (*A motto of South Carolina.*)
  2. Is cui librōs dedī eōs nōn remīsit.
  3. Certa āmittimus dum incerta petimus.
  4. Puellās et eārum mātrem in lūdō vīdī.
  5. Commūne perīculum concordiam facit.
  6. Eī puerī quōs aestāte vīdimus erant eius fīliī.
  7. Hostibus pulsīs, tamen disciplīnam nostram nōn remittēmus.

B. 1. Her father and mine are away.
  2. Give him a part of the money.
  3. We shall see him and his mother this summer.
  4. This man is my teacher; that man is her father.

381. Vocabulary

commū′nis, –e, *common* (commune, communistic)
dum, conj., *while*
incer′tus, –a, –um, *uncertain* [*cernō*]
is, e′a, id, *this, that; he, she, it*
*pars, par′tis, par′tium, f., *part* (party, partition)
remit′tō, –ere, remī′sī, remis′sus, (lit., *let back*), *relax, send back* [*mittō*]
spē′rō, –ā′re, –ā′vī, –ā′tus, *hope (for)* (despair)
spī′rō, –ā′re, –ā′vī, –ā′tus, *breathe* (spirit, inspiration)

382. English Word Studies: The Names of the Months

In early Roman times the year began March 1, and February was the last month. We still use the ancient Roman names of the months. *March* was named after Mars. *April* was the *opening* month (**aperiō**), when the earth seems to open up. *May* is the month when things become *bigger* (**maior**). *June* is Juno's month, *July* was originally called **Quīnctīlis**, the *fifth* month, but was renamed in honor of Julius Caesar after he had the calendar changed to our present system. Similarly *August* was originally **Sextīlis**, the *sixth* month, but was renamed after the Emperor Augustus. *September* was originally the *seventh* month and kept its name even after it later became the ninth; similarly, *October, November, December*. *January* was named after Janus, the god of beginnings. *February* was the time of purification (**fēbrua**), like the Christian Lent.

Drugstore run by Cupids in a wall painting at Pompeii. Compare pages 126–127.

Silenus holding the infant Bacchus. An ancient statue.

Lesson LIII

383. MIDĀS

Midās, nōbilis genere, rēx Phrygiae, multīs oppidīs expugnātīs, magnam auctōritātem habuit. Quondam Sīlēnus, magister deī Bacchī, in agrīs Phrygiae interceptus, ad eum rēgem ductus est. Quod Sīlēnus ab eōdem rēge multa beneficia accēpit, Bacchus parātus fuit rēgī dare id quod spērāvit. Midās dīxit: "Sī omnia quae parte corporis meī 5 tetigerō [1] in aurum vertentur, mihi grātum erit."

Hōc praemiō datō, omnia commūnia quae rēx tangēbat in aurum vertēbantur. Terram tangit: nōn iam terra est sed aurum. Aquam tangit: eōdem modō in aurum vertitur. Tum grātiās Bacchō prō magnō praemiō ēgit. 10

Tum rēx magnam cēnam parārī iussit et omnia genera cibōrum in mēnsā pōnī. Haec mēnsa ab eōdem tācta in aurum versa est. Dum magnā celeritāte servī cēnam parant, Midās familiārēs nōbilēs convocāvit. Grātō animō cēnam bonam quae parāta erat spectāvit. Dum cibum capit, cibus in aurum versus est. Vīnum in mēnsā pōnī iussit. 15 Hoc tangit et nōn iam idem est sed in aurum vertitur. Omnibus amīcīs ēgregia cēna grāta fuit sed nōn rēgī. Inter multōs cibōs Midās tamen edere [2] nōn potuit.

Tandem ad Bacchum, auctōrem malōrum, rēx miser prōcēdere mātūrāvit et fīnem supplicī petīvit—nam supplicium et impedīmen- 20 tum, nōn iam praemium erat id quod ā deō accēperat. Bacchus iussit eum in mediō flūmine Pactōlō [3] sē [4] lavāre. Praeceps rēx ad flūmen cucurrit, ubi sē lāvit, sē remīsit, sine cūrā spīrāvit, nam aurum remōtum erat. Arēna [5] flūminis in aurum versa est, et etiam nunc in hōc eōdem flūmine aurum est. 25

---

[1] From **tangō**.   [2] *eat.*   [3] *Pactō'lus.*   [4] *himself.*   [5] *sand.*

1. Why did Bacchus reward Midas? How?
2. What is meant by the modern expression, "the Midas touch"?
3. What is meant by comparing the gold buried at Fort Knox to that acquired by Midas?

384. The Demonstrative Īdem

The demonstrative **īdem,** meaning *same,* is a compound of **is** and **–dem,** with slight changes for ease of pronunciation:

	SINGULAR	
	M.	F.	N.
Nom.	√ īdem	eădem	ĭdem
Gen.	eiusdem	eiusdem	eiusdem
Dat.	eīdem	eīdem	eīdem
Acc.	⍱ eundem	⍱ eandem	ĭdem
Abl.	eōdem	eādem	eōdem

	PLURAL	
Nom.	eīdem (īdem)	eaedem	eădem
Gen.	√ eōrundem	√ eārundem	√ eōrundem
Dat.	eīsdem (īsdem)	eīsdem (īsdem)	eīsdem (īsdem)
Acc.	eōsdem	eāsdem	eădem
Abl.	eīsdem (īsdem)	eīsdem (īsdem)	eīsdem (īsdem)

Practice

Give the Latin in the singular and plural for *the same body* in the accusative, *the same summer* in the ablative, *the same year* in the genitive, *the same punishment* in the nominative, *the same part* in the dative.

385. Exercises

A. 1. Eōdem annō lībertās captīvīs data est.
2. Dux eum ad idem supplicium trahī iussit.
3. Dum omnia timēmus, glōriam spērāre nōn possumus.
4. Oppidō expugnātō, Caesar impedīmenta hostium intercēpit.
5. Hic homō nōbilī genere sed nōn magnīs factīs illum superat.
6. Hominēs līberī parēsque esse dēbent, quod eundem Deum habent.

Bacchus watches while Midas bathes in the River Pactolus to get rid of the Golden Touch. A seventeenth-century painting by the French artist Poussin.

Metropolitan Museum of Art

B. 1. His punishment scared the rest.
2. He will not send back the same book.
3. When I saw the same boy,[6] I was no longer afraid.
4. Their towns were captured one at a time the same year.

386. Vocabulary

expug′nō, –ā′re, –ā′vī, –ā′tus, (lit., *fight it out*), *capture by assault* [pugnō]
ge′nus, ge′neris, n., *birth, kind* (genus, generation)
ī′dem, e′ădem, ĭ′dem, *same* (identity)
interci′piō, –ere, –cē′pī, –cep′tus, *intercept* [capiō]
nō′bilis, –e, (lit., *"know-able"*), *noble* [nōscō]
suppli′cium, suppli′cī, n., *punishment* [plicō]
tan′gō, –ere, te′tigī, tāc′tus, *touch* (tactile, tangent)

387. English Word Studies

1. Explain the word *community*. **Supplicium** literally means *folding* (or *bending*) *down* for punishment. Explain *supplication*. What is an *inexpugnable* fortress?

2. Latin phrases in English:

ibid. (ibidem), *in the same place.*
id. (idem), *the same* (i.e., as mentioned above).
quid pro quo, *something for something* ("tit for tat").
Homo proponit, sed Deus disponit, *Man proposes, but God disposes.*
Explain **semper idem, genus homo.**

---

[6] Use ablative absolute.

Erich Lessing/PhotoEdit

The single arch on the left is all that remains of the Pons Aemilius (second century B.C.), the first stone bridge built within the city of Rome. Many think that the wooden Pons Sublicius (Horatius' bridge) stood nearby.

Lesson LIV

388. HORĀTIUS

Nunc in locīs commodīs sedēbimus et legēmus dē Horātiō,[1] virō fortī nōbilīque genere. Sī haec fābula, nōn tibi nōta, tē dēlectābit,[2] tū ipse lege eandem sorōribus frātribusque tuīs parvīs (sī frātrēs sorōrēsque habēs), quī circum tē sedēbunt et magnō cum studiō
5 audient.

Tarquiniī,[3] ā Rōmānīs pulsī, auxilium petīvērunt ā Porsenā,[4] rēge Etrūscōrum. Itaque Porsena ipse cum multīs mīlitibus Rōmam[5] vēnit. Rōmānī, dē salūte commūnī incertī, territī sunt, quod magna erat potestās Etrūscōrum magnumque Porsenae nōmen. Rōmānī quī
10 agrōs colēbant in oppidum migrāvērunt; portās clausērunt et oppidum ipsum praesidiīs dēfendērunt. Pars urbis Tiberī flūmine mūnīta est. Pōns sublicius[6] iter hostibus dabat, sed ēgregius vir prohibuit, Horātius Coclēs,[7] illō cognōmine appellātus quod in proeliō oculum āmīserat. Is, extrēmā pontis parte occupātā, mīlitēs hostium sōlus

---

[1] *Horatius (Horā'shus).*   [2] Translate by the present: *pleases.*
[3] *the Tar'quins,* Etruscan rulers of Rome in the sixth century B.C.
[4] *Por'sena.*   [5] *to Rome.*   [6] *bridge made of piles.*   [7] *Cō'clēs* ("One-Eye").

sine auxiliō intercēpit et sustinuit et Rōmānōs quī fugiēbant pontem 15
frangere iussit. Ipsa audācia hostēs terruit. Ponte frāctō, Horātius nōn
dubitāvit sed armīs impedītus praeceps in Tiberim dēsiluit et per multa
tēla integer ad Rōmānōs trānāvit. Eius virtūte oppidum nōn expugnātum est et potestās Porsenae frācta est. Grāta ob factum clārum eius
cīvitās fuit. Multī agrī eī pūblicē datī sunt, quōs ad terminum vītae 20
coluit. Exemplum virtūtis ab eō prōpositum Rōmānī semper memoriā
retinuērunt.

QUESTIONS

1. Why did Porsena come to Rome?
2. How was he prevented from entering the city?
3. How did Cocles get his name?
4. Is the destruction of bridges important in wars today?

389. The Intensive in English and Latin

In English, compound pronouns are formed by joining -*self* to *my,*
your, him, her, it and the plural -*selves* to *our, your, them.* These compounds may be used in an intensive or emphatic sense; as, *I saw the*
man myself.

In Latin, the pronoun **ipse** is a compound of **is** and the intensive
ending **–pse,** and therefore has purely intensive force: **Ipse hominem**
vīdī, *I saw the man myself.* Note that **ipse** may be used alone in the
nominative to emphasize an omitted subject. It is declined like **ille**
(367), except in the neuter nominative and accusative singular.

	SINGULAR		
	M.	F.	N.
Nom.	ipse	ipsa	ipsum
Gen.	ipsīus	ipsīus	ipsīus
Dat.	ipsī	ipsī	ipsī
Acc.	ipsum	ipsam	ipsum
Abl.	ipsō	ipsā	ipsō

(The plural is regular.)

Practice

Translate **frātris ipsīus, suppliciō ipsō, partēs ipsae, hic cīvis ipse,**
illārum nāvium ipsārum, sorōrī meae ipsī, eiusdem generis, eōrun-
dem auctōrum.

309

390. Exercises

A. 1. Nōnne idem ipsī cernitis, puerī?
2. Quae officia soror vestra ipsa suscipiet?
3. Deī quōs Rōmānī colēbant multī erant.
4. Quis est puer ille quī cum sorōre meā sedet?
5. Ille homō agricola appellātur quod agrōs colit.
6. Frātrēs et sorōrēs eiusdem familiae paria iūra habēre dēbent.

B. 1. These (men) are standing; those are sitting.
2. These letters were written by the king himself.
3. We ourselves shall get much money in a few years.
4. The same winter they saw and heard him themselves.

391. Vocabulary

co′lō, –ere, co′luī, cul′tus, *till, inhabit, worship*　　(cultivate)
fran′gō, –ere, frē′gī, frāc′tus, *break*　　(fracture, fraction)
frā′ter, frā′tris, m., *brother*　　(fraternize, fraternal)
ip′se, ip′sa, ip′sum, *self, very*
potes′tās, potestā′tis, f., *power*　　[*possum*]
se′deō, –ē′re, sē′dī, sessū′rus, *sit*　　(session, preside)
so′ror, sorō′ris, f., *sister*　　(sorority)

392. English Word Studies: The Norman-French Influence

In early lessons **(310, 321),** we saw how Latin words were introduced into the English language at its very beginning. A very important later period of influence followed the Norman invasion of England (1066). The language of the Norman conquerors was an old form of French, and thus itself descended from Latin. In a few centuries it had introduced many new words that often show great variation from the original Latin spellings. Especially common is the change from one vowel to two. Look up the Latin originals of *captain, courage, duke, homage, peer, prey, reign, treason, villain, visor.*

The opening pages of Sir Walter Scott's *Ivanhoe* reveal in language the changed cultural situation that followed the Norman conquest. The animals that the defeated and oppressed Saxons must tend are referred to by the Anglo-Saxon names *swine* and *kine.* But when these animals are served on the tables of the Norman masters, they are referred to by their more elegant, Latin-derived names, *pork* and *beef.*

Painting in an Etruscan tomb. Note the fisherman and the boat's lucky eye.

Alan Oddie/PhotoEdit

The Acropolis was originally the fortified center of Athens. The Parthenon, which we see here, was constructed in 447–438 B.C. It is considered by some experts to be the most perfectly pleasing building ever erected.

Lesson LV

393. *CICERŌ ET TĪRŌ*

Cicerō et Tīrō fuērunt Rōmānī clārī, alter maximus [1] ōrātor tōtīus Italiae, alter servus fīdus.[2] Quod Tīrō dīligentiā sapientiāque Cicerōnī magnum auxilium dabat, Cicerō eum tōtō corde amābat et posteā līberāvit. Neutrī grātum erat sine alterō ūllum iter facere. 5

Cicerō cum Tīrōne in Graeciā fuerat. Ubi ille in Italiam revertit, Tīrō sōlus in Graeciā relīctus est quod aeger [3] fuit. Cicerō ad eum trēs litterās in itinere ūnō diē [4] scrīpsit. Inter alia haec ipsa scrīpsit:

[1] *greatest.*   [2] *faithful.*   [3] *sick.*   [4] Ablative.

"Variē litterīs tuīs affectus sum, prīmā parte territus, alterā cōn-
10 firmātus. Hōc tempore tē [5] neque marī neque itinerī committere
dēbēs. Medicus tuus bonus est, ut [6] scrībis et ego audiō; sed eum nōn
probō; nam iūs [7] nōn dēbet stomachō [8] aegrō darī. Sed tamen et ad
illum et ad Lysōnem [9] scrīpsī. Lysōnis nostrī neglegentiam nōn probō,
quī, litterīs ā mē acceptīs, ipse nūllās remīsit; respondēre dēbet. Sed
15 Lysō Graecus est et omnium Graecōrum magna est neglegentia. In
nūllā rē [10] properāre dēbēs.

"Curium [11] iussī omnem pecūniam tibi dare quam cupis. Sī medicō
pecūniam dabis, dīligentia eius augēbitur. Magna sunt tua in mē
officia; [12] omnia superāveris, sī, ut spērō, salūtem tuam cōnfirmātam
20 vīderō. Ante, dum magnā dīligentiā mihi auxilium dās,[13] nōn salūtem
tuam cōnfirmāre potuistī; nunc tē nihil impedit. Omnia dēpōne; salūs
sōla in animō tuō esse dēbet."

Nōnne Cicerō dominus aequus amīcusque erat? Aliī dominiī erant
bonī, aliī malī. Omnī aetāte et in omnibus terrīs bonī et malī hominēs
25 fuērunt et sunt et fortasse semper erunt.

QUESTIONS

1. What was Tiro's relation to Cicero?
2. To whom did Cicero write about Tiro's illness?
3. Use a remark in this letter as a basis for discussion of national
   and racial prejudices.

394. Declension of Ūnus

The numeral **ūnus** and the other words in the vocabulary of this
lesson are irregular only in the genitive and dative singular of all
genders. In these cases they are declined like **ipse (389),** in all others
like **magnus.** If you need help in declining them, see **559.** Like **hic,
ille,** and **is,** these adjectives are emphatic and therefore usually precede their nouns.

Practice

1. Decline in the singular **alius tuus frāter.**
2. Give the Latin for the following in the genitive and dative
   singular: *neither sister, the whole town, the other leader, no
   winter, safety alone, one citizen.*

---

[5] *yourself.*   [6] *as.*   [7] *soup.*
[8] Use the English derivative.   [9] Tiro was staying at Lyso's house.
[10] *thing.*   [11] *Cu'rius,* a banker.   [12] *services.*
[13] In English the past tense is used.

395. Words Often Confused

1. **alius** = *another,* one of a group of *three or more.*
   alter = *the other,* i.e., *of two* and no more.
2. **tōtus** = *whole,* i.e., no part missing, not capable of being divided.
   omnis (singular) = *every.*
   omnēs (plural) = *all,* i.e., a complete collection of units or parts.
3. **nūllus** = *not any, no*—an adjective.
   nihil = *not a thing, nothing*—always a noun.
   nēmō [14] = *no man, no one*—always a noun.

396. Exercises

A. 1. Rēx neutrī fīliō potestātem committet.
2. Cōnsilia alterius ducis alterī nōn erant grāta.
3. Sorōrēs meae agrōs montēsque tōtīus īnsulae vīdērunt.
4. Is homō ipse ab aliīs dēfēnsus est sed nūllō modō ab aliīs.
5. Quīnque amīcī eius iam discessērunt et is sōlus nunc manet.
6. Accēpistīne ipse ūlla praemia prō meritīs tuīs? Nūlla accēpī neque ūlla exspectō. (See **216**.)

B. 1. Every man in our whole country ought to work.
2. To one sister I shall give money, to the other this book.
3. Have you seen my mother and sister? I have seen neither.
4. My brother spent part of that same summer alone in the woods.

[14] See **446**.

Roman theater at Leptis Magna, Libya, in northern Africa.

Wide World

a′lius, a′lia, a′liud,[16] *other, another*	(alias)
(a′lius . . . a′lius, *one . . . another;* a′liī . . . a′liī, *some . . . others*)	
al′ter, al′tera, al′terum,[17] *the other* (of two)	(alternate)
(al′ter . . . al′ter, *the one . . . the other*)	
neu′ter, neu′tra, neu′trum, *neither* (of two)	(neutral)
nūl′lus, nūl′la, nūl′lum, *no, none*	(nullify)
sō′lus, sō′la, sō′lum, *alone, only*	(sole, solitary)
tō′tus, tō′ta, tō′tum, *whole*	(total)
ūl′lus, ūl′la, ūl′lum, *any*	
ū′nus, ū′na, ū′num, *one*	(unify, unit)

All the adjectives above, except **alter** [17], have **–īus** in the genitive and **–ī** in the dative singular of all genders **(394).**

398. English Word Studies: Spelling

Latin words are often very helpful in fixing the spelling of English words in your mind. In this lesson we shall consider words in which a double consonant occurs.

If the Latin word has a double consonant, it is usually preserved in English, except at the end of a word: *terror,* but *deter* (from **terreō**); *carriage,* but *car* (**carrus**); *rebelled,* but *rebel* (**bellum**); *remitted,* but *remit* (**remittō).** *Letter* has two *t*'s and *literal* only one because the spelling of Latin **littera** varied.

Many prefixes bring about the doubling of consonants by assimilation. The most important are **ad–, con–, in–, ob–, ex–,** and **sub–.** If you will analyze the English word, you can often tell whether the consonant is to be doubled: **con–** and **modus** form **commodus;** prefix **ad–** and you get the English derivative *ac-com-modate* with two *c*'s and two *m*'s. Similarly *commend* has two *m*'s; *re-com-mend* has two *m*'s but only one *c* because **re–** cannot be assimilated. Other examples of doubling through assimilation are *im-material, ac-celerate, suf-ficient, ef-ficient* (but *de-ficient,* for **dē–** is not assimilated).

Find five more examples of doubling of consonants as a result of assimilation.

---

[15] **Uter,** *which* (of two), and **uterque,** *each, both,* are likewise irregular and belong to this group but are comparatively unimportant.

[16] The neuter nominative and accusative singular end in **–d,** not **–m** (cf. **ille**).

[17] The genitive singular of **alter** ends in **–īus** (short **–ĭ**).

Glimpses of Roman Life

399. ROMAN RELIGION

The earliest Romans believed that for almost every object and activity—the sky, the flow of rivers, the ripening of crops, even the hinges of a door—there was a mysterious and protecting spirit **(anima).** This is the *animism* common in primitive agricultural societies, filled with what we would call superstitions, magic, and taboos. Gradually these spirits began to take on clearer form and personality as gods. Worship was centered in the family around various household gods: the Lar (plural, Lares), probably originally a field spirit who had been domesticated to protect the whole homestead, Vesta, goddess of the hearth, the Penates, gods of the food supply, and the Genius, the guardian spirit of the head of the household. The family's simple offerings and prayers to these deities long remained the most vital part of Roman religion.

In addition, as Rome grew as a political community, public religious activity was an integral part of state affairs, and rapidly assimilated other gods and forms of worship from peoples near and far. From the Etruscans the Romans learned a style of temple building and the arts of foretelling the future. When Greek influence on Rome increased, the Romans identified their native gods with the chief Greek deities: the sky-god Jupiter with Zeus, the war-god Mars with Ares, the sea-god Neptune with Poseidon, the grain-goddess Ceres with Demeter, and so on. Still later, as all the world flocked to Rome, new religions were introduced from Egypt, Asia Minor, and even Persia, while the official state cult turned more and more to emperor-worship. But the generally tolerant and *polytheistic* (believing in many gods) Romans found *monotheism* (belief in a single god) strange. For nearly three centuries they persecuted the Christians because they scorned the pagan gods of the state and would not admit the divinity of the emperor, until Christianity itself was officially recognized by the Emperor

Anthony Paccione

Three columns of the Temple of Vespasian near the Roman Forum. To what order do their capitals belong? The various hatchets, knives, bowls and other implements used in religious sacrifices are shown on the frieze supported by the columns. In the left background are the ruins of the Temple of Saturn.

Constantine in 313 A.D. And as Christianity grew in strength, the great pagan gods faded from the ceremonies of the state, and the homely family rituals retreated to the peasant folk from whom they had sprung.

Just as remarkable as Roman religion's variety and ability to borrow other forms of worship was the closeness of its tie with politics. Originally the chief priest **(pontifex maximus)** had been the king himself; later the chief priest was elected, and he and all other priests were government officials. The state had charge of the building and restoration of temples, which were often less centers of worship than public treasuries, record offices, museums, and meeting places.

Another political feature of the ancient religion was the attempt to determine the will of the gods in various ways. The duty of those priests who were called augurs was to determine whether a certain important act (such as a military expedition) would be successful. This they did by watching the flight of birds. Certain movements were supposed to indicate success; others, failure. Another practice, borrowed from the Etruscans, was to sacrifice animals and examine their entrails in order to discover the will of the gods. These two methods were official and were used before important matters were undertaken. Eventually, many intelligent Romans lost faith in these practices, but they kept them up in order to influence the more ignorant classes. Private persons also resorted to numerous unofficial fortunetellers, such as astrologers, as some superstitious people do today.

With so many gods to worship, the Romans naturally had many holidays. Some of these were celebrated with amusements as well as with religious observances, as is true of our holidays today. The amusements about which you have read **(327)** developed in this way.

QUESTIONS

1. What part did family worship play in Roman life?
2. To what extent is astrology practiced today?
3. In what countries today is religion directly connected with the state?

An altar at Pompeii showing a sacrifice. The priest always covered his head. The man at the right has his heavy hammer ready for the sacrificial act. The small boy at the left, with pitcher and saucer, is a camillus (see p. 200).

A statuette (about ten inches tall) of a Lar, or family god. He dances lightly, and pours wine from a goat-shaped drinking horn onto the dish in his left hand, symbolizing the blessings of a happy and abundant household.

Metropolitan Museum of Art

UNIT X REVIEW

Lessons L–LV

The Story of Lucius (cont.)

400. ALIĪ DEĪ

Dē magnīs deīs iam lēgimus. Nunc dē multīs parvīs deīs legēmus. Concordiam, Victōriam, Salūtem, Pācem, Fortūnam, Virtūtem Rōmānī deās vocāvērunt, quod sacrae erant et ā Rōmānīs amābantur. Etiam pecūnia ā Rōmānīs amābātur et dea erat, sed tamen (ita scrībit 5 auctor Rōmānus Iuvenālis [1]) nōn in templō habitāvit.

Aliī deī erant deī familiārēs, quōs prīmōs Lūcius cognōverat. Lār familiāris erat is deus quī familiam cōnservābat. Penātēs erant eī deī quī cibum servābant. Vesta erat dea focī, in quō cibus parābātur. Ad focum erant parvae fōrmae deōrum. Ibi, omnibus līberīs et fa-10 miliāribus convocātīs, pater Lūcī ipse deīs grātiās agēbat et cibum dōnābat. Quondam nōn multus cibus erat, sed tamen pater deīs partem cibī dōnābat. Lūcius patrem rogat: "Cūr ille cibus deīs hōc tempore ā tē datur? Nōn multum habēmus." Pater respondit: "Cibō hōc datō, deī hominibus magna beneficia et longam vītam dabunt."

[1] *Jū'venal*, a poet of the second century A.D.

401. VOCABULARY

NOUNS			
1. aestās	4. genus	8. nihil	12. supplicium
2. cor	5. hiems	9. pars	
3. frāter	6. māter	10. potestās	
	7. mors	11. soror	

ADJECTIVES			
13. alius	16. incertus	20. praeceps	24. ūnus
14. alter	17. neuter	21. sōlus	
15. commūnis	18. nōbilis	22. tōtus	
	19. nūllus	23. ūllus	

PRONOUNS			
25. hic	26. īdem	28. ipse	
	27. ille	29. is	

VERBS			
30. colō	33. expugnō	36. remittō	39. spīrō
31. currō	34. frangō	37. sedeō	40. tangō
32. expellō	35. intercipiō	38. spērō	41. timeō

CONJUNCTION	42. dum

A household shrine in the house of the Vettii in Pompeii. Between the Lares is the Genius of the head of the house, wearing a toga drawn over his head. The snake too represents the Genius, or guardian spirit. Notice that the costume of the Lares is similar to that on page 318.

Bill Roberts/PhotoEdit

402. GRAMMAR SUMMARY

Case Uses

	In Latin The ablative with—	In English The objective with—
PLACE	1. Preposition **in.**	1. Preposition *in.*
MEANS	2. No preposition.	2. Preposition *with* or *by.*
ACCOMPANIMENT	3. Preposition **cum.**	3. Preposition *with.*
AGENT	4. Preposition **ab.**	4. Preposition *by.*
MANNER	5. No preposition or preposition **cum.**	5. Preposition *with,* etc.
RESPECT	6. No preposition.	6. Preposition *in.*
TIME	7. No preposition.	7. No preposition or preposition *at, in,* or *on.*

403. VOCABULARY (English Meanings)

NOUNS
1. *summer*
2. *heart*
3. *brother*
4. *birth, kind*
5. *winter*
6. *mother*
7. *death*
8. *nothing*
9. *part*
10. *power*
11. *sister*
12. *punishment*

ADJECTIVES
13. *other, another*
14. *the other*
15. *common*
16. *uncertain*
17. *neither*
18. *noble*
19. *no, none*
20. *steep*
21. *alone*
22. *whole*
23. *any*
24. *one*

PRONOUNS
25. *this*
26. *same*
27. *that*
28. *-self*
29. *this, that*

VERBS
30. *till, worship*
31. *run*
32. *drive out*
33. *capture by assault*
34. *break*
35. *intercept*
36. *relax, send back*
37. *sit*
38. *hope*
39. *breathe*
40. *touch*
41. *fear*

CONJUNCTION
42. *while*

404. UNIT PRACTICE AND EXERCISES

Form Drill

A. Make **hic, ille,** and **īdem** agree as demonstrative adjectives with the following nouns in the case required, as follows:

māteriae (gen.): **huius, illīus, eiusdem māteriae**

aestāte	**frātrēs** (nom.)	**patris**
capita (nom.)	**mortium**	**pretium** (acc.)
cor (acc.)	**partī**	**sorōrem**

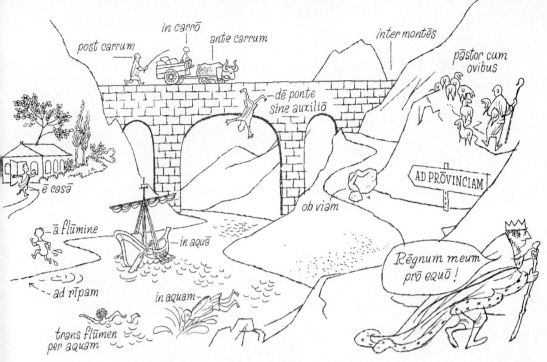

Use of Latin prepositions.

B. Supply the correct form of **is** in the following sentences and translate:

1. (*Him, her, it*) vīdī.
2. (*By him, by her*) ēvocātus sum.
3. Fīlium (*his, her*) docēbō.
4. Nōvistīne (*their*) patrem?
5. Hunc librum (*to him, to her, to them*) mandābō.

C. Decline **nūlla māter, alius auctor.**

405. ENGLISH WORD STUDIES

1. Give the Latin words suggested by the derivatives: *cordial, partial, sedentary, fraternity, inspiration, cult, generation, sorority, cursive, remiss, maternal, intercept, infinite, sediment.*

2. Find and use in sentences as many derivatives as possible from **trahō, audiō,** and **premō.**

Intercept.

UNIT XI

FAMOUS ROMANS

A frieze showing the execution of the Gauls by the Romans during the Gallic Wars. The captive Gauls are wearing gold neckpieces called "torques" which were usually a sign of wealth.

Albert Moldvay

Lesson LVI

406. QUĪNTUS CICERŌ ET POMPŌNIA

Pompōnius Atticus erat firmus amīcus M. Cicerōnis. Pompōnia, soror Atticī, erat uxor Quīntī, frātris M. Cicerōnis. Sed inter Pompōniam Quīntumque nōn semper concordia erat. Ūna gravis causa inter aliās erat haec, quod apud [1] Quīntum auctōritās Stātī [2] valēbat,
5 quem Pompōnia domō [3] expellere nūllō modō potuit; aliēnae auctōritātī cēdere nōn ·cupīvit. Neuter alterī cēdere potuit; neuter alterum movēre potuit. Cicerō Pompōniam accūsāvit, Atticus Quīntum. Cicerō ad Atticum hōc modō scrīpsit:

"Frātrem meum vīdī. Tōtus sermō inter nōs dē tē et sorōre tuā
10 fuit. Verba Quīntī nōn inimīca fuērunt. Tum ad Pompōniam contendimus. Quīntus eī amīcā vōce dīxit: 'Pompōnia, tū rogā mulierēs ad cēnam, ego puerōs rogātūrus sum.' (Hī puerī erant fīliī Cicerōnis et frātris eius.) Sed illa, audientibus nōbīs, 'Ego ipsa sum,' respondit, 'in hōc locō hospita.' Hoc dīxit quod īdem Stātius cēnam parārī iusserat.
15 Tum Quīntus, 'Audīsne?' inquit mihi, 'haec semper sustinēre cōgor.' Dīcēs: 'Haec vōx nihil est.' Sed magnum est [4]; vōce dūrā atque animō aliēnō eius oppressus et commōtus sum. Ad cēnam illa nōn adfuit; Quīntus tamen ad eam sedentem sōlam cibum mīsit; illa remīsit. Grave vulnus Quīntus accēpit neque ipse ūllam iniūriam fēcit. Cupiēns eam
20 plācāre nōn potuit. Gravibus cūrīs opprimor. Quid factūrī sumus? Contendere dēbēmus inter sorōrem tuam et frātrem meum pācem efficere."

QUESTIONS

1. Who was Atticus' brother-in-law?
2. Of whom was Pomponia jealous?

[1] *with.*   [2] *Statius* (*Stā'shus*), a freedman of Quintus.   [3] *from the house.*
[4] *it is a serious thing.*

407. Present Participle

In English, the *present active participle* ends in *–ing: I saw your brother reading a book.* In Latin, it is formed by adding **–ns** to the present stem. It is declined like a third declension adjective of one ending (cf. **pār, 345**), with the stem ending in **–nt–: portāns, portantis.** For full declension see **555.**

1. The ablative singular ending is regularly **–e**, but **–ī** is used whenever the participle is used simply as an adjective.
2. In verbs of the fourth conjugation, and **–iō** verbs of the third, **–ie–** appears throughout, forming the base **–ient–**, as **audiēns, audientis; capiēns, capientis.**
3. **Sum** has no present participle in common use; that of **possum** is **potēns.**

The present participle modifies a noun or pronoun. Like the present infinitive, it represents an act as happening at the time indicated by the main verb.

The present participle cannot be used with the verb **sum** to form a progressive tense, as is done in English with *be* **(25, 1, 193).** Latin has no present passive participle.

408. Future Active Participle

Unlike English, Latin has a future active participle, as we have already seen in the principal parts of some verbs. In most verbs it is formed by dropping the **–us** of the perfect participle and adding **–ūrus: portātūrus,** *going to carry;* **factūrus,** *going to make.* It is declined like **magnus.** Note that we have to use a phrase to translate it. It is often used with the verb **sum.**

Spareribs for the lady's dinner. A de luxe Roman butcher shop, with easy chair and footstool. The customer is watching the butcher closely. Cleaver and chopping block look very modern. From a sculptured relief in Dresden, Germany.

Practice

Form and translate the participles of **nāvigō, obtineō,** and **prōdūcō**
in the present and future.

409. Exercises

A. 1. Duo puerī pugnantēs ā magistrō captī sunt.
2. Rōmānīs tardē prōcēdentibus, barbarī fūgērunt.
3. Hieme nūllōs agricolās in agrīs labōrantēs vidēmus.
4. Cūr in hōc locō sine frātribus tuīs remānsūrus es?
5. Hī puerī, suppliciō gravī affectī, ā magistrō dīmissī sunt.
6. Vōcēs amīcōrum rogantium auxilium ā nōbīs numquam audītae sunt.
7. Oppressī in aliēnō locō, hostēs cum impedīmentīs ad montēs contentūrī erant.

B. (*Instead of clauses, use participles wherever possible.*)
1. The arms given to the other soldiers are heavy.
2. The number of (those) approaching was not large.
3. He is going to fold the letter which he has written.
4. He was dragged to death by you (while he was) defending the public cause.

410. Vocabulary

aliē′nus, –a, –um, another's, unfavorable   [*alius*]
conten′dō, –ere, –ten′dī, –tentū′rus, *struggle, hasten*   [*tendō*]
gra′vis, –e, *heavy, severe*   (gravity, gravitation)
op′primō, –ere, oppres′sī, oppres′sus, *overcome, surprise* [*premō*]
vōx, vō′cis, f., *voice, remark*   [*vocō*]

411. English Word Studies

1. What is a *neutral?* An *alien?* What is meant by the statement
in the Declaration of Independence "that all men . . . are endowed
by their Creator with certain *unalienable* [usually misquoted *inalien-
able*] rights; that among these are life, liberty, and the pursuit of
happiness"?

2. Latin phrases in English:

inter alia, *among other things.*
ipso facto, *by the fact itself, thereby.*
in loco parentis, *in place of a parent.*
una voce, *with one voice, unanimously.*
Vox populi vox Dei, *The voice of the people* (*is*) *the voice of God.*
obiter dictum, (*something*) *said by the way* (**ob iter**), *incidentally.*
Timeo Danaos et dona ferentes, *I fear the Greeks even when they bring
gifts* (Virgil). For the events that led to this remark see **116.**
Explain **in toto, vox humana.**

326

Temple dedicated to the Emperor Antoninus (second century A.D.) and to his wife Faustina. The ruins are some of the finest in the Roman Forum. Inside the temple has been built the Church of S. Lorenzo in Miranda. The inscription tells of the dedication of the temple to the imperial couple.

Lesson LVII

412. CINCINNÀTUS

Hostēs Minucium,[1] ducem Rōmānum, et mīlitēs eius in locō aliēnō magnā vī premēbant. Ubi id nūntiātum est, omnēs Rōmānī timentēs vim hostium cupīvērunt Cincinnātum [2] dictātōrem facere, quod is sōlus Rōmam ā perīculō nōn levī prohibēre et cīvitātem servāre
5 poterat. Ille trāns Tiberim eō tempore agrum parvum colēbat. Nūntiī missī eum in agrō labōrantem invēnērunt et cōnstitērunt. Salūte [3] datā acceptāque, Cincinnātus uxōrem parāre togam iussisse dīcitur; nam nōn oportēbat [4] sine togā nūntiōs audīre.

Hī nūntiī eum dictātōrem appellant et dīcunt: "Mīlitēs nostrī ab
10 hostibus premuntur et cīvēs terrentur. Perīculum nostrum nōn leve est. Hostēs nōn cōnsistent sed mox ad portās nostrās ipsās venient. Auxilium tuum rogāmus." Itaque Cincinnātus, vōcibus eōrum adductus, contrā hostēs contendit. Rōmānī, tēlīs iactīs, hostēs opprimunt et castra expugnant. Minuciō servātō, Cincinnātus dīcitur
15 hostēs sub iugum [5] mīsisse. Tum, nūllīs hostibus prohibentibus, mīlitēs ad urbem redūxit et triumphāvit. Vīs hostium frācta erat. Ductī sunt in pompā ante eum ducēs hostium, capta arma ostenta sunt; post eum mīlitēs vēnērunt praedam gravem ostendentēs. Et haec omnia Cincinnātus magnā celeritāte gessit: potestāte dictātōris in [6] sex mēnsēs
20 acceptā, sextō decimō diē [7] ad agrōs discessit, nōn iam dictātor sed triumphāns agricola. Eōdem mēnse agricola et dictātor et iterum agricola fuit.

QUESTIONS

1. Where was Cincinnatus' farm?
2. Who was with him when the messengers came?
3. How long did he stay away from his farm?

---

[1] *Minucius (Minū'shus)*.
[2] *Cincinnatus (Sinsinā'tus)*.
[3] *greeting*.
[4] *it was not proper*.
[5] *under the yoke*, i.e., an arch of spears. This act signified surrender.
[6] *for*.
[7] *sixteenth day*.

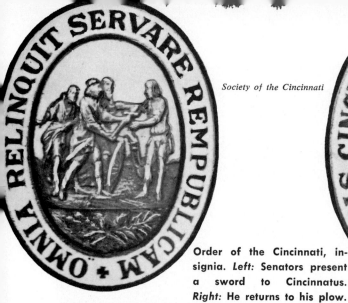

Society of the Cincinnati

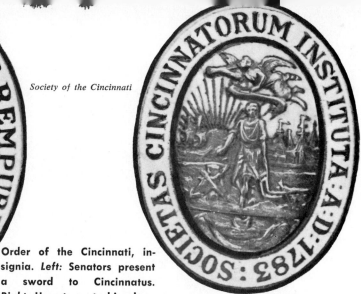

Order of the Cincinnati, insignia. *Left:* Senators present
a sword to Cincinnatus.
Right: He returns to his plow.

413. Perfect Active Infinitive

The *perfect active infinitive* is formed by adding **–isse** to the perfect stem: **portāvisse,** *to have carried;* **docuisse,** etc. It represents an act as having happened before the time indicated by the main verb: **Cincinnātus dīcitur hostēs sub iugum mīsisse,** *Cincinnatus is said* [NOW] *to have sent* [PREVIOUSLY] *the enemy under the yoke.*

Review infinitive used as subject and object **(129, 130);** infinitive with subject in the accusative as in English **(234).**

Practice

Form the perfect active infinitive of **dīmittō, intercipiō, videō, expediō.**

414. Exercises

A. 1. Ostendite omnibus bonum exemplum.
2. Vim prohibēre et pācem cōnservāre est nōbile.
3. Rēgis fīlia librum scrīpsisse sine auxiliō dīcitur.
4. Quis dīxit: "Dā mihi lībertātem aut dā mihi mortem"?
5. Rōmānī paucās nāvēs ad Britanniam mīsisse dīcuntur.
6. Mīlitēs cōnsistentēs arma levia cum magnā vī iēcisse dīcuntur.
7. Homō malus mē cōnsistere iussit et omnem meam pecūniam dare.

B. 1. We cannot breathe under water.
2. I saw your father folding a letter.
3. That king is said to have tilled the fields himself.
4. Those men are said to have come together in a strange land.

329

An ostrich and its keeper, from Armerina, Sicily. Mosaic was an important part of interior decoration and was found even in modest Roman homes.

415. Vocabulary

cōnsis′tō, –ere, cōn′stitī, cōnstitū′rus, *stand still, stop*   **[stō]**

dī′cō, –ere, dī′xī, dic′tus,[8] *say, tell*   (diction, dictaphone)

ia′ciō, –ere, iē′cī, iac′tus, *throw*   (jet, projectile)

le′vis, –e, *light (in weight)*   (levity)

*mēn′sis, mēn′sis, mēn′sium, m., *month*   (semester)

osten′dō, –ere, osten′dī, osten′tus, *(stretch out), show*   **[tendō]**

prohi′beō, –ē′re, –hi′buī, –hi′bitus, *prevent, keep from*   **[habeō]**

*vīs, —,[9] f., *force, violence;* plur. vī′rēs, vī′rium, *strength*   (vim)

416. Latin and English Word Studies

1. The suffix **–or** is added to the stem of the past participle and therefore is preceded by **t** or **s;** it indicates the doer of an action: **monitor** (*one who warns*), **scriptor** (*one who writes*), **inventor** (*one who finds*). It is used in English in the same way.

Eject.

A different suffix **–or** is added to the present base of a verb; it usually indicates a state of being or condition: **timor, amor, terror.** It is used in English.

Find five English words which are formed by adding one of these **–or** suffixes to the stems of verbs that you have studied. Explain *eject, injection, reject, ostentation, prohibition.*

2. The city of *Cincinnati,* Ohio, was named from the Society of the Cincinnati, formed by army officers at the end of the Revolutionary War. Why do you suppose the society took that name? What does its motto **Omnia reliquit servare rem publicam** mean? There is also a town named *Cincinnatus* (N.Y.).

---

[8] The imperative singular is **dīc.**   [9] Genitive and dative singular rare (see **552**).

Lesson LVIII

417. BELLA

Quae sunt causae bellī? Variī auctōrēs ostendērunt multās esse causās. Multa bella aut ob iniūriās aut prō lībertāte gesta esse vidēmus. In aliīs bellīs lībertās sociōrum dēfēnsa est. Haec bella iūsta fuērunt. Multī populī pugnant quod putant potestātem imperiumque vī bellō-
5 que augērī posse. Hī cupiunt patriam esse nūllī secundam. Sī supe-rantur, omnia saepe āmittunt; sī superant, aliēnās terrās occupant, quās in fōrmam prōvinciārum redigunt. Putāsne bella huius generis iūsta esse? Multī dīcunt omnia bella iūsta esse, aliī putant nūlla esse iūsta. Quid dē hōc putās? Nōvimus aliōs prō lībertāte, aliōs prō glōriā bella
10 gessisse. Quae fuērunt causae bellōrum nostrōrum? Audīvistīne dē bellō frīgidō?

Horātius,[1] poēta Rōmānus, scrībit dulce esse prō patriā vītam āmittere. Sī patria in perīculō est, nōnne putās mūnus nostrum esse eam dēfendere? Scīmus nōn levēs esse labōrēs mīlitum, gravia eōs
15 accipere vulnera, multōs ad mortem mittī; etiam scīmus eōs tamen nōn dubitāre omnēs labōrēs prō patriā grātō animō suscipere et sustinēre. Prō hīs mūneribus praemia aequa eīs solvere nōn possumus. Sed nec praemia nec beneficia exspectant; spērant cīvēs facta sua memoriā tentūrōs esse et aliōs semper parātōs futūrōs esse patriam dēfendere.
20 Hōc modō praemia solvere possumus.

Bellane ūllō tempore cōnstitūra sunt? Possuntne bella prohibērī? Quis scit? Sed spērāmus parvō spatiō temporis nōn iam bella futūra esse; spērāmus omnēs hominēs aliōrum iūra cōnservātūrōs esse.

QUESTIONS

1. Which wars were just?
2. What do soldiers hope for?
3. What are your answers to the questions asked in the text?

---

[1] *Horace.* The exact words of his famous phrase are: **Dulce et decōrum est prō patriā morī.**

Ewing Galloway

Horace's famous line on the entrance gate of Arlington National Cemetery, Arlington, Virginia, near Washington, where many illustrious heroes are buried.

418. Perfect Passive and Future Active Infinitive

1. The *perfect passive infinitive* is a compound formed by using the perfect participle with the present infinitive **esse: portātus esse,** *to have been carried;* **doctus esse** (cf. perfect passive indicative: **portātus sum**).

2. The *future active infinitive* is a compound formed by using the future active participle with the present infinitive **esse: portātūrus esse,** *to be going to carry;* **doctūrus esse,** *to be going to teach;* **futūrus esse,** *to be going to be.*

In both tenses the participle agrees with the subject of **esse: Spērō eam haec factūram esse,** *I hope that she will do these things.*

3. There was no future passive infinitive in common use in Latin.

Learn the infinitives, active and passive, of the model verbs **(566– 570)** and **sum (571).**

Practice

Form and translate the infinitives, active and passive, of **iaciō, solvō,** and **prohibeō.**

419. Infinitive with Verbs of Saying, etc.

In English, after verbs of *saying, thinking, knowing, hearing,* etc., if the words are not quoted directly, we use a clause often introduced by *that: He says (that) the boys are coming.* But sometimes we use the infinitive: *The boys are said to be coming; I know him to be a good man; I heard him say this; I believe this to be true.*

In Latin, the infinitive is *always* used with such words: **Dīcit puerōs venīre.** Note that **puerōs** is in the accusative because it is the subject of an infinitive **(234).** No introductory word is used.

420. Direct and Indirect Statement

1. **Dīxit, "Puerī veniunt,"** *He said, "The boys are coming."*
2. **Dīxit puerōs venīre,** *He said that the boys were coming.*

In the first sentence the exact words of the speaker are given, as shown by the use of quotation marks. Such a sentence is called a *direct statement.* In the second sentence the exact words are not given. Such a sentence is called an *indirect statement.* Indirect statements, with verbs in the infinitive and their subjects in the accusative, are used as objects of verbs of *saying, thinking, knowing, hearing,* etc.

Who or *Whom?* You can easily see how a knowledge of indirect statement in Latin will enable you to use *who* and *whom* correctly in English:

1. *Mr. Smith is a man who, I believe, is honest.*
2. *Mr. Smith is a man whom I believe to be honest.*

421. Exercises

A. 1. Dīcunt, "Cīvis iūstus lībertātem amat."
2. Cīvis iūstus lībertātem amāre dīcitur.
3. Dīcunt cīvem iūstum lībertātem amāre.
4. Putāmus nostra mūnera futūra esse levia.
5. Nōs omnēs scīmus in spatiō vītae esse cūrās et labōrēs.
6. Putāsne hunc pecūniam dēbitam solvisse aut solūtūrum esse?
7. Sciō et dīcō pecūniam ab illō homine dēbitam nōn solūtam esse.
8. Putō, Mārce, illum hominem numquam futūrum esse prīmum aut secundum ōrdine.

B. Translate the words in italics:
1. I know *him to be* wise.
2. I know the *signal was given.*
3. They say the *wagon was drawn* by mules.
4. I hear that your *sister will live* in Detroit.
5. I believe the *men have been led across* the river.

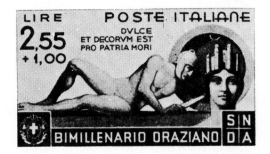

Italian stamp issued for Horace's 2000th birthday (1935) quotes his line on patriotism.

C. 1. Galba said, "My father is a soldier."
2. We all know that his father is a soldier.
3. I think that Galba himself will be a soldier.
4. I hear that Galba's brother was a sailor and was not scared by the sea.
5. He himself said, "I am going to be a soldier, for my father is a soldier."

422. Vocabulary

iūs′tus, –a, –um, *just*	**[iūs]**
la′bor, labō′ris, m., *work, hardship*	**[labōrō]**
mū′nus, mū′neris, n., *duty, service, gift*	(munificent)
pu′tō, –ā′re, –ā′vī, –ā′tus, *think*	(reputation)
sci′ō, scī′re, scī′vī, scī′tus, *know*	(science)
secun′dus –a, –um, *second*	(secondary)
sī, conj., *if*	
sol′vō, –ere, sol′vī, solū′tus, *loosen, pay*	(solution)

423. English Word Studies: Spelling

The base of the Latin present participle is **–ant, –ent,** or **–ient,** according to the conjugation **(407).** This is used as a suffix in English, with the same meaning as the participial ending *–ing.*

A common mistake in the spelling of English words is due to the confusion of *–ant* and *–ent.* Reference to the Latin helps:

1. Almost all English words derived from the first conjugation follow the Latin spelling with an *–a–: expectant, emigrant.*

2. Most English words that are derived from the other conjugations follow the Latin spelling with an *–e–: regent, agent, efficient, expedient.*

3. But some words in the latter group have an *–a–: tenant, defendant.*

Give eight English words with suffix *–ant* or *–ent* derived from Latin words previously studied. Explain *laboratory, omniscient, solvent, absolve, remunerate.*

Lesson LIX

424. CORIOLĀNUS

Mārcius, nōbilis Rōmānus, Coriolōs,[1] oppidum Volscōrum,[2] expugnāverat. Ob hoc mūnus "Coriolānus" appellātus est.

Post bellum ob variās causās plēbs īrā ācrī permōta clāmāvit Coriolānum esse hostem. Is, perīculum īnstāre sentiēns, fūgit ad
5 Volscōs quōs ipse superāverat. Volscī dīcuntur eum benignē [3] accēpisse, nam sēnsērunt eum esse ducem fortem ac iūstum et Rōmam nōn iam amāre. Etiam spērāvērunt eum contrā Rōmānōs pugnātūrum esse.

Mox Coriolānus, dux ā Volscīs lēctus, ad urbem Rōmam contendit,
10 omnēs in itinere superāns. Rōmānī, castrīs eius ad urbem positīs, bellō īnstantī territī sunt. Lēgātī dē pāce ad Coriolānum missī sunt sed ubi pervēnērunt ab eō remissī sunt. "Mātrem eius ad eum mittēmus," putāvērunt Rōmānī; "sī cūra urbis cor eius nōn tanget, amōre mātris ille certē tangētur et īra eius frangētur; tum fīnem labōrum
15 nostrōrum inveniēmus." Itaque māter et uxor Coriolānī cum duōbus parvīs fīliīs ad castra hostium pervēnērunt.

Coriolānus, verbīs ācribus mātris permōtus et lacrimīs omnium tāctus, dīcitur clāmāvisse: "Quid fēcistī, māter? Tū sōla Rōmam servāvistī sed mē vīcistī." Tum iussit Volscōs discēdere. Rōma lacrimīs,
20 nōn armīs servāta erat. Coriolānī facta semper in memoriā omnium haerēbunt.

QUESTIONS

1. How did Coriolanus get his name?
2. Where did he go when exiled?
3. Why did he spare Rome?

---

[1] *Corī'olī.*   [2] *Volsci (Vol'sī).*   [3] *kindly.*

425. How Indicative and Infinitive Differ in Tense

1. *It was thought that he was present.*
2. *He was thought to be present.*

In the first sentence, the verb in the subordinate clause is in the past indicative. In the second sentence, the infinitive *to be* refers to the same time but is in the present tense. The tenses of the indicative are determined by their *relation to present time,* but the tenses of the infinitive are determined by their *relation to the verbs on which they depend.* This is true in Latin as in English; remember it in translating a Latin infinitive into an English "that" clause.

426. How the Tenses of the Infinitive Differ

1. The present infinitive represents time or action as *going on,* from the standpoint of the introductory verb:

Dīcit } eōs vocāre, *He* { *says* / *said* } *(that) they* { *are* / *were* } *calling.*
Dīxit

Change **vocāre** to **vocārī** and translate.

2. The future infinitive represents an act that will occur *later,* from the standpoint of the introductory verb:

Dīcit } eōs vocātūrōs esse, *He* { *says* / *said* } *(that) they* { *will* / *would* } *call.*
Dīxit

From Fayoum in Egypt comes another type of Roman art, the mummy portrait. Painted on a wood panel with colors mixed into melted wax, the portrait was fastened to the person's mummy after death. The dry climate of Egypt has preserved about 600 of these portraits. Note how well the artist has executed the eyes and jewelry of this lady. From the second or third century A.D.

Courtesy Detroit Institute of Arts

3. The perfect infinitive represents time or action as *completed before* that of the introductory verb:

$\left.\begin{array}{l}\textbf{Dīcit} \\ \textbf{Dīxit}\end{array}\right\}$ **eōs vocāvisse,** *He* $\left\{\begin{array}{l}says \\ said\end{array}\right\}$ *(that) they* $\left\{\begin{array}{l}have \\ had\end{array}\right\}$ *called.*

Change **vocāvisse** to **vocātōs esse** and translate.

Note that the participle in the compound forms of the infinitive must agree with its subject (see 2 above).

427. Exercises

A.
1. Omnēs sēnsimus perīculum īnstāre.
2. Puer nōn clāmāre potuit, quod vōx haesit.
3. Quis dīxit socium meum sine frātre pervēnisse?
4. Servī spērāvērunt labōrem futūrum esse facilem.
5. Omnēs puerī certē sciunt Columbum ad Americam pervēnisse.
6. Rōmānī dīcēbant Caesarem esse fortem ducem nec superātum esse.
7. (*a*) Omnēs scīmus puerōs nostrōs esse ācrēs et fortēs. (*b*) *Substitute* scīvimus *for* scīmus *in* (*a*) *and translate.*

B. Translate the words in italics:
1. He knew *me to be* his friend.
2. He knew that *I was working* hard.
3. We saw that *we would* not *answer* in time.
4. He said that his *son was being taught* by new methods.
5. We hear that your *father has been sent* to Europe on a secret mission.

C.
1. We can prove that our cause is just.
2. Who said that we would not arrive?
3. My mother wrote that the city was beautiful.
4. The boy thought that (his) father had been saved.
5. The general says that the soldiers of the provinces were brave.

428. Vocabulary

ā′cer, ā′cris, ā′cre,[4] *sharp, keen*		(acid, acrid)
hae′reō, –ē′re, hae′sī, hae′sus, *stick*		(adhere, adhesive)
īn′stō, –ā′re, īn′stitī, —, *threaten*		[*stō*]
perve′niō, –ī′re, –vē′nī, –ventū′rus, (*come through*), *arrive*		
		[*veniō*]
sen′tiō, –ī′re, sēn′sī, sēn′sus, *feel, realize*		(sense, sensation)
***urbs, ur′bis, ur′bium,** f., *city*		(urbane, suburban)

[4] Cf. **345,** footnote 9.

The layout we see here is similar to that of many houses in Roman times. The peristyle, or garden, was surrounded by a portico, or columned walkway.

429. English Word Studies

1. By addition of the suffix **–ia (232)** to the base of the present participle, a suffix **–antia** or **–entia** is formed which becomes *–ance, –ence, –ancy,* or *–ency* in English (cf. the change of **–tia** to *–ce* [**237**]: **scientia,** *science*). The difficulty in spelling is again removed by reference to the Latin (cf. **423**).

Give eight English nouns with this suffix derived from Latin words previously studied. Explain *coherence, sensitive, consensus, intangible, dissension, inherent.* What is the difference between *adhesion* and *cohesion?*

2. Most of the names of American states are Indian, but several of them are of Latin origin or form. Vermont means *green mountain* **(viridis mōns),** Pennsylvania is *Penn's woods* **(silva),** Virginia is the *maiden's* land (named after Queen Elizabeth I, the virgin queen), Florida is the *flowery land* **(flōs, flōris),** Colorado is the land of the *colored* or *red* river, Montana is *mountainous* **(mōns),** Nevada is the land of snow **(nix, nivis).** Rhode Island is said to be named after the Greek island of Rhodes, meaning *rose.* New Jersey means "New Caesarea," named after the island of Jersey, one of many places named in honor of one of the Caesars. The titles *Kaiser* and *Czar* also came from **Caesar.**

States whose endings (only) are Latin are Carolina (Charles II), Georgia (George II), Louisiana (Louis XIV), and Indiana.

Glimpses of Roman Life

430. HOW THE ROMAN MADE HIS LIVING

In the early days of Rome nearly every man was a farmer; even later farming remained the chief occupation of the Romans, as it once was of people in most countries. It is not surprising therefore that Cincinnatus left his plow to lead the Romans in war and on its successful completion returned to his farm. In the early days many a war was won by the "embattled farmers." Nor is it surprising that farming was considered the foundation of Roman life, and that the sturdy Roman character was largely shaped by the hard work on the farm.

At first farms were small and were worked by the owner and his family. The increased use of slave labor led to increase in the size of farms and to a change in the attitude toward farming.

Industry was not so highly developed among the Romans as among us. There were no large factories. Much of the work was done by hand either at home or in small shops. The spinning of thread and its weaving into cloth were often done at home. Even the Emperor Augustus wore clothing made by slaves under his wife's direction. There were carpenters, workers in metal, masons and bricklayers, makers of tools, wagonmakers, brickmakers, and so on. The making of bricks and pottery came nearest to being industry in the modern sense.

The free workers were members of what may be called unions, whose chief purposes were to bring the members together for good fellowship and to provide burials for the members who died. Many slaves, too, came to be employed in industry.

The shops were very small—there were no department stores or chain stores. Usually a small room at the front of a private residence was used as a shop. The wares were often displayed outside. Sometimes the shopkeepers cluttered up the sidewalks and streets so much that traffic was interfered with until some strict official prevented this practice—even as today.

Pastoral scene in a Roman mosaic in Antioch, Turkey, once an important city.

Such were the occupations of the poorer classes. Rich men invested their money in wholesale trade, real estate, loans, government contracts, and foreign trade. Great profits could be made by buying from the government the right to collect the taxes in a province—everything collected over and above the cost of the contract went into the collector's pocket. The professions, with the exception of law and public life, were not well developed. Doctors and teachers were usually slaves or freedmen, i.e., former slaves. Law and politics were reserved largely for the upper classes.

DISCUSSION QUESTIONS

1. What professions are highly respected today?
2. What percentage of people today are engaged in farming?
3. How does mass production better the life of the worker?

UNIT XI REVIEW

Lessons LVI–LIX

The Story of Lucius (cont.)

431. VIRGINĒS VESTĀLĒS

Etiam cīvitās focum Vestae habuit. Templum Vestae in Forō urbis Rōmae stābat. Ibi sex puellae, Virginēs Vestālēs appellātae, ignem perpetuum Vestae semper servābant. Magna erat glōria Vestālium, et maximē ā populō Rōmānō amābantur. Eīs in viīs urbis vīsīs, omnēs
5 cōnstitērunt atque dē viā cessērunt. Facile erat eās cognōscere, quod omnēs semper albās vestēs gessērunt, neque ūlla alia mulier vestem eiusdem generis gessit. In circō loca ēgregia eīs dabantur. Sed dūrum fuit supplicium illīus Vestālis quae mala fuit: ea vīva sub terrā posita est.

EXACTING DUTIES

10 Iūlia, soror Lūcī, Vestālis erat et multa dē vītā Vestālium dīcēbat. Cum reliquīs Vestālibus in Ātriō[1] Vestae ad templum habitāvit sed tamen saepe patrem et mātrem et frātrēs vidēbat. Dīxit vītam Vestālium grātam esse sed labōrem numquam facilem esse: eās omnia magnā cūrā dīligentiāque facere cōgī. Dīxit Vestālēs ligna[2] in focō eōdem
15 modō semper pōnere et omnia certīs hōrīs in ōrdine facere. Itaque spatium disciplīnae longum erat. Puellae sex annōrum, ā patribus mātribusque Vestae datae, prīmōs decem annōs discipulae ēgērunt, tum decem annōs in officiīs ēgērunt et posteā parvās puellās docuērunt. Tamen post trīgintā annōs lībertās eīs data est et eae ad
20 amīcōs familiāsque redīre[3] potuērunt, sed multae in Ātriō Vestae mānsērunt. Sex sōlae Vestālēs in Ātriō ūnō tempore habitāvērunt.

---

[1] *ā'trium, house.* [2] *wood.* [3] Infinitive of **red-eō**, *go back*.

342

MISFORTUNE

Quondam Iūlia, aquam sacram portāns, vīdit aliam Vestālem ante portam sedentem lacrimantemque et ad eam cucurrit. Causā petītā, illa respondet, vōce haerente: "Sīvī [4] ignem sacrum exstinguī; labōre cōnfecta, somnō oppressa sum." Iūlia, corde malā fortūnā amīcae 25 tāctō, tamen illī nūllum cōnsilium dare potuit. Itaque illa pontificī omnia dīxit, et hic eam verberāvit—nihil aliud facere potuit, quod ita lēgēs iussērunt.

RIGHT OR WRONG

Hōc audītō, Lūcius ācrī vōce respondit illam miseram nōn me-rēre ob lassitūdinem poenā afficī et ōtium habēre dēbēre, sed eius 30 soror, Iūlia, quae aliam sententiam habuit, respondit: "Etiam amīca mea ipsa quae verberāta est sentit supplicium aequum fuisse. Mūnera nostra gravia sunt. Sī multā cūrā mūnera nōn efficiēmus, perīculum grave īnstābit. Itaque poena neglegentiae ācris esse dēbet. Sī ego ignem exstinguī sinam [5] (quod spērō numquam futūrum esse), 35 gravem poenam, etiam mortis, solvere dēbēbō."

[4] *I let* (perfect of **sinō**).   [5] Future of **sinō:** *I let*.

The Vestal Virgins at a banquet. This fragmentary relief from the Altar of Piety in Rome may represent the feast given for the Vestals when the Emperor Claudius dedicated the altar in 43 A.D.

Capitoline Museum

QUESTIONS

1. How would you explain the origin of the custom of keeping the sacred fire burning?
2. How many Vestals were there, including those in training?

432. GRAMMAR SUMMARIES

Participles

In Latin	In English
1. Present active **(portāns).**	1. Present active (*carrying*).
2. No present passive.	2. Present passive (*being carried*).
3. No perfect active.	3. Past active (*having carried*).
4. Perfect passive **(portātus).**	4. Past passive (*having been carried*).
5. Future active **(portātūrus).**	5. No future active.

Courtyard of the home of the Vestal Virgins in the Forum, near the Temple of Vesta. On the side are statues of the chief Vestals (cf. pp. 6, 345). Left, Basilica of Maxentius; right, a church built into the Temple of Venus and Rome.

James Sawders

One of the chief Vestal Virgins, like those shown on the facing page (this statue has been moved from the Roman Forum to a museum). The dignity of her dress and bearing indicate the great respect in which the Vestals were held, for the fire of the hearth was always something particularly sacred to the Romans.

Indirect Statement

In Latin	*In English*
1. No conjunction is used.	1. "That" is frequently used.
2. The subject is in the accusative.	2. The subject is in the nominative.
3. The verb is in the infinitive.	3. The verb is in the indicative.

433. VOCABULARY

NOUNS	2. mēnsis	4. urbs	6. vōx
1. labor	3. mūnus	5. vīs	

ADJECTIVES	8. aliēnus	10. iūstus	12. secundus
7. ācer	9. gravis	11. levis	

VERBS	16. haereō	20. ostendō	24. sciō
13. cōnsistō	17. iaciō	21. perveniō	25. sentiō
14. contendō	18. īnstō	22. prohibeō	26. solvō
15. dīcō	19. opprimō	23. putō	

CONJUNCTION	27. sī

434. VOCABULARY (English Meanings)

NOUNS
1. work
2. month
3. duty, service
4. city
5. force
6. voice

ADJECTIVES
7. sharp, keen
8. another's
9. heavy, severe
10. just
11. light
12. second

VERBS
13. stop
14. struggle, hasten
15. say, tell
16. stick
17. throw
18. threaten
19. overcome
20. show
21. arrive
22. prevent
23. think
24. know
25. feel, realize
26. loosen, pay

CONJUNCTION
27. if

435. UNIT PRACTICE AND EXERCISES

Form Drill

1. Decline **vōx ipsa, nūllus pēs, hic mēnsis.**
2. Give in all tenses the third plural active of **timeō;** the third singular passive of **opprimō.**
3. Form the participles, active and passive, of **regō, iaciō, sciō,** and **respondeō.**
4. Form the infinitives, active and passive, of **sentiō, intercipiō, ostendō,** and **mōnstrō.**

Exercises

A. Translate the words in italics. Be careful to make the participle agree with its noun in gender, number, and case:
1. *Running* water is usually fresh.
2. We saw the boys *dragging* a big sled.
3. They heard the sound of men *approaching*.
4. Are they *going to remain* in this country?
5. She was *going to say* something to her friend.
6. He forgot to mail the letter *after he had folded* it.
7. *When he had heard these words*, he felt encouraged.

Dancing girls in an ancient relief now in the Louvre, Paris.

Photo Hachette

Albert Moldvay

A modern statue by Thornycroft in London showing Queen Boudicca in her chariot. Boudicca led the Britons in a brief revolt against the Romans in 61 A.D. It failed, and she took poison.

B. Complete in Latin these indirect statements and translate:
1. Sciō (*the boys are reading*) librōs.
2. Spērō (*the boys will read*) librōs.
3. Putō (*the boys have read*) librōs.
4. Dīxit (*the books were being read*) ā puerīs.
5. Dīxit (*the books had been read*) ā puerīs.

436. ENGLISH WORD STUDIES

1. Explain the following and give the Latin words from which they are derived: *omnipotent, alienate, vocal, expulsive, oppressive, diction, ostensible, prohibit.*

2. Find and use in sentences as many English derivatives as possible from **dīcō** and **putō**.

3. The first word in each of the following lines is a Latin word From among the last five words in each line pick the one which is an English derivative of the first word.

scit	skit	sky	sigh	scientific	sit
tangō	tangerine	tang	intangible	tango	tactics
putātus	putty	put	repute	potato	pot
dīcere	contradict	dixie	dice	decree	decent
gravia	graft	graveyard	gravity	engrave	gray

UNIT XII

GREEK MYTHS AND ROMAN HISTORY

Here in the Roman Forum we see the three surviving columns of the Temple of Castor and Pollux (right), dedicated to the twins who, after fighting on the side of the Romans against the Tarquins, miraculously appeared at this site to announce the Roman victory. Further in the distance, we see the Arch of Titus.

Erich Lessing/PhotoEdit

Lesson LX

437. *QUATTUOR AETĀTĒS*

Antīquī dīxērunt prīmam aetātem esse auream. Sāturnus erat rēx
deōrum hominumque. Illō tempore poenae lēgēsque aberant, quod
omnēs hominēs iūstī erant. Nūllae nāvēs in marī erant, nec trāns
mare lātum hominēs nāvigābant. Bellum numquam erat nec mīlitēs
5 et arma. In ōtiō vītam hominēs agēbant, nam omnēs terrae concordiā
et pāce ligātae sunt. Hominēs in agrīs nōn labōrābant; terra nōn
culta ipsa frūmentum et omnia ūtilia dabat. Urbēs nōn erant. Neque
hiems neque aestās erat: semper erat vēr. Flūmina lactis [1] et vīnī
erant. Quod omnēs agrī commūnēs erant, terminī agrōrum nōn erant.
10 Aliēnōs agrōs hominēs nōn cupiēbant.

Sāturnō expulsō, Iuppiter rēx erat. Nunc incipit secunda aetās,
quae ex argentō est, dūrior quam prīma, grātior tamen quam tertia.
Tum aestās et hiems esse incipiunt; quattuor sunt spatia annī. Tum
prīmum in agrīs labōrāre hominēs incipiunt.

15   Tertia aetās ex aere [2] erat. Dūrior erat quam secunda.

Quārta aetās, quae ex ferrō est, dūrissima omnium est. Poenae
gravissimae statuuntur, sed hominēs interficiunt et rapiunt. Nautae
in omnī marī ad ultima loca nāvigant et ūtilia petunt quae in variīs
terrīs continentur. Bellīs numquam intermissīs, hominēs terrās aliēnās
20 vincere mātūrant. Nihil sacrum est; omnia rapiuntur. Hominēs in
agrīs labōrant; nam labor omnia vincit.

Haec dīcunt auctōrēs clārissimī Graecī dē quattuor aetātibus.
Vergilius,[3] poēta Rōmānus, putābat iterum aetātem auream futūram
esse. Etiam nunc multī putant vītam semper grātiōrem futūram esse.
25 Putātisne fortasse condiciōnem fortūnamque populōrum antīquōrum
meliōrem [4] fuisse quam condiciōnem nostram? Quō modō statuistis
hanc sententiam vēriōrem esse? Quae erit condiciō hominum post
mīlle annōs? Aliī dīcunt: "Tempora mūtantur, et nōs mūtāmur in illīs."
Aliī respondent hominēs semper eōsdem fuisse et futūrōs esse. Quae
30 est sententia vestra? Possuntne fortasse ambae [5] sententiae vērae
esse?

---

[1] *of milk.*   [2] *of bronze.*   [3] *Virgil.*   [4] *better.*   [5] *both.*

In this woodcut from an edition of Ovid, 1501, Prometheus creates man out of clay and sends him fire. Thus the Golden Age was born. The Silver Age is shown by men working in the fields and building homes. Fighting started in the Bronze Age but became worse in the Iron Age, when sailing on the seas began.

QUESTIONS

1. Why didn't men work in the Golden Age?
2. When did they begin?
3. When did crime begin?

438. Comparison of Adjectives

Adjectives change form to show *degree*. This is called *comparison*. There are three degrees: *positive, comparative, superlative*. The positive is the simple form of the adjective; the others indicate a greater degree. To *compare* an adjective is to give the three degrees.

In English, the comparative is formed by adding –*er* (–*r*) to the positive: *high-er, brave-r*. The superlative is formed by adding –*est* (–*st*) to the positive: *high-est, brave-st*. But adjectives of more than one syllable are often compared by the use of *more* and *most: more skillful, most skillful*.

In Latin, the comparative is formed by adding –**ior** (m. and f.), –**ius** (n.) to the base of the positive, and the superlative is formed by adding –**issimus, –a, –um**:

POSITIVE	COMPARATIVE	SUPERLATIVE
altus, –a, –um, *high* (base, **alt–**)	**altior, altius,** *higher*	**altissimus, –a, –um,** *highest*
fortis, –e, *brave* (base, **fort–**)	**fortior, fortius,** *braver*	**fortissimus, –a, –um,** *bravest*

Hints for Translating. The comparative may also often be translated *more, too, rather;* the superlative, *most, very, exceedingly:* **ūtilior,** *more useful;* **altissimus,** *very high.*

439. Declension of the Comparative

Adjectives are declined as follows in the comparative:

	SINGULAR		PLURAL	
	M., F.	**N.**	**M., F.**	**N.**
Nom.	altior	altius	altiōrēs	altiōra
Gen.	altiōris	altiōris	altiōrum	altiōrum
Dat.	altiōrī	altiōrī	altiōribus	altiōribus
Acc.	altiōrem	altius	altiōrēs	altiōra
Abl.	altiōre	altiōre	altiōribus	altiōribus

While comparatives are declined like adjectives of the third declension, they do not have **–ī** in the abl. sing., **–ium** in the gen. plur., or **–ia** in the nom. and acc. plur. neuter; i.e., comparatives are not **i**–stems.

In Latin, when **quam** is used, the two things compared are in the same case; but in English *than* is usually followed by the nominative because a verb is understood: **Fortiōrem virum quam illum nōn vīdī,** *A braver man than he (is) I have not seen.*

The Pont du Gard, in France, is a Roman aqueduct and bridge combined.

Homines interficiunt et rapiunt. A preliminary sketch for Pietro da Cortona's (1596–1669) "Age of Iron." The finished painting is in Florence, Italy.

Practice

1. Compare **grātus, nōbilis, clārus, levis, longus.**
2. Decline **tardus** in the comparative.
3. Decline **supplicium iūstius.**

440. Exercises

A. 1. Novissimum librum ad frātrem meum mittere statuī.
    2. Quid est ūtilius grātiusque quam librōs bonōs semper legere?
    3. Gallī vīribus corporis Rōmānōs superābant sed nōn erant fortiōrēs virī.
    4. Condiciōnēs pācis ab hostibus victīs semper dūrissimae esse habentur.
    5. Homō dē viīs mē rogāvit; ego respondī hanc esse plāniōrem quam illam.
    6. Eī duo itinera ostendimus—alterum facile, alterum longius et incertius.

B. 1. Nothing is more useful than water.
    2. Why are not the rivers of Italy very long?
    3. Does peace have nobler victories than war?
    4. I know that that river is swift but not very wide.
    5. More severe terms of peace than these will be determined (upon).

353

Fragments such as these present a classical jigsaw puzzle to the specialists who try to reassemble them into the objects they were in ancient times. These are a few of the thousands of pieces of sculpture found in a cave near Rome.

441. Vocabulary

ae′tās, aetā′tis, f., *age*	(eternal)
condi′ciō, condiciō′nis, f., *condition, terms*	(conditional)
quam, conj., *than*	
ra′piō, –ere, ra′puī, rap′tus, *carry off*	(rapacious)
sta′tuō, –ere, sta′tuī, statū′tus, (*make stand*), *establish,* *determine*	[stō]
ū′tilis, –e, *useful*	(utility, utilitarian)
vin′cō, –ere, vī′cī, vic′tus, *conquer*	(victor, invincible)

442. English Word Studies

It is important to distinguish different words that come from the same stem. "Plain" and "plane" both come from **plānus,** *level, flat.* A "plain" is a *level* field; a "plain" person is not above the average *level.* A "plane" is a *flat* surface (hence "plane" geometry); it is also a tool that makes surfaces *flat.* The *flat* surfaces of an "airplane" (or "hydroplane") enable it to glide through the air (or water). "Plane" is therefore used in a more literal sense than "plain."

Take **corpus:** a "corpse" is a dead *body;* a "corps" (pronounced "core") is a *body* of men forming part of an army. The former is literal, the latter, figurative. A "corporation" is a *body* of men united for commercial or other purposes. A "corpuscle" is a little *body* in the blood. "Corporal" punishment is punishment inflicted upon the *body,* i.e., a whipping; but something "corporeal" has a *body,* i.e., it is not imaginary. Similarly, a "principal" is the *leading* person in a school; a "principle" is a *leading* rule.

Now explain in the same way *statue* and *statute; urban* and *urbane; sensory* and *sentiment; respiration* and *inspiration.*

354

Lesson LXI

443. BAUCIS ET PHILĒMŌN

Iuppiter et Mercurius per Phrygiam, quae in Asiā est, iter fēcērunt, sed nēmō in tōtā illā gente eōs cognōvit. Omnēs eōs esse hominēs
humilēs iūdicāvērunt. Ad mīlle casās accessērunt; nam locum somnō
aptum petīvērunt. Sed omnēs, hīs vīsīs, casās celeriter clausērunt.
In tōtā regiōne ācriter repulsī sunt. Tamen ūna casa, parva et 5
humilis, eōs nōn reppulit. Ibi Baucis et Philēmōn [1] multōs annōs
ēgerant. Condiciōne humilī nōn affectī, paupertātem leviter ac
fortiter sustinuērunt. Duo tōta domus [2] fuērunt, et dominī et servī
ipsī; nam nūllōs servōs habuērunt.

[1] *Baucis (Bau'sis), Philē'mon.*   [2] *household* (predicate nominative).

**Casa humilis deos non reppulit. Philemon washes Jupiter's feet while Baucis pre-
pares supper. Painted by P. Gyselaer.**

Frick Art Reference Library

10 Cēnam humilem Baucis magnā dīligentiā celeritāteque parāvit; numquam celerius labōrāverat. Tum, omnibus īnstrūctīs, deōs ad cēnam vocāvit. Mēnsa, nōn pulchra sed ūtilis, paucīs sed bonīs cibīs īnstrūcta erat. Vīnum sūmunt, sed semper crāter [3] vīnum continēbat. Tum Philēmōn et Baucis, ad mēnsam sedentēs, clārē sēnsērunt deōs
15 adesse. Tum Iuppiter, "Deī sumus," inquit. "Tōtam hanc gentem poenam solūtūram esse statuimus, quod nēmō nōbīs auxilium dedit, sed vōs vīvētis. Ad montem prōcēdēmus." Itaque Baucis et Philēmōn, hāc ōrātiōne permōtī, ad montem tardē prōcessērunt. Ibi cōnstitērunt et vīdērunt tōtam regiōnem sub aquā esse, casam suam sōlam manēre.
20 Dum spectant, casa eōrum in pulchrum templum vertitur.

Tum Iuppiter, "Quid cupitis?" inquit; "id quod petitis dōnābō." Philēmōn, uxōre cōnsultā, respondit: "Nūllum mūnus nōbīs grātius aptiusque esse iūdicāmus quam esse sacerdōtēs [4] illīus templī et ē vītā eōdem tempore excēdere, quod in concordiā multōs annōs ēgimus."
25 Post hanc ōrātiōnem hoc mūnus Iuppiter eīs permīsit.

Post multōs annōs, Philēmōn et uxor, aetāte gravēs, ante sacrum templum stābant. Corpora eōrum in arborēs [5] tardē vertuntur; vōcēs haerent; nōn iam spīrant nec vīvunt. Neuter ante alterum ē vītā excessit. Multōs annōs hae duae arborēs ante templum stābant.

QUESTIONS

1. What was Jupiter looking for?

[3] *bowl.*   [4] *priests.*   [5] *trees.*

Even Mercury sometimes gets tired, in spite of his winged sandals.

Philemon et Baucis, aetate graves, ante sacrum templum stabant. Corpora eorum in arbores vertuntur. A woodcut from an edition of Ovid, 1563.

2. Why did it take so long to find it?

3. How did Philemon find out that his guests were gods?

444. Formation of Adverbs

1. Adverbs formed from adjectives of the first and second declensions are explained in **169**.

2. In the positive degree, adverbs formed from adjectives of the third declension generally add **–iter** to the base; as, adj., **fortis**, adv., **fortiter**; adj., **ācer**, adv., **ācriter**.

The comparison of adverbs is very similar to that of adjectives:

POSITIVE	COMPARATIVE	SUPERLATIVE
altē	**altius**	**altissimē**
fortiter	**fortius**	**fortissimē**

Note that in the comparative degree the adverb always has the same form as the neuter accusative singular of the comparative adjective.

Practice

Form and compare adverbs from the following adjectives already studied: **longus, ūtilis, levis, clārus, firmus, gravis, vērus.**

445. Exercises

A. 1. Sciō hoc flūmen esse longius quam illud.
 2. Pater meus omnia iūstē et celeriter iūdicat.
 3. Praemiō acceptō, magister ōrātiōne aptā respondit.
 4. Hī mīlitēs, ē castrīs ēductī, ad pugnam ā duce īnstruuntur.
 5. Tardius pervēnimus quod reliquī puerī celerius cucurrērunt.
 6. Hī hominēs, ab hostibus repulsī, in pāce vīvere statuērunt.

B. 1. We shall breathe more easily.
 2. No one approves a very long speech.
 3. The battle was sharply fought, but few men received severe wounds.
 4. We certainly hope that all nations will live in peace, (now that it has been) established.

446. Vocabulary

ap′tus, –a, –um, *fit, suitable* (adapt)
*gēns, gen′tis, gen′tium, f., *people, nation* [*genus*]
h̓u′milis, –e, *low, humble* (humility)
īn′struō, –ere, īnstrū′xī, īnstrūc′tus, *arrange, provide*
 [*struō, arrange*]
iū′dicō, –ā′re, –ā′vī, –ā′tus, *judge* (judicial)
nē′mō, dat. nē′minī, acc. nē′minem (no other forms), *no one*
 [*homō*]
ōrā′tiō, ōrātiō′nis, f., *speech* (orator)
re′giō, regiō′nis, f., *region* [*regō*]
repel′lō, –ere, rep′pulī, repul′sus, *drive back, repulse* [*pellō*]
vī′vō, –ere, vī′xī, vīc′tus, *be alive, live* (vivid, victuals)

447. English Word Studies: The Suffix –iō

In Latin the suffix **–iō** is added to verb stems, usually to that of the past participle. Since this generally ends in **–t** or **–s,** words of this origin are likely to end in **–tiō** or **–siō.** The suffix indicates an act or the result of an act: **ōrātiō** is the act of speaking, or the result, i.e., a speech. Nouns with this suffix have **–iōnis** in the genitive. Therefore the stem ends in **n.** The English form of the suffix, which is very common, is *–ion* (*–tion, –sion*): *region, oration, session.* It often has the force of the suffix *–ing.*

Give and define ten English words with the suffix *–ion* derived from Latin verbs which you have studied. Look up the origin and meaning of *gentle, gentile, genteel, jaunty.*

Praeceps puer miser in mare cecidit. Icarus on the door of the memorial to the Wright brothers at Kitty Hawk, N. C., honoring their first airplane flight in 1903.

Aycock Brown

Lesson LXII

448. DAEDALUS ET ĪCARUS

In īnsulā magnā Crētā Mīnōs [1] fuit rēx. Daedalus [2] cum fīliō parvō Īcarō [2] ibi captīvus fuit. Fugere nōn potuit quod mare prohibuit. "Neque per terram," inquit, "neque per mare fugere possum, sed caelum certē nōn clausum est. Illā viā difficillimā prōcēdēmus." Itaque ālās parāvit, simillimās ālīs vērīs avium.[3] Partēs ālārum cērā [4] ligāvit. 5 Īcarus ad patrem stābat, ālās levissimās tangēbat, opus patris impediēbat. Tandem fīnis labōris difficilis aderat; ālae parātae erant. Daedalus tempus aptum esse iūdicāvit. Tum ālās corporī fīlī iūnxit et eum hīs verbīs ācriter monuit:

"In mediō caelō prōcēdēmus; nam, sī humilius volābimus,[5] undae 10 ālās graviōrēs facient; sī altius volābimus, ignis ālās ūret [6] et in mare cadēs. Omnia nunc tibi explicābō."

Tum omnēs partēs ālārum fīliō ostendit et omnia in ōrdine explicāvit. Perīculum esse sēnsit et fīliō timuit, quī patrī dissimillimus erat. Ālīs propriīs īnstrūctus antecessit et fīlium post volāre iussit. 15

Agricolae territī ex agrīs eōs vīdērunt; multī putāvērunt eōs deōs aut deīs similēs esse. Celerrimē pater fīliusque āera [7] ālīs pepulērunt.[8]

[1] *Mī'nos* (nom. sing.).   [2] *Daedalus (Dĕd'alus), Ic'arus.*   [3] *of birds.*
[4] *wax.*   [5] *fly.*   [6] *will burn.*
[7] Accusative singular: *air.*   [8] *beat* (from **pellō**).

359

Multās regiōnēs multāsque gentēs relīquērunt. Tum puer nōn iam timidus patrem ducem relīquit. Ōrātiōnem patris memoriā nōn
20 tenuit et altius volāvit quod iūdicāvit nihil accidere posse. Sed multa accidērunt: celeriter sōl cēram solvit; nōn iam ālae haesērunt. Praeceps puer miser in mare cecidit; nōn iam vīvit. Ab illō posteā hoc mare nōmen proprium "Īcarium" accēpit.

Interim pater, nōn iam pater, in omnibus regiōnibus fīlium petīvit,
25 nōmen fīlī clāmāvit. Tandem ālās Īcarī in undīs vīdit sed corpus eius numquam invēnit.

Tum ipse ad Siciliam facile pervēnit et ibi multōs annōs ēgit. Sed fābula ab aliīs dicta huic dissimilis est: scrībunt eum in Italiam volāvisse et ibi in templō ālās posuisse. Hōc modō deīs prō salūte grātiās
30 ēgit.

Prīmus omnium hominum Daedalus, Nātūrā victā, per caelum lātum volāvit, sī auctōrēs Graecī et Rōmānī vērum dīxērunt. Nunc multī hominēs facile volant, etiam per immēnsum,[9] sed nēmō ālīs propriīs. Quid hominibus difficilius [10] est?

QUESTIONS

1. In what way did Icarus disobey his father?
2. Where did Daedalus land?

449. Comparison of –er Adjectives and Their Adverbs

The superlative of all adjectives ending in **–er** is formed by adding **–rimus, –a, –um** to the nominative singular masculine of the positive:

POSITIVE	COMPARATIVE	SUPERLATIVE
līber, lībera, līberum	līberior, līberius	līberrimus, –a, –um
ācer, ācris, ācre	ācrior, ācrius	ācerrimus, –a, –um
celer, celeris, celere	celerior, celerius	celerrimus, –a, –um

The corresponding adverbs are formed as follows:

POSITIVE	COMPARATIVE	SUPERLATIVE
līberē	līberius	līberrimē
ācriter	ācrius	ācerrimē
celeriter	celerius	celerrimē

[9] *the immeasurable,* i.e., *space.*   [10] See **438**, "Hints."

Practice

Compare **miser, pulcher, altus.** Form and compare the corresponding adverbs. Decline **illa līberior patria.**

450. Adjectives with Superlative in –limus

The superlative of five adjectives ending in **–lis** is formed by adding **–limus, –a, –um** to the base of the positive:

POSITIVE	COMPARATIVE	SUPERLATIVE
facilis, –e	facilior, facilius	facillimus, –a, –um
difficilis, –e	difficilior, difficilius	difficillimus, –a, –um
similis, –e	similior, similius	simillimus, –a, –um
dissimilis, –e	dissimilior, dissimilius	dissimillimus, –a, –um
humilis, –e	humilior, humilius	humillimus, –a, –um

Note. The superlative of other **–lis** adjectives, such as **nōbilis, –e, ūtilis, –e,** etc., is formed regularly—i.e., by adding **–issimus** to the base of the positive: **nōbil–issimus, –a, –um.**

The adverbs formed from the adjectives in the preceding list are generally formed regularly, but the adverb from **facilis** is **facile.**

In the superlative the corresponding adverbs end in **–ē: facillimē.**

Statue of Icarus made in 1951 by Helene Sardeau.

The New York Times

451. Dative with Adjectives

1. **Hic liber est similis illī,** *This book is similar to that.*
2. **Ille homō est frātrī meō inimīcus,** *That man is unfriendly to my brother.*

Observe that the dative is often used with Latin adjectives whose English equivalents are followed by *to*. The following have already been studied: **amīcus, inimīcus, similis, dissimilis, aptus, grātus.**

452. Exercises

A. 1. Hic equus similior meō est quam ille.
    2. Rōmānōrum deī dissimillimī nostrō Deō erant.
    3. Ille liber difficillimus est, nam pauca clārē explicat.
    4. Humilis homō nec altē cadere nec graviter potest.
    5. Nihil est nōbīs ūtilius quam bonus liber; nam est nōbilissimus amīcōrum.

B. 1. This region is fit for (to) some settlers, but not for others.
    2. As the bad men approached, the boys ran more quickly.
    3. The places in which our soldiers fell are most sacred.
    4. The teacher in a very beautiful speech unfolded the life of Caesar.

453. Vocabulary

ca′dō, –ere, ce′cidī, cāsū′rus, *fall*   (cadence, casualty)
  ac′cidō, –ere, ac′cidī, —, *fall to, befall, happen* (with dat.)
diffi′cilis, –e, *difficult*   **[*facilis*]**
ex′plicō, –ā′re, –ā′vī, –ā′tus, *unfold, explain*   **[*plicō*]**
fa′cile, adv., *easily*   **[*facilis*]**
iun′gō, –ere, iūn′xī, iūnc′tus, *join* (*to*)   (joint, junction)
pro′prius, –a, –um, (*one's*) *own*   (propriety, appropriate)
si′milis, –e, *like*   (resemble, similarity)
  dissi′milis, –e, *unlike*

454. English Word Studies

1. "Space" and "missile" terms are often taken from Latin and Greek. *Space* is from **spatium,** *missile* from **mittō.** Others are *capsule* (**capiō**), which "holds" the crew, *circumlunar* (**circum, lūna,** "moon"), *core* (**corpus**), *fission* (**findō,** "split"), *fusion* (**fundō,** "pour," "melt"), *gravity* (**gravis**), *intercontinental* (**inter, contineō**), *interstellar* (**inter, stēlla**), *jet* (**iaciō**), *orb, orbit* (**orbis,** "circle"), *propellant* (**prō, pellō**), *reaction* (**re, agō**), *supersonic* (**super, sonus,** "sound"), *trajectory* (**trāns, iaciō**).

A contrast of moods in marble. The boy Icarus watches confidently as his father Daedalus anxiously stitches the feathers to his arm. A statue in Venice by the Italian sculptor Canova (1757–1882).

Missile names are often based on characters in myths: *Apollo, Atlas* (who held the earth on his shoulders), *Gemini, Jupiter, Mercury, Saturn, Titan.* Can you find other space terms derived from Latin?

2. Lawyers use so many Latin phrases daily that they must be familiar with Latin. A few such phrases are:

subpoena, a summons to court *under penalty* for failure to attend.

in propria persona, *in one's own person* (not through someone else).

ex post facto, *resulting after the fact;* as a law which makes punishable acts committed before its passage.

in forma pauperis, *in the form* (or *manner*) *of a poor man;* to sue as a poor man and so avoid the costs of the suit.

Look through the court records and legal items in the newspapers for other Latin phrases.

Lesson LXIII

455. PYRRHUS ET EIUS VICTŌRIA

Rōmānī, quī erant optimī mīlitēs, gentēs quae proximae urbī erant vīcerant et in ulteriōrēs partēs Italiae pervēnerant; summā virtūte contrā maiōrem numerum hostium in extrēmīs ac difficillimīs regiōnibus Italiae bene pugnāverant. Posteā bellum novī generis, dissimile
5 aliīs, cum Pyrrhō, duce summō et rēge maximō Ēpīrī, gessērunt.

Pyrrhus in Italiam īnferiōrem ā Tarentīnīs, gente pessimā, vocātus erat, quī eō tempore cum Rōmānīs pugnābant. Is in Italiam mīlitēs trānsportāvit et elephantōrum auxiliō Rōmānōs fortiter pugnantēs reppulit, quod Rōmānī elephantōs maximōs nōn ante vīsōs timu-
10 ērunt. Peius [1] tamen Pyrrhō victōrī quam victīs Rōmānīs accidit, nam plūrimī Pyrrhī mīlitēs cecidērunt. Pyrrhus, ubi plūrima corpora Rōmānōrum interfectōrum in fronte vulnera habēre vīdit, haec verba fēcit: "Bene Rōmānī pugnāvērunt. Cum tālibus [2] mīlitibus tōtus orbis [3] facillimē ā mē vincī potest!" Familiāribus dē victōriā agentibus dīxit:
15 "Sī iterum eōdem modō vīcerō, nūllōs mīlitēs ex Italiā īnferiōre in Ēpīrum redūcam." Nam hanc victōriam nōn ūtilem esse iūdicāvit quod plūrēs mīlitēs āmīserat.

QUESTIONS

1. What was the cause of Pyrrhus' victories?
2. What is a "Pyrrhic victory"?

456. Irregular Adjectives Compared

In English, some adjectives in common use are compared irregularly, such as *good, better, best; bad, worse, worst.*

---

[1] *a worse thing.*   [2] *such.*   [3] *world.*

Roman coins revealing the Roman idea of liberty. Both figures hold the liberty cap. S C are for "senatus consulto," "by decree of the Senate." Cf. the Statue of Liberty (p. 275).

Below: An elephant fitted out for battle marches across a third-century B.C. Etruscan pottery platter. The calf, tagging along by the mother's tail, does not seem quite so terrifying. Both Pyrrhus and Hannibal used elephants against the Romans.

Villa Giulia, Rome

Rome, Tiber River. In the background is the tomb of the Emperor Hadrian (117–138 A.D.), later a castle and prison, now a museum.

In Latin, the following adjectives, among others, are compared irregularly and should be memorized:

POSITIVE	COMPARATIVE	SUPERLATIVE
bonus, –a, –um (*good*)	**melior, melius** (*better*)	**optimus, –a, –um** (*best*)
malus, –a, –um (*bad*)	**peior, peius** (*worse*)	**pessimus, –a, –um** . (*worst*)
magnus, –a, –um (*large*)	**maior, maius** (*larger*)	**maximus, –a, –um** (*largest*)
parvus, –a, –um (*small*)	**minor, minus** (*smaller*)	**minimus, –a, –um** (*smallest*)
multus, –a, –um (*much*)	**—, plūs** [4] (*more*)	**plūrimus, –a, –um** (*most*)

The adverbs formed from the adjectives above are compared, in general, according to the rule **(444)**; exceptions used in this book are noted in the vocabularies.

Extrēmus and **Summus.** In English we sometimes have to use nouns to translate adjectives like **extrēmus** and **summus: in extrēmā ōrātiōne,** *at the end of the speech;* **summus mōns,** *top of the mountain* (cf. **reliquī mīlitēs,** *rest of the soldiers;* **in mediō flūmine,** *in the middle of the river*). When used in this way, the adjective usually precedes its noun.

---

[4] Gen. **plūris;** there is no masculine and feminine singular, and no dative singular at all, the plural is **plūrēs, plūra,** gen. **plūrium,** etc. See **558.**

457. Exercises

A.
1. Puerī ad īnferiōrem partem flūminis iter facient.
2. Optimī cīvēs patriam semper optimē dēfendent.
3. Summus mōns ā nōbīs facillimē occupātus est.
4. Pessimī hominēs in ultimās regiōnēs mittī dēbent.
5. Hī septem puerī territī sunt quod perīculum maximum esse sēnsērunt.
6. Agricolae quī meliōrēs agrōs habent maiōrem cōpiam frūmentī habēbunt.
7. Nōnne spērās proximum mēnsem nōn futūrum esse dūriōrem quam hunc?

B.
1. The smallest boy is not the worst.
2. Can a horse run more swiftly than a man?
3. The smaller man fought more bravely than the larger.
4. We shall do this well and very quickly without your aid.

458. Vocabulary

bě′ně, adv., *well*	**[bonus]**
extrē′mus, –a, –um, *farthest, last, end of*	(extremist)
īnfe′rior, īnfe′rius, *lower*	(inferiority)
prox′imus, –a, –um, *nearest, next* (with dat.)	(proximity)
sum′mus, –a, –um, *highest, top of*	(sum, summit)
ulte′rior, ulte′rius, *farther*	(ulterior)

459. English Word Studies

1. A number of English words preserve the forms of the comparative and superlative of Latin irregular adjectives: *major* (cf. *mayor*), *maximum, minor, minus, minimum, plus, inferior, superior, ulterior, prior, anterior, posterior, interior, exterior, junior, senior.*

What is the difference between a *majority* and a *plurality* vote? Between a *majority* and a *minority* report?

2. Latin phrases in English:

excelsior, *higher* (motto of the state of New York).

esse quam videri, *to be rather than to seem* (*to be*) (motto of the state of North Carolina).

e pluribus unum, *one* (*country*) *out of many* (*states*) (motto of the United States, found on its coins).

Translate the motto of Oklahoma (also of the University of Illinois and the American Federation of Labor): **Labor omnia vincit.**

Pyrrhus. An ancient statue.

Lesson LXIV

460. PYRRHUS ET FABRICIUS

Fabricius,[1] quī erat īnferior genere quam aliī Rōmānī, tamen ab omnibus amātus est quod optimus fortissimusque mīles erat. Neque amīcōs neque inimīcōs suōs fallēbat. Praemia numquam sūmēbat. Itaque Rōmānī cīvitātis suae salūtem eī crēdidērunt et eum inter aliōs
5 lēgātōs ad Pyrrhum mīsērunt.

Multa quae dē Fabriciō et eius summā honestāte Pyrrhus audīverat vēra esse crēdidit. Itaque hunc lēgātum in castrīs suīs cōnspectum bene accēpit. Ad extrēmum eī dīxit: "Cūr nōn in Ēpīrum mēcum venīs et ibi manēs? Tibi quārtam rēgnī meī partem tribuam." Sed
10 Fabricius respondit sē neque partem rēgnī sibi tribuī cupere neque sūmptūrum esse.

Proximō annō Fabricius contrā Pyrrhum pugnāvit. Medicus rēgis mediā nocte ad eum vēnit et dīxit sē prō praemiō Pyrrhum interfectūrum esse. Fabricius, quī nēminem fefellerat, respondit sē nūl-
15 lum praemium prōpōnere et iussit hunc ligātum ad dominum redūcī et Pyrrhō omnia dīcī. Ubi rēx medicum ligātum cōnspexit, maximē mōtus dīxit: "Ille est Fabricius quī nōn facilius ab honestāte quam sōl ā cursū [2] suō āvertī potest!"

[1] *Fabricius (Fabrish'us).*   [2] Ablative; *course.*

1. Why did the Romans have so much confidence in Fabricius?
2. What offer did Pyrrhus make to Fabricius?
3. What reason did Pyrrhus have for being grateful to Fabricius?

461. *Reflexive Pronouns*

In English, as we have seen **(389)**, the emphatic pronouns *myself, ourselves,* etc., correspond to Latin **ipse:** *I myself saw him,* **Ipse eum vīdī.** These same English pronouns are used *reflexively* as objects of verbs or prepositions to refer to the subject of the verb: *I saw myself; He stuck a knife into himself.*

In Latin, the personal pronouns of the first and second persons may be used reflexively, but in the third person Latin has a special reflexive pronoun, **suī,** declined alike in the singular and plural:

Gen. **suī,**		*of himself, herself, itself, themselves*
Dat. **sibi,**	*to*	" " " "
Acc. **sē (sēsē),**		" " " "
Abl. **sē (sēsē),**	*with (from,* etc.)	" " " "

QUESTION

Why do reflexive pronouns have no nominative?

Fabricius before Pyrrhus. A painting by a Dutch artist of the seventeenth century. Presumably the bearded man next to Pyrrhus is Cineas (cf. section 354).

462. Use of Reflexive Pronouns

(ego)	**mē rogō,** *I ask myself*	**(nōs)**	**nōs rogāmus,** *we ask ourselves*
(tū)	**tē rogās,** *you ask yourself*	**(vōs)**	**vōs rogātis,** *you ask yourselves*
(is)	**sē rogat,** *he asks himself*	**(eī)**	**sē rogant,** *they ask themselves*

Practice

Give in all tenses the first singular of **līberō;** the second plural of **fallō;** the third singular of **interficiō,** using the correct reflexive pronoun with each.

463. Reflexive Adjectives

Corresponding to **meus, tuus, noster,** and **vester,** derived from **ego, tū, nōs,** and **vōs,** there is the reflexive adjective **suus, –a, –um,** *his own, her own, its own, their own,* derived from **suī.**

Caution. Remember that **suus** *always refers to the subject of the verb.* When *his, her,* etc., do not refer to the subject, then **eius,** etc., must be used **(379).** Note the difference in the following:

1. **Patrem eius vīdī,** *I saw his father.*
2. **Patrem suum vīdit,** *He saw his (own) father.*
3. **Patrem eius vīdit,** *He saw his* (i.e., someone else's) *father.*

From Ostia. The girl and a slave are apparently carrying geese to market. The prop is necessary because the marble horse is too heavy for its slender legs.

464. Exercises

A.
1. Frāter eius mātrem suam fefellit et posteā sē in mare iēcit.
2. Tū tē ipsum fallere semper potuistī sed mē numquam fefellistī.
3. Crēditisne Deum mare terramque prō sē aut prō nōbīs fēcisse?
4. Mūnera pūblica optimīs, nōn pessimīs, hominibus tribuī dēbent.
5. Arma sūmēmus et nōs fortiter dēfendēmus contrā pessimōs hostēs.
6. Puerum currentem cōnspexī, sed ille crēdidit sē ā mē nōn vīsum esse.

B. Translate the words in italics:
1. We saw *his* brother.
2. You will see *their* friends.
3. The girl loved *her* mother.
4. He wasted *his* money and *theirs*.
5. They will defend *themselves* and *us*.

C.
1. He says that he himself has four brothers.
2. We always praise ourselves and say the worst (things) about others.
3. Entrust yourselves and all your (possessions) to us.
4. The leader of the enemy, having caught sight of us, killed himself.

Stamp of the United States with the word "credo," "belief," derived from the Latin verb "credo," "I believe."

465. Vocabulary

cōnspi′ciō, –ere, –spe′xī, –spec′tus, *catch sight of, see*   [*spectō*]

con′trā, prep. with acc., *against*

crē′dō, –ere, crē′didī, crē′ditus, *believe, entrust* (with dat.) (credible)

fal′lō, –ere, fefel′lī, fal′sus, *deceive*   (fallacy, falsity)

lēgā′tus, –ī, m., *envoy*   [*lēgō, appoint*]

su′ī, reflex. pron., *of himself,* etc.   (suicide)

sū′mō, –ere, sūmp′sī, sūmp′tus, *take*   (assumption)

su′us, –a, –um, reflex. adj., *his own,* etc.

tri′buō, –ere, tri′buī, tribū′tus, *grant*   (contribute)

371

466. English Word Studies

In the fourteenth century there began a great revival of interest in the ancient Latin and Greek authors. This revival is known as the *Renaissance* (from **re-nāscor,** *to be born again*). Beginning in Italy, it spread over western Europe and reached England in the sixteenth century. Ever since then many new words have been added to English from Latin and Greek. These new words are easily distinguished by their similarity to the Latin originals. Over ninety per cent of the words in Caesar and Cicero have English derivatives.

One result of the introduction of new words directly from the Latin was the formation of a number of *doublets,* words derived at different periods from the same Latin word and having different meanings. Note the following (the earlier form precedes): *sample, example* **(exemplum);** *feat, fact* **(factum);** *Mr., master* **(magister);** *loyal, legal* **(lēx);** *mayor, major* **(maior);** *chance, cadence* **(cadō).** Show how these doublets got their meanings from the original Latin meaning. There is one set of *quintuplets* in English: *dais, desk, dish, disk, discus,* all from **discus.** Cf. **447** for a *quadruplet.*

An Italian skin diver brings up a lead anchor of ancient Roman times near Ponza, an island off the coast of Italy between Rome and Naples. The anchor weighs 440 lbs.

Wide World

Lesson LXV

467. RĒGULUS

Contrā Carthāginiēnsēs quī partem Āfricae incoluērunt arma ā
Rōmānīs sūmpta erant.[1] Rēgulus, dux Rōmānōrum, imperiō acceptō,
ad Āfricam nāvigāvit et hostēs superāvit. Multa mīlia captīvōrum in
Italiam mīsit sed ipse, opere difficilī nōn perfectō, in Āfricā remānsit.
Contrā trēs Carthāginiēnsium ducēs pugnāns victor fuit. Hostēs ā Rō-   5
mānīs pressī pācem petīvērunt. Quam [2] Rēgulus dīxit sē dūrissimīs
condiciōnibus datūrum esse. Itaque Carthāginiēnsēs auxilium ā Lace-
daemoniīs,[3] quī Graeciam incoluērunt, petīvērunt. Dux quī ā Lacedae-
moniīs missus erat cum quattuor mīlibus mīlitum et centum elephantīs
contrā Rōmānōs prōcessit. Rōmānīs victīs, Rēgulus captus est.   10

Rēgulus in Āfricā mānsit sed quīntō annō Carthāginiēnsēs superātī
eum ad urbem Rōmam mīsērunt. Eum iussērunt pācem ā Rōmānīs
obtinēre et permūtātiōnem captīvōrum facere. Is dīxit, pāce nōn factā,
sē ad eōs reversūrum esse. Illī crēdidērunt eum sē trāditūrum esse.

Itaque Rēgulus in Italiam pervēnit. Ductus in senātum Rōmānum 15
dīxit sē esse captīvum, nōn iam Rōmānum. Itaque etiam uxōrem,
quae eum cōnspexerat et ad eum cucurrerat, ā sē remōvit. Dīxit
hostēs, frāctōs multīs proeliīs, spem [4] nūllam nisi [5] in pāce habēre;
nōn esse ūtile multa mīlia captīvōrum prō sē ūnō, aetāte cōnfectō,
hostibus reddī. "Captīvōs Rōmānōs aurō emere nōn dēbēmus," ex- 20
plicat; "nam virtūs eōrum āmissa est, nec vēra virtūs aurō emī potest."
Senātus hōc cōnsiliō numquam ante datō permōtus pācem cum hosti-

---

[1] First Punic or Carthaginian War, 264–241 B.C. (cf. **233, 372, 491**). These
wars were for the supremacy of the world. Carthage was in northern Africa,
near present-day Tunis.

[2] In Latin, a relative is often used at the beginning of a sentence to connect with
the preceding sentence. In English, a demonstrative is used instead.

[3] *the Spartans.*   [4] *hope.*   [5] *except.*

Modern though the building looks, this model is of an ancient apartment house at Ostia, Rome's seaport. A good part of the building still stands.

bus nōn fēcit. Itaque Rēgulus, opere perfectō, Carthāginiēnsēs nōn fefellit sed in Āfricam revertit et sē Carthāginiēnsibus trādidit, ā quibus omnibus suppliciīs interfectus est. Posteā Rōmānī eī honōrēs tribuērunt.

Haec prīmō bellō Pūnicō accidērunt. Posteā Rōmānī, pāce frāctā, duo alia bella cum eīsdem hostibus gessērunt et imperium suum maximē auxērunt.

QUESTIONS

1. Why did Regulus remain in Africa?
2. What caused his later defeat?
3. Why did he urge the Romans not to make peace?

468. Declension of Duo and Trēs

The numbers from 4 to 100 are indeclinable in Latin. For **ūnus** see **394**. **Duo,** *two,* and **trēs,** *three,* are declined as follows:

	M.	F.	N.	M., F.	N.
Nom.	duo	duae	duo	trēs	tria
Gen.	duōrum	duārum	duōrum	trium	trium
Dat.	duōbus	duābus	duōbus	tribus	tribus
Acc.	duōs	duās	duo	trēs	tria
Abl.	duōbus	duābus	duōbus	tribus	tribus

469. Declension and Use of Mīlle

Mīlle, when used of one thousand, is usually an indeclinable adjective (like **centum**): **mīlle hominēs.** When used of two or more thousands, it is a neuter plural **i**–stem noun (cf. **mare, 340**). The word used with the plural forms of **mīlle** must be in the genitive: **duo mīlia hominum** (lit., *two thousands of men*), *two thousand men.*

	SINGULAR	PLURAL
Nom.	mīlle	mīlia
Gen.	mīlle	mīlium
Dat.	mīlle	mīlibus
Acc.	mīlle	mīlia
Abl.	mīlle	mīlibus

Practice

Give in Latin: *two boys, one hundred children, one thousand citizens, two thousand sailors, three thousand soldiers.*

A mosaic of a ship at Ostia. The oars were for steering. Ostia was a busy port since wheat from North Africa was imported there.

470. Exercises

A.
1. Nāvī frāctā, omnēs certē interficientur.
2. Duōs optimōs librōs ēmī quōs hāc aestāte legam.
3. Mīlle nautās cum tribus ducibus in maria ultima mīsimus.
4. Post duās pugnās hostēs cōnfectī nōn iam vim nostram sustinuērunt.
5. Centum mīlia agricolārum, agrīs suīs relīctīs, ad oppida contendērunt.

B.
1. Anna was third in rank, but her brother was fifth.
2. Three men were killed, and two received wounds.
3. The lower part of this river is between two nations.
4. All the boys easily completed the work in three hours.

471. Vocabulary

cen′tum, indeclinable adj., *hundred* (centennial, centipede)
e′mō, –ere, ē′mī, ēmp′tus, *take, buy* (redemption)
impe′rium, impe′rī, n., *command, power* (imperial, empire)
in′colō, –ere, inco′luī, incul′tus, *live, inhabit* [*colō*]
mīl′le, plur. **mī′lia,** *thousand* (millennium)
o′pus, o′peris, n., *work* (opus, operate)
perfi′ciō, –ere, –fē′cī, –fec′tus, *finish* [*faciō*]
trā′dō, –ere, trā′didī, trā′ditus, *give* or *hand over, surrender* [*dō*]

472. English Word Studies

1. Much difficulty is caused in English spelling by silent or weakly sounded letters. This difficulty is often solved by referring to the Latin original: *labor·a·tory, rep·e·tition, lib·r·ary, sep·a·rate, auxil·i·ary, compar·a·tive, de·b·t, rei·g·n, recei·p·t.* The Latin original often helps in other difficulties: *con·s·ensus, a·nn·uity, defi·c·it, acce·l·erate.*

Define the above words and give their Latin originals:

2. Much confusion is caused in English by the combinations *ei* and *ie.* Remember that the derivatives of compounds of **capiō** have *ei* as *receive.*

The Arch of Janus in Rome was erected during the time of Constantine. It was used as a shelter by cattle dealers. Small statues were placed in the niches of the arch.

Albert Moldvay

Glimpses of Roman Life

473. ROMAN SOCIAL AND ECONOMIC CONDITIONS

Until the Romans could control the food supply of the empire they had conquered, their economic system was quite unstable. And economic instability was one of the principal causes of the political dissension that reached its peak in the first century B.C.

From time to time the common people of Rome suffered from lack of food when the wheat crop failed, as also happens even in modern times. According to tradition, at one such time the senate, which was the ruling body, obtained a large amount of wheat and was planning to give it away to the poor. It was in connection with this plan that the plebeians were angry at Coriolanus, as we have already read (424). He advised the senate not to give the wheat free and criticized the plebeians sharply. All this happened in the fifth century B.C.—nearly twenty-five hundred years ago.

In the time of the Gracchi (second century B.C.) economic conditions became especially bad. The rich nobles had acquired large farms by taking over public lands and by forcing out the poor small farmers. These wandered over Italy with their families and many settled in Rome, where they had a hard time. They could not obtain work on the large farms because these were worked by slave labor. Tiberius Gracchus planned to force the large landowners to sell all but 500 acres of their lands at a reasonable price. He then intended to cut this land up into small farms to be rented at a low cost to the poor. He felt that the men who fought for their country had as much right to a home as the wild animals in the forests.

After Tiberius' death Gaius tried to carry out his brother's policies. In addition, he used the unemployed to build roads, stored large amounts of wheat to avoid shortages, gave relief to the poor by selling wheat well below cost, and established colonies. All of his measures have been tried in modern times. The poverty and unrest in southern Italy today is caused in part by the existence of large estates, though progress is being made in dividing them up into small farms.

The problems of dividing up the big estates, of furnishing relief by making available cheap or free wheat, and of helping the landless mobs who had flocked to the city continued to bother Roman leaders for another century after the death of the Gracchi. Julius Caesar, a popular leader who favored such measures, made himself a dictator and established government by emperors. Under his successor, Augustus, a great peace was established which brought prosperity and better living conditions for two hundred years. But the people paid for these advantages by a loss of their liberties and privileges: free speech, political rights, individual liberties of various sorts were gradually reduced.

DISCUSSION QUESTIONS

1. Discuss the policy of the Gracchi in giving public lands and wheat to the poor and using the unemployed in building roads. Give some modern parallels.
2. In what European countries has a program of social and economic reform resembling that of the Gracchi led to dictatorship?
3. How can any nation get a maximum of social reform without abandoning important liberties?

American Museum of Natural History

Left: Remains of an apartment house in Rome.

Below: Hadrian's Villa (see pp. 48, 204), showing an artificial island on which the Emperor had his private apartment.

Fototeca

UNIT XII REVIEW

Lessons LX–LXV

The Story of Lucius (cont.)

474. CAESARIS TRIUMPHUS

Quondam pater Lūcī ā Forō revertit et dīxit triumphum Caesaris futūrum esse et posteā magnōs lūdōs. C.[1] Iūlius Caesar tum erat maximus Rōmānōrum. Galliam, Alexandrīam, Pontum, Āfricam vīcerat. Decem annōs in Galliā ēgerat atque, multīs mīlibus hostium repulsīs, illam regiōnem in prōvinciam Rōmānam redēgerat. Pom- 5 peius,[2] cum Caesare prō summā potestāte contendēns, in fugam datus erat. Tum Caesar in Aegyptum prōcesserat et, Alexandrīnīs [3] pulsīs, Cleopātrae nōmen rēgīnae Aegyptiōrum dederat. Rēge Pontī celeriter victō, ex eius rēgnō nōtās illās litterās mīserat in quibus erant sōla verba, "Vēnī, vīdī, vīcī." Nunc, hōc opere perfectō, futūrī erant 10 quattuor triumphī, quod Caesar dē bellīs reverterat, cui summa potestās ā deīs commissa est.

WAITING

Lūcius numquam triumphum vīderat et dē eō multa rogāvit. Pater eī dīxit triumphum esse similem pompae in Circō habitae et 15 Caesarem per Circum et Sacram Viam ad Capitōlium prōcessūrum esse. Lūcius permōtus vix exspectāre poterat. Sed omnia ad eum quī exspectat veniunt; tempus triumphōrum aderat. Prīmus et clārissimus triumphus Caesaris erat Gallicus. Loca emī nōn potuērunt sed pater Lūcī familiāris Caesaris erat et optima loca obtinuit. Caesar in 20 Campō Mārtiō [4] mīlitēs īnstrūxit et ex praedā eīs praemia tribuit. Hōc factō, pompa tardē prōcēdere incipit.

---

[1] C. = Gāius.   [2] *Pompey.*   [3] *the people of Alexandria.*
[4] *Campus Martius (Mar'shus)*, a park in Rome.

Post longum tempus (ut [5] Lūcius putāvit) pompa aderat. Prīmī fuērunt cōnsulēs et senātōrēs, post quōs vēnērunt cornicinēs,[6] quī
25 Lūciō grātissimī fuērunt. Tum cōnspexit titulōs [7] ducum oppidōrumque captōrum cum fōrmīs exemplīsque [8] oppidōrum. Dē nōminibus nōn nōtīs multa rogāvit: "Quī sunt Aquītānī? Quī sunt Belgae?" Pater respondit: "Gallia est omnis dīvīsa [9] in partēs trēs; quārum ūnam incolunt Belgae, aliam Aquītānī, tertiam eī quī ipsōrum linguā Celtae,
30 nostrā Gallī appellantur. Hōrum omnium fortissimī sunt Belgae." "Quī sunt Helvētiī?" [10] "Helvētiī statuērunt per prōvinciam nostram iter facere quod maiōrēs fīnēs habēre cupīvērunt, sed ā Caesare prohibitī sunt." "Quis est Ariovistus?" "Ariovistus erat superbus rēx Germānōrum, ā Caesare ex Galliā expulsus." "Quī sunt Germānī?"
35 "Maxima pars Germānōrum trāns Rhēnum flūmen incolunt.[11] Etiam trāns Rhēnum Caesar mīlitēs suōs trādūxit et cum Germānīs contendit." "Quid est Britannia?" "Britannia est extrēma īnsula, ā barbarīs culta; etiam ad eam Caesar pervēnit. Sed sōlum [12] post centum annōs nostra erit."

HAIL! THE CONQUERING HERO COMES!

40 Posteā Lūcius cōnspexit arma captōrum prīncipum et prīncipēs ipsōs ligātōs, inter quōs erat Vercingetorīx.[13] Nunc populus maximē clāmat. "Quis est ille?" rogat Lūcius. Pater respondet: "Ille est ultimus dux Gallōrum, quī victōs Gallōs ad bellum permōvit, sed Caesarī trāditus est. Eō tempore quō pompa ad Capitōlium pervēnit, ille
45 interficiētur." Nunc clāmōrēs audiuntur: "Caesar adest! Caesar adest!" Currus imperātōris, quattuor equīs trāctus, cernitur. Caesar ipse togam pictam [14] gerit et scēptrum tenet. In currū [15] .stat servus corōnam super Caesaris caput tenēns. Sed subitō [16] omnēs terrentur: axe frāctō, Caesar paene [17] ē currū iactus est. Hic sōlus nōn com-
50 mōtus est. Dum cōnstitit ac novum currum exspectat, Lūcium cōnspicit et eum rogat: "Tū, quis es?" Lūcius respondet: "Ego sum

---

[5] *as.* [6] *buglers.* [7] *placards* (with names of towns, etc.).
[8] *models* (of wood, etc.). [9] From **dīvidō.** Use derivative.
[10] *Helvetians (Helvē'shians).*
[11] A plural verb may be used when the subject is grammatically singular but refers to more than one.
[12] *only.* [13] *Vercingetorix (Versinjet'orix).*
[14] *embroidered* (with gold). [15] Ablative. [16] *suddenly.* [17] *almost.*

Lūcius Iūlius. Patrem meum nōvistī. Mīles erō et multās gentēs vincam." Caesar rīdēns eius caput tetigit et dīxit: "Bene incipis. Putō tē imperātōrem futūrum esse." Pompa intermissa rūrsus [18] prōcēdit, et nunc mīlitēs Caesaris accēdunt, clāmantēs, "Iō triumphe! [19] Iō [55] triumphe!" Etiam carmina canunt. Inter alia Lūcius haec audit:

"Ecce [20] Caesar nunc triumphat quī subēgit Galliās."

Itaque omnēs discēdunt, Lūciō clāmante, "Iō triumphe! Iō triumphe!"

QUESTIONS

1. What was a triumph?
2. What two kings did Caesar defeat?
3. Who came first in the parade and who last?

Italian stamp honoring Horace's birthday (cf. p. 335). The lines from his Odes welcome the return of spring. This poem was a favorite of Thomas Jefferson.

475. VOCABULARY

NOUNS			
1. aetās	3. gēns	6. mīlle	9. ōrātiō
2. condiciō	4. imperium	7. nēmō	10. regiō
	5. lēgātus	8. opus	

ADJECTIVES	14. dissimilis	18. proprius	22. suus
11. aptus	15. extrēmus	19. proximus	23. ulterior
12. centum	16. humilis	20. similis	24. ūtilis
13. difficilis	17. īnferior	21. summus	

PRONOUN	25. suī		

VERBS	31. explicō	37. perficiō	43. tribuō
26. accidō	32. fallō	38. rapiō	44. vincō
27. cadō	33. incolō	39. repellō	45. vīvō
28. cōnspiciō	34. īnstruō	40. statuō	
29. crēdō	35. iūdicō	41. sūmō	
30. emō	36. iungō	42. trādō	

ADVERBS	46. bene	47. facile	

PREPOSITION	48. contrā		

CONJUNCTION	49. quam		

[18] *again.*　　　[19] Exclamation: *Triumph!*　　　[20] *look.*

476. VOCABULARY (English Meanings)

NOUNS			
	3. *nation*	6. *thousand*	9. *speech*
1. *age*	4. *command*	7. *no one*	10. *region*
2. *condition*	5. *envoy*	8. *work*	

ADJECTIVES			
	14. *unlike*	18. *one's own*	22. *his own*
11. *suitable*	15. *farthest, end of*	19. *next*	23. *farther*
12. *hundred*	16. *low, humble*	20. *like*	24. *useful*
13. *difficult*	17. *lower*	21. *highest, top of*	

PRONOUN	
	25. *of himself*

VERBS			
	31. *unfold*	37. *finish*	43. *grant*
26. *happen*	32. *deceive*	38. *carry off*	44. *conquer*
27. *fall*	33. *inhabit*	39. *drive back*	45. *live*
28. *catch sight of*	34. *arrange, provide*	40. *establish*	
29. *believe*	35. *judge*	41. *take*	
30. *buy*	36. *join*	42. *give over*	

ADVERBS		
	46. *well*	47. *easily*

PREPOSITION	
	48. *against*

CONJUNCTION	
	49. *than*

The triumph of Caesar in a fifteenth-century painting by the Italian artist Mantegna. The inscription means: "To Gen. Julius Caesar for conquering Gaul by military power, a triumph was decreed, (all) malice (against him) having been removed and overcome." "Devict" is for "devictam," "potencia" for "potentia."

477. UNIT PRACTICE AND EXERCISES

Comparison

1. Compare **aptus, celer, levis, iūstus.** Form and compare adverbs from **certus, ācer, humilis.**
2. Decline **ūtilior liber** and **melior aetās** in the singular.
3. Give in Latin in the singular and plural in the case indicated: *a most beautiful region* (nom.); *a worse time* (acc.); *a rather long journey* (dat.); *the smallest part* (abl.); *a larger ship* (gen.).

Left: Italian stamp for "twin" cities Paris and Rome, showing the twins Romulus and Remus. *Right:* Stamp of Liechtenstein with inscription: "Opus iustitiae pax Pius XII," "The work of justice (is) peace, Pius XII."

Reflexive Forms

Give in Latin: *he deceives him and himself; they praise them and themselves; they will ask their friends and hers; he defends himself; we praise him; she will see her father.*

478. ENGLISH WORD STUDIES

1. Give the Latin words suggested by the following English derivatives:

accident, appropriate, conditional, conspicuous, credible, fallacious, instructive, opera, proximity, rapture, regional, redemptive, repulsive, centipede, millepede

2. From your knowledge of Latin rearrange these French numerals in the proper sequence:

trois, sept, un, cinq, quatre, dix, huit, neuf, deux, six

3. Find and use in sentences as many English derivatives as possible from **nāvigō, doceō, vincō, sūmō.**

4. Complete each of the following sentences as in this sample: **Perficiō** is to *perfection* as **incipiō** is to *inception.*

a. **Emō** is to *redemption* as ? is to *repulsion.*
b. *Creditor* is to **crēdō** as *instructor* is to ?.
c. **Ūtilis** is to *utility* as ? is to *humility.*
d. *Statute* is to **statuō** as *institute* is to ?.
c. *Consistency* is to **cōnsistō** as ? is to **currō.**

UNIT XIII

MEN WHO MADE ROME GREAT

In its long history, Rome was blessed with many outstanding leaders. The best known of these is Julius Caesar (100–44 B.C.), soldier, statesman, and historian. Unquestionably he was a great military commander. His absolute physical courage, his self-confidence, his iron will, his fairness, and his generosity with praise and rewards made him an unparalleled leader of men. You will find a great deal more information about this unusual man in the *Second Book* of the *Latin for Americans* series.

An ancient statue of Marius in a museum in Rome. Here Marius is shown wearing the toga of the peaceful orator, not the uniform of a conquering general.

Lesson LXVI

479. MARIUS

C. Marius, vir humilis generis, ob ēgregiam virtūtem cōnsul ā Rōmānīs factus est. Plūrimī cīvēs putāvērunt eum esse maximum imperātōrem aetātis suae.

Iugurthā,[1] rēge Numidiae, quae terra in Āfricā est, victō, Marius
5 bellum contrā Cimbrōs et Teutonēs [2] suscēpit. Hī, quī extrēmōs fīnēs Germāniae incoluerant, Cimbrīs sē iūnxerant. Multōs mēnsēs hae duae gentēs novās terrās petīverant et ad prōvinciam Rōmānam pervēnerant. Tribus ducibus Rōmānīs ā barbarīs repulsīs, Marius mīlitēs trēs annōs exercuit. Posteā Teutonēs sub Alpibus proeliō
10 superāvit ac super centum mīlia interfēcit.

Cimbrī autem, quī nihil dē victōriā Rōmānōrum audīverant, per lēgātōs praemissōs ācriter sibi et Teutonibus agrōs petīvērunt. Marius rīdēns, "Illī tenent," inquit, "semperque tenēbunt terram ā [3] nōbīs acceptam." Proximō annō is cum mīlitibus bene exercitīs contrā eōs
15 pugnāvit. Nec minor erat pugna cum uxōribus eōrum quam cum virīs. Illae quae supererant sē līberōsque suōs interfēcērunt.

Multōs annōs Rōmānī hōs barbarōs īnstantēs timuerant, sed Alpēs post hanc victōriam Rōmam ā perīculō prohibēbant.

Postquam Rōmānī intellēxērunt necesse [4] esse bellum cum Mi-
20 thridāte [5] gerere, hoc negōtium Sullae commīsērunt. Sed postquam Sulla ex urbe discessit, Marius, quī ipse cupīvit hoc negōtium super omnia suscipere, summam potestātem obtinuit. Posteā Sulla cum mīlitibus quōs circum sē habuit Marium in fugam dedit. Mīlitibus praemissīs, paucōs mēnsēs Rōmae [6] Sulla mānsit. Postquam autem
25 ad bellum discessit, Marius Rōmam occupāvit.

---

[1] *Jugur'tha.*   [2] *Cimbri (Sim'brī), Teu'tons.*   [3] *from.*
[4] *necessary* (indeclinable).   [5] *Mithridā'tēs.*   [6] *at Rome.*

Quattuor annōs Sulla cum Mithridāte bellum gessit. Post mortem Marī in Italiam revertit. Omnēs hostēs prae sē agēns, circum multa oppida mīlitēs suōs dūxit. Dictātor factus, multa mīlia cīvium interficī iussit. Amīcus eum monuit: "Nōnne intellegis hoc nōn tibi ūtile esse? Sī omnēs interficiēs, et nēmō supererit, quōrum cīvium dictātor eris?" 30

QUESTIONS

1. What was the cause of the war with the Cimbri and Teutons?
2. Which did Marius defeat first? Where?
3. What was the cause of the quarrel between Marius and Sulla?
4. Give some examples of men in modern times who, like Marius, rose to high positions from humble beginnings.

480. Accusative of Extent

Duōs annōs remānsit, *He remained two years.*
Flūmen decem pedēs altum est, *The river is ten feet deep.*

Observe that

1. **duōs annōs** answers the question, *How long?*
2. **decem pedēs** answers the question, *How much?*
3. both express *extent* by the accusative;
4. the English and Latin constructions are identical and are not to be confused with the direct object.

481. Post, Posteā, and Postquam

The conjunction **postquam,** meaning *after,* must be distinguished carefully from the adverb **posteā,** meaning *afterwards,* and the preposition **post,** meaning *after* (or *behind*). Examine the following:

1. **Post hunc mēnsem plūrēs librōs legam,** *After this month I shall read more books.*
2. **Posteā multōs librōs lēgī,** *Afterwards I read many books.*
3. **Postquam opus perfēcī, multōs librōs lēgī,** *After I finished the work, I read many books.*

Observe that

1. the addition of **quam** to **post** makes **postquam** a conjunction, which is followed by a verb, usually in the perfect indicative;
2. **posteā** [7] means literally *after that,* i.e., *afterwards;*

---

[7] Sometimes **post** is used as an adverb like **posteā.**

3. the real difficulty is not in Latin but in the English use of *after,* as both a conjunction and a preposition.

Postquam vīdit quod *post* sē erat
quīnque mīlia pedum cucurrit.

482. Words Often Confused

The words in the following groups closely resemble one another in form or sound and must be carefully distinguished. See the Latin-English Vocabulary.

accēdō, accidō	cīvīs, cīvitās	ob, ab
aetās, aestās	gēns, genus	pars, pār
alius, alter, altus	ibi, ubi	pōnō (posuī), possum
cadō, cēdō	liber, līber, līberī	vīs, vir

483. Exercises

A. 1. Illī hominēs multōs mēnsēs sē exercuērunt.
2. Putō hunc montem esse mīlle pedēs altum.
3. Ego crēdō nōs in illō locō duōs annōs remānsisse.
4. Quis nōn cōnspexit nautās nāvigantēs "plānīs"[8] super caput?
5. Super tria mīlia Germānōrum, pāce factā, Rōmānīs sēsē iūnxērunt.
6. Postquam hostēs ā mīlitibus praemissīs victī sunt, paucī superfuērunt.
7. Postquam mīlitēs servōs cōnspexērunt, eōs circum viās prae sē ēgērunt.

B. 1. In summer we hasten to the fields.
2. The greater part of the winter we remain in town.
3. After the boy fell into the river, his sister ran shouting to her mother.

---

[8] i.e., *airplanes.*

4. My brother will arrive next year and remain with me [9] the whole summer.

5. We understand that you have been training yourselves for many months.

484. Vocabulary

autem, conj. (never first word), *however*

cir′cum, prep. with acc., *around*

exer′ceō, –ē′re, exer′cuī, exer′citus, *keep busy, train* (exercise)

intel′legō, –ere, –lē′xī, –lēc′tus, *understand* (intellect)

negō′tium, negō′tī, n., *business* [*ōtium*]

post′quam, conj., *after* [*post* + *quam*]

prae, prep. with abl., *before, in front of*

praemit′tō, –ere, –mī′sī, –mis′sus, *send ahead* [*mittō*]

su′per, prep. with acc., *over, above* [*superō*]

super′sum, –es′se, super′fuī, superfutū′rus, *be left* (*over*), *survive* [*sum*]

485. Latin and English Word Formation

Ne– is sometimes used as a negative prefix in Latin: **nēmō (ne–homō), negōtium (ne–ōtium), neuter (ne–uter), nūllus (ne–ūllus).** We do the same thing in English with *no: nothing, none* (*no-one*), *neither* (*no-either*).

Circum, contrā, prae, and **super** have their usual meanings when used as prefixes in Latin and English. In English **prae** becomes *pre–*, as *pre–pare, pre–fix;* **contrā** sometimes retains its form, sometimes becomes *counter–, as contra–dict, counter–act.* **Super** sometimes becomes *sur–* in English, in which form it must be distinguished from assimilated **sub:** *surplus, surmount* **(super),** but *surreptitious* **(sub).**

Find ten English words with these prefixes, compounded with Latin words which you have studied. Explain *intelligence, supervisor, surplus, precedent;* also *treason* and *tradition,* which are doublets derived from **trādō.**

[9] See **226**, footnote 5.

Treason.

Lesson LXVII

486. GRACCHĪ

Ti. et C. Gracchī erant Scīpiōnis Āfricānī nepōtēs.[1] Dīligentiā Cornēliae mātris puerī doctī sunt. Cornēlia crēdidit eōs certē summam potestātem obtentūrōs esse. Quondam hospita, domō Cornēliae petītā, ōrnāmenta sua pulcherrima manū prae sē tenēns dēmōnstrābat.
5 Tum Cornēlia līberōs suōs, quī cāsū aderant, manū tetigit atque hospitae dēmōnstrāns dīxit: "Haec sunt mea ōrnāmenta!"

Tiberius iam vir plēbī amīcus erat. Tribūnus plēbis factus [2] populō agrōs dare cupiēbat. Hī agrī pūblicī erant sed multōs annōs ā nōbilibus occupātī erant, quī dīxērunt sē eōs nōn reddītūrōs esse. Tamen
10 Tiberius populō eōs reddidit. Tum senātus convocātus dē Tiberiō cōnsuluit. Multī eum dēspicientēs interficere cupīvērunt. Tiberiō accēdente, Scīpiō Nāsīca,[3] senātor, clāmāvit: "Venīte mēcum sī reī [4] pūblicae salūtem cupitis." Tum ille et aliī quī circum eum stantēs incitātī sunt, Tiberium, impetū factō, interfēcērunt.
15 Posteā in somnō Gāius dīcitur vīdisse frātrem suum dīcentem: "Cūr dubitās, Gāī? Tū, quī superes, hoc negōtium perficere et vītam tuam populō dare dēbēs." Itaque Gāius opus Tiberī sē perfectūrum esse statuit neque eius cōnsilia dēsertūrum. Tribūnus factus plēbī frūmentum dabat et cīvitātem omnibus quī Italiam incolēbant. Mīlitēs autem
20 exercēre nōn potuit et intellēxit sē sine exercitū nihil efficere posse; ā multīs dēspectus et dēsertus et sine praesidiō fugere coāctus, interfectus est.

Itaque senātus mortem Gracchōrum effēcit. Sed cōnsilia hōrum mānsērunt, et Rōmānī multōs annōs eōs et eōrum cāsūs memoriā tenuērunt.

QUESTIONS

1. Who was the grandfather of Gaius Gracchus?
2. Who was the teacher of Tiberius Gracchus?
3. What was the political policy of Gaius?

---

[1] *grandsons.* Lesson LXVIII will tell you more about the great Roman general Scipio Africanus (*Sip'io Afrikā'nus*). [2] 133 B.C. [3] *Nasī'ca.* [4] Genitive of **rēs.**

487. Fourth Declension

As we have seen, the first declension is the *A*–declension, the second is the *O*–declension, the third is the consonant and *I*–declensions. These three declensions, especially the third, include most of the nouns. A few nouns belong to the *fourth declension,* which is the *U*–declension. Most of these nouns are derived from verbs.

	ENDINGS		EXAMPLE	
	SING.	PLUR.	SING.	PLUR.
Nom.	–us	–ūs	cāsus	cāsūs
Gen.	–ūs	–uum	cāsūs	cāsuum
Dat.	–uī	–ibus	cāsuī	cāsibus
Acc.	–um	–ūs	cāsum	cāsūs
Abl.	–ū	–ibus	cāsū	cāsibus

Gender. Most nouns of the fourth declension in **–us** are masculine; the only feminines in this book are **manus** and **domus.**

The declensions. The illustration indicates the relative size of each (see above) and the characteristic letters.

Practice   1   2   3   4

1. Decline **exercitus noster, hic impetus fortis.**
2. Name the case or cases of each of the following words: **senātū, impetum, manibus, ōrātiōne, domuī, exercituum, condiciōnibus.**

488. Exercises

   A. 1. Quid manū tuā tenēs?
      2. Paucī cūrās cāsūsque vītae leviter dēspicere possunt.
      3. Exercitus noster impetum in (*on*) ōrdinēs Gallōrum fēcit.
      4. Postquam cāsus ducī nūntiātus est, ille mortem suā manū petīvit.
      5. Maiōrēs gentēs iūra minōrum populōrum dēspicere nōn dēbent.
      6. Omnēs cīvēs in suīs propriīs domibus ā barbarīs interfectī sunt.

B. 1. I determined to move into another house.
2. I found a suitable house and approached it.
3. The house was deserted; I could see nothing.
4. I touched a body with my hand and cried out.
5. Next month I shall find a house in which there are no bodies.

489. Vocabulary

cā'sus, –ūs, m., *fall, chance, accident*	**[cadō]**
dēmōns'trō, –ā're, –ā'vī, –ā'tus, *show*	**[mōnstrō]**
dē'serō, –ere, dēse'ruī, dēser'tus, *desert*	(desertion)
dēspi'ciō, –ere, dēspe'xī, dēspec'tus, *look down on, despise*	
	[spectō]
do'mus, –ūs,[5] f., *house, home*	(domestic)
exer'citus, –ūs, m., *(trained) army*	**[exerceō]**
im'petus, –ūs, m., *attack*	**[petō]**
ma'nus, –ūs, f., *hand*	(manual, manufacture)
red'dō, –ere, red'didī, red'ditus, *give back*	**[dō]**
senā'tus, –ūs, m., *senate*	(senatorial)

490. English Word Studies

In an earlier lesson **(145)** we saw that many English words are simply the stem of a Latin noun, adjective, or verb, or the stem plus silent *–e.* A great many such words are derived from the Latin words in this book. A few are *facile, prime, just, cede, part.* In the case of verbs, the stem of the present indicative, present participle, or perfect participle, or of all three, may furnish an English word: *convene, convenient, convent; remove, remote; agent, act.*

As previously noted, there are sometimes changes in the base, such as the dropping of one of two final consonants, as in *remit, expel,* and particularly the addition of a vowel to the main vowel of the word, as in the following: *p·e·ace, mo·u·nt, re·i·gn, rema·i·n. Cont·a·in, ret·a·in,* etc., are from the compounds of **teneō.**

Find ten more words illustrating these principles. Explain *domestic, manual labor, manicure, despicable, impetuous.*

---

[5] Usually has abl. sing. **domō** and acc. plur. **domōs (552).**

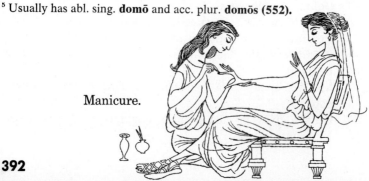

Manicure.

Lesson LXVIII

491. SCĪPIŌ

P. Cornēlius Scīpiō nōmen glōriamque meruit quod suum patrem, impetū hostium graviter vulnerātum, servāvit.[1] Tum, post pugnam Cannēnsem,[2] in quā Rōmānī interclūsī et gravissimē victī erant, omnibus probantibus, Scīpiōnī, puerō vīgintī annōrum, summum imperium datum est. Ille spem salūtis Rōmānīs reddidit. Postquam sex annōs in 5 Italiā exercituī praefuit, Rōmānī eum exercituī Hispānō praefēcērunt. Ille urbem Carthāginem Novam diē quō vēnit expugnāvit; ita celer erat. Quīntō annō exercitūs hostium ex Hispāniā expulit. Dēmōnstrāverat cīvibus suīs potestātem Carthāginiēnsium frangī posse. Neque aurum rapuerat neque miserīs nocuerat.   10

Hispāniā victā, hic prīnceps in Āfricam prōcēdere mātūrāvit et ibi Carthāginiēnsēs victōriīs terruit. Tum senātus Carthāginiēnsium Hannibalem ad patriam vocāvit. Sed Scīpiō eum Zamae[3] vīcit, et ille, clārissimus et maximus omnium ducum quī contrā Rōmānōs pugnāvērunt, ex patriā suā fūgit. Scīpiō ob hanc victōriam Āfricānus 15 appellātus est. Nōn iam Hannibal, cuius nōmen līberōs Rōmānōrum terruerat, īnstābat.

Multae rēs dē Scīpiōne Āfricānō trāduntur. Quondam, dum exercituī praeest, ille ad oppidum mūnītum in quō erant multī mīlitēs interclūsī exercitum addūxit. Scīpiō crēdidit oppidum capī posse, 20 sed paucī eandem spem habuērunt. Cāsū ūnus ē mīlitibus hominem ligātum, quī alterī mīlitī nocuerat, ad eum trāxit et rogāvit: "Quō diē locōque iubēs hunc hominem ad tē ad supplicium venīre?" Tum Scīpiō manum ad oppidum ipsum tetendit et iussit eum hominem

---

[1] Second Punic War (218–201 B.C.), greatest of the three wars against Carthage.

[2] of Cannae (Căn'ē). The Carthaginian plan of encirclement used in this battle was imitated by the Germans in their conquest of Poland in 1939 and in Belgium and France in 1940; the American army used it with great success in the Ruhr district of Germany in 1945.

[3] at Zama (202 B.C.), in Tunisia, territory fought over by American soldiers in 1943. There is a town in Mississippi named Zama.

Scipio crowns an African king. From the motion picture "Scipio Africanus."

25 in illō oppidō tertiō diē esse. Ita rēs facta est; tertiō diē, impetū
ācriter factō, oppidum expugnātum est eōdemque diē ibi ille suppliciō
hominem affēcit.

Saepe ante prīmam lūcem hic prīnceps populī Rōmānī domum
relinquēbat et in Capitōlium veniēbat et ibi sōlus multās hōrās sedē-
30 bat. Aliī putāvērunt Scīpiōnem, deīs dēspectīs, hanc rem ad speciem
facere; aliī autem crēdidērunt eum dē salūte cīvitātis deum cōnsulere.

QUESTIONS

1. How old was Scipio when he went to Spain?
2. Why was Scipio called Africanus?
3. What explanations were given of Scipio's visits to the temple?

492. Fifth Declension

The last of the noun declensions includes comparatively few words.
Rēs and **diēs,** however, occur constantly and should be memorized.
Most other nouns of the *fifth declension* have no plural; all are feminine
except **diēs,** which is usually masculine.

| | ENDINGS | | EXAMPLES | | | |
	SING.	PLUR.	SING.	PLUR.	SING.	PLUR.
Nom.	–ēs	–ēs	diēs	diēs	rēs	rēs
Gen.	–ēī or –ĕī	–ērum	diēī	diērum	reī	rērum
Dat.	–ēī or –ĕī	–ēbus	diēī	diēbus	reī	rēbus
Acc.	–em	–ēs	diem	diēs	rem	rēs
Abl.	–ē	–ēbus	diē	diēbus	rē	rēbus

Observe that **–e–** appears in every ending; this is the *E*–declension (cf. **487**). In **diēs** the **–ē–** is long in the genitive and dative singular, though it precedes a vowel (**512**, 1).

Practice

1. Decline **rēs similis** and **ūna spēs**.
2. Give each of the following in the form indicated: **diēs proximus** (abl. plur.); **prīnceps noster** (acc. sing.); **speciēs nova** (dat. sing.); **impetus maior** (acc. plur.); **manus pulchra** (gen. plur.); **melior lūx** (abl. sing.).

493. Developing "Word Sense"

Here are just a few of the English meanings that the single Latin word **rēs** can have in different contexts: *thing, matter, object, being, circumstance, affair, case, situation, condition, fortune, occurrence, deed, act, event, history, fact, reality, truth, substance, property, possessions, benefit, interest, profit, advantage, cause, reason, account, lawsuit,* etc. And when **rēs** is joined with adjectives, the list grows almost endlessly: **rēs secundae aut malae**, *prosperity or misery,* **rēs rūstica**, *agriculture,* **rēs dīvīna**, *sacrifice,* **rēs pūblica**, *state,* **rēs mīlitāris**, *warfare,* etc.

Memorize all these meanings? Never! Get the basic ones, inspect the context, and use common sense. Test case: what did the poet Ovid mean when he proudly described Rome as **caput rērum urbs Rōmāna?**

494. Exercises

A. 1. Amīcus certus in rē incertā cernitur.
2. Speciēs illōrum barbarōrum mē puerum terrēbat.
3. Virum quī huic operī praefuit illī urbī praeficiam.
4. Memoria diēī bene āctī est per sē magnum praemium.
5. Dēmōnstrāvī illum prīncipem nocuisse senātuī populōque Rōmānō.
6. Lēgātus Rōmānus dīxit exercitum suum domibus nōn nocitūrum esse.
7. Quid significant (*mean*) hae litterae, in signīs Rōmānīs vīsae, "S P Q R"? Rogā magistrum tuum sī nōn nōvistī.

Left: Stamp of British Guiana, with Latin motto: "Damus petimusque vicissim," "We give and seek in return." *Right:* Stamp of Barbados. Britannia holds Neptune's trident and drives his sea horses.

B. 1. Most (men) are deceived by the appearance of things.
2. Show him your new books; he will not do harm to them.
3. By chance I heard our leader say that there was hope of peace.
4. We put a senator (**senātor**) in charge of affairs; he desired to send men to the moon (**lūna**).

495. Vocabulary

di′ēs, diē′ī, m., *day*	(diary, diurnal)
interclū′dō, –ere, –clū′sī, –clū′sus, *cut off*	[*claudō*]
lūx, lū′cis, f., *light*	(lucid, translucent)
no′ceō, –ē′re, no′cuī, nocitū′rus, *do harm (to)* (with dat.)	
	(innocent)
praefi′ciō, –ere, –fē′cī, –fec′tus, *put in charge of* (with acc. and dat.)	[*faciō*]
prae′sum, –es′se, prae′fuī, praefutū′rus, *be in charge of* (with dat.)	[*sum*]
prīn′ceps, prīn′cipis, m., *leader*	[*prīmus* + *capiō*]
rēs, re′ī, f., *thing, matter, affair*	(real)
spe′ciēs, speciē′ī, f., *appearance*	[*speciō*]
spēs, spe′ī, f., *hope*	[*spērō*]

496. English Word Studies

1. English words which preserve the forms of the Latin fourth declension are: *census, consensus, impetus, prospectus, status, apparatus* (plural *apparatuses* or *apparatus;* the latter preserves the Latin plural). Note that *consensus* (from **sentiō**) is spelled with an –*s*– but *census* (from **cēnseō**) with a –*c*–. An ablative form of this declension is seen in *impromptu*.

The fifth declension is represented by *rabies, series, species*. The last two are used in the plural with no change of form (as in Latin).

The accusative singular is represented by *requiem*, the ablative singular by *specie*, and the ablative plural by *rebus*.

A.M., **ante merīdiem**, *before midday;* P.M., **post merīdiem**, *after midday;* M., **merīdiēs**, *midday*, come from the fifth declension.

2. Latin phrases in English:

bona fide, *in good faith.*
casus belli, *an occasion for war.*
prima facie, *on the first face (of it)*; as *prima facie* evidence.
in statu quo, *in the situation in which (it was before)*; **status quo,** *the situation in which (it was before).*
sine die, *without a day (being set)*; used of adjournment for an indefinite period by a parliamentary body.
Explain **per diem, post mortem, sui generis.**

One of several similar sculptures which have been called portraits of Scipio Africanus. Because of the shaven heads, they have also been identified as priests of Isis, an Egyptian goddess. But regardless of its true identity, this bust is a good example of the way realistic Roman sculpture did not flatter the subject.

National Museum, Naples

Lesson LXIX

497. CATŌ ET SCĪPIŌ

M. Catō, vir humilī genere, ad summōs honōrēs per sē ascenderat. Hic Scīpiōnī, virō nōbilissimā familiā, inimīcus erat et eum dēspexit. Itaque familiārem suum Petīlium iussit in senātū explōrāre ratiōnēs pecūniae praedaeque captae in bellō cum Antiochō[1] ā Scīpiōne gestō. Hōc modō Catō, cīvis magnae auctōritātis, senātum in duās partēs 5 dīvīsit, alteram quae Scīpiōnī nocēre cupiēbat, alteram quae eum prīncipem maximae virtūtis esse crēdēbat. Tum Scīpiō, cuius īra ex speciē gravī frontis clārē cernī poterat, librum prae sē tenuit et dīxit:

"In hōc librō ratiōnēs scrīptae sunt omnis pecūniae omniumque rērum quās accēpī. Hic est diēs quō mihi in animō erat[2] ratiōnēs 10 apud vōs legere atque explicāre. Nunc autem, quod Petīlius eās explōrāre et mihi imperāre cupit, apud vōs eās nōn explicābō."

Hōc dictō, librum suīs propriīs manibus dīscidit.[3]

QUESTIONS

1. In what respect were Cato and Scipio unlike?
2. Why did Scipio tear the book in pieces?
3. According to this story, what is the wrong way to get a person to do something?
4. What other Romans besides Cato rose to high positions from humble origins?

[1] *Antī'ochus,* a Syrian king.   [2] **mihi . . . erat,** *I intended.*   [3] *tore in pieces.*

397

498. Genitive and Ablative of Description

1. **virī magnae virtūtis,** *men of great courage.*
2. **spatium decem pedum,** *a space of ten feet.* *gen. pl.*
3. **hominēs inimīcō animō,** *men* with (or *of*) *an unfriendly spirit.*

Observe that in English we may say *men of* or **with** *an unfriendly spirit*. Both are descriptive. Note also that description is similarly expressed in Latin, i.e., either by the genitive or the ablative, but only when modified by an adjective.

While the *genitive* and the *ablative of description* are translated alike, Latin uses the genitive chiefly for *permanent* qualities, such as measure and number (see 2) and the ablative for *temporary* qualities, such as personal appearance.

The Roman senate house, with the three windows, is in the center (cf. p. 243). It was erected by Caesar and restored by later emperors. A church built into it in the seventh century was not removed until recently. Due to the silting over of the Forum, the doorway had been completely blocked and the church entrance was higher up. The original bronze doors are now in the Lateran church.

James Sawders

499. Exercises

A. 1. Lēgātus Gallōrum fuit vir clārissimō genere.
   2. "Dīvide et imperā" erat cōnsilium Rōmānōrum.
   3. Ille erat puer magnā grātiā apud familiārēs suōs.
   4. Hāc aestāte ascendam montem decem mīlium pedum.
   5. Eum montem sōlī virī maximae virtūtis explōrāvērunt.
   6. Frontem huius montis ascendere nōn poterō, quod ea est praeceps et difficillima.

B. 1. The general was a man of great influence.
   2. Do you desire to climb a mountain which has never been explored?
   3. We know that Italy is divided from Gaul by very high mountains.
   4. After a journey of two days, we arrived at **(ad)** a very beautiful city.

500. Vocabulary

a′pud, prep. with acc., *among*
ascen′dō, –ere, ascen′dī, ascēn′sus, *climb* (*up*), *ascend*
                                                   [*scandō, climb*]
dī′vidō, –ere, dīvī′sī, dīvī′sus, *divide*   (division)
explō′rō, –ā′re, –ā′vī, –ā′tus, *investigate, explore* [*plōrō, call out*]
*frōns, fron′tis, fron′tium, f., *forehead, front*   (frontal)
im′perō, –ā′re, –ā′vī, –ā′tus, *command* (with dat. of person)
                                                  [*imperium*]
ra′tiō, ratiō′nis, f., *account, reason*   (rational, reason)

501. Latin and English Word Formation

The suffixes **–ilis** and **–bilis** are added to verb stems to form adjectives. They indicate what *can be done:* **facilis** is "doable," *easy.* The suffix **–ilis** usually becomes *–ile* in English: *facile, fertile.* The more common suffix **–bilis** becomes, *–ble, –able, –ible* in English: *amiable, comparable, credible, divisible, noble, visible.*

Several suffixes meaning *pertaining to* are added to nouns and adjectives to form adjectives: **–āris** (English *–ar*), **–ārius** (*–ary*), **–ānus** (*–an, –ane*), **–icus** (*–ic*). Examples of their use in Latin and English are: **familiāris, frūmentārius, Rōmānus, pūblicus;** *singular, ordinary, human, humane, generic.*

The suffix **–tūdō** (English *–tude*) is added to adjective stems to form nouns and means *state of being;* **magnitūdō,** *magnitude.*

Find fifteen other examples of these suffixes in English words derived from Latin words already studied.

Seal of the United States, reverse, with mottoes that are based on Virgil: God "has smiled on our undertakings," "a new series of generations." You will find the seal on a dollar bill.

Harris & Ewing

Glimpses of Roman Life

502. THE ROMAN CITIZEN

According to tradition, Rome was founded in 753 B.C. April 21 is still celebrated as the birthday of Rome. The first rulers were kings, but the last king was driven out in 509 B.C. because he was a tyrant. The new government was headed by two consuls of equal power, one to be a check on the other. Their term of office was limited to a year. The Roman historian Livy sees the origin of Roman liberty in this restriction. But this government was not democratic, for it was in the control of a small group of noble families called patricians. For two hundred years the common people (plebs—plebeians) strugged for equality and justice and gradually won most of the rights of their more fortunate fellow citizens. At first they could not hold office and did not even have fair trials in court. Their struggle for democracy and liberty is of great interest to us. First they secured the right to elect special officials, called tribunes, who could veto the acts of the patrician officials. Then they obtained a set of written laws, called the Twelve Tables, which served as a kind of constitution or bill of rights. In 326 B.C. imprisonment and slavery for debt were abolished. This step Livy calls a second beginning of liberty for the plebeians. In 287 B.C. the plebeians succeeded in establishing the principle that a vote of the plebs should have the authority of law. Such a vote was called a **plebiscitum,** from which we get our word *plebiscite*. In these ways a fairly democratic form of government was assured for some time.

While these struggles were going on inside the country, wars were being fought and the Roman empire was being formed. The heroic deeds of Horatius, Cincinnatus, Fabricius, Regulus, Scipio, and many others accounted for Roman success and developed the Roman virtues of courage, honesty, organizing ability, patriotism, devotion to family, strict justice, plain living, and the determination to see things through and never to give up. From all this grew the great system of Roman law and government, one of the greatest of modern inheritances from Rome. The Romans organized law and government on a large scale. Their success in this may be compared to the organization of industry during the last hundred years. Europe and Latin America still use Roman law. Even the English common law, the basis of the United States' legal system, owes much to the law of the Romans. It has been said that Roman law is "a basic platform on which we can build a united world."

No wonder the possession of Roman citizenship was highly prized and that the people said with pride *"Civis Romanus sum."* This citizenship, bestowed in a solemn ceremony, brought the protection of Roman law everywhere in the world. It also brought the responsibility of protecting the Roman state against its enemies. Similarly today citizenship in any country brings both advantages and duties.

"It is clear that the spirit of '76 had a most diversified origin. . . . In listing the 'founding fathers,' it is not enough to include merely American patriots of the caliber of Jefferson, Franklin, and the Adamses. . . . Demosthenes and Aristotle, Brutus, Cicero, and Tacitus belong there, as do many others of similar stamp and influence. . . . In fact, they were often scarcely less significant as intellectual guides than such influential English standbys as Edward Coke and John Locke. Not less than the Washingtons and the Lees, these ancient heroes helped to found the independent American commonwealth."

DISCUSSION QUESTIONS

1. The Romans had two consuls as a check on each other. What system of "checks and balances" do we have in our government?
2. The restriction of the consulship to one year was regarded as the origin of Roman liberty. Have we any similar restriction for our highest officials?
3. Are persons sometimes imprisoned for debt today? Have there been changes in our laws on the subject in the last one hundred years?
4. What are some of the privileges and duties of citizenship today?

401

Wearers of the toga represented in this beautiful relief from the Altar of Peace erected in Rome during the reign of Augustus. Heads are covered for sacrifice.

UNIT XIII REVIEW

Lessons LXVI–LXIX

The Story of Lucius (concluded)

503. CĪVIS NOVUS ITER FACIT

Iam Lūcius puer quīndecim annōrum erat. Nunc pater eius dīxit eum dēbēre proximīs Līberālibus[1] togam praetextam dēpōnere et virīlem togam sūmere. Hōc tempore plūrimī puerī Rōmānī togās praetextās dēpōnēbant. (Puerī Rōmānī togās praetextās gerēbant, sed 5 virī tōtās albās gerēbant. Brācae,[2] quae ā virīs nunc geruntur, ā barbarīs, nōn ā Rōmānīs, illīs diēbus gerēbantur.)

THE NEW CITIZEN

Līberālia aderant. Multī amīcī convēnērunt. Lūcius, postquam togam praetextam ante Larēs posuit, novam virīlem togam sūmpsit. Omnēs familiārēs cum eō ad Forum pedibus prōcessērunt, et posteā 10 ad Capitōlium, ubi nōmen eius in numerō cīvium scrīptum est. Nunc poterat dīcere, "Cīvis Rōmānus sum!" Tum omnēs cum Lūciō domum[3] revertērunt, ubi optima cēna parāta erat. Multī cibī dē

---

[1] The *Liberalia*, a festival which was held March 17.   [2] *trousers.*

[3] As in English, "place to which" is expressed without a preposition with **domum:** *home.*

402

ultimīs terrīs portātī erant, aliī dē Graeciā, aliī dē Asiā, aliī dē Āfricā. Amīcī cēnam variō sermōne prōdūxērunt et cum Lūciō dē officiīs cīvium, dē bellō et pāce, dē negōtiīs, dē multīs aliīs rēbus ēgērunt. 15 Lūcius nunc intellēxit mūnera et officia cīvis Rōmānī.

THE JOURNEY

Paulō [4] post Lūcius, iam vir, cum patre iter fēcit. Itaque per portam Capēnam [5] ex urbe discessērunt. Raedā ibi inventā, in Appiā Viā prōcessērunt. Sepulchrīs ad viam cōnspectīs, Lūcius dīxit: "Pater, cūr sepulchra ad viās pōnuntur? Hoc numquam intellegere potuī." 20 Pater respondit: "Hōc modō omnēs ea vidēre possunt." Lūcius dīxit sē nocte [6] inter sepulchra iter facere nōn cupere.

GOOD ROADS AND GREAT MEN

Quod iter facile et commodum erat, Lūcius dīxit: "Nōnne crēdis Appiam Viam optimam omnium esse?" Pater respondit: "Omnēs nostrae viae optimae sunt. Ob eam causam hostēs vīcimus, fīnēs 25 lātiōrēs parāvimus, potestātem patriae nostrae auximus, et nunc gentēs regimus. Aliī pictūrās pulchriōrēs pingunt,[7] aliī ōrant [8] causās melius, sed nōs regimus populōs." "Etiam apud nōs causae optimē ōrantur," respondit Lūcius. "Quis melior ōrātor fuit aut est aut erit quam Cicerō? Hic ōrātor etiam cōnsul fuit et populum Rōmānum 30 rēxit. Ego eum ōrātiōnem habentem in Forō audīvī et eius ōrātiōnēs in lūdō lēgī." "Lēgistīne ōrātiōnēs in Catilīnam, illum quī cīvitātem vī opprimere statuit?" "Illās et aliās lēgī. In prīmā dīxit dē Catilīnā: 'Ō tempora! Ō mōrēs! [9] Senātus haec intellegit, cōnsul videt; hic tamen vīvit.' " "Optimē!" dīxit pater. "In secundā, sī memoria mē nōn fallit, 35 dīxit, postquam Catilīna ex urbe discessit: 'Abiit,[10] excessit, ēvāsit,[11] ērūpit!' [12] Ex Cicerōnis linguā fluēbat ōrātiō dulcior quam mel."

SCENES BY THE WAY

Tum altōs et pulchrōs arcūs [13] aquaeductūs [14] cernunt, quī optimam aquam dē montibus in urbem dūcit. Pater Lūciō dīxit prīmum aquaeductum ab Appiō factum esse. Appius fuit ille quī Appiam 40

---

[4] *shortly.* [5] A gate in the wall of Rome. [6] *at night.* [7] *paint.* [8] *plead.*
[9] *customs.* [10] *he has gone away.* [11] **Ēvadō, ēvāsus**—derivative?
[12] **Ērumpō, ēruptus**—derivative? [13] Accusative plural.
[14] Genitive singular.

Viam mūnīvit. Ita prōcēdunt, nunc agrōs et vīllās, montēs silvāsque spectantēs, nunc hominēs in viā ipsā, et ad terminum itineris perveniunt.

EPILOGUE

Nōn iam vīvunt Lūcius et eius amīcī, nōn iam vīvunt Caesar et
45 Cicerō, prīncipēs summae auctōritātis, sed lingua eōrum vīvit, vīvunt eōrum dicta et facta, lēgēs et mōrēs,⁹ glōria et fāma. Haec omnia in eōrum librīs inveniuntur. Eīs quī itinera parva per illōs librōs faciunt Rōmānī ipsī vīvere videntur.

QUESTIONS

1. Why did the Romans emphasize a boy's entry to adult life? Can you think of any parallels in modern times?
2. Compare the Roman and the American ages for reaching full citizenship. Who gained more freedom—the Roman or the American? Who gained more responsibilities?

504. Synonyms

We rarely find a word in any language which has exactly the same meaning as another word. Words which have almost the same meaning are called *synonyms*. **Homō** and **vir** both mean *man,* but **homō** sometimes means any *human being;* **vir,** a *"he-man,"* or *hero.*

The following synonyms have occurred in previous lessons:

1. **ante** = *before* (of time and place), adverb or preposition (with accusative).
   prae = *before* (of place only), preposition (with ablative).

2. **terra** = *land* (as opposed to water), also some particular *land* or *country.*
   fīnēs = *borders,* therefore a *land* or *country* with reference to its boundaries.
   patria = *fatherland,* the *land* of one's birth.

3. **dux [dūcō]** = *a leader* in any field, but often in a military sense.
   prīnceps [prīmus + capiō] = the *first* or *chief* man in a group—usually nonmilitary.

4. **videō** = *see,* the most common word.
   cernō = *see clearly.*
   cōnspiciō = *catch sight of.*
   spectō, *look at.*

5. **labor** = *hard work, toil, suffering.*
   opus = usually *a piece of work.*
   negōtium = *lack of leisure* **[ōtium],** *business.*

6. **potestās** = *power* in general.
auctōritās = *influence*.
rēgnum = *royal power*.
imperium = *military power, command*.

505. GRAMMAR SUMMARY

Accusative with Ad or In

When *to* implies literally *motion toward* a place or person, we have seen that the accusative with **ad** or **in** is used. This is true after the following "motion" verbs, previously studied:

accēdō, cēdō, contendō, dūcō, fugiō, mātūrō, mittō, moveō, nāvigō, portō, prōcēdō, prōdūcō, properō, redigō, redūcō, trānsportō, veniō.

Dative of Indirect Object

When *to* does not imply actual motion but indicates the person *to whom* something is given, told, shown, etc., the dative is used. The following verbs, already studied, are transitive and may have an accusative as the *direct object* and a dative as the *indirect object*:

committō, dīcō, dō, dōnō, iungō, mandō, mōnstrō, nūntiō, ostendō, permittō, prōpōnō, reddō, relinquō, respondeō, submittō, trādō, tribuō.

Some of these verbs have as the direct object either a neuter pronoun or an infinitive: **dīcō, respondeō, nūntiō.**

With some other verbs the dative is regularly used: **noceō.**

506. VOCABULARY

NOUNS	4. exercitus	8. manus	12. rēs
1. cāsus	5. frōns	9. negōtium	13. senātus
2. diēs	6. impetus	10. prīnceps	14. speciēs
3. domus	7. lūx	11. ratiō	15. spēs

VERBS	20. dīvidō	25. interclūdō	30. reddō
16. ascendō	21. exerceō	26. noceō	31. supersum
17. dēmōnstrō	22. explōrō	27. praeficiō	
18. dēserō	23. imperō	28. praemittō	
19. dēspiciō	24. intellegō	29. praesum	

CONJUNCTIONS	32. autem	33. postquam	
PREPOSITIONS	35. circum	37. super	
34. apud	36. prae		

507. VOCABULARY (English Meanings)

NOUNS
1. chance
2. day
3. home
4. army
5. front
6. attack
7. light
8. hand
9. business
10. first man
11. account
12. thing
13. senate
14. appearance
15. hope

VERBS
16. ascend
17. show
18. desert
19. look down on
20. divide
21. train
22. explore
23. command
24. understand
25. cut off
26. do harm to
27. put in charge
28. send ahead
29. be in charge of
30. give back
31. be left over

CONJUNCTIONS 32. however   33. after

PREPOSITIONS 35. around   37. above
34. among   36. in front of

508. UNIT PRACTICE AND EXERCISES

Form Drill

1. Decline **senātus noster, diēs longior.**
2. Give the genitive and accusative singular and the genitive plural of:

   id negōtium, haec potestās, impetus fortis, īdem prīnceps, quae ratiō, rēs ipsa, cāsus peior, domus ūlla.

3. Give in all tenses the third singular active of **noceō;** the third plural passive of **dēserō;** the first plural active of **imperō;** the third plural passive of **dēspiciō;** the second singular active of **audiō.**
4. Identify by giving voice, tense, and, when possible, mood, person, and number:

   praemīsit, incoluisse, exercērī, interclūdēns, dēserunt, redde, dēmōnstrāte, explōrārī, dīvidī, imperāns, superestis, praeerimus, praeficiēmus, ascendam, vīvite, dīvīsus, interclūdentur, intellēctum est, permissūrus.

509. ENGLISH WORD STUDIES

1. Give the Latin words and prefixes suggested by the following English derivatives: *ascendancy, casualty, circumnavigate, demonstration, familiarity, indivisible, innocuous, intellectual, lucid, opponent, preview, subjunctive, superscription, transcend, virtue.*

2. Find and use in sentences as many English derivatives as possible from **pōnō, veniō,** and **pellō.**

A Roman, L. Antistius Sarculo, and his wife. A tombstone from Rome, now in London. It was erected by their freedmen, Rufus and Anthus, at their expense.

510. IN BRITANNIĀ—A Play in Latin

Persōnae

Dīvicus
Cocurō
Osbus } Britannī
Caractō
Aliī Britannī

Brigida, *fīlia Dīvicī*
Sulpicius Rūfus, *Rōmānus*
Antōnia, *uxor Rūfī*
Medicus
Servī et Servae

Locus: In tabernā Dīvicī, in Britanniā. (*Aliī Britannī dormiunt, aliī bibunt.*)

Cocurō: Brigida! Vīnum!

Brigida: Ecce! (*Vīnum Cocurōnī dat.*)

Cocurō: Vīnum Rōmānum est. Vīnum Rōmānum amō—nōn autem Rōmānōs.

Osbus: Rōmānōs nōn ōdī.[1] Per Rōmānōs in Britanniā nunc sunt 5 viae bonae, castra mūnīta, multī mercātōrēs, melior cibus.

Cocurō: Rōmānī autem nōn sunt Britannī. Sī hīc[2] manēbunt, Britannia erit Rōmāna.

Dīvicus: Rōmāna erat mulier quae quondam Brigidam meam servāvit.   10

Brigida: Bene dīcit. Graviter aegra eram. Mulier Rōmāna servum suum, medicum doctum, ad mē mīsit. Ille mē cūrāvit.

Osbus: Quis erat illa mulier?

Brigida: Antōnia.

Dīvicus: Uxor Sulpicī Rūfī est, cuius vīlla est proxima.   15

Brigida: Benignī sunt.

Cocurō: Rōmānīs nōn cōnfīdō. Medicīs nōn cōnfīdō.

Osbus: Nōn paucī Rōmānī puellās nostrās in mātrimōnium dūcunt. Cavē,[3] Brigida!

Dīvicus: Brigida Caractōnī spōnsa est.   20

Cocurō: Vir fortis est—et Britannus.

Osbus: Etiam Rōmānī fortēs sunt. Mīlitēs Rōmānī Britannōs ab hostibus dēfendunt.

[1] *I do not hate.*   [2] *here.*   [3] *beware.*

COCURŌ: Britannī sē dēfendere possunt. (*Clāmōrēs audiuntur.*)

25 BRIGIDA: Pater! Clāmōrem audiō! Quid est?

(*Accēdit Caractō cum aliīs Britannīs. In tabernam dūcunt Sulpicium Rūfum et Antōniam, cum servīs eōrum.*)

CARACTŌ: Ecce, Dīvice! Nōnne clārī sunt captīvī?

DĪVICUS: Caractō! Quid ēgistī?

30 CARACTŌ: Hī Rōmānī in viā iter faciēbant. Magnam pecūniam habent. Itaque nōs illōs cēpimus.

BRIGIDA: Caractō! Latrō es!

CARACTŌ: Latrō? Minimē! Rōmānī fīnēs Britannōrum occupāvērunt. Omnia quae habent sunt nostra.

35 SULPICIUS: Latrō pessime, quid cupis?

ANTŌNIA: Ecce ōrnāmenta mea! Omnia tua erunt, sī nōs dīmittēs.

CARACTŌ: Ōrnāmenta nōn cupiō; plūs cupiō.

SULPICIUS: Plūs? Quid dīcis?

CARACTŌ: Pecūniam habēs. Ubi nūntiābitur familiae tuae amīcīs-

40 que tuīs vōs captōs esse, illī prō vōbīs magnum praemium dabunt.

BRIGIDA: Caractō! Hī Rōmānī sunt fīnitimī nostrī et amīcī. Hic vir est Sulpicius Rūfus. Haec mulier, Antōnia, mē quondam servāvit. Ecce—ille servus est medicus quī mē cūrāvit!

CARACTŌ: Omnēs Rōmānī hostēs Britannōrum sunt.

45 ALIĪ BRITANNĪ: Hostēs sunt!

OSBUS: Caractō! Mīlitēs Rōmānī venient. Vōs capient.

DĪVICUS: Caractō! Nisi [4] hōs Rōmānōs līberābis, Brigida uxor tua nōn erit.

CARACTŌ: Quid? Brigida mihi spōnsa est.

50 DĪVICUS: Nōn iam tibi spōnsa est.

BRIGIDA: Uxor latrōnis nōn erō.

BRITANNĪ: Caractō! Praeda magna erit!

ALIĪ BRITANNĪ: Caractō! Mīlitēs Rōmānī mox aderunt!

SULPICIUS: Mīlitēs Rōmānī latrōnēs interficiunt.

55 ANTŌNIA: Vōbīs nōn nocuimus. Nōs dīmitte!

BRIGIDA: Eōs dīmitte!

CARACTŌ: Prō tē, Brigida—illōs dīmittō. Discēdite omnēs!

ANTŌNIA: Tibi grātiās agimus, Brigida!

(*Discēdunt Rōmānī et Britannī et servī et servae.*)

60 DĪVICUS: Fortis vir es, Caractō—nimis [5] autem audāx.

CARACTŌ: Brigida mē retinēbit, mē docēbit, domina mea erit.

---

[4] *unless.*   [5] *too* (with **audāx**).

GRAMMATICAL APPENDIX

PRONUNCIATION

511. Vowels

In Latin, as in English, the *vowels* are *a, e, i, o, u*.[1]

At one time the English vowels were pronounced like the Latin, but the pronunciation of English has changed greatly. In French, Spanish, Italian, German, and other languages, which also have adopted the Latin alphabet, the vowels are still pronounced very much as in Latin.

Each of the Latin vowels may be pronounced long or short, the difference being one of *time*. This is called *quantity*. There is also a difference of *sound* between the long and the short vowels, except **a**. This is called *quality*. The pronunciation is approximately as follows:

LONG	SHORT	LONG AND SHORT AS IN
ā as in *father*	**a** as first *a* in *aha*	*Martha* (**ā, ă**)
ē as in *they* or *a* in *late*	**e** as in *let*	*lateness* (**ē, ĕ**)
ī as in *police* or *ea* in *seat*	**i** as in *sit*	*seasick* (**ī, ĭ**)
ō as in *note*	**o** as in *for*	*phonograph* (**ō, ŏ**)
ū as in *rule* or *oo* in *fool*	**u** as in *full*	*two-footed* (**ū, ŭ**)

In this book long vowels are regularly marked $-$; short vowels are usually unmarked, but ⌣ is sometimes used.

Caution. It is very important to distinguish the *sounds* of the long and short vowels. To confuse **ī** and **ĭ**, or **ē** and **ĕ** in Latin is as bad a mistake as for a person to say, *I heard the din in the hall,* when he meant the "dean," or *I forgot the debt,* when he meant the "date."

---

[1] In English sometimes also *y*, as in *by*. But the *y* in *yes, young, etc.,* is a consonant.

The English equivalents of **e** and **o** are only approximate. Avoid pronouncing ŏ like *o* in *not* or in *note*.

512. Quantity of Vowels

The quantity (and quality) of vowels must be learned as part of the word. There are, however, a few general rules:

1. A vowel is usually short before another vowel or **h** (because **h** is weakly sounded).

2. A vowel is short before **nt, nd,** final **m** and **t,** and usually final **–r.**

513. Diphthongs

The first three of the following *diphthongs* (two vowels making one sound) are the most common ones.

ae like *ai* in *aisle*   **eu** like *eh–oo* (pronounced quickly)
au like *ou* in *out*   **ui** like *oo–ee* (pronounced quickly); only in **cui**
oe like *oi* in *oil*   and **huic**
ei like *ei* in *freight*

514. Consonants

All letters other than vowels and diphthongs are *consonants.*

The Latin consonants have, generally speaking, the same sounds as in English. The following differences, however, should be noted:

b before **s** or **t** has the sound of **p.**
c is always hard as in *cat,* never soft as in *city.*
g is always hard as in *go,* never soft as in *gem.*
i (consonant) has the sound of *y* in *year.* **i** is a consonant between vowels and at the beginning of a word before a vowel. Some books use **j** for consonant **i.**
s always has the sound of *s* in *sin;* never of *s* in *these.*
t always has the sound of *t* in *ten;* never of *t* in *motion.*
v has the sound of *w* in *will.*
x has the sound of *x* in *extra.*
    (**ch = k; ph = p; th = t**)

Doubled consonants are pronounced separately: **an–nus.**

In both English and Latin the combination **qu** forms a single consonant and the **u** is not a vowel here. Occasionally **gu** and **su** are treated the same way, as in English *anguish* and *suave.*

515. English Pronunciation of Latin

Latin words which have become thoroughly English should be pronounced as English words; for example in *terra firma,* the *i* is pronounced as in *firm,* not as in *miracle;* in *alumni,* the *i* is pronounced as in *mile.*

410

516. Syllables

Every Latin word has as many syllables as it has vowels or diphthongs: **vir–tū–te, proe–li–um.**

A single consonant between two vowels or diphthongs is pronounced with the second: **fī–li–us, a–git.** Compound words are divided into their component parts and are exceptions to this rule: **ad–es.**

When two or more consonants occur between vowels or diphthongs, the division is made before the last consonant: **por–tus, vīnc–tī, an–nus.** An exception to this rule occurs whenever a mute **(p, b, t, d, c, g)** is followed by a liquid **(l, r)**, in which case the mute combines with the liquid and both are pronounced with the second vowel: **pū–bli–cus, cas–tra.**

The next to the last syllable of a word is called the *penult* (Latin **paene,** *almost;* **ultima,** *last*); the one before the penult (i.e., the third from the end) is called the *antepenult.*

517. Quantity of Syllables

Some syllables of course take longer to pronounce than others, just as some vowels are longer than others.

1. A syllable is *naturally* long if it contains a long vowel or a diphthong: **fā–mae.**

2. A syllable is long *by position* if it contains a short vowel followed by two or more consonants or the double consonant **x** (= **cs**): **sil–vīs, por–tō.**

Note. Exception is made in the case of a mute followed by a liquid **(516). H** is so weakly sounded that it does not help make a syllable long.

Caution. Distinguish carefully between long *syllable* and long *vowel;* in **ĕxĕmplum** the first two syllables are long, though the vowels are short.

518. Accent

The accented syllable of a word is the one that is pronounced with more stress or emphasis than the others; so in the word *an'swer,* the accent is on the first syllable. In Latin the accent is easily learned according to fixed rules:

1. Words of two syllables are accented on the first: **frā′ter.**

2. Words of three or more syllables are accented on the penult if it is long, otherwise on the antepenult: **lēgā′tus, exem′plum; dī′cĕre, sī′mĭlis.**

Note that the accented syllable is not necessarily long.

519. Basic Grammatical Terms

The material here given may be reviewed in connection with the Lessons. For the use of those who prefer to review basic grammar before taking up the Lessons, a number of explanations are given here which will also be found in the body of the book. Teachers can easily devise English exercises for drill with classes which need it. Or the sentences on these pages may be used for that purpose.

520. The Sentence. Subject and Predicate

A *sentence* is a group of words which completely express a thought. Every sentence consists of two parts—the *subject,* about which something is said, and the *predicate,* which says something about the subject: *The sailor* (subject) *saved the girl* (predicate), **Nauta puellam servāvit.**

A subject or predicate is said to be *modified* by those words which affect or limit its meaning.

521. Parts of Speech

The words of most languages are divided, according to their use, into eight classes called *parts of speech,* These are:

Nouns	Adjectives	Adverbs	Conjunctions
Pronouns	Verbs	Prepositions	Interjections

522. Nouns

A *noun* (from Latin **nōmen,** *name*) is a word that names a person, place, or thing: *Anna,* **Anna;** *island,* **īnsula;** *letter,* **littera.**

Nouns may be classified as:

1. *Common* (applied to any one of a group): *city,* **urbs;** *girl,* **puella.**

2. *Proper* (applied to a particular one of a group): *Rome,* **Rōma;** *Julia,* **Iūlia.**

Note. Proper nouns always begin with a capital letter.

523. Pronouns

A *pronoun* (Latin **prō,** *for;* **nōmen,** *name*) is a word used instead of a noun. The noun whose place is taken by a pronoun is called an *antecedent* (Latin **ante,** *before;* **cēdō,** *go*).

1. *Personal* pronouns distinguish the three persons: the person speaking (*I,* **ego;** *we,* **nōs**—first person), the person spoken to (*you,* **tū, vōs**—second person), the person or thing spoken of (*he,* **is;** *she,* **ea;** *it,* **id;** *they,* **eī**—third person).

2. *Interrogative* pronouns are used to ask questions: *who,* **quis;** *which, what,* **quid.**

3. *Relative* pronouns relate to a preceding (antecedent) word and join to it a dependent clause: *who,* **quī;** *which, what, that,* **quod.**

4. *Demonstrative* pronouns point out persons or objects definitely—often accompanied with a gesture: *this,* **hic;** *that,* **ille;** *these,* **hī;** *those,* **illī.**

524. Adjectives

An *adjective* is a word used to describe a noun or pronoun or to limit its meaning:

1. *Descriptive* adjectives are either *common* or *proper: good,* **bonus;** *Roman,* **Rōmānus.** Proper adjectives begin with a capital letter.

2. *Limiting* adjectives can be divided into six groups:

412

a. *Article—definite* (*the*), *indefinite* (*a, an*). There is no word in Latin for "the" or "a."

b. *Numerals—cardinals* (*one, two, three,* etc., **ūnus, duo, trēs,** etc.), *ordinals* (*first, second, third,* etc., **prīmus, secundus, tertius,** etc.).

c. *Possessive* adjectives (formed from personal pronouns): *my, mine,* **meus;** *our, ours,* **noster;** *your, yours,* **tuus, vester;** *his, her, its,* **eius;** *their, theirs,* **eōrum.**

When interrogative, relative, and demonstrative pronouns are used as adjectives, they are called respectively:

d. *Interrogative* adjectives: *what street?* **quae via?**

e. *Relative* adjectives: *He spent a year in Italy, in which country he saw many beautiful things,* **Annum in Italiā ēgit, in** *quā* **terrā multa pulchra vīdit.**

f. *Demonstrative* adjectives: *that road,* **illa via.**

In English, the demonstrative adjectives are the only ones that have different forms in the singular and plural: *this, these; that, those.*

525. Verbs

A *verb* is a word that tells what a subject does or is: *He fought,* **Pugnāvit;** *He is good,* **Bonus est.**

1. According to use, verbs are either *transitive* or *intransitive.*

a. A *transitive* verb is one which tells what a person or thing does to another person or thing: *Anna is carrying water,* **Anna aquam** *portat.*

b. An *intransitive* verb is one whose action is limited to the subject: *Anna is working,* **Anna** *labōrat.*

Contrast "set" (transitive) with "sit" (intransitive), and "lay" (transitive) with "lie" (intransitive).

2. Intransitive verbs are either *complete* or *linking* (copulative).

a. A *complete* verb is one which is complete in meaning without an object or other word: *He sails,* **Nāvigat.**

b. A *linking* verb is one which links a noun or adjective to the subject: *They are good,* **Bonī sunt.**

The chief linking verbs in English are *be, appear, seem, become, feel, look, taste, smell.*

3. An *auxiliary* verb (Latin **auxilium,** *help*) is one used in the conjugation of other verbs: *I am learning; Did you see? They have given.*

526. Adverbs

An *adverb* is a word used to modify the meaning of a verb, adjective, or other adverb: *He is working now,* **Nunc labōrat.**

527. Prepositions

A *preposition* is a word used to show the relation of a noun or pronoun, called its *object,* to some word (usually the verb) in the sentence: *He sails to the island,* **Ad īnsulam nāvigat.**

528. Conjunctions

A *conjunction* is a word used to join words, phrases **(544),** and clauses **(545).** Conjunctions are classified according to their use as:

1. *Coördinate,* connecting words or sentences of equal rank (*and,* **et;** *but,* **sed;** *or,* **aut;** *nor,* **neque**).

2. *Subordinate,* connecting a subordinate clause of a sentence with the principal clause (*if,* **sī;** *while,* **dum;** *because,* **quod,** etc.).

3. *Correlative,* used in pairs (*both . . . and,* **et . . . et;** *neither . . . nor,* **neque . . . neque,** etc.).

529. Interjections

An *interjection* is a word used to show emotion. It has no direct relation to any other word in the sentence: *O! Alas! Ah! Oh!*

530. Inflection

The change of form which words undergo to indicate differences in their use is called *inflection: boy—boys,* **puer—puerī;** *see, saw, seen,* **videō, vīdī, vīsus.** The inflection of nouns, pronouns, and adjectives is called *declension.* They are *declined* to indicate change in number and case, and sometimes gender. Personal pronouns also indicate person.

531. Number

A noun or pronoun is *singular* when it refers to one person or thing: *girl,* **puella;** *house,* **casa;** *mouse,* **mūs;** *tooth,* **dēns.** It is *plural* when it refers to more than one: *girls,* **puellae;** *houses,* **casae;** *mice,* **mūrēs;** *teeth,* **dentēs.**

532. Gender

Gender is a distinction in the form of words corresponding to a distinction of sex. It is shown by change of word, by change of ending, or by use of a prefix: *father—mother,* **pater—māter,** *master—mistress,* **dominus—domina;** *he-goat—she-goat.* The first words given in each group are *masculine,* the second are *feminine.* Most nouns in English have no gender and are therefore *neuter* ("neither" masculine nor feminine). In Latin, however, many such nouns are masculine or feminine. The gender is indicated, not by the meaning of the word, but usually by its ending: **via,** f., *way;* **equus,** m., *horse.*

533. Case

Case is a change in the form of a noun, pronoun, or adjective to show its use in the sentence: *She* (subject) *is here,* **Ea adest;** *I saw her* (object), **Eam vīdī.**

534. Subject and Object

1. The *subject* of a verb is that about which something is said **(520).**

2. The *direct object* is that which is directly affected by the action indicated in the transitive active verb: *Anna carries water,* **Anna** *aquam* **portat.** The term *object* is also applied to a word dependent upon a preposition **(527).**

535. Names and Uses of the Cases

1. *Nominative.* A noun or pronoun used as the subject of a verb is in the *nominative* case: *The farmer calls,* **Agricola vocat.**

2. *Accusative (Objective).* A noun or pronoun used as the object of a verb or preposition is in the *accusative* (or *objective*) case: *I sent a book to him,* **Ad eum librum mīsī.**

3. *Dative.* The noun or pronoun that indicates to or for whom the direct object is given, shown, or told is called the *indirect object* and is put in the *dative* case: *I gave him a book,* **Eī librum dedī.**

4. *Genitive (Possessive).* Possession is expressed by the *genitive* (or *possessive*) case: *the boy's book,* **puerī liber.**

536. Conjugation

The inflection of verbs is called *conjugation*. Verbs are *conjugated* by putting together their various forms that indicate *person, number, tense, voice,* and *mood.*

537. Person and Number

A verb must agree with its subject in person and number: *The girl is good,* **Puella est bona;** *The girls are good,* **Puellae sunt bonae.**

538. Tense

Tense means time. There are six tenses:

1. The *present* represents an act as taking place now: *He goes.*

2. The *past* represents an act as having already taken place: *He went yesterday.*

3. The *future* represents an act that will occur later: *He will go to-morrow.*

4. The *present perfect* represents an act as completed, but from the point of view of the present: *He has just gone.*

5. The *past perfect* represents an act as completed at some definite time in the past: He *had gone* (before something else occurred).

6. The *future perfect* represents an act as completed at or before some definite time in the future: *He will have gone* (before something else will occur).

539. Progressive, Interrogative, Negative, and Emphatic Verb Forms

1. *Progressive* (time or action continuous; used with some form of the auxiliary "be"): *They are studying, they were studying, they will be studying, they have been studying, they had been studying, they will have been studying.*

2. *Interrogative, Negative,* and *Emphatic* (with some form of the auxiliary "do," used only in the present and past):

   a. Used in questions: *Do (did) you know this?*
   b. Negative: *I do (did) not know it.*
   c. Emphatic: *I do (did) believe it.*

540. Voice

A transitive verb is in the *active voice* when it represents the subject as the doer or agent: *Anna loves Clara,* **Anna Clāram** *amat.*

A transitive verb is in the *passive voice* when it represents the subject as the receiver of the action: *Clara is loved,* **Clāra** *amātur.*

Intransitive verbs are used only in the active voice in English.

541. Mood

1. The *indicative mood* is used to state a fact or to ask a question: *Rome is a great city,* **Rōma** *est* **magna urbs;** *Where is Anna?* **Ubi** *est* **Anna?**

2. The *imperative mood* is used to express commands: *Look at the waves, Spectā* **undās.**

542. Infinitive

The *infinitive* is a verbal noun. It is a form of the verb to which *to* is usually prefixed in English: *to go, to sing.* It has tense and voice, but not person, number, or mood.

543. Participle

The participle is a verbal adjective. As an adjective it modifies a noun or pronoun: *a losing fight.* As a verb it may have an object or adverbial modifiers: *suddenly losing his balance, he fell off.* It has four forms in English:

	ACTIVE	PASSIVE
Present:	*seeing*	*being seen*
Past:	*having seen*	*seen, having been seen*

544. Phrases

A *phrase* is a group of words without subject and predicate.

One important kind of phrase is the *prepositional phrase,* that is, a preposition together with its object: *in great danger,* **in magnō perīculō.**

545. Clauses

A *clause,* like a phrase, is a part of a sentence but differs from a phrase in having a subject and a predicate.

Clauses are classified as:

1. *Principal,* the leading or independent statement in a sentence: *The girl whom you saw on the street* is *my sister, Puella* **quam in viā vīdistī soror mea est.**

2. *Subordinate,* a dependent statement modifying some word in the principal clause: *The girl whom you saw on the street is my sister,* **Puella quam in viā vīdistī soror mea est.**

546. Sentences

1. A *simple sentence* contains one principal clause: *My friend, the farmer, has many horses,* **Amīcus meus, agricola, multōs equōs habet.**

2. A *compound sentence* contains two or more principal clauses connected by a coördinate conjunction, such as "and," "but," etc.: *My friend, the farmer, has many horses, but I have not seen them,* **Amīcus meus, agricola, multōs equōs habet, sed eōs nōn vīdī.**

3. A *complex sentence* contains one principal clause to which one or more subordinate clauses are joined by subordinate conjunctions or by relative or interrogative pronouns: *My friend, the farmer, has many horses which I have not seen,* **Amīcus meus, agricola, multōs equōs habet quōs nōn vīdī.**

Children and cupids rolling hoops and playing leapfrog.

BASIC FORMS

547. Nouns

<table>
<tr><td colspan="3">First Declension (66) [1]
via, viae, f., road</td><td colspan="2">Second Declension (66)
servus, servī, m., slave</td></tr>
<tr><td></td><td>SINGULAR</td><td>PLURAL</td><td>SINGULAR</td><td>PLURAL</td></tr>
<tr><td>NOM.</td><td>via</td><td>viae</td><td>servus</td><td>servī</td></tr>
<tr><td>GEN.</td><td>viae</td><td>viārum</td><td>servī</td><td>servōrum</td></tr>
<tr><td>DAT.</td><td>viae</td><td>viīs</td><td>servō</td><td>servīs</td></tr>
<tr><td>ACC.</td><td>viam</td><td>viās</td><td>servum</td><td>servōs</td></tr>
<tr><td>ABL.</td><td>viā</td><td>viīs</td><td>servō</td><td>servīs</td></tr>
<tr><td>(VOC.)</td><td></td><td></td><td>(serve)</td><td></td></tr>
</table>

548.   Second Declension (106, 117)

<table>
<tr><td colspan="2">ager, agrī, m., field</td><td colspan="2">puer, puerī, m., boy</td><td colspan="2">signum, signī, n., sign</td></tr>
<tr><td></td><td>SING.   PLUR.</td><td></td><td>SING.   PLUR.</td><td></td><td>SING.   PLUR.</td></tr>
<tr><td>NOM.</td><td>ager   agrī</td><td></td><td>puer   puerī</td><td></td><td>signum   signa</td></tr>
<tr><td>GEN.</td><td>agrī   agrōrum</td><td></td><td>puerī   puerōrum</td><td></td><td>signī   signōrum</td></tr>
<tr><td>DAT.</td><td>agrō   agrīs</td><td></td><td>puerō   puerīs</td><td></td><td>signō   signīs</td></tr>
<tr><td>ACC.</td><td>agrum   agrōs</td><td></td><td>puerum   puerōs</td><td></td><td>signum   signa</td></tr>
<tr><td>ABL.</td><td>agrō   agrīs</td><td></td><td>puerō   puerīs</td><td></td><td>signō   signīs</td></tr>
</table>

549.   Third Declension (301,335)

<table>
<tr><td colspan="2">mīles, mīlitis, m., soldier</td><td colspan="2">lēx, lēgis, f., law</td><td colspan="2">corpus, corporis, n., body</td></tr>
<tr><td></td><td>SING.   PLUR.</td><td></td><td>SING.   PLUR.</td><td></td><td>SING.   PLUR.</td></tr>
<tr><td>NOM.</td><td>mīles   mīlitēs</td><td></td><td>lēx   lēgēs</td><td></td><td>corpus   corpora</td></tr>
<tr><td>GEN.</td><td>mīlitis   mīlitum</td><td></td><td>lēgis   lēgum</td><td></td><td>corporis   corporum</td></tr>
<tr><td>DAT.</td><td>mīlitī   mīlitibus</td><td></td><td>lēgī   lēgibus</td><td></td><td>corporī   corporibus</td></tr>
<tr><td>ACC.</td><td>mīlitem   mīlitēs</td><td></td><td>lēgem   lēgēs</td><td></td><td>corpus   corpora</td></tr>
<tr><td>ABL.</td><td>mīlite   mīlitibus</td><td></td><td>lēge   lēgibus</td><td></td><td>corpore   corporibus</td></tr>
</table>

550.   Third Declension I-Stems (340)

<table>
<tr><td colspan="3">cīvis, cīvis, m. and f., citizen</td><td colspan="2">mare, maris, n., sea</td></tr>
<tr><td></td><td>SINGULAR</td><td>PLURAL</td><td>SINGULAR</td><td>PLURAL</td></tr>
<tr><td>NOM.</td><td>cīvis</td><td>cīvēs</td><td>mare</td><td>maria</td></tr>
<tr><td>GEN.</td><td>cīvis</td><td>cīvium</td><td>maris</td><td>marium</td></tr>
<tr><td>DAT.</td><td>cīvī</td><td>cīvibus</td><td>marī</td><td>maribus</td></tr>
<tr><td>ACC.</td><td>cīvem</td><td>cīvēs(-īs)</td><td>mare</td><td>maria</td></tr>
<tr><td>ABL.</td><td>cīve</td><td>cīvibus</td><td>marī</td><td>maribus</td></tr>
</table>

551.   Fourth Declension (487)   Fifth Declension (492)

<table>
<tr><td colspan="2">cāsus, cāsūs, m., chance</td><td colspan="2">diēs, diēī, m., day</td><td colspan="2">rēs, reī, f., thing</td></tr>
<tr><td></td><td>SING.   PLUR.</td><td></td><td>SING.   PLUR.</td><td></td><td>SING.   PLUR.</td></tr>
<tr><td>NOM.</td><td>cāsus   cāsūs</td><td></td><td>diēs   diēs</td><td></td><td>rēs   rēs</td></tr>
<tr><td>GEN.</td><td>cāsūs   cāsuum</td><td></td><td>diēī   diērum</td><td></td><td>reī   rērum</td></tr>
<tr><td>DAT.</td><td>cāsuī   cāsibus</td><td></td><td>diēī   diēbus</td><td></td><td>reī   rēbus</td></tr>
<tr><td>ACC.</td><td>cāsum   cāsūs</td><td></td><td>diem   diēs</td><td></td><td>rem   rēs</td></tr>
<tr><td>ABL.</td><td>cāsū   cāsibus</td><td></td><td>diē   diēbus</td><td></td><td>rē   rēbus</td></tr>
</table>

[1] The numbers in parentheses refer to the sections in which these forms are discussed.

418

552.   Irregular Nouns **(415, 446, 489)**

	SING.	PLUR.	SING.	SING.	PLUR.
NOM.	vīs	vīrēs	nēmō	domus	domūs
GEN.	———	vīrium	(nūllīus)	domūs(-ī)	domuum(-ōrum)
DAT.	———	vīribus	nēminī	domuī(-ō)	domibus
ACC.	vim	vīrēs(-īs)	nēminem	domum	domōs(-ūs)
ABL.	vī	vīribus	(nūllō)	domō(-ū)	domibus
(LOC.)				(domī)	

Adjectives and Adverbs *bonus, magnus & malus can only have 1st + 2nd endings*

553.   First and Second Declensions **(66,106,117)**

	SINGULAR			PLURAL		
	M.	F.	N.	M.	F.	N.
NOM.	magnus	magna	magnum	magnī	magnae	magna
GEN.	magnī	magnae	magnī	magnōrum	magnārum	magnōrum
DAT.	magnō	magnae	magnō	magnīs	magnīs	magnīs
ACC.	magnum	magnam	magnum	magnōs	magnās	magna
ABL.	magnō	magnā	magnō	magnīs	magnīs	magnīs
(VOC.)	(magne)					

	SINGULAR			PLURAL		
NOM.	līber	lībera	līberum	noster	nostra	nostrum
GEN.	līberī	līberae	līberī	nostrī	nostrae	nostrī
DAT.	līberō	līberae	līberō	nostrō	nostrae	nostrō
ACC.	līberum	līberam	līberum	nostrum	nostram	nostrum
ABL.	līberō	līberā	līberō	nostrō	nostrā	nostrō

Plural, **līberī, līberae, lībera,** etc.   Plural, **nostrī, –ae, –a,** etc.

554.   Third Declension **(345)**
                              THREE ENDINGS

	SINGULAR			PLURAL		
	M.	F.	N.	M.	F.	N.
NOM.	ācer	ācris	ācre	ācrēs	ācrēs	ācria
GEN.	ācris	ācris	ācris	ācrium	ācrium	ācrium
DAT.	ācrī	ācrī	ācrī	ācribus	ācribus	ācribus
ACC.	ācrem	ācrem	ācre	ācrēs(-īs)	ācrēs(-īs)	ācria
ABL.	ācrī	ācrī	ācrī	ācribus	ācribus	ācribus

TWO ENDINGS   ONE ENDING

	SINGULAR		PLURAL		SINGULAR		PLURAL	
	M.F.	N.	M.F.	N.	M.F.	N.	M.F.	N.
NOM.	fortis	forte	fortēs	fortia	pār	pār	parēs	paria
GEN.	fortis	fortis	fortium	fortium	paris	paris	parium	parium
DAT.	fortī	fortī	fortibus	fortibus	parī	parī	paribus	paribus
ACC.	fortem	forte	fortēs(-īs)	fortia	parem	pār	parēs(-īs)	paria
ABL.	fortī	fortī	fortibus	fortibus	parī	parī	paribus	paribus

555. PRESENT PARTICIPLE (407)

	SINGULAR		PLURAL	
	M.F.	N.	M.F.	N.
NOM.	portāns	portāns	portantēs	portantia
GEN.	portantis	portantis	portantium	portanium
DAT.	portantī	portantī	portantibus	portantibus
ACC.	portantem	portāns	portantēs(–īs)	portantia
ABL.	portante(–ī)	portante(–ī)	portantibus	portantibus

556. Comparison of Regular Adjectives and Adverbs (438, 444, 449, 450)

POSITIVE		COMPARATIVE		SUPERLATIVE	
ADJ.	ADV.	ADJ.	ADV.	ADJ.	ADV.
altus	altē	altior	altius	altissimus	altissimē
fortis	fortiter	fortior	fortius	fortissimus	fortissimē
līber	līberē	līberior	līberius	līberrimus	līberrimē
ācer	ācriter	ācrior	ācrius	ācerrimus	ācerrimē
facilis	facile	facilior	facilius	facillimus	facillimē

557. Comparison of Irregular Adjectives (456)

POSITIVE	COMPARATIVE	SUPERLATIVE
bonus, –a, –um	melior, –ius	optimus, –a, –um
malus, –a, –um	peior, –ius	pessimus, –a, –um
magnus, –a, –um	maior, –ius	maximus, –a, –um
pavus, –a, –um	minor, –us	minimus, –a, –um
multus, –a, –um	—, plūs	plūrimus, –a, –um

558. Declension of Comparatives (439, 456)

	SINGULAR		PLURAL		SINGULAR	PLURAL	
	M.F.	N.	M.F.	N.	N.[1]	M.F.	N.
NOM.	altior	altius	altiōres	altiōra	plūs	plūrēs	plūra
GEN.	altiōris	altiōris	altiōrum	altiōrum	plūris	plūrium	plūrium
DAT.	altiōrī	altiōrī	altiōribus	altiōribus	——	plūribus	plūribus
ACC.	altiōrem	altius	altiōrēs	altiōra	plūs	plūrēs	plūra
ABL.	altiōre	altiōre	altiōribus	altiōribus	plūre	plūribus	plūribus

559. DECLENSION OF NUMERALS (394, 468, 469)

	M.	F.	N.	M.F.	N.
NOM.	ūnus	ūna	ūnum	trēs	tria
GEN.	ūnīus	ūnīus	unius	trium	trium
DAT.	ūnī	ūnī	ūnī	tribus	tribus
ACC.	ūnūm	ūnam	ūnum	trēs	tria
ABL.	ūnō	ūnā	ūnō	tribus	tribus

[1] **Plūs** has no masculine or feminine singular.

	M.	F.	N.	M.F.N. (*adj.*)	N. (*noun*)
NOM.	duo	duae	duo	mīlle	mīlia
GEN.	duōrum	duārum	duōrum	mīlle	mīlium
DAT.	duōbus	duābus	duōbus	mīlle	mīlibus
ACC.	duōs	duās	duo	mīlle	mīlia
ABL.	duōbus	duābus	duōbus	mīlle	mīlibus

Alius has **aliud** in the nom. and acc. sing. neuter; plural regular

560.   Numerals **(20, 307)**

	ROMAN NUMERALS	CARDINALS	ORDINALS
1.	I.	ūnus, –a, –um	prīmus, –a, –um
2.	II.	duo, duae, duo	secundus (alter)
3.	III.	trēs, tria	tertius
4.	IIII *or* IV.	quattuor	quārtus
5.	V.	quīnque	quīntus
6.	VI.	sex	sextus
7.	VII.	septem	septimus
8.	VIII.	octō	octāvus
9.	VIIII *or* IX.	novem	nōnus
10.	X.	decem	decimus
11.	XI.	ūndecim	ūndecimus
12.	XII.	duodecim	duodecimus
13.	XIII.	tredecim	tertius decimus
14.	XIIII *or* XIV.	quattuordecim	quārtus decimus
15.	XV.	quīndecim	quīntus decimus
16.	XVI.	sēdecim	sextus decimus
17.	XVII.	septendecim	septimus decimus
18.	XVIII.	duodēvīgintī	duodēvīcēsimus
19.	XVIIII *or* XIX	ūndēvīgintī	ūndēvīcēsimus
20.	XX.	vīgintī	vīcēsimus
21.	XXI.	vīgintī ūnus *or* ūnus et vīgintī	vīcēsimus prīmus *or* ūnus et vīcēsimus
30.	XXX.	trīgintā	trīcēsimus
40.	XXXX *or* XL.	quadrāgintā	quadrāgēsimus
50.	L.	quīnquāgintā	quīnquāgēsimus
60.	LX.	sexāgintā	sexāgēsimus
70.	LXX.	septuāgintā	septuāgēsimus
80.	LXXX.	octōgintā	octōgēsimus
90.	LXXXX *or* XC.	nōnāgintā	nōnāgēsimus
100.	C.	centum	centēsimus
101.	CI.	centum (et) ūnus	centēsimus (et) prīmus
200.	CC.	ducentī, –ae, –a	ducentēsimus
300.	CCC.	trecentī, –ae, –a	trecentēsimus
400.	CCCC.	quadringentī, –ae, –a	quadringentēsimus
500.	D.	quīngentī, –ae, –a	quīngentēsimus
600.	DC.	sescentī, –ae, –a	sescentēsimus
700.	DCC.	septingentī, –ae, –a	septingentēsimus
800.	DCCC.	octingentī, –ae, –a	octingentēsimus
900.	DCCCC.	nōngentī, –ae, –a	nōngentēsimus
1000.	M.	mīlle	mīllēsimus
2000.	MM.	duo mīlia	bis mīllēsimus

561.   Personal **(227)**

	SING.	PLUR.	SING.	PLUR.	M.	F.	N.
NOM.	ego	nōs	tū	vōs	is	ea	id
GEN.	meī	nostrum (nostrī)	tuī	vestrum(–trī)	(For declension
DAT.	mihi	nōbīs	tibi	vōbīs	see **563**—de-
ACC.	mē	nōs	tē	vōs	monstrative **is**)
ABL.	mē	nōbīs	tē	vōbīs			

562.   Reflexive **(461)**

	FIRST PERSON	SECOND PERSON	THIRD PERSON SING. AND PLUR.
GEN.	meī	tuī	suī
DAT.	mihi	tibi	sibi
ACC.	mē	tē	sē(sēsē)
ABL.	mē	tē	sē(sēsē)

Reflexives are not used in the nominative and have no nominative form.

563.   Demonstrative **(367,378,384,389)**

	SINGULAR			PLURAL		
	M.	F.	N.	M.	F.	N.
NOM.	hic	haec	hoc	hī	hae	haec
GEN.	huius	huius	huius	hōrum	hārum	hōrum
DAT.	huic	huic	huic	hīs	hīs	hīs
ACC.	hunc	hanc	hoc	hōs	hās	haec
ABL.	hōc	hāc	hōc	hīs	hīs	hīs
NOM.	is	ea	id	eī(iī)	eae	ea
GEN.	eius	eius	eius	eōrum	eārum	eōrum
DAT.	eī	eī	eī	eīs (iīs)	eīs (iīs)	eīs (iīs)
ACC.	eum	eam	id	eōs	eās	ea
ABL.	eō	eā	eō	eīs (iīs)	eīs (iīs)	eīs (iīs)

	SINGULAR			PLURAL		
	M.	F.	N.	M.	F.	N.
NOM.	īdem	eadem	idem	eīdem (īdem)	eaedem	eadem
GEN.	eiusdem	eiusdem	eiusdem	eōrundem	eārundem	eōrundem
DAT.	eīdem	eīdem	eīdem	eīsdem (īsdem)	eīsdem (īsdem)	eīsdem (īsdem)
ACC.	eundem	eandem	idem	eōsdem	eāsdem	eadem
ABL.	eōdem	eādem	eōdem	eīsdem (īsdem)	eīsdem (īsdem)	eīsdem (īsdem)

	SINGULAR			PLURAL		
	M.	F.	N.	M.	F.	N.
NOM.	ille	illa	illud	illī	illae	illa
GEN.	illīus	illīus	illīus	illōrum	illārum	illōrum
DAT.	illī	illī	illī	illīs	illīs	illīs
ACC.	illum	illam	illud	illōs	illās	illa
ABL.	illō	illā	illō	illīs	illīs	illīs

	SINGULAR			PLURAL		
	M.	F.	N.	M.	F.	N.
	ipse	ipsa	ipsum	ipsī	ipsae	ipsa
	ipsīus	ipsīus	ipsīus	ipsōrum	ipsārum	ipsōrum
	ipsī	ipsī	ipsī	ipsīs	ipsīs	ipsīs
	ipsum	ipsam	ipsum	ipsōs	ipsās	ipsa
	ipsō	ipsā	ipsō	ipsīs	ipsīs	ipsīs

564. Relative **(270)**

	SINGULAR			PLURAL		
	M.	F.	N.	M.	F.	N.
NOM.	quī	quae	quod	quī	quae	quae
GEN.	cuius	cuius	cuius	quōrum	quārum	quōrum
DAT.	cui	cui	cui	quibus	quibus	quibus
ACC.	quem	quam	quod	quōs	quās	quae
ABL.	quō	quā	quō	quibus	quibus	quibus

565. Interrogative **(284)**

	SINGULAR		PLURAL		
	M.F.	N.	M.	F.	N.
NOM.	quis	quid	quī	quae	quae
GEN.	cuius	cuius	quōrum	quārum	quōrum
DAT.	cui	cui	quibus	quibus	quibus
ACC.	quem	quid	quōs	quās	quae
ABL.	quō	quō	quibus	quibus	quibus

A bakery in Herculaneum, with mills for grinding the grain; the bakers ground their own. One upper millstone is gone; the other has only a small piece left.

First Conjugation

Principal Parts: **portō, portāre, portāvī, portātus**

ACTIVE		PASSIVE	
	INDICATIVE		

PRESENT *I carry,* etc. *I am carried,* etc.
(25, 194)

portō	portāmus	portor	portāmur
portās	portātis	portāris(–re)	portāminī
portat	portant	portātur	portantur

IMPERFECT *I was carrying,* etc. *I was (being) carried,* etc.
(186, 194)

portābam	portābāmus	portābar	portābāmur
portābās	portābātis	portābāris(–re)	portābāminī
portābat	portābant	portābātur	portābantur

FUTURE *I shall carry,* etc. *I shall be carried,* etc.
(49,194)

portābō	portābimus	portābor	portābimur
portābis	portābitis	portāberis(–re)	portābiminī
portābit	portābunt	portābitur	portabuntur

PERFECT *I carried, have carried,* etc. *I was carried, have been carried,* etc.
(95, 240)

portāvī	portāvimus	portātus $\begin{cases} \text{sum} \\ \text{es} \\ \text{est} \end{cases}$	portātī $\begin{cases} \text{sumus} \\ \text{estis} \\ \text{sunt} \end{cases}$
portāvistī	portāvistis	(–a, –um)	(–ae, –a)
portāvit	portāvērunt(–ēre)		

PAST PERFECT *I had carried,* etc. *I had been carried,* etc.
(222, 241)

portāveram	portāverāmus	portātus $\begin{cases} \text{eram} \\ \text{erās} \\ \text{erat} \end{cases}$	portātī $\begin{cases} \text{erāmus} \\ \text{erātis} \\ \text{erant} \end{cases}$
portāverās	portāverātis	(–a, –um)	(–ae, –a)
portāverat	portāverant		

FUTURE PERFECT *I shall have carried,* etc. *I shall have been carried,* etc.
(222, 241)

portāverō	portāverimus	portātus $\begin{cases} \text{erō} \\ \text{eris} \\ \text{erit} \end{cases}$	portātī $\begin{cases} \text{erimus} \\ \text{eritis} \\ \text{erunt} \end{cases}$
portāveris	portāveritis	(–a, –um)	(–ae, –a)
portāverit	portāverint		

INFINITIVE **(23, 249, 413, 418)**

PRESENT portāre, *to carry* portārī, *to be carried*
PERFECT portāvisse, *to have carried* portātus esse, *to have been carried*

FUTURE portātūrus esse, *to be going to carry*

PARTICIPLE **(239, 407, 408)**

PRESENT portāns, *carrying*
PERFECT portātus, *(having been) carried*
FUTURE portātūrus, *going to carry*

IMPERATIVE **(69)**

PRESENT *carry*
portā portāte

567.   Second Conjugation

PRINCIPAL PARTS: **doceō, docēre, docuī, doctus**

INDICATIVE

PRESENT (81, 194)	doceō	docēmus	doceor	docēmur
	docēs	docētis	docēris(–re)	docēminī
	docet	docent	docētur	docentur

IMPERFECT (186, 194)	docēbam	docēbāmus	docēbar	docēbāmur
	docēbās	docēbātis	docēbāris(–re)	docēbāminī
	docēbat	docēbant	docēbātur	docēbantur

FUTURE (81, 194)	docēbō	docēbimus	docēbor	docēbimur
	docēbis	docēbitis	docēberis(–re)	docēbiminī
	docēbit	docēbunt	docēbitur	docēbuntur

PERFECT (95, 240)	docuī	docuimus	doctus (–a, –um) { sum es est	doctī (–ae, –a) { sumus estis sunt
	docuistī	docuistis		
	docuit	docuērunt(–ēre)		

PAST PERFECT (222, 241)	docueram	docuerāmus	doctus (–a, –um) { eram erās erat	doctī (–ae, –a) { erāmus erātis erant
	docuerās	docuerātis		
	docuerat	docuerant		

FUTURE PERFECT (222, 241)	docuerō	docuerimus	doctus (–a, –um) { erō eris erit	doctī (–ae, –a) { erimus eritis erunt
	docueris	docueritis		
	docuerit	docuerint		

INFINITIVE (249, 413, 418)

PRESENT	docēre	docērī
PERFECT	docuisse	doctus esse
FUTURE	doctūrus esse	

PARTICIPLE (239, 407, 408)

PRESENT	docēns	
PERFECT		doctus
FUTURE	doctūrus	

IMPERATIVE (69)

| PRESENT | docē | docēte |

568.
Third Conjugation

PRINCIPAL PARTS: **pōnō, pōnĕre, posuī, positus**

INDICATIVE

PRESENT **(141, 194)**	pōnō	pōnimus	pōnor	pōnimur
	pōnis	pōnitis	pōneris(–re)	pōniminī
	pōnit	pōnunt	pōnitur	pōnuntur
IMPERFECT **(186, 194)**	pōnēbam	pōnēbāmus	pōnēbar	pōnēbāmur
	pōnēbās	pōnēbātis	pōnēbāris(–re)	pōnēbāminī
	pōnēbat	pōnēbant	pōnēbātur	pōnēbantur
FUTURE **(164, 194)**	ponam	pōnēmus	pōnar	pōnēmur
	pōnēs	pōnētis	pōnēris(–re)	pōnēminī
	pōnet	pōnent	pōnētur	pōnentur

PERFECT **(141, 240)**	posuī	posuimus	positus (–a, –um) { sum / es / est }	positī (–ae, –a) { sumus / estis / sunt }
	posuistī	posuistis		
	posuit	posuērunt(–ēre)		

PAST PERFECT **(222, 241)**	posueram	posuerāmus	positus (–a, –um) { eram / erās / erat }	positī (–ae, –a) { erāmus / erātis / erant }
	posuerās	posuerātis		
	posuerat	posuerant		

FUTURE PERFECT **(222, 241)**	posuerō	posuerimus	positus (–a, –um) { erō / eris / erit }	positī (–ae, –a) { erimus / eritis / erunt }
	posueris	posueritis		
	posuerit	posuerint		

INFINITIVE **(141, 249, 413, 418)**

PRESENT	pōnere	pōnī
PERFECT	posuisse	positus esse
FUTURE	positūrus esse	

PARTICIPLE **(239, 407, 408)**

PRESENT	pōnēns	
PERFECT		positus
FUTURE	positūrus	

IMPERATIVE **(141)**

PRESENT	pōne	pōnite

ACTIVE		PASSIVE

Fourth Conjugation

PRINCIPAL PARTS: **mūniō, mūnīre, mūnīvī, mūnītus**

INDICATIVE

PRESENT (147, 194)	mūniō mūnīs mūnit	mūnīmus mūnītis mūniunt	mūnior mūnīris(–re) mūnītur	mūnīmur mūnīminī mūniuntur
IMPERFECT (186, 194)	mūniēbam mūniēbās mūniēbat	mūniēbāmus mūniēbātis mūniēbant	mūniēbar mūniēbāris(–re) mūniēbātur	mūniēbāmur mūniēbāminī mūniēbantur
FUTURE (175, 194)	mūniam mūniēs mūniet	mūniēmus mūniētis mūnient	mūniar mūniēris(–re) mūniētur	mūniēmur mūniēminī mūnientur

PERFECT (147, 240)	mūnīvī mūnīvistī mūnīvit	mūnīvimus mūnīvistis mūnīvērunt(–ēre)	mūnītus (–a, –um) { sum / es / est	mūnītī (–ae, –a) { sumus / estis / sunt
PAST PERFECT (222, 241)	mūnīveram mūnīverās mūnīverat	mūnīverāmus mūnīverātis mūnīverant	mūnītus (–a, –um) { eram / erās / erat	mūnītī (–ae, –a) { erāmus / erātis / erant
FUTURE PERFECT (222, 241)	mūnīverō mūnīveris mūnīverit	mūnīverimus mūnīveritis mūnīverint	mūnitus (–a, –um) { erō / eris / erit	mūnītī (–ae, –a) { erimus / eritis / erunt

INFINITIVE **(249, 413, 418)**

PRESENT	mūnīre	mūnīrī
PERFECT	mūnīvisse	mūnītus esse
FUTURE	mūnītūrus esse	

PARTICIPLE **(239, 407, 408)**

PRESENT	mūniēns	
PERFECT		mūnītus
FUTURE	mūnītūrus	

IMPERATIVE **(147)**

PRESENT	mūnī	mūnīte

570.   Third Conjugation–iō Verbs

PRINCIPAL PARTS: **capiō, capĕre, cēpī, captus**

INDICATIVE

PRESENT	capiō	capimus	capior	capimur
(147,194)	capis	capitis	caperis (–re)	capiminī
	capit	capiunt	capitur	capiuntur
IMPERFECT	capiēbam	capiēbāmus	capiēbar	capiēbāmur
(186,194)	capiēbās	capiēbātis	capiēbāris	capiēbāminī
	capiēbat	capiēbant	capiēbātur	capiēbantur
FUTURE	capiam	capiēmus	capiar	capiēmur
(175,194)	capiēs	capiētis	capiēris (–re)	capiēminī
	capiet	capient	capiētur	capientur
PERFECT	cēpī	cēpimus	captus sum	captī sumus
(147,240)	cēpistī	cēpistis	captus es	captī estis
	cēpit	cēpērunt (-ēre)	captus est	captī sunt
PAST	cēperam	cēperāmus	captus eram	capti erāmus
PERFECT	cēperās	cēperātis	captus eras	capti erātis
(222,241)	cēperat	cēperant	captus erat	capti erant
FUTURE	cēperō	cēperimus	captus erō	capti erimus
PERFECT	cēperis	cēperitis	captus eris	capti eritis
(222,241)	cēperit	cēperint	captus erit	capti erunt

INFINITIVE **(249, 413, 418)**

PRESENT	capere	capī
PERFECT	cēpisse	captus esse
FUTURE	captūrus esse	

PARTICIPLE **(239, 407, 408)**

PRESENT	capiēns	
PERFECT		captus
FUTURE	captūrus	

IMPERATIVE **(147)**

PRESENT	cape	capite

428

PRINCIPAL PARTS: **sum, esse, fuī, futūrus**

PRINCIPAL PARTS: **possum, posse, potuī, ——**

INDICATIVE

PRESENT (111)	*I am, you are,* etc.	
	sum	sumus
	es	estis
	est	sunt

IMPERFECT (186)	*I was,* etc.	
	eram	erāmus
	erās	erātis
	erat	erant

FUTURE (128)	*I shall be,* etc.	
	erō	erimus
	eris	eritis
	erit	erunt

PERFECT (128)	*I was,* etc.	
	fuī	fuimus
	fuistī	fuistis
	fuit	fuērunt (–ēre)

PAST PERFECT (222)	*I had been,* etc.	
	fueram	fuerāmus
	fuerās	fuerātis
	fuerat	fuerant

FUTURE PERFECT (222)	*I shall have been,* etc.	
	fuerō	fuerimus
	fueris	fueritis
	fuerit	fuerint

INDICATIVE (313)

PRESENT	*I am able, I can,* etc.	
	possum	possumus
	potes	potestis
	potest	possunt

IMPERFECT	*I was able, I could,* etc.	
	poteram	poterāmus
	poterās	poterātis
	poterat	poterant

FUTURE	*I shall be able,* etc.	
	poterō	poterimus
	poteris	poteritis
	poterit	poterunt

PERFECT	*I was able, I could,* etc.	
	potuī	potuimus
	potuistī	potuistis
	potuit	potuērunt (–ēre)

PAST PERFECT	*I had been able,* etc.	
	potueram	potuerāmus
	potuerās	potuerātis
	potuerat	potuerant

FUTURE PERFECT	*I shall have been able*	
	potuerō	potuerimus
	potueris	potueritis
	potuerit	potuerint

INFINITIVE (111, 413, 418)

PRESENT	esse, *to be*
PERFECT	fuisse, *to have been*
FUTURE	futūrus esse, *to be going to be*

INFINITIVE (315, 413)

PRESENT	posse, *to be able*
PERFECT	potuisse, *to have been able*
FUTURE	——

PARTICIPLE (408)

FUTURE	futūrus, *going to be*

PARTICIPLE (407)

PRESENT	potēns (*adj.*), *powerful*

IMPERATIVE

PRESENT	*be*	
	es	este

BASIC SYNTAX

572. Agreement

1. *Adjectives.* Adjectives and participles agree in number, gender, and case with the nouns which they modify **(15, 106, 239)**.

2. *Adjectives as Nouns.* Adjectives are often used as nouns **(216)**.

3. *Verbs.* Verbs agree in person and number with their subjects **(22, 25)**. When two subjects are connected by **aut, aut . . . aut, neque . . . neque,** the verb agrees with the nearer subject **(202)**.

4. *Relative Pronoun.* The relative pronoun agrees in gender and number with its antecedent, but its case depends upon its use in its own clause **(272)**.

5. *Appositives.* Appositives regularly agree in case **(142)**.

Noun Syntax

573. Nominative

1. *Subject.* The subject of a verb is in the nominative **(9)**.

2. *Predicate.* A noun or adjective used in the predicate after a linking verb (*is, are, seem,* etc.) to complete its meaning is in the nominative **(10)**.

574. Genitive

1. *Possession.* Possession is expressed by the genitive **(44)**.

2. *Description.* The genitive, if modified by an adjective, may be used to describe a person or thing **(498)**.

575. Dative

1. *Indirect Object.* The indirect object of a verb is in the dative. It is used with verbs of *giving, reporting, telling,* etc. **(54)**.

2. *With Special Verbs.* The dative is used with a few intransitive verbs, such as **noceō (505)**.

3. *With Adjectives.* The dative is used with certain adjectives, as **amīcus, pār, similis,** and their opposites **(451)**.

576. Accusative

1. *Direct Object.* The direct object of a transitive verb is in the accusative **(16)**.

2. *Extent.* Extent of time or space is expressed by the accusative **(480)**.

3. *Place to Which.* The accusative with **ad** (*to*) or **in** (*into*) expresses "place to which" **(114)**.

4. *Subject of Infinitive.* The subject of an infinitive is in the accusative **(234)**.

5. *With Prepositions.* The accusative is used with the prepositions **ad, ante, apud, circum, contrā, inter, ob, per, post, super,** and **trāns;** also with **in** and **sub** when they show the direction toward which a thing moves.

577. Ablative

1. *From Which.* The ablative with **ab, dē,** or **ex** expresses "place from which" **(103).**

2. *Agent.* The ablative with **ā** or **ab** is used with a passive verb to show the person (or animal) by whom something is done **(200).**

3. *Accompaniment.* The ablative with **cum** expresses accompaniment **(170).**

4. *Manner.* The ablative of manner with **cum** describes how something is done. **Cum** may be omitted if an adjective is used with the noun **(279).**

5. *Means.* The means by which a thing is done is expressed by the ablative without a preposition **(61).**

6. *Description.* The ablative without a preposition is used (like the genitive) to describe a person or thing **(498).**

7. *Place Where.* The ablative with **in** expresses "place where" **(87).**

8. *Time When.* "Time when" is expressed by the ablative without a preposition **(373).**

9. *Respect.* The ablative without a preposition is used to tell in what respect the statement applies **(355).**

10. *Absolute.* A noun in the ablative used with a participle, adjective, or other noun in the same case and having no grammatical connection with any other word in its clause is called an ablative absolute **(323).**

11. *With Prepositions.* The ablative is used with the prepositions **ab, cum, dē, ex, prae, prō, sine;** also with **in** and **sub** when they indicate place where.

578. Vocative

The *vocative* is used in addressing a person **(100).**

Verb Syntax

579. Tenses

1. *Imperfect. Repeated, customary,* or *continuous* action in the past is expressed by the imperfect **(187).**

2. *Perfect.* An action completed in the past is expressed by the perfect. It is translated by the English past, occasionally by the present perfect **(95, 187).**

580. Participles

1. The tenses of the participle (present, perfect, future) indicate time *present, past,* or *future* from the standpoint of the main verb **(239, 407, 408).**

2. Perfect participles are often used as simple adjectives and, like adjectives, may be used as nouns **(312).**

3. The Latin participle is often a one-word substitute for a subordinate clause in English introduced by *who* or *which, when* or *after, since* or *because, although,* and *if* **(318).**

581. Infinitive

1. The infinitive is a verbal indeclinable neuter noun, and as such it may be used as the subject of a verb **(129)**.

2. With many verbs the infinitive, like other nouns, may be used as a direct object **(130)**.

3. The infinitive object of some verbs such as **iubeō** and **doceō** often has a noun or pronoun subject in the accusative **(234)**.

4. Statements that convey indirectly the thoughts or words of another, used as the objects of verbs of *saying, thinking, knowing, hearing, perceiving,* etc., require verbs in the infinitive with subjects in the accusative **(419)**.

582. LATIN FORMS AND PHRASES IN ENGLISH

You will be reminded daily that Latin is a living language. Almost every time you open a book, a magazine, or even a newspaper you will find an abbreviation or a phrase in Latin. A knowledge of the forms on these pages, their meanings, and how to use them correctly is one of the marks of an educated person. Partial lists are given below of 1) Latin phrases, mottoes, and quotations; 2) Latin abbreviations; 3) unchanged Latin forms in English; 4) bases of the Latin words used in English; 5) bases plus –e used in English. The last three groups especially represent only a small part of the total number. The figure after each phrase or word gives the section in which it is treated. The words without numbers are not specifically mentioned in the lessons.

I. Phrases, Mottoes, Quotations

ab ovo usque ad mala, **294**

ad astra per aspera, **156**

ad infinitum, **156**

ad maiorem Dei gloriam, *to the greater glory of God*

ad nauseam, **64**

Alis volat propriis, **448**

Alma Mater, **376**

alter ego, *second self*

Amantium irae amoris integratio est, **5**

amicus curiae, **190**

Annuit coeptis, **502**

ante bellum, **316**

aqua vitae, **64**

argumentum ad hominem, *argument to the man,* i.e., one that appeals to the person addressed

Arma non servant modum, **358**

Ars longa, vita brevis, "Art is long, time is fleeting"

Audi et alteram partem, *Hear the other side too*

aut Caesar aut nihil, **376**

auxilio ab alto, **167**

bona fide, **496**

Carpe diem, *Seize the day,* i.e., the opportunity

casus belli, **496**

Cave canem, *Look out for the dog*

consilio et armis, **190**

corpus delicti, *the body of the crime,* i.e., the facts of the crime

cui bono? **288**

cum grano salis, *with a grain of salt*

cum laude, *with honor*

de facto, **316**

Dei gratia, **252**

de jure, **343**

de novo, **133**

Deo gratias, **252**

Disciplina praesidium civitatis, **353**

Divide et impera, **499**

Dominus providebit, **358**

dramatis personae, *characters of the play*

Dulce et decorum est pro patria mori, **417**

Dum spiro spero, **380**

Dux femina facti, **304**

Elizabeth regina, **205**

Ense petit placidam sub libertate quietem, **358**

e pluribus unum, **1, 459**

Errare est humanum, **129**

esse quam videri, **459**

Est modus in rebus, *There is a middle ground in things*

Et tu, Brute, **316**

ex animo, **156**

Exeunt omnes, *All leave*

ex officio, **167**

ex parte, *on (one) side*

Experientia docet, **156**

ex post facto, **454**

extempore, **358**

Ex uno disce omnes, *From one learn (about them) all*

Facilis descensus Averno, *Easy is the descent to Avernus,* i.e., the Lower World

facta, non verba, *deeds, not words,* **314**

Fata viam invenient, **343**

Fortes Fortuna adiuvat, **358**

Fortuna caeca est, **47**

genus homo, **387**

Homo proponit, sed Deus disponit, **387**

homo sapiens, *man having sense,* i.e., human being

hostis humani generis, *enemy of the human race*

Ilium fuit, **288**

imperium et libertas, *empire and freedom*

in absentia, **288**

In Deo speramus, **205**

in forma pauperis, **454**

In hoc signo vinces, **5**

in libris libertas, **353**

in loco parentis, **411**

in medias res, *into the middle of things*

in memoriam, **133**

in nomine Domini, *in the name of the Lord*

in omnia paratus, **358**

in perpetuum, **288**

in propria persona, **454**

in re, *in the matter of*

in statu quo, **496**

inter alia, **411**

inter nos, **288**

in toto, **411**

Ipse dixit, *He himself said it*

ipsissima verba, *the very words*

ipso facto, **411**

ius gentium, *the law of nations*

iustitia omnibus, **376**

Labor omnia vincit, **459**

lex scripta, **304**

Littera scripta manet, *The written letter lasts*

lux ex oriente, *light from the east*

Magna Charta, **47**

magna cum laude, *with high honor*

magnum bonum, **190**

magnum opus, *a great work*

Manus manum lavat, *Hand washes hand,* i.e., one hand washes the other

mare clausum, *a closed sea*

materia medica, *medical material*

me iudice, **343**

mens sana in corpore sano, *a healthy mind in a healthy body*

mihi cura futuri, my concern is the future

mirabile dictu, *wonderful to say*

modus operandi, *method of operating*

Montani semper liberi, **167**

multum in parvo, **133**

ne plus ultra, *no more beyond,* i.e., nothing better

non compos mentis, *not in possession of one's senses*

nosce te ipsum, *know thyself*

novus homo, **304**

novus ordo seclorum, **502**

nunc pro tunc, *now as of then*
obiter dictum, **411**
Omnia reliquit servare rem publicam, **416**
O tempora, O mores! *O times, O customs!* **503**
Otium sine litteris mors est, *Leisure without literature is death*
Pater Noster, **376**
pauci quos aequus amat Iuppiter, **205**
pax in bello, **304**
Pax vobiscum! **288**
per annum, **252**
per capita, **343**
per diem, **496**
per se, *by itself*
persona non grata, **64**
Possunt quia posse videntur, **5**
post mortem, **496**
prima facie, **496**
primus inter pares, **376**
pro bono publico, **220**
pro forma, **220**
pro patria, **220**
quid pro quo, **387**
rara avis, *a rare bird*
semper idem, **387**
semper paratus, **314**
sic semper tyrannis, **252**

sine die, **496**
sine qua non, **288**
subpoena, **454**
sub rosa, **252**
sui generis, **496**
summa cum laude, *with highest honor*
summum bonum, *the highest good*
sursum corda, *(lift) up (your) hearts*
Te Deum, **316**
Tempus fugit, **343**
terra firma, **205**
terra incognita, **316**
Timeo Danaos et dona ferentes, **411**
Ultima Thule, **321**
una voce, **411**
urbs et orbis, **1**
Vanitas vanitatum, **358**
Veni, vidi, vici, **5**
Verbum sapienti sat est, *A word to the wise is sufficient*
Vestis virum facit, *Clothes make the man*
via media, **190**
vice versa, *in reverse*
victoria, non praeda, **167**
virginibus puerisque, *for girls and boys*
virtute et armis, **358**
vox humana, **411**
Vox populi vox Dei, **411**

II. Abbreviations

A. B. (Artium Baccalaureus), *Bachelor of Arts*
A. D., **376**
ad fin., **353**
ad lib. (ad libitum), *at pleasure*
Ag (argentum), *silver*
A. M., **496**
Au (aurum), *gold*
Cf., **47**
d. (denarius), *penny*
D. V. (Deo volente), *God willing*
e.g. (exempli gratia), *for example*
et al. (et alii), *and others*
etc., **47**
fec. (fecit), *he made (it)*
ibid., **387**
id., **387**
i.e., **47**

in loc. (in loco), *in the place*
inv. (invenit), *he invented (it)*
£ (libra), *pound* (British money)
lb. (libra), *pound*
LL. D. (Legum Doctor), *Doctor of Laws*
loc. cit. (loco citato), *in the place cited*
M., **496**
M. D. (Medicinae Doctor), *Doctor of Medicine*
N. B. (Nota bene), *Note well*
no. (numero), *by number*
op. cit. (opere citato), *in the work cited*
per cent. (per centum), *per cent, per hundred*
Ph. D. (Philosophiae Doctor), *Doctor of Philosophy*

434

P.M., **496**
pro tem., **343**
prox. (proximo mense), *next month*
P. S., **353**
q. v. (quod vide), *which see*
℞ (Recipe), *Take* (in prescriptions)

S. P. Q. R. (Senatus Populusque Romanus), *The Senate and People of
Rome,* **494**
s. v. (sub verbo), *under the word*
ult. (ultimo mense), *last month*
vs. (versus), *against*

III. Latin Forms in English [1]

actor, **338**
addendum, **120**
affidavit, **98**
agenda, **120**
alibi
Alma, **92**
alumna, **12**
alumnus, **35**
amanuensis, **348**
amoeba, **28**
antenna, **12**
anterior, **459**
apex, **338**
apparatus, **496**
appendix, **338**
arbiter, **109**
area, **12**
arena, **12**
Augustus, **92**
aurora
axis, **343**
bacillus, **35**
bacterium, **120**
basis, **343**
bonus, **35**
camera, **12**
campus, **35**
cancer, **109**
candelabrum, **120**
Cecilia, **92**
census, **496**
circus, **35**
Clara, **92**
Claudia, **92**
consensus, **496**
consul, **338**
copula, **12**
Cornelia, **92**

Cornelius, **92**
corona, **12**
curriculum, **120**
datum, **120**
deficit, **190**
delirium, **120**
dictum, **120**
discus, **35**
doctor, **214, 338**
duplex, **348**
erratum, **316**
excelsior, **459**
exterior, **459**
facsimile, **348**
factor, **338**
focus, **35**
formula, **12**
forte, **348**
forum
fungus, **35**
genius, **35**
genus, **338**
gladiolus, **35**
gratis, **85**
habitat, **85**
honor
ignoramus, **85**
impedimenta
impetus, **496**
impromptu, **496**
index, **338**
inertia
inferior, **459**
insignia, **348**
insomnia
integer, **109**
interceptor
interior, **459**

inventor, **416**
Julia, **92**
Julius, **92**
junior, **459**
labor, **338**
larva, **12**
Lavinia, **92**
Leo, **92**
locus
major, **459**
mandamus, **85**
Marcia, **92**
maximum, **120, 459**
medium
memorandum, **120**
militia
minimum, **120, 459**
minister, **109**
minor, **459**
minus, **459**
minutiae, **12**
miser, **109**
monitor, **416**
nausea
nebula, **28**
neuter, **109**
nostrum
nova, **28**
octavo
omnibus, **348**
onus
opera
opus
papilla, **28**
par, **348**
pauper, **348**
plus, **459**
posterior, **459**

[1] Many other nouns in *–a, –us, –um,* and *–or.* For a list of 7000 Latin words
in English see *Classical Journal,* 48 (1952), pp. 85–108.

prior, **459**
prospectus, **496**
quarto
quietus, **35**
Quintus, **92**
rabies, **496**
radius, **35**
ratio, **338**
rebus, **496**
recipe
regalia, **348**
requiem, **496**
Rufus, **92**
saliva

senior, **459**
September, etc., **348**
series, **496**
simile, **348**
simplex, **348**
sinister, **109**
specie, **496**
species, **496**
specimen
spectrum, **120**
stamen, **338**
status, **496**
Stella, **92**
stimulus, **35**

stratum, **120**
superior, **459**
Sylvester, **92**
tenet, **85**
terror, **416**
ulterior, **459**
vertebra, **28**
vertex, **338**
vesper, **109**
veto, **85**
via, **85**
victor, **92, 338**
viscera **338**

IV. English Words From Latin Base [1]

accept
act, **490**
agent, **490**
alien
apt
ascend
audit
client
consist
consult
contend
convenient, **490**
convent, **490**
credit
cult

debit
deception
defend, **145**
desert
duct
effect
excess
expedient
export
familiar
firm
form, **145**
fort
front
habit

incipient
instant
intellect
intercept
invent
just, **490**
laud, **145**
oration, **447**
part, **490**
perfect
pomp
position
press
prohibit
prospect, **220**

public, **145**
quart
rapt
ration
region, **447**
remiss
script
sermon
session, **447**
sign, **145**
tangent
tend
timid
urban
verb

V. English Words From Latin Base Plus –e [2]

Belle, **92**
cause, **145**
cede, **145, 490**
commune
conserve
convene, **490**
cure, **145**
defense
discipline
divide

explore
extreme
facile, **490**
false
fame, **145**
fortune, **145**
grave
legate
liberate
mandate

mode
nature
plane, **442**
prime, **490**
probe
produce, **220**
pulse
reduce
remote, **490**
remove, **490**

response
senate
sense
sole
solve
statue
statute
tribute
urbane
verse

[1] Many other words with suffixes –*al,* –*an,* –*ant,* –*ar,* –*ent,* –*ic,* –*id,* –*ion.*
[2] Many other words derived from the present stem and perfect participle of
verbs and many nouns and adjectives with suffixes –*tude,* –*ure,* –*ile,* –*ane,*
–*ive,* –*ose.*

Albert Moldvay

In Roman times, public fountains were the principal source of water for local residents. Today, more elaborate fountains, such as this one in Perugia, Italy add beauty and charm to parks and other public places.

583. LATIN SONGS

THE STAR-SPANGLED BANNER

Ōh, potestne cernī, praefulgente diē,
 Salūtātum signum circā noctis adventum?
Lātī clāv(ī) et stēllae, dēcertant(e) aciē,
 Glōriōsē cingunt oppidī mūnīmentum!
Iaculumque rubēns, globus sūrsum rumpēns
Per noctem mōnstrant vexillum fulgēns.
 Stēllātumne vexillum volāns tegit nōs,
 Patriam līberam fortiumque domōs?
 (For "America" see **5**, 3)

 Tr. F. A. Geyser

ADESTE FIDĒLĒS [1]

Adeste, fidēlēs,
 Laetī triumphantēs;
Venīte, venīte in Bethlehem;
 Nātum vidēte
 Rēgem angelōrum;
Venīte adōrēmus, venīte adōrēmus,
Venīte adōrēmus Dominum.

Cantet nunc "Iō!"
 Chorus angelōrum;
Cantet nunc aula caelestium:
 "Glōria, glōria
 In excelsīs Deō!"
Venīte, etc.

Ergō quī nātus
 Diē hodiernā,
Iēsū, tibi sit glōria;
 Patris aeternī
 Verbum carō factum!
Venīte, etc.

[1] Sung to the tune of the Portuguese Hymn, "O Come, All Ye Faithful."

The greatest of all medieval student songs.
In 1860 the composer Brahms used its
melody in the glorious climax to his
"Academic Festival Overture."

GAUDEAMUS IGITUR

Student Song

1. Gau - de - a - mus   i - gi - tur,   Iu - ve -nes dum
2. Vi - vat a - ca - de - mi - a,   Vi - vant pro - fes -
3. Vi - vat et res   pu - bli - ca   Et qui il - lam

su - mus;   Post iu - cun - dam   iu - ven - tu - tem,
so - res,   Vi - vat mem-brum quod - li - bet,
re - git;   Vi - vat nos - tra   ci - vi - tas;

Post mo -les - tam se - nec - tu - tem, Nos ha - be - bit
Vi - vant mem-bra quae - li - bet,   Sem - per sint in
Vi - vat haec so - da - li - tas   Quae nos huc col-

hu - mus, Nos ha - be - bit hu - mus.
flo - re, Sem - per sint in flo - re.
le - git, Quae nos huc col - le - git.

INTEGER VITAE

Horace, Odes I. 22 (ca. 25 b.c.)　　　Dr. F. F. Flemming, ca. 1811

1. In - te - ger vi - tae sce - le - ris - que
2. Si - ve per Syr - tes i - ter aes - tu -
3. Nam - que me sil - va lu - pus in Sa -

pu - rus Non e - get Mau - ris ia - cu - lis ne -
o - sas, Si - ve fac - tu - rus per in - hos - pi -
bi - na, Dum me - am can - to La - la - gen et

qu(e) ar - cu Nec ve - ne - na - tis gra - vi - da sa -
ta - lem Cau - ca - sum vel quae lo - ca fa - bu -
ul - tra Ter - mi - num cu - ris va - gor ex - pe -

git - tis, Fus - ce, pha - re - tra,
lo - sus Lam - bit Hy - das - pes.
di - tis, Fu - git in - er - mem.

The theme of this ode is that the virtuous man needs no defense. The poem was later converted into a Christian hymn; the idea was one that Christians also accepted.

VOCABULARY

LATIN–ENGLISH

Proper names are not included unless they are spelled differently in English or are difficult to pronounce in English. Their English pronunciation is indicated by a simple system. The vowels are as follows: ā as in *hate,* ă as in *hat,* ē as in *feed,* ĕ as in *fed,* ī as in *bite,* ĭ as in *bit,* ō as in *hope,* ŏ as in *hop,* ū as in *cute,* ŭ as in *cut.* In the ending *ēs* the *s* is soft as in *rose.* When the accented syllable ends in a consonant, the vowel is short; otherwise it is long.

A

ā, ab, *prep. w. abl.,* from, away from, by

absum, abesse, āfuī, āfutūrus, be away, be absent

ac, *see* **atque**

accēdō, –ere, accessī, accessūrus, approach

accidō, –ere, accidī, —, fall to, befall, happen (*w. dat.*)

accipiō, –ere, accēpī, acceptus, receive

accūsō, –āre, –āvī, –ātus, blame, accuse

ācer, ācris, ācre, sharp, keen

ācriter, *adv.,* sharply

ad, *prep. w. acc.,* to, toward, for, near

addūcō, –ere, addūxī, adductus, lead to, influence

adsum, –esse, adfuī, adfutūrus, be near, be present

aeger, aegra, aegrum, sick

Aegyptiī,–ōrum, *m. pl.,* the Egyptians

Aegyptus, –ī, *f.,* Egypt

Aenēās, –ae, *m.,* Aeneas (Enē′as)

Aeolus, –ī, *m.,* Aeolus (E′olus)

aequē, *adv.,* justly

aequus, –a, –um, even, just, calm

aestās, aestātis, *f.,* summer

aetās, aetātis, *f.,* age

Aetna, –ae, *f.,* (Mt.) Etna

afficiō, –ere, affēcī, affectus, affect, afflict with

Āfricānus –ī, *m.,* Africa′nus

ager, agrī, *m.,* field, farm, country

agō, –ere, ēgī, āctus, drive, do, treat, discuss, live *or* spend (*of time*); **grātiās agō,** thank

agricola, –ae, *m.,* farmer

āla, –ae, *f.,* wing

albus, –a, –um, white

aliēnus, –a, –um, another's, unfavorable

alius, alia, aliud, other, another; **alius . . . alius,** one . . . another; **aliī . . . aliī,** some . . . others

Alpēs, –ium, *f. pl.,* the Alps

altē, *adv.,* high, far

alter, altera, alterum, the other (*of two*); **alter . . . alter,** the one . . . the other

altus, –a, –um, high, tall, deep

Americānus, –a, –um, American; **Americānus –ī,** *m.,* an American

amīcitia, –ae, *f.,* friendship

amīcus, –a, –um, friendly; **amīcus, –ī,** *m.,* **amīca, –ae,** *f.,* friend

āmittō, –ere, āmīsī, āmissus, let go, lose

amō, –āre, –āvī, –ātus, love, like

amor, –ōris, *m.,* love

amphitheātrum, –ī, *n.,* amphitheater

Anglicus, –a, –um, English

animus, –ī, *m.,* mind, courage

annus, –ī, *m.,* year

ante, *adv. and prep. w. acc.,* before (*of time or space*)

antecēdō, –ere, –cessī, –cessūrus, go before, take the lead

antīquus, –a, –um, ancient

appellō, –āre, –āvī, –ātus, call

Appius, –a, –um, *adj.*, of Appius, Appian; **Appius**, –pī, *m.*, Appius

aptus, –a, –um, fit, suitable (*w. dat.*)

apud, *prep. w. acc.*, among, with

aqua, –ae, *f.*, water

aquaeductus, –ūs, *m.*, aqueduct

Aquītānus, –ī, *m.*, an Aquitā'nian

arcus, –ūs, *m.*, arch, bow

arēna, –ae, *f.*, sand, arena

argentum, –ī, *n.*, silver

arma, –ōrum, *n. pl.*, arms, weapons

ascendō, –ere, ascendī, ascēnsus, climb (up), ascend

Athēna, –ae, *f.*, *a Greek goddess* = Minerva

atque (ac), *conj.*, and

ātrium, ātrī, *n.*, atrium, hall

auctor, –ōris, *m.*, maker, author

auctōritās, –tātis, *f.*, authority, influence

audācia, –ae, *f.*, boldness

audāx, *gen.* audācis, daring

audiō, –īre, –īvī, –ītus, hear

augeō, –ēre, auxī, auctus, increase

aureus, –a, –um, golden

aurīga, –ae, *m.*, charioteer

aurum, –ī, *n.*, gold

aut, or; **aut . . . aut**, either . . . or

autem, *conj.* (*never first word*), however

auxilium, –lī, *n.*, aid; *pl.* reinforcements

āvertō, –ere, āvertī, āversus, turn from

avus, –ī, *m.*, grandfather

axis, –is, *m.*, axle

B

barbarus, –a, –um, foreign, barbarous; **barbarus**, –ī, *m.*, foreigner, barbarian

Belgae, –ārum, *m. pl.*, the Belgians; the Belgian people

bellum, –ī, *n.*, war

bene, *adv.*, well, well done; *comp.* **melius**, better; *superl.* **optimē**, best, very good

beneficium, –cī, *n.*, kindness, benefit

benignus, –a, –um, kind

bibō, –ere, bibī, ——, drink

bonus, –a, –um, good; *comp.* **melior, melius**, better; *superl.* **optimus, –a, –um**, best

Britannia, –ae, *f.*, Britain

Britannus, –ī, *m.*, a Briton

C

C., *abbreviation for* **Gāius**

cadō, –ere, cecidī, cāsūrus, fall

Caecilius, –lī, *m.*, Caecilius (Sēsil'ius)

caelum, –ī, *n.*, sky

Caesar, –aris, *m.*, Caesar

canis, –is, *m.*, dog

canō, –ere, cecinī, cantus, sing

capiō, –ere, cēpī, captus, take, seize, capture; **cōnsilium capiō**, adopt a plan

Capitōlium, –lī, *n.*, the Capitol, *temple of Jupiter at Rome;* the Capitoline Hill

captīvus, –ī, *m.;* **captīva**, –ae, *f.*, prisoner

caput, capitis, *n.*, head

carmen, –minis, *n.*, song

carrus, –ī, *m.*, cart, wagon

Carthāginiēnsēs, –ium, *m. pl.*, the Carthaginians (Carthajin'ians)

Carthāgō, –ginis, *f.*, Carthage, *a city in Africa;* **Carthāgō Nova**, New Carthage, *in Spain*

casa, –ae, *f.*, house

castra, –ōrum, *n. pl.*, camp

cāsus, –ūs, *m.*, fall, chance, accident

Catilīna, –ae, *m.*, Catiline

causa, –ae, *f.*, cause, reason, case

cēdō, –ere, cessī, cessūrus, move, retreat, yield

celer, celeris, celere, swift

celeritās, –tātis, *f.*, swiftness

celeriter, *adv.*, quickly

Celtae, –ārum, *m. pl.*, Celts, *a people of Gaul*

cēna, –ae, *f.*, dinner

centum, hundred

Cerēs, –eris, *f.*, Ceres (Sē'rēs), *goddess of agriculture*

cernō, –ere, crēvī, crētus, separate, discern, see

certē, *adv.*, certainly

certus, –a, –um, fixed, sure

cibus, –ī, *m.*, food

Cicerō, –ōnis, *m.*, Cicero (Sis'ero)

Circē, –ae, *f.*, Circe (Sir'sē), *a sorceress*

circum, *prep. w. acc.*, around

circus, –ī, *m.*, circle, circus, *esp. the Circus Maximus at Rome*

cīvis, cīvis, *m.*, citizen

cīvitās, –tātis, *f.*, citizenship, state

clam, *adv.*, secretly

clāmō, –āre, –āvī, –ātus, shout, cry out
clāmor, –ōris, m., shout
clārē, adv., clearly
clārus, –a, –um, clear, famous
claudō, –ere, clausī, clausus, close
cognōmen, –minis, n., cognomen, surname
cognōscō, –ere, –nōvī, –nitus, learn, recognize; perf., know, understand
cōgō, –ere, coēgī, coāctus, drive together, collect, compel
colō, –ere, coluī, cultus, till, inhabit, worship
colōnus, –ī, m., settler
Colossēum, –ī, n., the Colosse'um, an amphitheater at Rome
committō, –ere, –mīsī, –missus, join together, commit, entrust; proelium committō, begin battle
commodē, adv., suitably
commodus, –a, –um, suitable, convenient
commoveō, –ēre, –mōvī, –mōtus, disturb
commūnis, –e, common
comprehendō, –ere, –hendī, –hēnsus, understand
concordia, –ae, f., harmony
condiciō, –ōnis, f., condition, terms
cōnficiō, –ere, –fēcī, –fectus, do up, complete, exhaust
cōnfīdō, –ere, cōnfīsus, have confidence (in)
cōnfirmō, –āre, –āvī, –ātus, make firm, encourage, establish
cōnservō, –āre, –āvī, –ātus, save, preserve
cōnsilium, –lī, n., plan, advice
cōnsistō, –ere, cōnstitī, cōnstitūrus, stand still, stop
cōnspiciō, –ere, –spexī, –spectus, catch sight of, see
cōnsul, –ulis, m., consul, the highest Roman official
cōnsulō, –ere, –suluī, –sultus, consult
contendō, –ere, –tendī, –tentūrus, struggle, hasten
contineō, –ēre, –uī, –tentus, hold (together), contain
contrā, prep. w. acc., against
conveniō, –īre, –vēnī, –ventūrus, come together
convocō, –āre, –āvī, –ātus, call together
cōpia, –ae, f., supply, abundance

cor, cordis, n., heart
corōna, –ae, f., crown
corpus, –poris, n., body
crēdō, –ere, –didī, –ditus, believe, entrust (w. dat.)
Crēta, –ae, f., Crete
cum, prep. w. abl., with
cupiditās, –tātis, f., desire
cupiō, –ere, cupīvī, cupītus, desire
cūr, adv., why
cūra, –ae, f., care, concern; (cum) magnā cūrā, very carefully
cūrō, –āre, –āvī, –ātus, care for, cure
currō, –ere, cucurrī, cursūrus, run
currus, –ūs, m., chariot

D

dē, prep. w. abl., from, down from, about
dea, –ae, f., goddess
dēbeō, –ēre, dēbuī, dēbitus, owe, ought
decem, ten
dēfendō, –ere, dēfendī, dēfēnsus, defend
dēligō, –ere, dēlēgī, dēlēctus, select
dēmōnstrō, –āre, –āvī, –ātus, show
dēpōnō, –ere, dēposuī, dēpositus, put or lay aside
dēscendō, –ere, dēscendī, dēscēnsus, descend
dēserō, –ere, dēseruī, dēsertus, desert
dēsiliō, –īre, dēsiluī, dēsultūrus, jump down
dēspiciō, –ere, dēspexī, dēspectus, look down on, despise
deus, –ī, m., god
dēvorō, –āre, –āvī, –ātus, swallow
dīcō, –ere, dīxī, dictus, say, tell
dictātor –ōris, m., dictator
dictum, –ī, n., word
diēs, diēī, m., day
difficilis, –e, difficult
digitus, –ī, m., finger
dīligentia, –ae, f., diligence
dīmittō, –ere, dīmīsī, dīmissus, let go, send away
discēdō, –ere, –cessī, –cessūrus, go away, depart
disciplīna, –ae, f., training, instruction
discipulus, –ī, m., discipula, –ae, f., learner, pupil
dissimilis, –e, unlike
dīvidō, –ere, dīvīsī, dīvīsus, divide
dō, dare, dedī, datus, give, put; poenam dō, pay the penalty

doceō, –ēre, docuī, doctus, teach
dominus, –ī, *m.,* master; domina, –ae, *f.,* mistress
domus, –ūs, *f.,* house, home
dōnō, –āre, –āvī, –ātus, give, present
dormiō, –īre, –īvī, –ītus, sleep
dubitō –āre, –āvī, –ātus, hesitate, doubt
dūcō, –ere, dūxī, ductus, lead, draw
dulcis, –e, sweet
dum, *conj.,* while
duo, –ae, –o, two
duodecim, twelve
dūrus, –a, –um, hard, harsh
dux, ducis, *m.,* leader, general

E

ē, ex, *prep. w. abl.,* from, out from, out of
ecce, look, here!
ēdūcō, –ere, ēdūxī, ēductus, lead out
efficiō, –ere, effēcī, effectus, make (out), bring about, complete
ego, meī, I
ēgregius, –a, –um, distinguished, excellent
elephantus, –ī, *m.,* elephant
emō, –ere, ēmī, ēmptus, take, buy
Ēpīrus, –ī, *f.,* Ēpī'rus, *a province in Greece*
equus, –ī, *m.,* horse
ērumpō, –ere, ērūpī, ēruptus, burst forth
et, *conj.,* and, even; et . . . et, both . . . and
etiam, *adv.,* also, even, too
Etrūscī, –ōrum, *m. pl.,* the Etruscans
Eumaeus, –ī, *m.,* Eumaeus (Ūmē'us)
Eurōpa, –ae, *f.,* Europe
ēvādō, –ere, ēvāsī, ēvāsūrus, go out, escape
ēvocō, –āre, –āvī, –ātus, summon
excēdō, –ere, excessī, excessūrus, depart
exemplum, –ī, *n.,* example
exerceō, –ēre, exercuī, exercitus, keep busy, train
exercitus, –ūs, *m.,* (trained) army
exit, he goes out
expediō, –īre, –īvī, –ītus, set free
expellō, –ere, expulī, expulsus, drive out
explicō, –āre, –āvī, –ātus, unfold, explain
explōrō, –āre, –āvī, –ātus, investigate, explore

expugnō, –āre, –āvī, –ātus, capture by assault
exspectō, –āre, –āvī, –ātus, look out for, await, wait
exstinguō, –ere, exstīnxī, exstīnctus, extinguish
extrēmus, –a, –um, farthest, last, end of

F

fābula, –ae, *f.,* story
facile, *adv.,* easily
facilis, –e, easy
faciō, –ere, fēcī, factus, do, make; verba faciō, speak, make a speech
factum, –ī, *n.,* deed
fallō, –ere, fefellī, falsus, deceive
fāma, –ae, *f.,* report, fame
familia, –ae, *f.,* family
familiāris, –e, of the family, friendly; *as noun,* friend
fāmōsus, –a, –um, famous, notorious
fātum, –ī, *n.,* fate; *often personified,* the Fates
ferrum, –ī, *n.,* iron
fīlius, –lī, *m.,* son; fīlia, –ae, *f.,* daughter
fīnis, fīnis, *m.,* end; *pl.,* borders, territory
fīnitimus, –a, –um, neighboring, near; *as noun,* neighbor
firmus, –a, –um, strong, firm
flūmen, flūminis, *n.,* river
fluō, –ere, flūxī, flūxus, flow
focus, –ī, *m.,* hearth
fōrma, –ae, *f.,* shape, image, form
fortasse, *adv.,* perhaps
fortis, –e, strong, brave
fortiter, *adv.,* bravely
fortūna, –ae, *f.,* fortune
forum, –ī, *n.,* market place; Forum (*at Rome*)
frangō, –ere, frēgī, frāctus, break
frāter, frātris, *m.,* brother
frīgidus, –a, –um, cold
frōns, frontis, *f.,* forehead, front
frūmentum, –ī, *n.,* grain
fuga, –ae, *f.,* flight
fugiō, –ere, fūgī, fugitūrus, flee
fulmen, –minis, *n.,* lightning
futūrus, *see* sum

G

Gāius, –ī, *m.,* Gā'ius
Gallia, –ae, *f.,* Gaul, *ancient France*
Gallicus, –a, –um, Gallic

Gallus, -ī, *m.,* a Gaul
gēns, gentis, *f.,* people, nation
genus, generis, *n.,* birth, kind
Germānia, -ae, *f.,* Germany
Germānus, -ī, *m.,* a German
gerō, -ere, gessī, gestus, carry on, wear
gladiātor, -ōris, *m.,* gladiator
glōria, -ae, *f.,* glory
glōriōsus, -a, -um, glorious
Graecia, -ae, *f.,* Greece
Graecus, -a, -um, Greek; **Graecus, -ī,** *m.,* a Greek
grātē, *adv.,* gratefully
grātia, -ae, *f.,* gratitude, influence; **grātiam habeō,** feel grateful; **grātiās agō,** thank
grātus, -a, -um, pleasing, grateful
gravis, -e, heavy, severe
graviter, *adv.,* heavily, seriously

H

habeō, -ēre, habuī, habitus, have, hold, consider; **grātiam habeō,** feel grateful (*w. dat.*); **ōrātiōnem habeō,** deliver an oration
habitō, -āre, -āvī, -ātus, live
haereō, -ēre, haesī, haesus, stick
Hannibal, -alis, *m.,* Hannibal, *a Carthaginian general*
herba, -ae, *f.,* grass, plant
Hibernia, -ae, *f.,* Ireland
hic, haec, hoc, this; *as pron.,* he, she, it
hiems, hiemis, *f.,* winter
Hispānia, -ae, *f.,* Spain
Hispānus, -a, -um, Spanish
homō, hominis, *m.,* man, human being
honestās, -tātis, *f.,* honor
honor, -ōris, *m.,* honor, office
hōra, -ae, *f.,* hour
hospita, -ae, *f.,* guest
hostis, hostis, *m.,* enemy (*usually pl.*)
humilis, -e, low, humble

I

iaciō, -ere, iēcī, iactus, throw
iam, *adv.,* already; **nōn iam,** no longer
ibi, *adv.,* there
īdem, eadem, idem, same
ignis, -is, *m.,* fire
ille, illa; illud, that; *as pron.,* he, she, it
impedīmentum, -ī, *n.,* hindrance; *pl.,* baggage
impediō, -īre, -īvī, -ītus, hinder
imperātor, -ōris, *m.,* commander, general

imperium, -rī, *n.,* command, power
imperō, -āre, -āvī, -ātus, command (*w. dat.*)
impetus, -ūs, *m.,* attack
in, *prep. w. acc.,* into, to, against; *w. abl.,* in, on
incertus, -a, -um, uncertain
incipiō, -ere, incēpī, inceptus, take to, begin
incitō, -āre, -āvī, -ātus, urge on, arouse
incolō, -ere, incoluī, incultus, live, inhabit
īnferior, īnferius, lower
inimīcus, -a, -um, unfriendly; *as noun, m.,* enemy
iniūria, -ae, *f.,* wrong, injustice, injury
iniūriōsus, -a, -um, harmful
inquit, said (he)
īnsānus, -a, -um, insane
īnstō, -āre, īnstitī, —, threaten
īnstruō, -ere, īnstrūxī, īnstrūctus, arrange, provide, draw up
īnsula, -ae, *f.,* island
integer, -gra, -grum, untouched, fresh
intellegō, -ere, -lēxī, -lēctus, understand
inter, *prep. w. acc.,* between, among
intercipiō, -ere, -cēpī, -ceptus, intercept
interclūdō, -ere, -clūsī, -clūsus, cut off
interficiō, -ere, -fēcī, -fectus, kill
interim, *adv.,* meanwhile
intermittō, -ere, -mīsī, -missus, let go, stop, interrupt
inveniō, -īre, invēnī, inventus, come upon, find
iō, *interj.,* hurrah!
ipse, ipsa, ipsum, -self, very
īra, -ae, *f.,* anger
is, ea, id, this, that; *as pron.,* he, she, it
ita, *adv.,* so
Italia, -ae, *f.,* Italy
itaque, *adv.,* and so, therefore
iter, itineris, *n.,* journey, road, march
iterum, *adv.,* again
iubeō, -ēre, iussī, iussus, order
iūdicō, -āre, -āvī, -ātus, judge
Iūlius, -lī, *m.,* Julius; **Iūlia, -ae,** *f.,* Julia
iungō, -ere, iūnxī, iūnctus, join (to)
Iūnō, -ōnis, *f.,* Juno, *a goddess, wife of Jupiter*
Iuppiter, Iovis, *m.,* Jupiter, *king of the gods*

iūs, iūris, *n.,* right
iūstē, *adv.,* justly
iūstus, −a, −um, just

L

labor, −ōris, *m.,* work, hardship
labōrō, −āre, −āvī, −ātus, work
lacrima, −ae, *f.,* tear
lacrimō, −āre, −āvī, −ātus, weep
lanterna, −ae, *f.,* lantern
Lār, Laris, *m.,* Lar, *a household god*
lassitūdō, −tūdinis, *f.,* weariness
lātē, *adv.,* widely
Latīnus, −a, −um, Latin, belonging to Latium; Latīnī, −ōrum, *m.,* the Latins
Latīnus, −ī, *m.,* Latī'nus
latrō, −ōnis, *m.,* bandit
lātus, −a, −um, wide
laudō, −āre, −āvī, −ātus, praise
lavō, −āre, lāvī, lautus, wash
lēgātus, −ī, *m.,* envoy
legō, −ere, lēgī, lēctus, gather, choose, read
levis, −e, light (*in weight*)
leviter, *adv.,* lightly
lēx, lēgis, *f.,* law
liber, librī, *m.,* book
līber, −era, −erum, free
līberē, *adv.,* freely
līberī, −ōrum, *m.,* children
līberō, −āre, −āvī, −ātus, free
lībertās, −tātis, *f.,* freedom
ligō, −āre, −āvī, −ātus, bind
lingua, −ae, *f.,* tongue, language
littera, −ae, *f.,* letter (*of the alphabet*), *pl.,* letter (*epistle*), letters (*if modified by an adjective such as* multae), literature
locus, −ī, *m.* (*pl.* loca, locōrum, *n.*), place
longus, −a, −um, long
Lūcīlius, −lī, *m.,* Lucilius (Lūsil'ius)
lūdō, −ere, lūsī, lūsus, play
lūdus, −ī, *m.,* game, school
Lūsitānia, −ae, *f.,* Portugal
lūx, lūcis, *f.,* light, daylight

M

M., *abbreviation for* Mārcus
magister, −trī, *m.,* teacher
magnus, −a, −um, large, great; *comp.* maior, maius, greater; *superl.* maximus, −a, −um, greatest, very great
maior, *see* magnus

malus, −a, −um, bad; *comp.* peior, peius, worse; *superl.* pessimus, −a, −um, very bad, worst; malum, −ī, *n.,* trouble
mandō, −āre, −āvī, −ātus, entrust
maneō, −ēre, mānsī, mānsūrus, remain
manus, −ūs, *f.,* hand
Mārcius, −cī, *m.,* Marcius (Mar'shus)
mare, maris, *n.,* sea
marītus, −ī, *m.,* husband
Mārs, Mārtis, *m.,* Mars, *god of war*
māter, mātris, *f.,* mother
māteria, −ae, *f.,* matter, timber
mātrimōnium, −nī, *n.,* marriage
mātūrō, −āre, −āvī, −ātus, hasten
maximē, *adv.,* very greatly, especially
maximus, *see* magnus
medicus, −ī, *m.,* doctor
Mediterrāneum (Mare), Mediterranean Sea
medius, −a, −um, middle (of)
mel, mellis, *n.,* honey
melior, *see* bonus
memoria, −ae, *f.,* memory; memoriā teneō, remember
mēnsa, −ae, *f.,* table
mēnsis, −is, *m.,* month
mercātor, −ōris, *m.,* merchant
Mercurius, −rī, *m.,* Mercury
mereō, −ēre, meruī, meritus, deserve, earn
mēta, −ae, *f.,* goal, turning post (*in the Circus*)
meus, −a, −um, my, mine
migrō, −āre, −āvī, −ātūrus, depart
mīles, mīlitis, *m.,* soldier
mīlle, *pl.* mīlia, thousand
Minerva, −ae, *f., a goddess*
minimē, *adv.,* not at all
minimus, minor, *see* parvus
miser, −era, −erum, unhappy, poor
mittō, −ere, mīsī, missus, let go, send
modus, −ī, *m.,* manner
moneō, −ēre, monuī, monitus, remind, warn
mōns, montis, *m.,* mountain
mōnstrō, −āre, −āvī, −ātus, point out, show
mors, mortis, *f.,* death
mōs, mōris, *m.,* custom
moveō, −ēre, mōvī, mōtus, move
mox, *adv.,* soon
mulier, mulieris, *f.,* woman
multus, −a, −um, much; *pl.,* many; *comp.* plūrēs, plūra, more; *superl.* plūrimus, −a, −um, most

mūniō, –īre, –īvī, –ītus, fortify; **viam mūniō,** build a road
mūnus, mūneris, *n.,* duty, service, gift
mūtō, –āre, –āvī, –ātus, change

N

nam, *conj.,* for
nārrō, –āre, –āvī, –ātus, relate
nātūra, –ae, *f.,* nature
nātūrālis, –e, natural
nauta, –ae, *m.,* sailor
nāvigō, –āre, –āvī, –ātus, sail
nāvis, nāvis, *f.,* ship
–ne, *introduces questions*
nec, *see* **neque**
neglegentia, –ae, *f.,* negligence
negōtium, –tī, *n.,* business
nēmō, *dat.* **nēminī,** *acc.* **nēminem** (*no other forms*), no one
Neptūnus, –ī, *m.,* Neptune, *god of the sea*
neque (*or* **nec**), and not, nor; **neque . . . neque,** neither . . . nor
neuter, –tra, –trum, neither (*of two*)
nihil, nothing
nōbilis, –e, noble
nōbīscum = cum nōbīs
noceō, –ēre, nocuī, nocitūrus, do harm to (*w. dat.*)
nōmen, nōminis, *n.,* name
nōn, *adv.,* not; **nōn iam,** no longer
nōs, we, *pl. of* **ego**
nōscō, –ere, nōvī, nōtus, learn; *perf.,* have learned, know
noster, –tra, –trum, our
nōtus, –a, –um, known, familiar
novem, nine
novus, –a, –um, new, strange
nox, noctis, *f.,* night
nūllus, –a, –um, no, none
numerus, –ī, *m.,* number
numquam, *adv.,* never
nunc, *adv.,* now
nūntiō, –āre, –āvī, –ātus, report, announce
nūntius, –tī, *m.,* messenger

O

ob, *prep. w. acc.,* toward, on account of, for
obtineō, –ēre, obtinuī, obtentus, hold, obtain
occultus, –a, –um, secret
occupō, –āre, –āvī, –ātus, seize
Ōceanus, –ī, *m.,* ocean
octō, eight

oculus, –ī, *m.,* eye
officium, –cī, *n.,* duty
omnis, omne, all, every
oppidum, –ī, *n.,* town
opprimō, –ere, oppressī, oppressus, overcome, surprise
optimē, *see* **bene**
optimus, *see* **bonus**
opus, operis, *n.,* work
ōrātiō, –ōnis, *f.,* speech
ōrātor, –ōris, *m.,* orator
ōrdō, ōrdinis, *m.,* order, rank
ōrnāmentum, –ī, *n.,* jewel, costume
ostendō, –ere, ostendī, ostentus, (stretch out), show
ōtiōsus, –a, –um, leisurely, idle
ōtium, ōtī, *n.,* leisure, peace

P

P., *abbreviation for* **Pūblius**
pār, *gen.* **paris,** equal
parātus, –a, –um, prepared, ready
parō, –āre, –āvī, –ātus, get, get ready, prepare
pars, partis, *f.,* part, side
parvus, –a, –um, small; *comp.* **minor, minus,** less; *superl.* **minimus, –a, –um,** least
pāstor, –ōris, *m.,* shepherd
pater, patris, *m.,* father
patria, –ae, *f.,* fatherland, country
paucī, –ae, –a, few
Paulus, –ī, *m.,* Paul
paupertās, –tātis, *f.,* poverty
pāx, pācis, *f.,* peace
pecūnia, –ae, *f.,* sum of money, money
peior, *see* **malus**
pellō, –ere, pepulī, pulsus, drive, drive out, defeat
Penātēs, –ium, *m.,* the Penā'tēs, *household gods*
Pēnelopē, –ae, *f.,* Penĕl'ope, *wife of Ulysses*
per, *prep. w. acc.,* through, by
perficiō, –ere, –fēcī, –fectus, finish
perīculum, –ī, *n.,* danger
permittō, –ere, –mīsī, –missus, let go through, allow, entrust (*w. dat.*)
permoveō, –ēre, –mōvī, –mōtus, move (deeply)
permūtātiō, –ōnis, *f.,* exchange
perpetuus, –a, –um, constant
persōna, –ae, *f.,* character
perveniō, –īre, –vēnī, –ventūrus, come through, arrive

pēs, pedis, *m.,* foot; **pedibus,** on foot
pessimus, *see* **malus**
petō, –ere, petīvī, petītus, seek, ask (for)
Philippus, –ī, *m.,* Philip
philosophia, –ae, *f.,* philosophy
Phrygia, –ae, *f.,* Phrygia (Frij'ia), *a country of Asia Minor*
pictūra, –ae, *f.,* picture
pila, –ae, *f.,* ball
plācō, –āre, –āvī, –ātus, calm
plāgōsus, –a, –um, fond of whipping
plānus, –a, –um, level
plēbs, plēbis, *f.,* the common people
plicō, –āre, –āvī, –ātus, fold
plūrēs, plūra, more, *see* **multus**
plūrimus, *see* **multus**
plūs, *see* **multus**
Plūtō, –ōnis, *m.,* Plu'tō
poena, –ae, *f.,* penalty, punishment
poēta, –ae, *m.,* poet
Polyphēmus, –ī, *m.,* Polyphē'mus, *a man-eating giant*
pompa, –ae, *f.,* parade
pōnō, –ere, posuī, positus, put, place; **castra pōnō,** pitch camp
pōns, pontis, *m.,* bridge
pontifex, –ficis, *m.,* priest
Pontus, –ī, *m., a country in Asia Minor*
populus, –ī, *m.,* people; *pl.,* peoples, nations
porta, –ae, *f.,* gate
portō, –āre, –āvī, –ātus, carry
portus, –ūs, *m.,* harbor
possum, posse, potuī, —, can, be able
post, *adv. and prep. w. acc.,* behind (*of place*); after (*of time*)
posteā, *adv.,* afterwards
postquam, *conj.,* after
potestās, –tātis, *f.,* power
prae, *prep. w. abl.,* before, in front of
praeceps, *gen.* **praecipitis,** headlong, steep
praeda, –ae, *f.,* loot
praeficiō, –ere, –fēcī, –fectus, put in charge of
praemittō, –ere, –mīsī, –missus, send ahead
praemium, –mī, *n.,* reward
praesidium, –dī, *n.,* guard, protection
praesum, –esse, –fuī, –futūrus, be in charge of
praetextus, –a, –um, (woven in front), bordered; **toga praetexta,** crimson-bordered toga

premō, –ere, pressī, pressus, press, press hard
pretium, –tī, *n.,* price
prīmō, *adv.,* at first
prīmum, *adv.,* for the first time
prīmus, –a, –um, first
prīnceps, –cipis, *m.,* leader
prō, *prep. w. abl.,* in front of, before, for
probō, –āre, –āvī, –ātus, test, prove, approve
prōcēdō, –ere, –cessī, –cessūrus, go forward, advance
prōdūcō, –ere, –dūxī, –ductus, lead out, prolong
proelium, –lī, *n.,* battle
prohibeō, –ēre, –hibuī, –hibitus, prevent, keep from
properō, –āre, –āvī, –ātūrus, hasten
prōpōnō, –ere, –posuī, –positus, put forward, offer
proprius, –a, –um, (one's) own
prōvideō, –ēre, –vīdī, –vīsus, foresee
prōvincia, –ae, *f.,* province
proximus, –a, –um, nearest, very near, next
pūblicē, *adv.,* publicly
pūblicus, –a, –um, public
Pūblius, –lī, *m.,* Pub'lius
puella, –ae, *f.,* girl
puer, puerī, *m.,* boy
pugna, –ae, *f.,* battle
pugnō, –āre, –āvī, –ātus, fight
pulcher, –chra, –chrum, beautiful
Pūnicus, –a, –um, Punic, Carthaginian
putō, –āre, –āvī, –ātus, think
Pyrrhus, –ī, *m.,* Pyr'rhus, *king of Epirus*

Q

quam, *conj.,* than
quārtus, –a, –um, fourth
quattuor, four
–que (*joined to second word*), and
quī, quae, quod, *relat. pron.,* who, which, what, that; *interrog. adj.,* what
quīndecim, fifteen
quīnque, five
quīntus, –a, –um, fifth
quis, quid, *interrog. pron.,* who, what
quod, *conj.,* because
quondam, *adv.,* once (upon a time)

R

raeda, –ae, *f.,* carriage, omnibus
rapiō, –ere, rapuī, raptus, carry off
ratiō, –ōnis, *f.,* account, reason
recipiō, –ere, recēpī, receptus, take back, recover, receive
reddō, –ere, reddidī, redditus, give back
redigō, –ere, redēgī, redāctus, drive back, reduce
redūcō, –ere, redūxī, reductus, lead back, bring back
rēgīna, –ae, *f.,* queen
regiō, –ōnis, *f.,* region
rēgnum, –ī, *n.,* royal power, kingdom
regō, –ere, rēxī, rēctus, rule, guide
relinquō, –ere, relīquī, relīctus, leave (behind), abandon
reliquus, –a, –um, remaining, rest (of)
remaneō, –ēre, remānsī, remānsūrus, remain
remedium, –dī, *n.,* remedy
remittō, –ere, remīsī, remissus, relax, send back
removeō, –ēre, remōvī, remōtus, remove
repellō, –ere, reppulī, repulsus, drive back, repulse
rēs, reī, *f.,* thing, matter, affair; **rēs pūblica,** public affairs, government
respondeō, –ēre, respondī, respōnsus, answer
restō, –āre, restitī, —, remain
retineō, –ēre, retinuī, retentus, hold (back), keep
reverentia, –ae, *f.,* respect
revertō, –ere, revertī, reversūrus, return
rēx, rēgis, *m.,* king
Rhēnus, –ī, *m.,* the Rhine river
rīdeō, –ēre, rīsī, rīsus, laugh (at)
rogō, –āre, –āvī, –ātus, ask
Rōma, –ae, *f.,* Rome
Rōmānus, –a, –um, Roman; *as noun,* a Roman
ruīna, –ae, *f.,* ruin

S

saccus, –ī, *m.,* sack
sacer, –cra, –crum, sacred
saepe, *adv.,* often
salūs, salūtis, *f.,* health, safety
sapientia, –ae, *f.,* wisdom
Sāturnus, –ī, *m.,* Saturn, *a god*

saxum, –ī, *n.,* rock
scēptrum, –ī, *n.,* scepter
scientia, –ae, *f.,* knowledge, science
sciō, –īre, scīvī, scītus, know
Scīpiō, –ōnis, *m.,* Scipio (Sip'io)
scrībō, –ere, scrīpsī, scrīptus, write
sēcum = cum sē
secundus, –a, –um, second
sed, *conj.,* but
sedeō, –ēre, sēdī, sessūrus, sit
semper, *adv.,* always
senātor, –ōris, *m.,* senator
senātus, –ūs, *m.,* senate
sententia, –ae, *f.,* feeling, opinion, motto
sentiō, –īre, sensī, sensus, feel, realize
sēparō, –āre, –āvī, –ātus, separate
septem, seven
sepulchrum, –ī, *n.,* tomb
sermō, –ōnis, *m.,* talk
servō, –āre, –āvī, –ātus, save, guard, preserve
servus, –ī, *m.;* **serva, –ae,** *f.,* slave
sex, six
sī, *conj.,* if
Siçilia, –ae, *f.,* Sicily (Sis'ily)
signum, –ī, *n.,* sign, standard, signal
silva, –ae, *f.,* forest, woods
similis, –e, like
sine, *prep. w. abl.,* without
singulī, –ae, –a, *pl. only,* one at a time
socius, –cī, *m.,* comrade, ally
sōl, sōlis, *m.,* sun
sōlus, –a, –um, alone, only
solvō, –ere, solvī, solūtus, loosen, pay
somnus, –ī, *m.,* sleep
sordidus, –a, –um, dirty
soror, –ōris, *f.,* sister
spatium, –tī, *n.,* space, time, lap (*in a race*)
speciēs, speciēī, *f.,* appearance
spectō, –āre, –āvī, –ātus, look (at)
spērō, –āre, –āvī, –ātus, hope (for)
spēs, speī, *f.,* hope
spīrō, –āre, –āvī, –ātus, breathe
spondeō, –ēre, spopondī, spōnsus, promise, engage
statua, –ae, *f.,* statue
statuō, –ere, statuī, statūtus, establish, determine
stō, stāre, stetī, stātūrus, stand
stomachus, –ī, *m.,* stomach
studiōsus, –a, –um, eager, studious
studium, –dī, *n.,* eagerness, interest; *pl.,* studies

449

sub, *prep.*, under, close to (*w. acc. after verbs of motion; w. abl. after verbs of rest or position*)

subigō, –ere, –ēgī, –āctus, subdue

submittō, –ere, –mīsī, –missus, let down, furnish

suī, *reflexive pron.*, of himself, herself, itself, themselves

sum, esse, fuī, futūrus, be

summus, –a, –um, highest, top of

sūmō, –ere, sūmpsī, sūmptus, take

super, *prep. w. acc.*, over, above

superbia, –ae, *f.*, pride

superbus, –a, –um, haughty

superō, –āre, –āvī, –ātus, overcome, excel

supersum, –esse, –fuī, –futūrus, be left over, survive

supplicium, –cī, *n.*, punishment

suscipiō, –ere, –cēpī, –ceptus, undertake

sustineō, –ēre, –tinuī, –tentus, hold up, maintain, endure

suus, –a, –um, *reflexive adj.*, his, her, its, their; his own, her own, its own, their own

T

taberna, –ae, *f.*, shop, tavern

tamen, *adv.*, nevertheless

tandem, *adv.*, at last

tangō, –ere, tetigī, tāctus, touch

tardē, *adv.*, slowly

tardus, –a, –um, slow, late

Tarentīnī, –ōrum, *m. pl.*, the people of Tarentum

Tēlemachus, –ī, *m.*, Telĕm'achus

tēlum, –ī, *n.*, weapon

templum, –ī, *n.*, temple

tempus, temporis, *n.*, time

tendō, –ere, tetendī, tentus, stretch

teneō, –ēre, tenuī, tentus, hold, keep; memoriā teneō, remember

terminus, –ī, *m.*, end, boundary

terra, –ae, *f.*, land, earth

terreō, –ēre, terruī, territus, scare, frighten

tertius, –a, –um, third

texō, –ere, texuī, textus, weave

theātrum, –ī, *n.*, theater

Ti., *abbreviation for* Tiberius

Tiberis, –is, *m.*, the Tī'ber, *a river in Italy*

Tiberius, –rī, *m.*, Tibē'rius

timeō, –ēre, timuī, —, fear, be afraid

timidē, *adv.*, timidly

timidus, –a, –um, timid

Tīrō, –ōnis, m., Tī'rō

toga, –ae, *f.*, toga (*cloak*)

tōtus, –a, –um, whole

trādō, –ere, –didī, –ditus, give *or* hand over, surrender, relate

trādūcō, –ere, –dūxī, –ductus, lead across

trahō, –ere, trāxī, trāctus, draw, drag

trānō, –āre, –āvī, –ātus, swim across

trāns, *prep. w. acc.*, across

trānsportō, –āre, –āvī, –ātus, transport

trēs, tria, three

tribūnus, –ī, *m.*, tribune, *a Roman official*

tribuō, –ere, tribuī, tribūtus, grant

trīgintā, thirty

triumphō, –āre, –āvī, –ātus, triumph

triumphus, –ī, *m.*, triumph

Troia, –ae, *f.*, Troy

Troiānus, –a, –um, Trojan; *as noun*, a Trojan

tū, tuī, you

tum, *adv.*, then

tuus, –a, –um, your, yours (*referring to one person*)

U

ubi, *adv.*, where; when

Ulixēs, –is, *m.*, Ūlys'sēs

ūllus, –a, –um, any

ulterior, ulterius, farther

ultimus, –a, –um, last, farthest

unda, –ae, *f.*, wave

ūnus, –a, –um, one

urbs, urbis, *f.*, city

ūtilis, –e, useful

uxor, –ōris, *f.*, wife

V

valeō, –ēre, valuī, valitūrus, be strong, be well; *imper.* valē, farewell

vāllum, –ī, *n.*, wall

variē, *adv.*, variously

varius, –a, –um, changing, varying, various

veniō, –īre, vēnī, ventūrus, come

ventus, –ī, *m.*, wind

Venus, –eris, *f.*, Vēnus, *goddess of love and beauty*

vēr, vēris, *n.*, spring

verberō, –āre, –āvī, –ātus, beat

verbōsus, –a, –um, wordy

verbum, –ī, *n.*, word; verba faciō, make a speech

Vergilius, –lī, *m.,* Virgil
vertō, –ere, vertī, versus, turn
vērus, –a, –um, true
Vestālis, –e, Vestal, of Vesta
vester, –tra, –trum, your, yours (*referring to two or more persons*)
vestis, –is, *f.,* garment, clothes
via, –ae, *f.,* way, road, street
victor, –ōris, *m.,* victor
victōria, –ae, *f.,* victory
videō, –ēre, vīdī, vīsus, see; *passive,* seem
vīgintī, twenty
villa, –ae, *f.,* country home
vincō, –ere, vīcī, victus, conquer
vīnum, –ī, *n.,* wine

vir, virī, *m.,* man
virgō, –ginis, *f.,* virgin, maiden
virīlis, –e, of a man
virtūs, –tūtis, *f.,* manliness, courage
vīs, —, *f.,* force, violence; *pl.,* **vīrēs, –ium,** strength
vīta, –ae, *f.,* life
vīvō, –ere, vīxī, vīctus, be alive, live
vīvus, –a, –um, alive
vix, *adv.,* scarcely
vocō, –āre, –āvī, –ātus, call, invite
vōs, *pl. of* **tū**
vōx, vōcis, *f.,* voice, remark
Vulcānus, –ī, *m.,* Vulcan, *god of fire*
vulnerō, –āre, –āvī, –ātus, wound
vulnus, vulneris, *n.,* wound

The Bank of England, which the English call "the old lady of Threadneedle Street," wears a Roman dress.

A

able (be), possum, posse, potuī, —
about, dē, *w. abl.*
absent (be), absum, abesse, āfuī, āfutūrus
across, trāns, *w. acc.*
advice, cōnsilium, –lī, *n.*
affair, rēs, reī, *f.*
affect, afflict, afficiō, –ere, affēcī, affectus
afraid (be), timeō, –ēre, timuī, —
after, *use abl. abs.;* post *(prep. w. acc.)*; postquam *(conj.)*
aid, auxilium, –lī, *n.*
all, omnis, –e
ally, socius, –cī, *m.*
alone, sōlus, –a, –um
always, semper
and, et, –que, atque
another, alius, –a, –um
answer, respondeō, –ēre, respondī, respōnsus
appearance, speciēs, speciēī, *f.*
approach, accēdō, –ere, accessī, accessūrus *(w.* ad)
approve, probō, –āre, –āvī, –ātus
arms, arma, –ōrum, *n.*
arouse, incitō, –āre, –āvī, –ātus
arrive, perveniō, –īre, –vēnī, –ventūrus
as, *use abl. abs.*
ask, rogō, –āre, –āvī, –ātus
await, exspectō, –āre, –āvī, –ātus
away (be), absum, –esse, āfuī, āfutūrus

B

bad, malus, –a, –um
battle, pugna, –ae, *f.;* proelium, –lī, *n.*
be, sum, esse, fuī, futūrus
beautiful, pulcher, –chra, –chrum
because, quod; *use particip. or abl. abs.*
begin, incipiō, –ere, –cēpī, –ceptus
between, inter, *w. acc.*
bind, ligō, –āre, –āvī, –ātus
body, corpus, corporis, *n.*
book, liber, librī, *m.*
boy, puer, puerī, *m.*
brave, fortis, –e; **bravely,** fortiter
breathe, spīrō, –āre, –āvī, –ātus
brother, frāter, frātris, *m.*

but, sed
by, ā, ab, *w. abl.*

C

call, vocō, –āre, –āvī, –ātus; appellō, –āre, –āvī, –ātus; **call out,** ēvocō; **call together,** convocō
camp, castra, –ōrum, *n.*
can, possum, posse, potuī, —
cannot, nōn possum
capture, expugnō, –āre, –āvī, –ātus
care, cūra, –ae, *f.*
carefully, cum cūrā
carry, portō, –āre, –āvī, –ātus; **carry on,** gerō, –ere, gessī, gestus
catch sight of, cōnspiciō, –ere, –spexī, –spectus
cause, causa, –ae, *f.*
certainly, certē
chance, cāsus, –ūs, *m.*
(put in) charge of, praeficiō, –ere, –fēcī, –fectus
children, līberī, –ōrum, *m.*
citizen, cīvis, cīvis, *m.*
citizenship, cīvitās, –tātis, *f.*
city, urbs, urbis, *f.*
clearly, clārē
climb, ascendō, –ere, ascendī, ascēnsus
close, claudō, –ere, clausī, clausus
colonist, colōnus, –ī, *m.*
come, veniō, –īre, vēnī, ventūrus; **come together,** conveniō, –īre, –vēnī, –ventus
compel, cōgō, –ere, coēgī, coāctus
complete, cōnficiō, –ere, –fēcī, –fectus
comrade, socius, –cī, *m.*
constant, perpetuus, –a, –um
contain, contineō, –ēre, –uī, –tentus
convenient, commodus, –a, –um
country, patria, –ae, *f.*
courage, animus, –ī, *m.*
cry out, clāmō, –āre, –āvī, –ātus

D

danger, perīculum, –ī, *n.*
daughter, fīlia, –ae, *f.*
day, diēs, diēī, *m.*
death, mors, mortis, *f.*
deceive, fallō, –ere, fefellī, falsus
deep, altus, –a, –um
(deeply) move, permoveō, –ēre, –mōvī, –mōtus

defend, dēfendō, –ere, dēfendī, dēfēnsus
depart, excēdō, –ere, excessī, excessūrus
desert, dēserō, –ere, dēseruī, dēsertus
deserve, mereō, –ēre, meruī, meritus
desire, cupiō, –ere, cupīvī, cupītus
determine, statuō, –ere, statuī, statūtus
dinner, cēna, –ae, *f.*
discipline, disciplīna, –ae, *f.*
dismiss, dīmittō, –ere, dīmīsī, dīmissus
divide, dīvidō, –ere, dīvīsī, dīvīsus
do, faciō, –ere, fēcī, factus; **do harm
to,** noceō, –ēre, nocuī, nocitūrus (*w.
dat.*)
drag, draw, trahō, –ere, trāxī, trāctus
drive, agō, –ere, ēgī, āctus
duty, officium, –cī, *n.*

E

eagerness, studium, –dī, *n.*
easy, facilis, –e; **easily,** facile
end, fīnis, fīnis, *m.;* terminus, –ī, *m.*
endure, sustineō, –ēre, –tinuī, –tentus
enemy, inimīcus, –ī, *m.* (*personal*);
hostis, –is, *m.* (*national*)
entrust, mandō, –āre, –āvī, –ātus; committō, –ere, –mīsī, –missus; crēdō,
–ere, crēdidī, crēditus
equal, pār, *gen.* paris
establish, cōnfirmō, –āre, –āvī, –ātus
every, omnis, –e
example, exemplum, –ī, *n.*
excel, superō, –āre, –āvī, –ātus
excellent, ēgregius, –a, –um
explore, explōrō, –āre, –āvī, –ātus

F

fall, cadō, –ere, cecidī, cāsūrus
fame, fāma, –ae, *f.*
familiar, nōtus, –a, –um
family, familia, –ae, *f.*
famous, clārus, –a, –um
farmer, agricola, –ae, *m.*
father, pater, patris, *m.*
fear, timeō, –ēre, timuī, —
feel grateful, grātiam habeō
few, paucī, –ae, –a
field, ager, agrī, *m.*
fifth, quīntus, –a, –um
fight, pugnō, –āre, –āvī, –ātus
find, inveniō, –īre, invēnī, inventus
first, prīmus, –a, –um
fit, aptus, –a, –um
flee, fugiō, –ere, fūgī, fugitūrus

fold, plicō, –āre, –āvī, –ātus
food, cibus, –ī, *m.*
foot, pēs, pedis, *m.;* **on foot,** pedibus
for (*conj.*), nam; (*prep.*), prō, *w. abl.;*
ob, *w. acc.*
foreigner, barbarus, –ī, *m.*
foresee, prōvideō, –ēre, –vīdī, –vīsus
forest, silva, –ae, *f.*
fortify, mūniō, –īre, –īvī, –ītus
four, quattuor
free (*adj.*), līber, –era, –erum; (*v.*),
līberō, –āre, –āvī, –ātus; expediō,
–īre, –īvī, –ītus
freedom, lībertās, lībertātis, *f.*
fresh, integer, –gra, –grum
friend, amīcus, –ī, *m.*
friendly, amīcus, –a, –um
friendship, amīcitia, –ae, *f.*
from, out from, ē, ex, *w. abl.;* **(away)
from,** ā, ab, *w. abl.*
furnish, submittō, –ere, –mīsī, –missus

G

gate, porta, –ae, *f.*
Gaul, Gallia, –ae, *f.;* **a Gaul,** Gallus,
–ī, *m.*
general, dux, ducis, *m.*
get, get ready, parō, –āre, –āvī, –ātus
girl, puella, –ae, *f.*
give, dōnō, –āre, –āvī, –ātus; dō, dare,
dedī, datus
go away, discēdō, –ere, –cessī, –cessūrus
god, deus, –ī, *m.*
good, bonus, –a, –um
grain, frūmentum, –ī, *n.*
(be *or* **feel) grateful,** grātiam habeō
great, magnus, –a, –um
guard, praesidium, –dī, *n.*

H

hand, manus, –ūs, *f.*
harm, do harm to, noceō, –ēre, nocuī,
nocitūrus (*w. dat.*)
harmony, concordia, –ae, *f.*
harsh, dūrus, –a, –um; **harshly,** dūrē
hasten, mātūrō, –āre, –āvī, –ātus; properō, –āre, –āvī, –ātūrus
have, habeō, –ēre, –uī, –itus
he, is; hic; ille; *often not expressed*
head, caput, capitis, *n.*
health, salūs, salūtis, *f.*
hear, audiō, –īre, –īvī, –ītus
heavy, gravis, –e
her (*poss.*), eius; (*refl.*), suus, –a, –um

hesitate, dubitō, –āre, –āvī, –ātus
high, altus, –a, –um
himself (*intens.*), ipse; (*reflex.*), suī
hinder, impediō, –īre, –īvī, –ītus
his (*poss.*), eius; (*reflex.*) suus, –a, –um
hold, teneō, –ēre, tenuī, tentus
hope (*v.*), spērō, –āre, –āvī, –ātus; (*noun*), spēs, speī, *f.*
horse, equus, –ī, *m.*
hour, hōra, –ae, *f.*
house, casa, –ae, *f.;* domus, –ūs, *f.*
how (in what manner), quō modō

I

I, ego, meī; *often not expressed*
if, *abl. abs.*
in, in, *w. abl.*
increase, augeō, –ēre, auxī, auctus
influence, addūcō, –ere, addūxī, adductus; (*noun*), grātia, –ae, *f.;* auctōritās, –tātis, *f.*
injustice, iniūria, –ae, *f.*
instruction, disciplīna, –ae, *f.*
interest, studium, –dī, *n.*
into, in, *w. acc.*
island, īnsula, –ae, *f.*
it, id; hoc; illud; *this is often not expressed*

J

journey, iter, itineris, *n.*
just, aequus, –a, –um; iūstus, –a, –um

K

kill, interficiō, –ere, –fēcī, –fectus
king, rēx, rēgis, *m.*
kingdom, rēgnum, –ī, *n.*
know, *perfect tense of* nōscō, –ere, nōvī, nōtus, *or of* cognōscō, –ere, –nōvī, –nitus; sciō, –īre, scīvī, scītus

L

land, terra, –ae, *f.;* **native land,** patria, –ae, *f.*
large, magnus, –a, –um
late, tardus, –a, –um
lead, dūcō, –ere, dūxī, ductus; **lead across,** trādūcō; **lead a life,** vītam agō; **lead back,** redūcō; **lead out,** ēdūcō, prōdūcō
leader, dux, ducis, *m.;* prīnceps, prīncipis, *m.*
learn, nōscō, –ere, nōvī, nōtus; cognōscō, –ere, –nōvī, –nitus

leisure, ōtium, –ī, *n.*
letter (*of alphabet*), littera, –ae, *f.;* (*epistle*), litterae, –ārum, *f.*
level, plānus, –a, –um
life, vīta, –ae, *f.*
like, amō, –āre, –āvī, –ātus
little, parvus, –a, –um
live a life, vītam agō; **dwell,** habitō, –āre, –āvī, –ātus
long, longus, –a, –um; **no longer,** nōn iam
look at, spectō, –āre, –āvī, –ātus
loot, praeda, –ae, *f.*
lose, āmittō, –ere, āmīsī, āmissus
love, amō, –āre, –āvī, –ātus
lower, īnferior, īnferius

M

maintain, sustineō, –ēre, –uī, –tentus
make, faciō, –ere, fēcī, factus
man, vir, virī, *m.;* homō, hominis, *m.*
manner, modus, –ī, *m.*
many, multī, –ae, –a
master, dominus, –ī, *m.*
messenger, nūntius, –tī, *m.*
middle of, medius, –a, –um
money, pecūnia, –ae, *f.*
month, mēnsis, –is, *m.*
most, plūrimī, –ae, –a
mother, māter, mātris, *f.*
motto, sententia, –ae, *f.*
mountain, mōns, montis, *m.*
move, moveō, –ēre, mōvī, mōtus; migrō, –āre, –āvī, –ātus; cēdō, –ere, cessī, cessūrus
much, multus, –a, –um; magnus, –a, –um
my, meus, –a, –um

N

name, nōmen, nōminis, *n.*
nation, gēns, gentis, *f.*
native land, patria, –ae, *f.*
nature, nātūra, –ae, *f.*
neighboring, fīnitimus, –a, –um
neither (*adj.*), neuter, –tra, –trum
neither . . . nor (*conj.*), neque . . . neque
never, numquam
nevertheless, tamen
new, novus, –a, –um
next, proximus, –a, –um
no longer (*adv.*), nōn iam; **no one** (*noun*), nēmō, *dat.* nēminī, *m.*

noble, nōbilis, –e
nor, neque
not, nōn
nothing, nihil, *indecl. n.*
now, nunc
number, numerus, –ī, *m.*

O

obtain, obtineō, –ēre, obtinuī, obtentus
on, in, *w. abl.;* **on account of,** ob, *w. acc.*
one at a time, singulī, –ae, –a; **one . . . the other,** alter . . . alter
opinion, sententia, –ae, *f.*
order, iubeō, –ēre, iussī, iussus
other, alius, –a, –ud; **the other (of two),** alter, –era, –erum
ought, dēbeō, –ēre, dēbuī, dēbitus
our, noster, –tra, –trum
ourselves (*intens.*), ipsī; (*reflex.*), nōs
out of, ē, ex, *w. abl.*
owe, dēbeō, –ēre, dēbuī, dēbitus

P

part, pars, partis, *f.*
peace, pāx, pācis, *f.*
people, populus, –ī, *m.*
pitch camp, castra pōnō
place, locus, –ī, *m.; pl.* loca, –ōrum, *n.*
plan, cōnsilium, –lī, *n.*
pleasing, grātus, –a, –um
poor, miser, –era, –erum
praise, laudō, –āre, –āvī, –ātus
prepare, parō, –āre, –āvī, –ātus
present (be), adsum, esse, adfuī, adfutūrus
present, dōnō, –āre, –āvī, –ātus; prōpōnō, –ere, –posuī, –positus
preserve, servō, –āre, –āvī, –ātus; cōnservō
price, pretium, –tī, *n.*
prisoner, captīvus, –ī, *m.*
prove, probō, –āre, –āvī, –ātus
province, prōvincia, –ae, *f.*
public, pūblicus, –a, –um
punishment, poena, –ae; *f.;* supplicium, –cī, *n.*
put, pōnō, –ere, posuī, positus; **put in charge of,** praeficiō, –ere, –fēcī, –fectus

Q

queen, rēgīna, –ae, *f.*
quickly, celeriter

R

rank, ōrdō, ōrdinis, *m.*
rather, *expressed by comparative*
read, legō, –ere, lēgī, lēctus
ready, parātus, –a, –um; **get ready,** parō, –āre, –āvī, –ātus
receive, accipiō, –ere, accēpī, acceptus
region, regiō, –ōnis, *f.*
reinforcements, auxilia, –ōrum, *n.*
remain, maneō, –ēre, mānsī, mānsūrus; remaneō
remember, memoriā teneō
remove, removeō, –ēre, remōvī, remōtus
report, nūntiō, –āre, –āvī, –ātus
rest (of), reliquus, –a, –um
reward, praemium, –mī, *n.*
right, iūs, iūris, *n.*
river, flūmen, flūminis, *n.*
road, via, –ae, *f.;* iter, itineris, *n.*
rule, regō, –ere, rēxī, rēctus
run, currō, –ere, cucurrī, cursūrus

S

sacred, sacer, –cra, –crum
safety, salūs, –ūtis, *f.*
sail, nāvigō, –āre, –āvī, –ātus
sailor, nauta, –ae, *m.*
same, īdem, eadem, idem
save, servō, –āre, –āvī, –ātus; cōnservō
say, dīcō, –ere, dīxī, dictus
scare, terreō, –ēre, terruī, territus
sea, mare, maris, *n.*
see, videō, –ēre, vīdī, vīsus
seek, petō, –ere, petīvī, petītus
seize, occupō, –āre, –āvī, –ātus
send, mittō, –ere, mīsī, missus; **send away,** dīmittō; **send back,** remittō
settler, colōnus, –ī, *m.*
severe, gravis, –e
shape, fōrma, –ae, *f.*
sharply, ācriter
she, ea; haec; illa; *often not expressed*
ship, nāvis, nāvis, *f.*
shout, clāmō, –āre, –āvī, –ātus
show, mōnstrō, –āre, –āvī, –ātus; dēmōnstrō
(catch) sight of, cōnspiciō, –ere, –spexī, –spectus
signal, signum, –ī, *n.*
since, *use abl. abs.;* quod (*conj.*)
sister, soror, sorōris, *f.*
sit, sedeō, –ēre, sēdī, sessūrus
slave, servus, –ī, *m.*

small, parvus, –a, –um

soldier, mīles, mīlitis, *m.*

some . . . others, aliī . . . aliī

son, fīlius, –lī, *m.*

speech, ōrātiō, –ōnis, *f.;* **make a speech,** verba faciō

spend (years), agō, –ere, ēgī, āctus

stand, stō, –āre, stetī, stātūrus

standard, signum, –ī, *n.*

state, cīvitās, –tātis, *f.*

strange, novus, –a, –um

street, via, –ae, f.

stretch, tendō, –ere, tetendī, tentus

studies, studia, –ōrum, *n.*

suitable, commodus, –a, –um

summer, aestās, –tātis, *f.*

supply, cōpia, –ae, *f.*

swift, celer, celeris, celere

swiftly, celeriter

swiftness, celeritās, –tātis, *f.*

T

take, capiō, –ere, cēpī, captus

teach, doceō, –ēre, docuī, doctus

teacher, magister, –trī, *m.*

terms, condiciō, –ōnis, *f.*

than, quam

thank, grātiās agō (*w. dat.*)

that (*demonst.*), ille, illa, illud; is, ea, id; (*relat.*) quī, quae, quod

their, eōrum, eārum, eōrum

themselves (*intens.*), ipsī, –ae, –a; (*reflex.*), suī

then, tum

there, ibi

they, eī, eae, ea; illī, illae, illa; *often not expressed*

thing, rēs, reī, *f.; often not expressed*

think, putō, –āre, –āvī, –ātus

third, tertius, –a, –um

this (*demonst.*), hic, haec, hoc; is, ea, id

three, trēs, tria

through, per, *w. acc.*

till, colō, –ere, coluī, cultus

timber, māteria, –ae, *f.*

time, tempus, –oris, *n.; ***one at a time,** singulī, –ae, –a

to, ad, *w. acc.; dat. of indir. obj.*

too, *expressed by comparative*

touch, tangō, –ere, tetigī, tāctus

town, oppidum, –ī, *n.*

train, exerceō, –ēre, exercuī, exercitus

transport, trānsportō, –āre, –āvī, –ātus

two, duo, duae, duo

U

under, sub, *w. acc. or abl.*

understand, intellegō, –ere, –lēxī, –lēctus

undertake, suscipiō, –ere, –cēpī, –ceptus

unfold, explicō, –āre, –āvī, –ātus

unhappy, miser, –era, –erum

upon, in, *w. abl.*

urge on, incitō, –āre, –āvī, –ātus

useful, ūtilis, –e

V

varying, varius, –a, –um

very, *expressed by superlative;* **very carefully,** magnā cūrā

victory, victōria, –ae, *f.*

W

wagon, carrus, –ī, *m.*

wait, exspectō, –āre, –āvī, –ātus

war, bellum, –ī, *n.*

warn, moneō, –ēre, –uī, –itus

watch, spectō, –āre, –āvī, –ātus

water, aqua, –ae, *f.*

we, nōs; *often not expressed*

well, bene

what (*pron.*), quis, quid; (*adj.*), quī, quae, quod

which, quī, quae, quod

who (*rel. pron.*), quī, quae, quod; (*interrog. pron.*), quis, quid

whole, tōtus, –a, –um

why, cūr

wide, lātus –a, –um

winter, hiems, hiemis, f.

with, cum, *w. abl.; sometimes abl. alone*

without, sine, *w. abl.*

woods, silva, –ae, *f.*

word, verbum, –ī, *n.*

work (*verb*), labōrō, –āre, –āvī, –ātus; (*noun*), opus, operis, *n.*

worse, peior, peius; **worst,** pessimus, –a, –um

wound, vulnus, vulneris, *n.*

write, scrībō, –ere, scrīpsī, scrīptus

Y

year, annus, –ī, *m.*

you, tū (*sing.*); vōs (*pl.*); *often not expressed*

your, tuus, –a, –um; vester, –tra, –trum; **yourselves** (*reflex.*), vōs

INDEX

Numbers in roman type refer to the sections of the text; those in *italic,* to pages showing illustrations.

458

descriptive genitive and ablative, 498, 574, 577
Diana, 245, 360
dice, *253*
Dido, 198, 215, 221; *151*
dining room, 294; *76*
Diocletian, Arch of, *301*
diphthongs, 513
direct object, 16, 505, 534, 576
direct statement, 420
dishes, *225, 423;* see also **tableware**
dō, 267
dolls, *327*
domes, *91, 118, 119, 148, 153, 296, 297*
Domitian, *85*
domus, declension of, 489, 552; construction, 503
Domus Tiberiana, *10*
Doric style, *9, 17, 146, 147, 163, 172*
doublets, 466, 485
Dougga, *192, 303*
Dover, *275*
Dresden, *325*
dress, *206; 156, 157, 201, 203, 223, 266, 270, 275, 292, 343, 345, 346, 348, 384, 386, 402*
Drusus, Arch of, *1*
duck, *228*
Dunedin, *174*
duo, declension of, 468, 559

ē, ex, 102, 103; as prefix, 104
economic conditions, Roman, 473
education, see **schools**
ego, declension of, 227, 561
egoist, *178*
Egypt, *337*
Eisenhower, D. D., *251*
eject, *331*
election posters, 157; *120, 121*
elephants, 455, 467; *365*
Elizabeth II, *114*
elongated, *26*
emphatic verb forms, 25, 539
enamel, *151*
endings, 9, 11, 38
England, *68, 71, 76, 77, 114, 185, 225, 237, 275, 347, 451*
English, see **word studies**
est, 7
Etna, Mt., *18*
Etruscans, 3, 377, 388, 399; *292, 310, 365*
Eumaeus, 339
Eurylochus, 322
Evora, *195*
extent of time or space, accusative of, 480, 576
extrēmus, use of, 456

Fabius Maximus, 233

Fabricius, 460, 502; *369*
Fannia, Tomb of, *293*
farming, see **agriculture**
Faustina, Temple of, *84, 159, 327*
Faustulus, 349; *277*
Fayoum, *337*
fifth declension, 492, 551
Finland, *235*
fire protection in Rome, 73
first conjugation, 25, 256, 566
first declension, 9, 66, 547
  adjectives, 15, 66, 106, 117, 553
Fiumicino, *30*
floors, 359; *14, 47, 71, 109, 200, 228, 285, 330*
Florence, *186, 353*
food and meals, 294, 443; *76, 78, 122, 223, 224, 325, 343*
Forum, the, 73, 207, 431; *1, 11, 27, 36, 38, 57, 84, 113, 159, 161, 215, 290, 316, 322, 327, 344, 348, 398;* Boarium, *243;* of Augustus, *215;* of Caesar, *214;* of Trajan, *214, 215*
fountains, *24, 25, 223*
fourth conjugation, 147, 175, 306, 569
fourth declension, 487, 551
France, *41, 50, 64, 168, 218, 219, 250*
Frankfort, Ky., *170*
Frascati, *30*
freedmen, 121; *95, 407*
French, Latin words in, 72, 115, 478
frescoes, 89; see also **wall paintings**
furniture, 359; *76, 157, 273, 285, 325*
future active infinitive, 418, 426
future active participle, 408
future perfect tense, 222, 538; passive, 241
future tense, 22, 538; active, 49, 81, 164, 175; passive, 194

games, 5, 226, 277, 327, 328; *105, 126, 175, 252, 253, 330, 417*
gardens, 359; *25, 48, 76, 339*
gates, see **arches**
Gaudeāmus Igitur, 584
Gaul, 59, 289, 317, 474; see also **France**
Gemini, *290*
gender, 31, 38, 532
  in the first declension, 31
  in the second declension, 31, 117
  in the third declension, 301, 347
  in the fourth declension, 487
  in the fifth declension, 492
genitive case, 44, 125, 153, 535, 574
  of description, 498
  of nouns and adjectives in –ius, 97; in –ium, 119
  of possession, 44, 535
Genius, 399; *319*
Germany, 168, 289; *325*

Gettysburg Address, 5
Giants, 366; *294*
girls, see children
gladiators, *105;* gladiatorial shows, 157, 277, 327; *120;* see also amphitheaters
glass, 359; *101*
glimpses of Roman life, see Roman life
gods, 269, 399, 400; *71, 200*
good, *56*
government, Roman, 377, 473, 502
Gracchi, 473, 486
grammar, basic, 519
grammar summaries, 38, 78, 125, 161, 208, 209, 256, 331, 363, 402, 432, 505
Greece, *82, 168, 311*
Greek, 1; *7, 191*
Gregory, Pope, 321
Gyselaer, P., *355*

Hadrian, *384;* tomb of, *366;* villa of, *48, 204, 378*
hair, 206; *157, 158, 203, 330*
Hannibal, 233, 491; *365*
harbors, *165*
hats, 206
Helen, *290*
Herculaneum, *197, 224, 423*
hic, declension of, 367, 563
hieroglyphics, *85*
holidays, Roman, 327, 399, 503
Homer, *81*
homō and vir, 504
hoops, *417*
Horace, 174, 417, 584; *333, 335, 381*
Horatius, 388, 502; *308*
horses, *80, 88, 89, 133, 259, 347, 370*
hotels, Roman, 36, 157; see also inns
house, Roman, 359; *76, 96, 100, 105, 109, 120, 121, 284, 285, 292, 300, 339, 374, 378*
House of Representatives, *23*
hunting, *14*
hymn, Christian, *440*

i-stem adjectives, 345, 554
i-stem nouns, 340, 550
Icarus, 448; *359, 361, 363*
īdem, declension of, 384, 563
ideographic writing, 3
idioms, 180
ille, declension of, 367, 563
Illinois, *153*
impecunious, *43*
impediment, *251*
imperative, 69, 541
    present active, 69; plural in *–ĭte,* 141; of *–ĭō* verbs, 147; of fourth conjugation, 147; irregulars of third conjugation, 147, 155, 415

imperfect tense, active, 186; passive, 194; distinguished from perfect, 187, 209, *579; 143*
impluvium, 359; *109, 285*
in, 87, 114, 125; *87;* as prefix, 115
In Britanniā, 510
incitō, meanings of, 247
India, *44*
indicative mood, 69, 541; tenses of, 425
indirect object, 54, 153, 505, 535, 575; *46*
indirect statement, 419, 420, 432, 581
industry, Roman, 430
infinitive, 23, 542, 581
    as object, 130, 216, 234, 255
    as predicate nominative, 129
    as subject, 129, 216, 255
    formation of, 23, 249, 413, 418
    in indirect statements, 419, 420
    tenses of, how they differ, 426
inflection, 7, 530; *17*
inflections (basic forms), summary of, 547
inkwells, *190, 242*
in libris libertas, *280*
inns, 36; *224*
inscriptions, *5, 6, 7, 37, 50, 76, 85, 91, 95, 105, 110, 114, 120, 152, 166, 177, 180, 239, 245, 248, 251, 280, 327, 333, 335, 365, 371, 381, 382, 383, 395, 400, 425*
Integer Vītae, 584
intensive pronoun, in English and Latin, 389, 563
intercept, *321*
interjections, 529
interrogative pronouns and adjectives, 284, 523, 524, 565
intransitive verbs, 199, 525
–iō verbs (third conjugation), 147, 175, 570
Ionic style, *146, 149, 153, 170, 279*
ipse, declension of, 389, 563
irregular adjectives, 394, 397, 456, 557
irregular comparison of adjectives, 456, 557
irregular nouns, 415, 446, 489, 552
irregular verbs, 571
is, 227, 378, 379, 563
Isis, priest of, *397*
isolation, *15*
Issus, *80*
it, 131, 231
Italian, Latin words in, 72
Italy, 179, 191, 215, 238; *21, 28, 30, 52, 86, 103, 136, 139, 162, 164, 166, 168, 177, 181, 204, 212, 245, 254, 335, 353, 354, 363, 372, 378, 381, 425;* see also **Herculaneum, Ostia, Pompeii, Rome, Sicily**

Muses, *138*
musician, *439, 440*
mute consonants, 516
Mysteries, Villa of the, *284, 292*

names, English, 92; of months and states, 382, 429; see also **word studies**
Narcissus, 121
Nausicaa, 334; *263, 266*
–ne, 135
nēmō, declension of, 446, 552
Neptune, 191, 334, 360, 366, 399; *145, 179, 200, 275, 395*
New York, *81, 156, 167, 275*
New Zealand, *174*
Nîmes, *41, 169, 218*
Niobe, 245; *186*
noceō, dative with, 505, 575
nominative case, 9, 10, 535, 573; absolute, 323
nōnne, 135
Norman-French influence, 392
nouns, 9, 38, 522; see also **first declension,** etc.
Nuceria, *289*
nūllus, nihil, nēmō, 395
number, 9, 22, 38, 531, 537
numerals, 20, 307, 332, 394, 468, 469, 524, 559, 560; *20*
Numitor, 349

obelisk, *85, 296*
object, direct, 16, 505, 534, 576; indirect, 54, 505, 535, 575; *46;* infinitive as, 130
objective case, 9, 16, 535
Odyssey, see **Ulysses**
Olympic Games, *86, 162, 366*
Op Art, *300*
opponent, *205*
Orbilius, 174
orchestra, *212*
order of words, see **word order**
ordinal numerals, 560
Ostia, *30, 47, 78, 164, 165, 254, 370, 374, 375*
Ovid, *351, 357*

Pactolus, 383; *307*
Padua, *42*
painting, prints, and drawings, modern, *2, 81, 118, 145, 171, 183, 234, 269, 277, 285, 307, 348, 351, 353, 355, 357, 369, 382;* see also **wall paintings**
Palatine Hill, 73; *10, 84, 257, 322, 348*
Pales, 73
palla, 206
Pannini, G. P., *118*
Pantheon, *91, 118, 296*
Papinian, *23*

papyrus rolls, 253; *2, 135, 138, 191, 242*
parade, *103;* see also **triumphs**
parchment, 253
Paris, *50, 383*
Parthenon, 269
participial stem, 265
participles, 239, 432, 543, 555, 580; used as adjectives and nouns, 312, 407, 580; as clauses, 318, 323, 580; in ablative absolute, 323; tenses of, 580; see **present participle,** etc.
parts of speech, 521
passive voice, 192, 193, 194, 199, 540; *147*
past particple, 239
past perfect tense, 222, 538; passive, 241
past tense, 22, 94, 125, 187, 209, 538
patricians, 502
pediment, *50;* see also **temples, capitols**
Penates, 399, 400
Penelope, 339, 344; *269, 270, 273*
penult, 516
perfect infinitive, active, 413, 426; passive, 418
perfect participle, 239, 580; stem of, 265, 447; used as adjective and noun, 312; used as clause, 318
perfect stem, 95, 265
perfect tense, 94, 95, 125, 579
distinguished from imperfect, 187, 209; *143*
formation of active, 95; of passive, 240
peristyle, 359; *109, 339, 378*
person, 22, 537
personal endings, 22, 25, 95; passive, 194
personal pronouns, 22, 227, 379, 523, 561
Peruzzi, 269
Phaeacia, 334; Phaeacian ship, *265*
Philemon, 443; *355, 357*
Phocas, Column of, *xii*
Phoenicians, 3
phrases (prepositional), 544
phrases and quotations, see **word studies**
Phrygia, 383, 443
pictographic writing, 3
Piranesi, G. B., *xii, 1*
Pistrucci, B., *294*
place, prepositions of, 87, 103, 114, 125, 577; *79*
Plautus, 327; *254*
plays, Latin, 261, 510; *95*
plebeians, 502
Pliny, 311; *239*
plūs, 456, 558
Pluto, 163, 366; *129*
Plymouth Rock, *160*
podium, *183*
Pollux, *290*
Polyphemus, 300; *231, 234*
polytheism, 399